Secondary Reading, Writing, and Learning

MARIAN J. TONJES
Western Washington University

Allyn and Bacon
Boston London Toronto Sydney Tokyo Singapore

This book is dedicated to my sons,
Jeffrey Charles and Kenneth Warren Tonjes.

Copyright © 1991 by Allyn and Bacon
A Division of Simon & Schuster, Inc.
160 Gould Street
Needham Heights, Massachusetts 02194

Series Editor: Sean W. Wakely
Senior Editorial Assistant: Carol L. Chernaik
Cover Administrator: Linda Dickinson
Cover Designer: Suzanne Harbison
Composition Buyer: Superscript Associates
Manufacturing Buyer: Megan Cochran
Production Administrator: Superscript Associates
Editorial-Production Service: Total Concept Associates

Library of Congress Cataloging-in-Publication Data

Tonjes, Marian J.
   Secondary reading, writing, and learning / Marian J. Tonjes.
     p. cm.
   Includes bibliographical references and index.
   ISBN 0-205-12401-1
   1. Language arts (Secondary) 2. Reading (Secondary) 3. English
language–Study and teaching (Secondary) 4. English language–
Composition and exercises–Study and teaching (Secondary)
5. Study, Method of. I. Title.
LB1631.T66 1991
428′.00712–dc20   90-21286
                                          CIP

Printed in the United States of America

10 9 8 7 6 5 4 3 2 1   94 93 92 91 90

Contents

2 Affective Concerns and Individual Differences   25

3 The Text: Organizational Patterns and Readability Factors   69

4 Vocabulary Concepts and Word Study   99

5 Expository Comprehension

6 Literary Comprehension

■ Preface

ATTENTION: INSTRUCTORS AND READERS

The terms *study-reading, study-writing,* and *study-learning* are used in this book to mean reading, writing, and learning for academic purposes in secondary school situations. These are directly affected by the kinds of interactions occurring among students, the text or task, and the classroom environment that the teacher mediates.

Reading courses and requirements for secondary teachers differ widely at universities across the country. Developmental reading has given way at times to content-area reading, leaving a gap that this text, it is hoped, will fill. This is not just another general content-area text. There are already many books in the field to meet that introductory need for all subjects for grades 4 through 12. This book is intended primarily for those secondary teachers—middle and high school—who require extensive reading, writing, and study strategies in their classrooms. This would include such areas as English, history, and science, as well as all potential reading specialists and consultants. It is recommended, but not essential, that if this book is used at the preservice level, a prior reading course be a prerequisite.

Thus, the two overall aims of this secondary text are, first, to guide teachers in ways of helping their students become more self-aware, self-monitoring, independent learners—in other words, to become more metacognitively aware, and, second, to incorporate active learning into classroom activities.

WHAT IS DIFFERENT ABOUT THIS TEXT?

1. A wide variety of innovative study aids have been included with each chapter, so that readers can make a selection as needed. These include the following:

     a. Graphic organizers or overviews
     b. Chapter outlines of topics and subtopics
     c. Cognitive competencies—what readers will be able to do
     d. Key items (concepts and vocabulary)
     e. Preorganizer activities to motivate and alert readers to what is to come
     f. Postorganizer activities to pull together information, synthesize it, and allow readers to react for long-term retention

2. Quizzes and tests can be readily constructed using these study aids.
3. There is a more in-depth look at vocabulary concerns.
4. Comprehension is divided into two chapters—expository and literary.
5. Study-reading strategies are also divided into two chapters, based on a four-part model.
6. There is a separate chapter on study-writing.
7. School programs, practices, and staff development are discussed in a separate chapter.
8. Appendixes cover the following areas: Barrett's taxonomy, basic academic competencies, reading selections for rate adaptability practice, a history of the English dictionary, and an assessment instrument listing.
9. A separate manual is provided for instructors using this text.
10. This text practices what it preaches, with direct application of what it teaches.

FOCUS/GENERALIZATION/SIGNIFICANCE: A GENERAL STUDY-READING COMPREHENSION STRATEGY

The following general comprehension strategy is deceptively simple in appearance. It has been used in numerous secondary and university classes, where students have admitted that this exercise forced them to read the text in a more deliberate, active way, keeping their mind on key ideas rather than getting mired in unrelated details. They found that they also had to try to find some relevance in the learnings, to think about applying theory to their classroom situations. "Focus/Generalization/Significance" should be tried with each chapter until it becomes second nature. Brief class discussions of students' selections may be interesting and provocative.

    As you read each chapter, keep in mind three basic things: the overall focus, a learning generalization, and the significance to you of the information presented. Taking focus first, one way to show you comprehend the overall major theme is to retitle the chapter using only synonyms. The title should be a superordinate one, including all major facets. Next, every chapter should contain several important learning generalizations. You can test your own generalizations by seeing if you can discuss a number of detailed items of information under each one. A generalization should not contain more than one example, if any, nor should it be so general that it says little of value. It is the balance between generality and specificity that makes a good generalization. Third, whereas generalizations are cognitive statements, significance statements should be affective in nature, concerned with attitudes and feelings about the learning. Looking back over a chapter, select several notions that intrigued, amazed, angered, interested, or bored you. Identify your emotional reaction to the information.

Examples of the three elements of the strategy follow:

- *Focus:* One possible focus for a chapter originally titled "Teaching and Remediating for Individual Differences" might be "Meeting Needs of All Students." Note that every word is different. Sometimes, using synonyms is sufficient for retitling the chapter.
- *Generalization:* One generalization from a chapter on vocabulary might be, "For those adolescents who never mastered word attack skills, it is necessary to reteach or remind them about various ways to get at meaning: context, structural analysis, phonics, and dictionary." Note that there is just enough detail to clarify what the generalization is driving at, so that you can proceed to discuss each of the four aspects in more detail. If the statement were merely, "Word attack skills may still be important for secondary students," it would need the addition of a main reason, such as, "because not knowing key words may hamper appropriate comprehension." Generalizations, as used here, are only one sentence long.
- *Significance:* Significance statements may start with "I feel" rather than "I think" because they represent an opinion about the value of the learnings: "I feel that students need to realize how interesting vocabulary development can be, because then they will be more likely to continue learning new words." Here, you are giving an opinion, which can be discussed further. To take another example, "The notion of amelioration and pejoration was fascinating to me because I had not realized how word meanings can change over time." As you finish reading each chapter, you may wish to jot down responses to share and discuss later in class. This type of discussion can act as a brief summary review.

Note that this strategy can be useful in determining some test questions or in planning individual conferences.

Focus (reword chapter title):

_____

Generalizations (cognitive learning statements)

1. _____

2. _____

3. _____

Significance (affective feelings about learning)

1. _____

2. _____

3. _____

TO THE INSTRUCTOR

The pretest that follows can be used at the beginning and end of the course to give students a way of comparing their entering knowledge with what they learned during the course.

Name _____

Subject area _____

Pretest (Background Knowledge You Bring to the Text)

1. Without looking at the Contents or thumbing through the text, predict and list here as many aspects of secondary reading, writing, and learning as you think will be discussed in this course.

2. At this point, what is your definition of secondary study-reading, study-writing, and study-learning?

3. The following terms are merely a sampling from the various chapters. Briefly define each. When you do not know, make an educated or humorous guess. (Remember, this is a *pretest* to determine a rough idea of entering knowledge, *not* one to see how much you have learned in this course.)

   (Preface) focus/generalization/significance _____

   _____

   (Chapter 1) functional literacy _____

   _____

   schema theory _____

   _____

   (Chapter 2) affective domain _____

   _____

   ludic reading _____

   _____

   (Chapter 3) organizational patterns _____

   _____

   integrative cues _____

   _____

(Chapter 4) diachronic linguistics _____

_____

structural analysis _____

_____

(Chapter 5) advance organizer _____

(Chapter 6) Barrett's taxonomy _____

_____

marginal gloss _____

_____

(Chapter 7) graphical literacy _____

_____

"new brain" theory _____

_____

(Chapter 8) SQ3R _____

_____

effective rate _____

_____

(Chapter 9) inquiry-centered writing _____

_____

Porpe _____

_____

(Chapter 10) cloze procedure _____

_____

Content IRI _____

_____

(Chapter 11) staff development model _____

_____

cooperative learning _____

_____

4. Read these two brief excerpts and judge their difficulty level for secondary students who are at either the middle school or the high school level. Also, state the level you are or will be teaching.

Excerpt #1 _____

Excerpt #2 _____

Excerpt 1 Deductive and Inductive Aspects of Logical Argument

Implicit in the foregoing analysis of the structure of argument is the notion that science uses a combination of inductive and deductive processes of reasoning. As Peter Senn has indicated, "Inductive reasoning keeps us alone, close to observation and the facts. Deductive reasoning makes us pay attention to the logic of our arguments and statements." Let us examine these processes more carefully.

The deductive form of argument is distinguishable from the inductive form because, in contrast to the latter, it is conclusive or demonstrative. R. B. Braithwaite has captured the essential differences in the two forms as follows:

> In deduction the reasonableness of belief in the premises as it were overflows to provide reasonableness for the belief in the conclusion. This happens because the conclusion is a logical consequence of the premises, and cannot be false while the premises are true. The empirical circumstances under which the premises collectively would be true are included in the circumstances under which the conclusion would be true; so a belief that the circumstances are such as to make the premises true involves, implicitly, if not explicitly, a belief that the circumstances are such as to make the conclusion true. If the former belief is a reasonable one, the latter belief will also be reasonable.

Reprinted by permission from *Teaching for Thinking in High School Social Studies* by Richard C. Phillips, copyright © 1974 by Addison-Wesley Publishing Company, Menlo Park, California, p. 213

Excerpt 2

The sign on the wall seemed to quaver under a film of sliding warm water. Eckels felt his eyelids blink over his stare, and the sign burned in this momentary darkness:

Time Safari, Inc.
Safaris to Any Year in the Past.
You Name the Animal.
We Take You There.
You Shoot It.

A warm phlegm gathered in Eckels' throat; he swallowed and pushed it down. The muscles around his mouth formed a smile as he put his hand slowly out upon the air, and in that hand waved a check for ten thousand dollars to the man behind the desk.

"Does this safari guarantee I come back alive?"

"We guarantee nothing," said the official, "except the dinosaurs." He turned. "This is Mr. Travis, your Safari Guide in the Past. He'll tell you what and where to shoot. If he says no shooting, no shooting. If you disobey instructions, there's a stiff penalty of another ten thousand dollars, plus possible government action, on your return."

Eckels glanced across the vast office at a mass and tangle, a snaking and humming of wires and steel boxes, at an aurora that flickered now orange, now silver, now blue. There was a sound like a gigantic bonfire burning all of Time, all the years and all the parchment calendars, all the hours piled high and set aflame.

A touch of the hand and this burning would, on the instant, beautifully reverse itself. Eckels remembered the wording in the advertisements to the letter. Out of chars and ashes, out of dust and coals, like golden salamanders . . .

5. Using the same excerpts, number and list potential study reading problems some of your students might have in mastering this material.

Excerpt #1   *Excerpt #2*

6. Using the same numbers as above, state one thing for each item you would do as a teacher to assist students with these problems.

Acknowledgments

Many, many thanks go to the following people who have so graciously assisted in producing this text:

- To my reviewers: Laura Boyd, Western Michigan University; Betty McEady-Gillead, San Francisco State University; Sharon Kossack, Florida International University; Anthony Manzo, University of Missouri, Kansas City; and Judith Meagher, University of Connecticut for your helpful and thorough comments.
- To my editor, Sean Wakely, for your patience and persistence.
- To my colleagues, for the time many of you took from your busy schedules to comment and give feedback.
- To my students, for reacting to all or parts of the text.
- To Western Washington University, Bureau of Faculty Research and to Dabney Bankert, for support with typing and editing for tight deadlines.
- To the University of Guam, Vice-President Robert A. Underwood, Dean Donald Schuster, and Department Chairman Gregg C. San Nicolas, for supporting my writing efforts, giving me released time and a student assistance while I taught there for a year as a visiting professor.

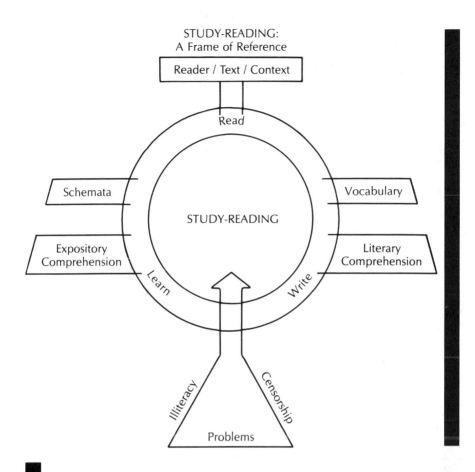

STUDY-READING:
A Frame of Reference

Reader / Text / Context

Read

Schemata

Vocabulary

STUDY-READING

Expository
Comprehension

Literary
Comprehension

Learn

Write

Illiteracy

Censorship

Problems

1

Study-Reading:
A Frame of Reference

CHAPTER OUTLINE

COGNITIVE COMPETENCIES

After study-reading this chapter, you should be able to:

1. *Justify* the continuance of study incorporating reading and writing across the curriculum and throughout the secondary school years.

2. *Differentiate* between general reading and study-reading, giving a personal example of each.

3. *Critique* several secondary school requirements as outlined in Goodlad's study.

4. *Demonstrate* your understanding of schema theory by describing an example in your subject area.

5. *Summarize* the problems of illiteracy and censorship.

6. *Problem-solve* a possible solution for each of the problems stated in number 5.

KEY TERMS

censorship
cultural literacy
literacy/illiteracy

prose/document/quantitative
   literacy
reading versus study-reading
schema (schemata) theory

Preorganizer 1
Looking Back: Reexperiencing Our Reading Past

For many of you starting this text, reading has always seemed to be something taken for granted. Its many complex aspects may not have occurred to you at a conscious level since your early years of learning the how-to of reading. Before starting to consider the varied aspects of reading to learn, or study-reading, try to think back to how you were taught to read. Allow the following questions to help lead you back.

_____ Did the teacher place all of you in high, average, and low groups (Bluebirds, Robins, and Squirrels)?

_____ Did the teacher call on people in a round-robin fashion?

_____ Did you learn by sounding out word parts and whole words?

_____ Did you experience events, write about them, "publish" homemade books or newspapers, and read each other's work?

_____ Were you given choices of what to read and then scheduled to meet with the teacher for an individual conference?

_____ Did you work with a reading kit of graded, color-coded cards in which you moved up the ladder by colors?

_____ Were you taught to speed-read using machines?

_____ Were you considered one of the good readers?

_____ How did you feel about your place in the reading hierarchy?

_____ What happened to those who were in the low group?

Sharing ideas and feelings with your group or class about your past experiences with various reading practices can serve as a starting point for considering secondary study-reading, -writing, and -learning. Following your discussion, what specific questions do you want answered in this text?

_____

_____

_____

Study-Reading: A Frame of Reference

Preorganizer 2
Looking Forward: What to Anticipate in This Text

For the next few months you will be considering problems and potentials of helping students to become more adept readers, writers, and learners. First, after a close look at the chapter outlines at the beginning of each chapter, rank-order the chapters in terms of their personal significance to you. Upon completing each chapter, you may wish to modify your choices. Second, try to set your own purpose prior to reading each chapter. Setting purposes helps readers focus and concentrate more meaningfully.

1
Study-Reading:
A Frame of Reference

*. . . people do not know how long it takes to learn to read.
I have been at it all my life and I can not say I have
reached the goal.*
JOHANN WOLFGANG GOETHE

INTRODUCTION

As middle and high school teachers, what problems do you face with your students' reading, writing, and study abilities? How do you cope with these problems? This book is dedicated to helping you address and attempt to solve these problems. In this first chapter we start with a frame of reference concerning study-reading, looking at *who* should be involved, *why* they should, *what* is involved, *how* we got here, *where* we are, and finally *what* are some of the problems still facing us. If you have examined the chapter outline, you will already have grasped the organizational pattern.

STUDY-READING: WHO SHOULD BE INVOLVED?

For the past thirty years or more we have given lip service to the fact that reading is a K–12 concern in which all teachers and administrators should be involved. When middle and high school classroom teachers, backed by supportive administrators, assume and share responsibilities for incorporating study-reading into their everyday curriculum, their job actually becomes easier because students are more likely to be successful and thus more motivated to learn.

6

Even so, if you were to talk today to a wide variety of secondary teachers and administrators, asking them what special problems they find most difficult to face with their students, many would still lament their students' general lack of study-reading and writing ability. They would tell you that many of their students are not motivated to read their texts or to write thoughtful papers. They would tell you that too many lack the abilities needed to master their subject, especially above the literal ("I've got the facts") level, on the higher, more demanding levels requiring analysis, synthesis, evaluation, and creativity. They would tell you that too many students do not have appropriately refined study skills, such as locating relevant reference material, organizing and outlining, note-taking, concentrating, and test-taking.

The answer is simple. If you are taking it merely on faith now, it is hoped that by the end of this course you will agree wholeheartedly that if you teach study-reading,-writing, and -learning skills concurrently with subject information, your students will become better able—and more willing—to handle their assignments. That's what this book is all about.

WHY SECONDARY STUDY-READING, -WRITING, AND -LEARNING?

Today, we as teachers face the awesome responsibility of educating our students to become more adept at thinking analytically, critically, and reactively; at being better able to solve problems and make wise decisions that can lead toward a better society. To reach this goal, our students need to become independent, self-motivated learners instead of relying solely on teachers and television for their information. The ability to make informed choices comes mostly through wide reading and exposure to a variety of viewpoints. Those who rely on television news, for example, are subject to the newscasters' biases. One example of manipulation of the news through overemphasis occurred in 1986, when the U.S. media, for lack of other newsworthy events, continually overemphasized terrorist bombings, threats, and other activities, until people grew fearful of traveling to Europe and tourism fell sharply there. (The media in Europe, by contrast, treated the terrorist acts as routine news and then went on to other topics.)

Reading is an essential avenue of communication and a prerequisite to academic achievement and even to personal adjustment. All of us can benefit from becoming more sophisticated in higher level reading, writing, and thinking skills. Those students who have not mastered basic skills in the earlier grades will, of course, need special attention from remedial specialists, but regular secondary classroom teachers have the dual responsibility of assisting all other students in mastering their materials and showing them how best to accomplish any given task.

As Hill (1979) outlined, the process and impact of reading shapes our intellectual processes, enabling us to amass many terms, concepts, and organizational skills, and to sharpen our higher cognitive processes.[1] This is just as true for the process and impact of writing. Being able to read easily and well may also increase our potential for personal fulfillment, give us therapeutic solutions to our personal problems, or provide an avenue for vicarious escape and relaxation. A lifetime of this kind of pleasure is denied those who either read poorly or are unmotivated to read at all.

Study-writing is also an essential communication tool and, unfortunately, one that we have too often neglected. Writing can help us become better readers, as we are more able to recognize text aids, for example.

Learning study skills (study-learning) are generally taught, if at all, at the senior high or freshman college level. And yet we know that this how-to knowledge cannot only produce better students but also can save them needed time over the long run for other beneficial activities.

In the final analysis, when we assist students in study-reading, -writing, and -learning, we actually make our teaching easier—and no one should quarrel with the worth of that.

WHAT IS INVOLVED IN STUDY-READING, -WRITING, AND -LEARNING?

Before going any further, this is a good time to look at some basic definitions and explanations that will undergird the rest of this text. First, there have been many definitions of reading over the years, but recently it has been redefined on the basis of current research findings. A four-part definition in the shape of a bookmark follows as shown in Figure 1.1.[2] It includes some key words: (1) constructing meaning . . . dynamic interaction; (2) existing knowledge; (3) information suggested . . . ; (4) context. . . .

More specifically, the statement, "Reading is the process of constructing meaning," is based in part on the theory of how we store and retrieve information, often referred to as *schema theory*, or the way we organize information for later retrieval.

"Through the dynamic interaction among the *reader*, the *text*, and the *context* of the reading situation" (emphasis added) refers to changing aspects which affect reading because, first, readers bring to their reading some background information, some awareness of strategies to use, and some knowledge of text structure. (Awareness and monitoring of strategies to use when reading has been called *metacognition* and will be discussed more thoroughly in the chapter on literary comprehension.) While reading, we

FIGURE 1.1
Definition of Study-Reading

> Reading is
> the process
> of *constructing meaning*
> through the
> *dynamic interaction*
> among the reader's
> *existing knowledge,*
> the
> *information suggested*
> by the
> written language,
> and the
> *context*
> of the
> reading situation.

Source: From *New Dimensions in Reading Instruction,* copyright © 1985 by the Michigan Reading Association. Used with permission.

think about meaning and monitor our own comprehension of that meaning. "Text structure" means the way ideas are organized in a text, such as a narrative that tells a story (story grammar) or expository writing (the type of writing found in textbooks), which seeks to explain and organize facts, information, and concepts. "Context of the reading situation" refers to the environment that surrounds the reader and the text, such as one in which teachers help readers establish purposes for reading through specific teaching activities.

Study-Reading: Definitions

As used in this text, *study-reading* involves all the regular activities of reading—decoding print, assigning correct meanings to terms, comprehending ideas, using study techniques—plus some additional ones. In order to study-read, students must take action based on a recognized purpose, action that will help them comprehend at the needed level and be able to store information and retrieve it later on. Thus, study-reading not only involves constructing meaning from print on the basis of our existing knowledge; it also requires categorizing that information in such a way that it will be readily accessible. Study-reading may require using advanced thinking skills and strategies to analyze or take something apart, synthesize or put pieces of information back together in a new way, or evaluate and justify responses. Study-reading also requires that readers differentiate among expository, descriptive, and literary types of writing. Finally, study-reading and study-writing by students are included here as subcategories under the general term of study-reading.

Study-writing is concerned with students' ability to express themselves in writing, to get a message across in the clearest way. It is closely related to study-reading in that both require knowledge of language background experiences and include essential roles of planning, composing, editing, and monitoring (see Chapter 9 on study-writing).

Study-learning involves all those activities and strategies students engage in when attempting to master a particular subject: locating information, organizing it, interpreting it, and applying it to other situations (see chapters 7 and 8 on study-learning).

Schema Theory

The term *schemata* (the plural of *schema*) refers to beliefs, concepts, expectations, processes—everything readers take from their past experiences to make sense of their world as they read. This background knowledge includes specific aspects of a subject area: general knowledge of the world (e.g., causes or social relationships) that help readers go beyond the print and make inferences or identify with people and events. Knowledge of writing style and its effect, conventions used for organizing and signaling organization of the text—such as grammar in literature or expository writing patterns—can reduce readers' processing demands as they attempt to comprehend. They are looking at how material is organized overall, rather than trying just to look at separate facts.[3]

Schema theory questions the conventional view that pupils should learn to reproduce the exact statement found in the text. It casts doubt on the idea that books have explicit meanings that can be understood without the need for interpretive frameworks. According to schema theory, a text is gobbledygook unless the reader can breathe meaning into it. Thus, students who can not apply schemata in an appropriate fashion may have trouble learning and recalling text information when study-reading.

Schemata, then, help readers (1) assimilate new information (e.g., *flan* is added to our existing schema for the category *desserts*); (2) see what is important (with a schema for reading math problems, readers must decide which operations to use to find the answer); (3) make inferences that elaborate (in a sports schema, a reader differentiates ball size when reading about a golf ball or about a batter hitting a baseball); (4) summarize by aiding in the separation of important ideas from less important ones (with a fable schema, readers would give more weight in their summary to the moral than to the character, action, or event); (5) aid memory, as our schema influences interpretation, and it is our interpretation of the text rather than the text itself that we will recall. Our schema first influences our interpretation and, when activated, helps us recall later what was read.

> The powerful thing about schemata is that once any element in a network of schemata is specific, it can be understood as it relates to the entire complex. With a schema of school, if "test" is mentioned you will know it refers to a measure of knowledge or aptitude, not a shell, or trial or reaction to a chemical.[4]

If we think of our human memory as resembling a library or storehouse, we can picture it as a system for storing and retrieving information. In order to retrieve a book or information, it must have been initially stored in some meaningful, organized, or systematic way. When we forget something, it is like attempting to locate a book in the library. The book is there somewhere, but we just don't know how to find it. When we speak of short-term memory, it means we have not processed the material by putting it into a relevant category for later retrieval.

HOW DID WE GET HERE? A NUTSHELL HISTORY OF READING IN AMERICAN SECONDARY SCHOOLS

In an attempt to better understand today's study-reading problems, let us glance briefly at some major historical antecedents in the evolution of the American secondary school. This section is adapted with permission from *Reading and Learning from Text* by Harry Singer and Dan Donlan (1980), pages 3–5.[5]

In the nineteenth century, the American secondary school evolved from one with a selective, classical, narrow curriculum to one that included a heterogeneous group of students and a broad, comprehensive curriculum. It is well to note that in 1880 fewer than 10 percent of 14- to 17-year-olds were enrolled in high school, and those were basically the most successful students. More than a hundred years later, that figure has risen to approximately 85 percent. In 1880 students had few electives, and the principal mode of instruction was lecture and rote memorization. Today we have a plethora of class offerings and a large and varied instructional arsenal of strategies and methods, such as problem solving, simulation, inquiry, individualized learning centers, and cooperative learning.

Over the past century, secondary schools have tried such innovations as progressive and life adjustment education, flexible scheduling, team teaching, and differentiated staffing. During this tumultuous era, we have had the Great Depression (plus smaller recessions), two world wars, a number of police actions, the Cold War, the civil rights movement, and the hue and cry for accountability in education. All of these have had profound effects on secondary schooling.

As our schools evolved, so did instruction in reading to learn, or study-reading. During World War I, too many draftees could not pass literacy tests. Thus, secondary reading instruction began out of necessity and has continued to be a permanent part of the secondary curriculum. From the 1940s to the 1960s, developmental reading, which emphasized a continuum of reading instruction from K to 12, was beginning to be practiced throughout the country. In the 1960s federal funds were available to subsidize secondary reading laboratories, which continued to focus more on basic skills of *learning to read* than on study-reading or *reading to learn.* Today, we tend to use secondary reading consultants to help faculty incorporate relevant content reading skills, rather than to function merely as teachers of remedial reading to students.[6] But we still have a long way to go to reach the goal of all teachers incorporating aspects of study-reading into their daily classes.

WHERE WE ARE: SOME SCHOOL PROBLEMS AND REQUIREMENTS TODAY

In his 1984 book *A Place Called School,* Goodlad reported on an extensive study of schools today.[7] For example, some interesting and disturbing findings in English and social studies include such things as overemphasis on mechanics and drill, little on problem solving. The dominant emphasis today in English/language arts is on teaching basic skills or mastery of mechanics such as capitalization, punctuation, syllabication, and parts of speech. Goodlad found that most secondary reading instruction taught by reading teachers is still remedial, involving drill in mechanics or word recognition. Nowhere did he find development of study skills such as listening skills.

The study showed, too, that there is less certainty in schools today about the importance of social studies or about what should be included in this category. At the middle school or junior high level, students take U.S. history, world geography, and state history. In high school the basic courses are American history and government, plus some electives. Rarely are there courses offered in comparative studies of cultures with a global, international content. Class activity mainly involves listening to teacher lectures, reading texts, completing worksheets or workbooks, and taking tests. Overall, there are few problem-solving activities, cooperative learning ventures, or student-planned and -executed projects. Obviously, much remains to be done. A recent movement in Washington State, looking at learning for the twenty-first century, has prompted a number of schools to try out cooperative learning with more active student involvement.

LOOKING BEYOND ENGLISH AND SOCIAL STUDIES

Most people would agree that the amount of reading required today for success, or even survival, in our technologically advanced society has grown rapidly. One example, comparing job-related reading in aviation, shows that one 1911 flight manual was barely a single page in length, whereas in 1952 the U.S. Navy required 1,800 pages of documentation for a Cougar aircraft, and the F-14 now requires 260,000 pages.[8] Those who fall behind in reading competency will have an increasingly difficult time in the world of tomorrow.

One partial solution to the problem of increased reading requirements has been to make writing easier to understand. "Plain language" laws have been enacted in a number of states for consumers' legal contracts, insurance policies, and income tax forms. (Concerns of readability or readable writing will be discussed in Chapter 3.) This is really only a stop-gap measure, as more and more occupations require higher reading skills. But with secondary teachers doing their part to increase literacy, our major problems in this area should soon be dissipated.

LITERACY AND ILLITERACY IN TODAY'S WORLD

- John is 16, white, a remedial student, reluctant, disabled, in tenth grade, reading at a seventh-grade level; he has an IQ of 100 (group-tested) and a small physique; he wears glasses, never volunteers in class, and is often overlooked.
- Anne is 14, white, pseudosophisticated, bored in class, boy-crazy, an eighth-grade student reading at grade level with an IQ of 125; she is pretty and is a cheerleader.
- Carol is 17, black, gifted, college-bound, a superior student, in twelfth grade with an IQ of 145 (group-tested); she is athletic, artistic, and articulate, and is reading at a high college level.
- Jose is 15, culturally diverse, and a potential dropout, an English as a second language (ESL) student from Mexico. He is in ninth grade, has an IQ of 90 (group-tested), is mechanically inclined with a *macho* attitude, but is polite and quiet in class. He is reading at a third-grade level in English—he has never been tested in Spanish.

"Hagar the Horrible" by Dik Browne, March 20, 1988. Reprinted with special permission of King Features Syndicate, Inc.

These descriptions are composites modeled on real secondary students found in all of our classrooms today. The information and labels given here cannot represent all the many variations, potentials, and problems that exist, but they give us an idea of actual individual differences. Try to use them as models for problems as you read on in the text. Think first of how the theory might apply, how and what you would diagnose, and then of what strategies you would like to try. Later you may wish to volunteer to tutor a similar type of secondary student for a more realistic, concrete application of theory as well as further practical experience.

Larrick in "Illiteracy Starts Too Soon" (1987) made a telling statement when she talked about the U.S. Postal Service's 1984 commemorative stamp titled "A Nation of Readers," which shows Lincoln reading to his son. Someone suggested that perhaps the postal authorities had to go back a hundred years in order to depict a father reading to his child. The modern-day duo might instead be watching television.[9]

Statistics vary as to the number of illiterate persons in the United States, but we cannot ignore their basic message:

1. About 25 million American adults cannot read the poison warning on a pesticide can, or a letter from their child's teacher.
2. About 35 million additional adults read at a level below their survival needs in our society.
3. These 60 million together represent more than one-third of the entire adult population of the United States.
4. The United States ranks forty-ninth in its level of literacy among the 159 members of the United Nations.
5. Functional illiteracy is rising, with an estimated 2.3 million adults yearly joining the ranks of the functionally illiterate.[10]

These are alarming figures indeed. Remember that one reason functional illiteracy is rising is that today's jobs require higher levels of reading ability than previously, as seen in the earlier example on aviation.

Definitions of Literacy

"Until recently the Library of Congress subject heading for literacy read 'literacy—see illiteracy.'"[11]

We can define the term *literacy* as the ability to read, communicate, compute, make judgments, and problem-solve or act on our judgments. Being *functionally literate* means having the ability to read such vital material as job applications and manuals, newspapers, graphics, directions, menus, and the like. In other words, it means being able to use written information to function in society, to achieve goals, and to develop potential.

Illiteracy is not a recent phenomenon; it has been with us many years. As Chall, Meron, and Hilferty reported in 1987, there are specific levels of literacy that need to be clarified when we report on or read about the status of literacy.[12]

1. *Lowest level (illiterate):* Unable to read, or able to read only the simplest text and street signs (27 million adults)
2. *Middle level (functionally illiterate):* Able to read only at eighth-grade level or below, able to read the local newspaper or articles in digest magazines (45 million adults)
3. *High school level:* Able to read technical manuals in industry or the military, and national news magazines (72 million adults)

Whatever the discrepancies in numbers in reports of illiteracy, it is easy to see that literacy or the lack of it continues to be a problem in today's world, even with compulsory schooling in the United States and elsewhere.

In a recent issue of the International Reading Association's newsletter *Reading Today*, a description was given of the report of the National Assessment of Educational Progress (NAEP).[13] The NAEP found that young adults, aged 21 to 25, do have basic literacy skills but may falter on more complex reading tasks needed in our technologically advanced society. Work situations may require far more reading than high schools require. Their study, which was backed with a $2 million grant from the U.S. Department of Education, characterized literacy skills in three ways:

1. *Prose literacy:* Skills and strategies needed to understand and use information from texts frequently found in the home or community
2. *Document literacy:* Skills and strategies needed to locate and use information in nontextual materials, including tables, graphs, charts, indexes, forms, and schedules
3. *Quantitative literacy:* Knowledge and skills needed to apply arithmetic operations (addition, subtraction, multiplication, and division, either singly or sequentially) in combination with printed material, as in balancing a checkbook or completing an order form

Tests and Literacy

It is generally agreed that we still need an adequate definition of what constitutes being minimally competent. This is really a matter of judgment. Even when we agree on a definition, we must still decide on the criterion level of competence. Minimal Competency Testing (MCT) is now used in a majority of states at the end of high school to determine whether students meet certain basic standards of literacy. But educators stand on both sides of the fence concerning the practical worth of these tests.

Although we are still in the process of developing better assessments, we lag in developing better uses and better public understanding of what tests can and cannot tell us. One misuse of test scores today may be an overemphasis on literacy as one of our nation's largest problems. Many conclusions about literacy are based on Scholastic Aptitude Test (SAT) scores. SATs, which are given to less than half the high school seniors in the United States, measure reading comprehension and vocabulary at a relatively difficult level. Their purpose is to predict how well students will do in college.

Academic institutions continue to use SAT scores because they are predictors of degrees of literacy. The high correlation between reading comprehension scores and SAT scores means that SAT scores are among the most useful indicators of higher academic potential. Some believe that SAT scores, not standard reading test scores, should be primary instruments to assess reading comprehension.

When we do use standardized tests for accountability purposes, the ones we select should at least do the following: attempt to assess the broadest definition of study-reading and provide information about what students can *do,* rather than just how well they compare to others. They should give information about *how* students study-read, not just how well they read.

Cultural Literacy

In recent years the general population has been hearing about a fourth type of literacy. That is *cultural literacy,* as described by E. D. Hirsch in a book by that name. Political and cultural implications may well affect future curriculum policy. Hirsch maintains that cultural literacy—the grasp of background knowledge we may assume our students have—is the key to effective education. Interesting but controversial is the extensive list titled "What Literate Americans Know" compiled by Hirsch, Kett, and Trefil.[14]

A Final Thought on Literacy

In a 1987 presentation at the annual convention of the International Reading Association, Frank Smith cautioned us not to oversell problems of literacy, not to be carried away by overemphasizing the negative aspects.[15] We tend to do this at times in education. As a secondary teacher, you are directly involved with problems of literacy and illiteracy, whether you wish to be or not.

CENSORSHIP PROBLEMS

Another major problem confronting us today is censorship of school reading materials. A strong movement in the United States is attempting to censor what our students read. In 1987 Ken Donelson developed a list of six typical statements or questions asked by these would-be censors, which all educators need to be ready to confront.[16] For practice in dealing with this sensitive issue, you may wish to debate these representative statements and questions in class. This list is reprinted here with permission from "Six Statements/Questions from the Censors" by Ken Donelson, *Phi Delta Kappan,* November 1987, pp. 208–214.

Censors' Statements and Questions

1. Libraries don't have balanced materials on all sides of an issue. Where are pro-life, pro-family, pro-defense, anti-homosexual, pro-creationist, pro back-to-basics books?
2. We need to get back to educational, moral patriotic fundamentals. Our country was founded by Christians in these fundamentals and needs to return to them. Why don't educators join such good people as Jerry Farwell, Phyllis Schlafly or other conservatives in the crusade to save America?
3. Why do libraries provide children with sex books like the notorious and perverted *Our Bodies, Ourselves*, and promote such filth? Books by authors like Judy Blume are so offensive and fill our children's heads with such thoughts, as of masturbation and birth control. When will educators return to promoting the classics rather than trash?
4. Why don't educators admit that they censor? They call it selecting and editing. Parents are the only honest group—calling it censoring.
5. Educators, willingly or not, promote permissiveness and moral relativism of secular humanism. Don't they realize how dangerous it is? When will they learn? [*Secular humanism*, according to Mel and Norma Gabler, as summarized by Lahaye, involves a belief in the following: (a) evolution is an unquestioned scientific fact; (b) children are their own authorities; (c) there are no absolute rights or wrongs; (d) there is no salvation or heaven and hell; faith is in man, not God; (e) public sex education is necessary, but without moral standards; modesty is belittled, as are purity, chasity, and abstinence; abortion, premarital sex, and homosexuality are accepted; (f) children should have the right to read anything; (g) there is no hope beyond the grave; (h) world citizenship is preferable to national patriotism; (i) socialism is superior to private ownership.[17]]
6. Educators have caved in to feminists and minorities about purging offensive materials—offensive to feminists and minorities. Why not be fair and remove the very few books we ask for?

For many, these are frightening questions. There is a need for all teachers to become knowledgeable about these attacks on our educational system and to be ready to defend our position against censorship. But first we need to be aware of our own communities' values concerning issues such as evolution versus creationism, racial concerns, and reproductive issues. That way, it may be possible to keep damaging attacks from getting out of hand.

Jenkinson gives us suggestions and guidance for dealing with would-be censors, which are adapted here with permission from "Protecting Holden Caulfield and His Friends from the Censors" by Edward B. Jenkinson, *English Journal*, 74 (January 1985), pp. 32–33, copyright © 1985 by the National Council of Teachers of English.

Ten Steps for Teachers When Confronted with Censors

1. Make sure that every book selected for classroom study or for supplementary reading lists meets solid educational objectives. Know every book on your reading list so that you can talk about it intelligently if challenged. Also, make sure that you have previewed every film you show and that you have sound objectives for using that film.

2. When you review the materials selection policies for your school system, play the devil's advocate. Challenge every statement as if you were trying to find some excuse for removing books from classrooms and libraries. Then work with your colleagues to strengthen the policies.

3. Review procedures for handling complaints against teaching materials. Make certain that the procedures do not give anyone the authority to remove a book without the review and recommendation of a reconsideration committee. Also, make certain that the procedures call for the important first step in which the person lodging the complaint has the opportunity to talk informally with the person—librarian or teacher—responsible for the "objectionable" work.

4. Make certain that the school system has adequately informed citizens of its educational philosophy, its curriculum, its goals and objectives, its policies and procedures, and so on.

5. Make certain that anyone who has a complaint about a book or a teaching method is given a fair hearing. (One of the largest protest groups in the nation was formed by a person who was "put down" by a teacher when the parent asked about a book.)

6. Insist on a public hearing when a citizen demands that a book be removed from classroom or library.

7. Help form a group of citizens who are supportive of the schools, of intellectual freedom, and of first-rate education. (Such informal groups have proved to be important in censorship incidents. Ministers who support intellectual freedom are invaluable assets to such a group.)

8. Become acquainted with the publications of protest groups. Learn their buzz-words and be prepared to refute their charges.

9. Be prepared to help the administration refute unfounded charges about classroom activities and the school system's supposed indoctrination of students in the "religion" of secular humanism.

10. Do the best job possible. That does not mean that you will never be the victim of schoolbook protest, but it may cut the likelihood

of trouble in half. It will also help you acquire friends among students and parents who will rally around you in time of need.

SUMMARY

Chapter 1 has examined study-reading from various angles to give us a frame of reference. *Who* should be involved (secondary teachers who use extensive reading, with supportive administrators); *why* study-reading is necessary (our responsibility to educate our students in ways leading to a better society, to help them become independent, self-motivated learners exposed to a variety of viewpoints through reading and motivated to continue to learn through this avenue of communication); *what* is involved (some basic definitions of reading, study-reading, study-learning, study-writing, and schema theory); *how* we got to this point (a nutshell history of reading in American secondary schools); *where* we are (school requirements today as noted by Goodlad's extensive study); and, finally, two major problem areas of concern—illiteracy in today's world and censorship.

NOTES

1. Walter R. Hill, *Secondary School Reading: Process, Program, Procedure* (Boston: Allyn and Bacon, 1979), pp. 18–21.

2. Michigan Curriculum Review Committee and Michigan Reading Association, *New Dimensions in Reading Instruction* (1985).

3. This discussion of schema is adapted with permission from John D. McNeil, *Reading Comprehension: New Directions for Classroom Practice*, 2nd ed. (Glenview, IL: Scott, Foresman, 1987), p. 5.

4. Ibid., p. 7.

5. Harry Singer and Dan Donlan, *Reading and Learning from Text* (Boston: Little, Brown, 1980), pp. 3–5. Adapted with permission.

6. Ibid.

7. John Goodlad, *A Place Called School: Prospects for the Future* (New York: McGraw-Hill, 1984), pp. 206–216.

8. George R. Klare, "Readability," in P. David Pearson, ed., *Handbook of Reading Research* (New York: Longman, 1984), p. 681.

9. Nancy Larrick, "Illiteracy Starts Too Soon," *Phi Delta Kappan* (November 1987), 184–189.

10. Ibid.

11. Myron C. Tuman, *A Preface to Literacy: An Inquiry into Pedagogy, Practice and Progress* (Tuscaloosa: University of Alabama Press, 1987), p. 9.

12. Jeanne S. Chall, Elizabeth Meron, and Ann Hilferty, "Adult Literacy: New and Enduring Problems," *Phi Delta Kappan* (November 1987), 190–196.

13. "Literacy," *Reading Today*, Newsletter of the International Reading Association, reporting on the National Assessment of Education Progress Report, Vol. 4 (December 1986–January 1987).

14. E. D. Hirsch, Jr., *Cultural Literacy: What Every American Needs to Know* (Boston: Houghton Mifflin, 1987).

15. Frank Smith, "Overselling Literacy", speech presented to the International Reading Association, Toronto, May 1988.

16. Ken Donelson, "Six Statements/Questions from the Censors," *Phi Delta Kappan*, November 1987, 208–214, reprinted with permission of the publisher; and Mel Gabler and Norma Gabler, "Mind Control through Textbooks," *Phi Delta Kappan*, 64 (October 1982).

17. Tim LaHaye, *The Battle for the Public Schools* (Old Tappen, NJ: Ravell, 1983), p. 80.

RECOMMENDED READINGS

Alverman, D. E., Moore, D. W., and Conley, M. W., eds. *Research within Reach: Secondary School Reading.* Newark, DE: International Reading Association, 1987.

Brown, A. L., Campione, J. C., and Day, J. D. "Learning to Learn: On Training Students to Learn from Texts." *Educational Researcher*, 10 (1981), 14–21.

Carroll, John B., and Chall, Jeanne S., eds. *Toward a Literate Society: The Report of the Committee on Reading of the National Academy of Education.* New York: McGraw-Hill, 1975.

Goodlad, John. *A Place Called School: Prospects for the Future.* New York: McGraw-Hill, 1984.

Graham, P. "Literacy: A Goal for Secondary School." *Daedalus*, 11 (1981), 119–134.

Harste, Jerome C., and Mikulecky, Larry J. "The Context of Literacy in Our Society." In *Becoming Readers in a Complex Society.* Eighty-third Yearbook of the National Society for the Study of Education. Chicago: University of Chicago Press, 1984.

Holdaway, D. *The Foundations of Literacy.* Sydney, Australia: Ashton Scholastic, 1979.

Jenkinson, Edward B. *Censors in the Classroom.* Carbondale: Southern Illinois University Press, 1979.

Langer, Judith A. "The Reading Process." In Allen Berger and H. Alan Robinson, eds., *Secondary School Reading: What Research Reveals for Classroom Practice.* Urbana, IL: National Conference on Research in English, and ERIC Clearinghouse on Reading and Communication Skills, 1982, pp. 39–51.

Morris, A., and Stewart-Dore, N. *Learning to Learn from Text: Effective Reading in the Content Areas.* North Ryde, Australia, 1984.

Rush, R. Timothy, Moe, Alden J., and Storlie, Rebecca L. *Occupational Literacy Education.* Newark, DE: International Reading Association, 1986.

Singer, Harry, and Ruddell, Robert B., eds. *Theoretical Models and Processes of Reading*, 3rd ed. Newark, DE: International Reading Association, 1985, p. 858.

Tovey, Duane R., and Kerber, James E., eds. *Roles in Literacy Learning: A New Perspective.* Newark, DE: International Reading Association, 1986.

Postorganizer 1
Developing a Text Schema

Before reading further in this text, it would be helpful to begin to formulate a relevant schema (a graphic organizer or cognitive map), on paper or in your mind, of major concepts and their interrelationships. One way to do this is first to study the chapter outline, as suggested previously, and then skim through the entire text rapidly to get an overview with no details. Try sketching out the schema using chapter titles for your initial focus. Check with a partner and make an initial revision. Date this text schema paper and return to it upon completion of the text for confirmation and change. Examples of graphic organizers are found at the beginning of each chapter.

Postorganizer 2
Things to Think About Now and Later

1. Is your schema activated in terms of:

_____ purpose?

_____ background knowledge?

_____ attention?

_____ focus?

_____ interest?

prior to, during, and after reading? _____

What is your purpose? _____

How much do you think you know already? _____

Do you pay close attention, or does your mind wander? _____

Do you keep in mind the focus (or thesis) of chapters so that you can fit the parts into the whole?

_____

Is the information of interest to you? _____

Do you see its relevance to your own life? _____

2. Are any relevant background experiences activated during reading?

_____

If so, what are they? _____

When reading materials for different purposes, do you show adaptability in activating, focusing, maintaining, and refining your interpretations?

_____

Are you aware of strategies to use when coping with a variety of text and

reading purposes? _____ Which ones? _____

3. To what extent is your understanding of texts and purposes adequate

for reading? _____

4. When your understanding diverges from what is generally thought to be the author's intention, do you justify your different interpretation?

_____

5. Can you recognize your own perspective about the topic as well

as others' perspectives? _____

Are you aware of your own level of understanding of a text read for dif-

ferent purposes? Explain. _____

What cognitive level did you use to read this chapter?

_____

Do you recognize new learnings and make potential applications to

what you already know? _____

Do you make a mental note of new learnings? _____

What potential applications from new learnings can you make here?

_____

Study-Reading: A Frame of Reference

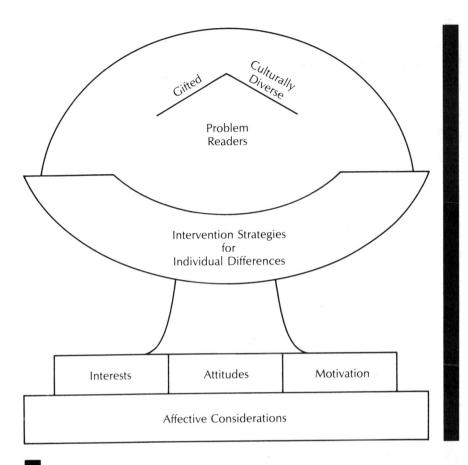

Gifted

Culturally
Diverse

Problem
Readers

Intervention Strategies
for
Individual Differences

Interests	Attitudes	Motivation

Affective Considerations

2

Affective Concerns
and Individual Differences

CHAPTER OUTLINE

Preorganizers
Introduction
Affective Domain
Reading Interests
  Vicarious Experiences
  What Do We Read?
  Research Generalizations on Adolescent Reading Interests
  Interest Inventories
  Techniques for Increasing Interests
Reader Attitudes and Motivation
  Ludic or Pleasure Reading
  Bibliotherapy
Individual Differences: Gifted Readers
  Challenging Gifted Readers
  The Must-Read List
  Approaches to Teaching Literature to the Gifted
  Social Studies and Sciences for the Gifted
  Cooperative Learning
Cultural Diversity and Cooperative Pluralism
  NELB and Black Populations
  Nonstandard English
  Cultural Meanings and Reading
  Bilingualism and ESL Programs
  Two Studies
Problem Readers
  Physical Factors
  Case Studies in Dyslexia
  Cognitive Factors
  Experimental Factors
  Two Principles of Remedial Instruction
  Problem Readers in the Regular Class
  Developmental Stages in Reading: Aid for Remedial Teachers
  Remedial Readers and Metacognitive Deficiencies
  Intervention Strategies
  Quick Tips for Helping Remedial Readers
Summary
Notes
Recommended Readings
Postorganizers

COGNITIVE COMPETENCIES

1. *List* three significant learning generalizations concerning affective dimensions, and state why each is significant.

2. *Create* another "Let's Read" list of vicarious experiences awaiting readers, using the chapter list as a guide.

3. *Research* secondary student reading interests in your school or a nearby secondary school, and compare the results to what other authorities have found.

4. *Interview* and *write up* a brief case study type of description of a gifted reader, a secondary remedial reader, and a culturally diverse student. You may wish to interview other teachers to obtain your information.

5. *Devise* a one-page plan of attack for incorporating effective enrichment, remedial, and culturally relevant strategies in your subject classroom.

KEY TERMS

affective domain
bibliotherapy
bilingualism
cooperative pluralism
cultural diversity
dyslexia

ESL programs
interest inventories
ludic reading
metacognitive deficiencies
NELB
reciprocal teaching

Preorganizer 1
Personal Attitudes toward Reading

1. Before reading this chapter, ponder your position, your own attitude toward reading in general. How much do you really value being able to read? Would you usually opt to read rather than become involved in another activity? What are several reasons that you read? What are your own reading preferences? It is important actually to write your response now for later comparison. Write your comments here:

   _____

   _____

   _____

2. Now jot down the title of one book that you have read purely for fun and enjoyment in the past month.

   _____

   (Don't worry if you cannot remember the exact title or author.)

3. What type of article in a magazine did you read with interest this past week?

   _____

4. What is your favorite section of the newspaper (e.g., sports)?

   _____

5. What one book has made a difference in your life? _____

   When and why (optional)? _____

   _____

6. What book would you recommend today to your colleagues that you consider a "must-read"? _____

   _____

   Why? _____

   _____

   Thinking about these issues now is important to your teaching. If you are not highly motivated to read something, it will be more difficult for

Affective Concerns and Individual Differences

you to convince your secondary students of the importance of reading in their lives. It's a case of "Do as I say, not as I do." As we all know, secondary students are quite canny in discovering this about their teachers and other significant adults in their lives.

If you stop to ponder this, you may well agree that reading has, at the very least, the advantage of selectivity and availability over most other pursuits. By the end of this chapter, any doubters should be convinced that the affective side is crucial to successful teaching and learning for all our students.

Preorganizer 2
Affective Objectives

What are your attitudes, feelings, and involvement?

Levels	You as a reader will:
(receive)	1. Show you are concentrating on reading the chapter, and thinking about its importance for the quiz or discussion, by such behaviors as keeping your eyes on the page, sitting silently, and not moving.
(respond)	2. Voluntarily write notes on your reading or highlight significant statements in the chapter.
(value)	3. State orally to peers in class how important the material read is to you or how significant it is to teaching, willingly giving reasons for your position.
Types	
(motivation)	4. Show you are motivated to use strategies discussed in the chapter by volunteering to describe how you would adapt them to your own class.
(interest)	5. Display interest in the topic by such behaviors as asking questions, giving personal examples, or listening carefully to the discussion.
(self-concept)	6. Show acceptance of your own ability and self-worth by actively risking discussion of difficult areas and trying to connect to new areas.

Affective Concerns and Individual Differences   **29**

Preorganizer 3
How to Turn Off Students to Reading/Writing

Here are some things of which teachers should beware. Check those items that apply to your own past schooling. As you read on, consider reasons why you should *not* perpetuate the same techniques with your students.

_____ Ask the class to read aloud in a round-robin manner, one by one, up and down the rows. Correct all mispronunciations. *Note:* Students should *never* be asked to read aloud for an audience what they have not first read silently and had the opportunity to practice. Oral reading to a group should be a form of oral interpretation or dramatics.

_____ After a silent reading assignment, ask only low-level, literal, "I've got the facts" questions, never allowing for personal inference, criticism, or creative embellishment, and not allowing students to search for answers in the texts. *Note:* Too many teachers ask what students perceive as "Guess what's in my head" questions. This means there is only one correct response, so the tendency when unsure is to duck behind another student's head to get out of the teacher's "line of fire."

_____ Use reading or writing as a punishment for misbehavior—for example, having a student write something fifty times or read in the detention room, with all its negative connotations. *Note:* We want our students to associate reading and writing with pleasant experiences, so that they will voluntarily choose to read or write on their own.

_____ Refuse to accept reading of current best-sellers in school, telling students instead that if they finish early you will give them more content-related work. *Note:* Ridiculing students openly because you have discovered they are hiding their own books inside their text will only embarrass them and bring about negative feelings.

_____ Insist that every unknown word be immediately looked up in the dictionary or glossary and written down. *Note:* Giving the class long lists of words to be looked up, defined, and used in a sentence is the single most effective turn-off to vocabulary development.

_____ Assign silent reading in class and then talk to individuals in a voice loud enough to disturb concentration. *Note:* Concentration is difficult for many students, who may require either absolute quiet or continuous background sound, such as classical music.

What other things had teachers done in the past to turn off students to reading or writing? _____

_____

_____

2
Affective Concerns
and Individual Differences

*There is hardly any grief that an hour's reading
will not dissipate.*
MONTESQUIEU

INTRODUCTION

When we consider that the affective domain in the area of schools takes into account all of our interests, attitudes, and motivations toward reading, writing, studying, and learning, it is surprising that more emphasis is not placed on it, for it actually undergirds all that we attempt to accomplish.

Spiegal (1981) reports that it has been estimated that one-half of the adult population in the United States has never read a book to the finish.[1] It is my strong belief that none of us want a world where our future adults are "aliterate"—able to read but chosing not to do so. This chapter looks at the interests, attitudes, and motivations of all secondary students—gifted, culturally diverse, remedial, and disabled.

AFFECTIVE DOMAIN

In 1964 Krathwohl, Bloom, and Masia developed a taxonomy of educational objectives in the affective domain.[2] The first three levels—receiving, responding, and valuing—directly apply to every classroom at every grade level. The last two levels of the taxonomy, organizing and characterization, which take into account consistency of values and total commitment, might better serve as long-term goals of schools.

At the lowest level, *receiving,* students are attending, but not with enthusiasm. A step higher, *responding,* means first responding only when asked to do so, then responding voluntarily, and finally showing satisfaction and interest in responding. We all hope our students will reach the third level, *valuing,* because we want them to see the relevance and significance of what we are teaching and to be willing to admit this publicly.

READING INTERESTS

Vicarious Experiences

If we are motivated to read, have a positive attitude toward it, and have an opportunity to read about those things that interest us, we will share in a world of riches. Just consider some of the vicarious experiences awaiting us, according to our interests:

Let's *be stirred* by a historical romance by Victoria Holt!

Let's *track down* a criminal with Agatha Christie, Ruth Rendell, or Simenon!

Let's *tickle our fancy* or *expand our creative imagination* with the science fiction of Frank Herbert or Ray Bradbury!

Let's *indulge* in the fantasy of Tolkien!

Let's *be kept in suspense* by Robert Ludlum or Clive Cussler!

Let's *empathize* with the horror of Anne Frank's life!

Let's *discover* hidden personal sides to famous British historical figures with Jean Plaidy!

Let's *laugh* along with Erma Bombeck!

Let's *project* into the future with Isaac Asimov!

Let's *explore* new worlds with Carl Sagan!

Let's *enjoy* the external beauty of Shakespere's sonnets!

Let's *scale* vast mountains with Hillary!

Let's *move back* in American history with Anya Seton or in British history with Sharon Penman!

Let's *travel* around the world with any good travel guide!

Let's *read!*

As Karlin (1984) reminds us, certain books have profound effects on a whole generation. *McGuffey's Readers* shaped moral behavior for many years; *Uncle Tom's Cabin* influenced attitudes toward slavery; and Sylvia Ashton

Warner's *Teacher* and *Spinster* helped to spark public interest in a different approach to schooling, which focused on individual needs and interests.[3] A varied reading diet can be as important as a varied food diet, affecting and enriching our lives in countless ways.

Why Do We Read?

There are numerous reasons for reading, each purpose affecting how we pursue the task. First, we read to learn—to obtain information and better understand our world, to become knowledgeable about certain topics. Most school reading falls into this category and can be thought of as study-reading. Next, we read (or should) for pleasure: for vicarious experiences, escape from reality, enjoyment and visualization of beautiful language; for excitement, suspense, and relief from boredom; or to learn how to fix, build, or create something. Finally, we may read for better understanding of ourselves and others through bibliotherapy (therapeutic response through books). We may empathize with or even become in our imagination a character in a story, thereby hoping to find answers to our problems, to cope with our daily lives, to gain insight into our own beliefs and values.

What Do Adolescents Read?

Adolescents have been found to read the following categories of material:

- *Vocational:* Careers, types of work
- *Social:* Getting along with others in work or play
- *Special interests:* Artistic pursuits, hobbies, sports, crafts
- *Literary:* Historical fiction, romance, mystery, spy thrillers
- *Technical/scientific:* Learning about our environment

Interests may also change frequently as adolescents mature. Although we cannot predict with absolute accuracy the interests of any specific individual within an age category, we can look at what they most frequently choose as a group. Carlsen (1980), for example, found that many interests can span a number of years.[4] Mysteries may be of high interest at all ages. After looking over Table 2.1 as a sample, you might wish to survey your own students and adapt the list each year accordingly. When interviewing, try to ascertain what it is that makes a book a favorite. Compare your students to the list in Table 2.1.

TABLE 2.1
Adolescent Reading Interests[5]

Ages 11–14	Ages 15–16	Ages 17–18
Animals	Nonfiction adventure	Search for personal
Adventures	Biography and	values
Sports	autobiography	Social significance
Mysteries	Adolescent life	Strange and unusual
Supernatural	War stories	human experience
Growing up around the	Historical novels	Transition to adulthood
world	Many from the 11–14	Many from the 11–14 and
Home and family life	list	15–16 lists
Slapstick humor		
Historical settings		
Science fiction		

Source: From *Books and the Teen-age Reader* by Robert G. Carlsen, 2nd revised edition. Copyright © 1980 by Bantam Books, New York. Used with permission.

Research Generalizations on Adolescent Reading Interests

Early (1984) has drawn several generalizations from research on adolescent interests in reading,[5] but not all authorities are in agreement. You may wish to react to these generalizations in class, stating your reasons for agreeing or disagreeing.

• Almost all adolescents report some interest in reading newspapers and magazines. (Is that because they are shorter than books? More up to date?)

• Clear differences do exist between female and male reading interests, but exceptions can be found. (We all recognize the cliché that girls like to read about romance, boys about sports or adventure.)

• In general, urban, suburban, and rural adolescents are all interested in the same kinds of reading. (This might come as somewhat of a surprise to those who would predict wider differences between rural and urban children, based on their background experience.)

• Age and grade levels in secondary schools seem to make little difference in reading interests. (There is a great deal of overlap.)

Early concludes that gender is the only variable that does make a difference in what adolescents choose to read. Do you agree?

Interest Inventories

An efficient way to learn more about your students' hobbies, activities, or interests is to administer some type of interest inventory. There are three types of interest inventories: general activities, reading interests, and subject-specific ones. A general inventory to discover student hobbies and activities might be useful in an English or reading class, for example. Figure 2.1, the Tonjes Interest Inventory (TII), lists 73 items, from sports to music, from gardening to types of reading.

A second kind of interest inventory is concerned with specific reading interests when reading for pleasure. At the beginning of a term, when you are diagnosing or determining the cognitive levels of your students, you may also wish to discover what they most like to read. Here is a sample that can be adapted to your classroom, as shown in Figure 2.2.

Following a survey of general areas of interest, you may wish to discover specific interests of your students which could be tied to your discipline. An example of a U.S. history interest inventory is shown in Figure 2.3. This could be adapted to any class requiring outside collateral reading.

Techniques for Increasing Interest

There are many ways to increase student interest in reading and writing while at the same time carrying out the content purpose of the lesson. Variety is encouraged, as any overused technique loses its potency. Many of these ideas were adapted from a list compiled by Shepherd (1982) and are used here by permission.[6] As a class exercise, it might be useful to categorize these 29 suggestions and possibly prioritize them.

_____ 1. Establish a library corner in the classroom containing collateral reading materials pertaining to your subject.

_____ 2. Take time to discuss books you are reading with students, tying them to personal experience as a model for them.

_____ 3. In English and reading classes, allow secondary students to illustrate their own stories and units. Some less able readers will find success here where they have not succeeded with writing alone.

_____ 4. Set up a "book of the quarter" by departments in such areas as science fiction, biography, historical fiction, humor, cookbooks, how-to books, and so on. Share with your class some of the things the faculty are discussing, thus serving as models of your own interest in reading.

list continues on page 40

FIGURE 2.1
Tonjes Interest Inventory (TII)

Name _____ Date _____

A. Circle each activity that you enjoy.

1. football	26. sailing	51. carpentry
2. baseball/softball	27. canoeing	52. auto remodeling
3. basketball	28. power boating	53. motorcycling
4. soccer	29. fishing	54. disco dancing
5. hockey	30. hunting	55. square dancing
6. la crosse	31. bicycling	56. card games
7. volleyball	32. backpacking	57. packaged games
8. tennis	33. archery	(e.g., Trivial Pursuit)
9. badminton	34. gymnastics	58. chess
10. racketball	35. reading newspapers	59. parties
11. handball	36. reading magazines	60. picnics
12. golf	37. reading novels	61. singing
13. track	38. reading nonfiction	62. playing a musical
14. wrestling	39. Ping-Pong	instrument
15. jogging	40. pool, billiards	63. listening to music
16. surfing	41. bowling	64. raising animals
17. skin diving	42. movies	65. gardening
18. water skiing	43. watching television	66. jigsaw puzzles
19. swimming	44. acting	67. crossword puzzles
20. diving	45. attending museums	68. drawing, painting
21. roller skating	46. concerts	69. attending plays
22. ice skating	47. ballet	70. sculpting
23. downhill skiing	48. cooking	71. writing
24. cross-country skiing	49. sewing	72. composing
25. horseback riding	50. ham radio	73. photography
		74. _____

B. List any other recreational activities not on this list you have engaged in during the past year and enjoyed.

75. _____   77. _____

76. _____   78. _____

C. Look over the activities you have selected and decide which three you most prefer. List in order of preference.

1. _____

2. _____

3. _____

D. Add up the number of activities you enjoy. _____

What is one thing you learned about yourself from taking this interest inventory? I learned that _____

What will you do with this information now, to enhance learning? Explain. _____

Source: From Marian J. Tonjes and Miles V. Zintz, *Teaching Reading, Thinking, Study Skills in Content Classrooms,* 2nd ed., p. 94. Copyright © 1987 Wm. C. Brown Publishers, Dubuque, Iowa. All Rights Reserved. Reprinted by permission.

FIGURE 2.2
Secondary Questionnaire: Personal Leisure Reading

Check the answers that best describe what is true for you. There are no wrong responses. This questionnaire will be kept confidential. Its purpose is to help best meet your particular interests.

1. Outside of schoolwork, what kind of reading do you actually do most often?

_____ newspaper   _____ novels

_____ magazines   _____ nonfiction (e.g., biography, personal accounts)

_____ comic books

_____ short stories   _____ other (state)

_____

2. Which of the above do you enjoy most, when you have the time, access, or money?

_____

3. Where do you do most of your leisure reading?

_____ study hall   _____ town library

_____ school library   _____ other (specify)

_____ at home   _____ I don't do any leisure reading.

4. When do you most often read for pleasure?

_____ weekday evenings   _____ any time

_____ weekends   _____ other (specify)

_____ vacations   _____ It is never a pleasure.

5. When reading, do you prefer absolute silence, or to have music or the TV playing?

_____

Do you prefer to read alone or with others? _____

6. How long do you usually read for pleasure at one stretch?

_____ 15 minutes   _____ 1 hour

_____ 30 minutes   _____ longer, and if so, how long?

_____

7. Approximately how many books do you own personally?

_____ none   _____ 1–5   _____ 6–10   _____ 11–20

_____ 20–40   _____ over 40   _____ prefer not to answer

8. If you were stranded on a desert island with only one object, which would you choose? You may wish to rank-order these items, with item 1 being the most important.

_____ game	_____ Bible
_____ pocket calculator	_____ anthology of poetry and short stories
_____ diary with pencil	_____ encyclopedia in one volume
_____ musical instrument	_____ dictionary
_____ tape recorder, tape, and solar batteries	_____ novel

9. How long does it take you to read all of your homework each day?

_____ 15 minutes	_____ 1 hour
_____ 30 minutes	_____ longer, and if so how long?
	_____

10. Which do you prefer doing, reading or writing? _____

Why? _____

11. Do you usually finish what you start to read? _____

12. Do you ever lose yourself in a story so that you forget your surroundings?

_____

13. Do your parents or other adults try to influence what you read? _____

14. When reading just for fun, do you read as slowly and carefully as you do for classwork?

_____

15. Have you ever been proud of something you wrote and wanted to share it with others?

_____

16. Do you prefer watching TV or movie adaptations to reading the same story?

_____

17. Is there a book you have read that was better than the TV or movie adaptation? _____

If so, which one? _____

Why was it better when read rather than viewed? _____

_____

_____

18. If a friend were in the hospital, what two entertaining books would you like to send along?

1. _____

2. _____

FIGURE 2.3
U.S. History Interest Inventory

Directions:

We will be studying U.S. history from colonial times to the present, divided into six units. You will be expected to read at least one outside article for each unit. The purpose of this inventory is to help me assist you in finding material of special interest to you. Please mark your preference within each unit, 1, first choice; 2, second choice; 3, third choice. Fill in the blank only if you have a preference not included here. In that case, check with me.

Colonial Times (1600–1760)

_____ a. Biography

_____ b. Family life

_____ c. Freedom and justice

_____ d. _____

Revolutionary War Era (1760–1785)

_____ a. Politics

_____ b. Battles

_____ c. The British position

_____ d. _____

Civil War Era (1850–1876)

_____ a. Battles

_____ b. Politics

_____ c. Slavery

_____ d. _____

Western/Frontier Life

_____ a. Native Americans

_____ b. Pioneers

_____ c. Wild West tales

_____ d. _____

World War II (1939–1945)

_____ a. Atomic/hydrogen bombs

_____ b. War in the Pacific

_____ c. War in Europe

_____ d. _____

Recent History (1945–today)

_____ a. Black movement

_____ b. Women's rights

_____ c. Presidents' power

_____ d. _____

_____ 5. Allow students to compose a drama or readers' theater script of a short story or historical episode to present to the class or assembly.

_____ 6. Use the notion of *story teasers,* which involves reading or summarizing part of the story, stopping at the most crucial point. If you have captured the students' interest, they will have to read the story for themselves in order to find out what happens.

_____ 7. When assigning research reading, use a problem-solving approach that includes students having to refine study-reading skills – skills such as checking validity of information and critiquing according to their own stated criteria.

8. Allow students to work in pairs or small groups in preparing annotated bibliographies of references or readings on their chosen topics related to your class.

9. Assign committees to be in charge of bulletin board displays related to units or stories, changing committees for every unit.

10. On a back table, set up a sampling of provocative-appearing reading material on the topic of a study. Include eye-catching artifacts, a background shape, photographs, and the like. Give a brief overview of each.

11. Tie in units or stories with their location in the country and the world by placing a pin in a map and attaching a ribbon to the pin with the label of the unit or story on it.

12. Pose personalizing questions about the reading that require students to bring in their own background experiences, beliefs, and values. Here are some examples:
    a. How would you have solved this problem?
    b. How do you think this might be true of life today?
    c. Why do you suppose the author was concerned with
    _____? What was the author's purpose?
    d. If you had lived back then, what would you have been like? Describe yourself physically (including your clothes) and also emotionally.

13. Have students research life in the United States or Canada in the year they were born, noting prices of goods, clothing styles, music preferences, movies or TV, world leaders, and special historical events and concerns of that time. Compare all this to today's world.

14. After students read a biography, ask them to write their own, making it as interesting as possible, thinking of past events that were humorous, frightening, or especially exciting. Students may also include their own beliefs and opinions. One option might be to have the class guess whose life it is after listening to you read one of the biographies aloud.

15. Keep a file easily available to your class of brief reviews of favorite books (*not* book reports) written by former students.

These could be categorized with labels such as history, mystery, science fiction, biography, humor, and poetry.

16. Select a current national or local issue and assign students to read newspapers and articles in order to prepare a panel discussion with a possible resolution. One option could be an English debate in which one side must try to convince members of the other side to join them, with key ideas pulled together at the end by the moderator.

17. Using the "hooked on books" notion of Daniel Fader, get the parents and the community to contribute paperback books to build a classroom library. Students should help serve on the screening committee.

18. Use a variation of the cloze procedure for reporting on outside reading. Delete a key word from each title handed in and signed, and have the rest of the class guess the correct word. The person who submitted the title verifies the responses. After they have correctly completed the title, have students conjecture what the book is about.

19. Have students keep a graph of the number and types of collateral reading they have completed.

20. Allow classroom time for browsing after new books are added to the collection. Teach or remind students how to browse, such as by reading quickly through the first chapter and then spot-reading a paragraph here or there throughout the book (but not the ending).

21. Use choral reading with poetry and stories that include much conversation. Discuss with students how tone, pitch, and stress may affect meaning. Practice first with a short sentence that changes meaning depending on stress.

22. Give students a verbal description and have them draw what they think is being described. Point out how pictures, though accurate, may differ, and have them speculate as to why this is so.

23. Organize a book-of-the-month club for an after-school activity in which students all read a pertinent book they have had a voice in selecting, then discuss it in small groups.

24. Ask students to imagine that a particular text or book they are reading has just been found three thousand years from

now. What information would the people learn about how we live, our problems and concerns? What misconceptions mnight they have about us? (Archaeologists have said we will be remembered as the white bowl people.)

25. Have students interview other students about their past and present reading interests and how these interests have changed or expanded. Report on these interviews or make a composite graph on the board.

26. Practice oral interpretation for a polished performance. Teachers should read to students to inform, entertain, and model the art. Make first selections brief, practice, and then get students to read to each other. Plays are especially good for this. Remedial students particularly enjoy reading aloud plays found in magazines such as *Scholastic*.

27. Make tapes of performances.

28. Use sustained silent reading (SSR) with outside reading on a regular basis, reminding students that there will be no interruptions of any kind and no moving around the room. Hang a sign outside the door saying No Interruptions—SSR. Remember that teachers must read a book of their choice too in order to serve as a model. Start with short spans such as 10 to 15 minutes and build up gradually. Use a kitchen timer so no one has to be a clock-watcher. When students forget their outside reading book, provide them with one from your collateral reading collection.

29. Have a "read-in" every Friday using all kinds of reading material, including newspapers and magazines of general and specific subject area interest. At the end of class, have the students count the number of pages read and enter this information in their reading log, including the title and author. Every second or third week, have students meet in small groups or in conference with the teacher to discuss their experiences, feelings, and questions.

30. Include here another motivational idea that can spark reader interest _____

_____

_____

_____

READER ATTITUDES AND MOTIVATION

People tend to pursue those areas that are of interest to them and bring them some measure of satisfaction. Why is it that some adolescent students read regularly, willingly, enthusiastically, on their own initiative, in their own free time? Why is it that others avoid reading whenever possible? Naturally, we will assume that past experiences play a great role in students' motivation and attitude toward reading. Another reason for avoidance, we might predict, will often be lack of skill in reading.

Ludic or Pleasure Reading

Five studies conducted over a six-year period by Nell (1988) were concerned with the psychology of reading for pleasure, or ludic reading.[7] These studies focused on light fiction because this has been found to account for most ludic reading, and because light fiction lends itself most readily to losing ourselves in the story, forgetting the world around us.

The term *ludic reading* comes from the Latin word *ludo,* meaning "I play," and reminds us that pleasure reading is a play activity, pursued voluntarily for its own sake. We might define ludic readers as those who choose to read at least one book a month for relaxation, escape, and pleasure. How many ludic readers are there in your classes? Among your faculty?

Nell's findings were as follows:

1. That readers perceive literary merit to be inversely related to reading pleasure
2. That there was a substantial variability of rate during natural pleasure reading
3. That those pages that were most liked were read at significantly lower rates
4. That readers greatly prize the control they maintain over their own reading
5. That being able to conjure up vivid imagery may be a prerequisite.

When analyzing motivation for ludic reading, we realize it is not the words alone on the page that motivate us, but our own interaction with the message in the text.

There is a delicate balance between selecting reading over alternative activities. We must continually compare the rewards of reading to those of other enticements and decide whether it is time to switch to something else. With ludic reading, our students must be assured that it makes sense to stop reading a particular book if they are bored with it, or fail to see the frame of reference, or dislike the writer's style. Pleasure reading should be just that, so reading just to finish a book makes little sense.

Brainstorming with a class to elicit their reasons for choosing reading over other activities will no doubt bring forth thoughts like these:

1. Having personal control over the book
2. Reading at our own desired rate
3. Rereading for a variety of purposes
4. Using our own imagination
5. Stopping and starting as we wish
6. Having a wide selection from which to choose

Students may then stop and think more seriously about the values of reading.

Bibliotherapy

Bibliotherapy (therapy through books) is a potentially powerful tool, a process whereby readers come to identify with a story, or a particular character in a story, connecting in some way what they are reading to their own personal problems and thus gaining insight, catharsis, or comfort. By reading a book that depicts a particular problem, it is possible for students to understand better and begin to deal with troubles such as death, divorce, alcoholism, and unwanted pregnancy, which may cause them to come to class unmotivated, unresponsive, and upset, unable to concentrate and learn.

Because most teachers are not trained counselors, there are certain dangers and cautions that must be observed. First, you should be familiar with a book's message before recommending it. For example, if a student has cancer, a book about accepting death from cancer is counterproductive if the student is successfully fighting the cancer. When suggesting a particular book to a student in need, never use it as an assignment. Any follow-up discussion should be up to the individual student. Students may wish to share their fears or to ask questions, or they may not. If they choose to talk to you, it is wise to be an empathetic listener, not giving advice but possibly suggesting referral to the school counselor. If that is threatening, it is best just to listen and then assure the student of the confidentiality of the matter. A sample of bibliotherapy references can be found at the end of this chapter.

Affective dimensions are so important to successful teaching and learning that they cannot be overemphasized. In the next section of this chapter, we will look briefly at the individual differences of our students, from gifted to culturally diverse to remedial or problem readers. The affective factors should be kept in mind for all students.

INDIVIDUAL DIFFERENCES: GIFTED READERS

Challenging Gifted Readers

An area that is often overlooked is finding ways of challenging gifted readers. Good books can stimulate thought and provide a knowledge base needed for problem solving and creative thinking. William Bennett, former U.S. secretary of education and former chairman of the National Endowment for the Humanities, conducted a survey of 325 journalists, teachers, business officials, and parents. From their responses, he compiled a list of authors and their literary works that all American students should study.[8] This list lends itself particularly well to challenging gifted secondary students. How many of these have you read sometime in the past?

The Must-Read List

1. Shakespeare (particularly *Macbeth* and *Hamlet*)
2. American historical documents (particularly the Declaration of Independence, the Constitution, and the Gettysburg Address)
3. Twain *(Huckleberry Finn)*
4. The Bible
5. Homer *(The Odyssey, The Iliad)*
6. Dickens *(Great Expectations, A Tale of Two Cities)*
7. Plato *(The Republic)*
8. Steinbeck *(The Grapes of Wrath)*
9. Hawthorne *(The Scarlet Letter)*
10. Sophocles *(Oedipus)*
11. Melville *(Moby Dick)*
12. Orwell *(1984)*
13. Thoreau *(Walden)*
14. Frost (poems)
15. Whitman *(Leaves of Grass)*
16. Fitzgerald *(The Great Gatsby)*
17. Chaucer *(The Canterbury Tales)*
18. Marx *(The Communist Manifesto)*
19. Aristotle *(Politics)*
20. Dickinson (poems)

21. Dostoevsky *(Crime and Punishment)*
22. Faulkner (various works)
23. Salinger *(Catcher in the Rye)*
24. De Tocqueville *(Democracy in America)*
25. Austen *(Pride and Prejudice)*
26. Emerson (essays and poems)
27. Machiavelli *(The Prince)*
28. Milton *(Paradise Lost)*
29. Tolstoy *(War and Peace)*
30. Virgil *(The Aeneid)*

The Great Books Foundation was formed in 1947 as a private, nonprofit educational organization. It publishes 19 series of books for grades 2 through 12 and for adults, and conducts training sessions for discussion group leaders. The Great Books approach has been used successfully for many years, particularly by colleges such as St. John's in Annapolis, Maryland, and Sante Fe, New Mexico. Classic books are used in lieu of regularly assigned texts. The Junior Great Books program for grades 2 through 12 prescribes specific readings particularly suited to gifted readers.

In this approach, after a basic question is asked at the interpretive level, leaders ask follow-up questions for one of the following purposes:

1. To explore implications
2. To require support for a response
3. To correct factual errors
4. To elicit additional opinions or responses
5. To encourage debate or further discussion
6. To clarify
7. To develop the most important ideas
8. To encourage examination of a response
9. To turn a discussion back to the reading

For further information about this organization and training, write or call:

The Great Books Foundation
40 East Huron Street
Chicago, IL 60611
Phone: 1-800-222-5870

Approaches to Teaching Literature to the Gifted

Qualitative differentiation is a major goal of programming for the gifted. Plauche-Parker gives us four teaching suggestions.[9]

1. Regardless of age, read aloud often to students, using the best literature your students can readily enjoy. Vary the styles, types of material, and methods of presentations to hold interest. Follow these readings with discussion.
2. Introduce each selection in a variety of ways, using media, artifacts, guest speakers, and the like. Go over unfamiliar vocabulary or concepts.
3. Divide students into small groups for follow-up discussion. It is possible to train volunteers in formulating good discussion questions. Teachers can then serve as facilitators, circulating, observing, and coaching.
4. Culminating activities can include the following:
    a. Role playing, dramas, improvising sequels to stories using creative dramatics
    b. Viewing a stage or television drama and writing critical reviews
    c. Writing poetry, prose, or drama as motivated by what has been read

Social Studies and Science for the Gifted

When considering social studies programs for the gifted at the secondary level, it is necessary to provide special opportunities for them through seminars, honors classes, acceleration (where classes are taken ahead of schedule), or concurrent enrollment in college-level courses. It is a good idea to allow the whole community to serve as a laboratory for social studies experience especially for the gifted.

For the secondary science classroom, we still need a stronger focus on the process of inquiry-based activities, scientific investigation, and the moral and ethical dimensions of scientific discoveries. Some fascinating problems yet to be solved are the origins of life, of the solar system, and of the universe; the mechanisms causing aging and death; and how the nervous system processes information.

Cooperative Learning

Gifted students can profit highly by being allowed to work together. They are stimulated by challenges to their ideas, which may make them realize they need to refine and clarify their thinking. In some models of cooperative learning, competition between groups and extrinsic rewards play a major role; in others these might be considered detrimental. When processing the results of small-group discussions, teachers should be nonjudgmental and encourage a variety of responses. The idea is to challenge students to arrive at consensus. The class must realize that they are also responsible for understanding students' explanations and must indicate to the students when they need clarification.

CULTURAL DIVERSITY AND COOPERATIVE PLURALISM

There have been some significant changes recently in how we perceive and work with those students from nondominant cultures and those who speak nonstandard dialects. At one time we referred to these students as *culturally disadvantaged* because they were not from the mainstream culture. We then changed the term to *cultural differences*, which was a step in the right direction. More recently, we have been trying to embrace *cultural diversity* as enriching to all of us, rather than just a problem to be faced. And many, like Goodlad, are now talking about a philosophy of *cooperative (or cultural) pluralism*.

As Goodlad pointed out at a recent speech at the University of Washington, up until now we have looked at multicultural education as involving two cultures, rather than embracing the whole of humanity.[10] The notion of cooperative pluralism gives us the opportunity to join with other groups and movements so that we can begin to live together in understanding, mutual appreciation, and peace. Instead of looking only at specific segments of a culture, we look at the whole system of *people*. We must focus on the interfacing of *people* rather than just the culture of specific ethnic groups. In other words, instead of a fragment, we learn about "us" in an interrelated and connected perspective. This means we concentrate on building skills for actively translating ideals into congruent behavior. And secondary teachers are in a good position to assist in this call for cooperative pluralism.

Goodlad (1984) makes another important point, which also deserves careful thought and discussion.[11]

> The school fails in its function unless it exists in a state of productive tension with the home: home and family create a press of one ethnic identity, one religion, one social class;
>
> Schools press toward a common identification, a sense of homogeneity which encompasses and integrates diverse elements. From this sense of function for schools emerged the concept of the common school. Schools created to assure reinforcement of only one set of values or to serve only one race, one neighborhood, one economic class fail in this function.

Striving toward more open-mindedness is an important goal, then, for all teachers in meeting needs of culturally diverse students.

NELB and Black Populations

There has been a significant increase in the number of culturally diverse students enrolled in our schools, and the trend is expected to continue.[12] In 1980 the *non–English language background* (NELB) population in the United States was approximately 34.6 million. Language-minority children under age 18 numbered 8 million, or 17 percent of the school-age population of the United States. The NELB survey did not include blacks. In 1983 there were more than 28 million blacks, representing 12 percent of the population, and one out of 15 children of school age was either black or NELB. To provide equal educational opportunity for all, we must be prepared to deal with a wide range of linguistic and cultural backgrounds. In her epilogue, Cantoni-Harvey (1987) says it well:

> Minority education must achieve a better balance between its remedial aspects and the rich cross-cultural dimensions it can add to every context in which learning takes place. Minority education needs to develop not only a new image but a new identity which should emphasize the strengths of the students it serves instead of focusing on their limitations. Proper attention must continue to be paid to the needs of those learners who are not fully proficient in English or are inadequately prepared to master the context taught in their classes; however, the unique contributions that can be made by these students should be recognized and gratefully accepted. What they may still lack . . . is balanced by what they can offer to the expanding pool of knowledge shared by their peers; they have much to gain from our schools, but also much to contribute.[13]

Nonstandard English

Those students who speak a dialect, as many blacks do, are speaking a consistent variation of the English language, which is logical and has specific rules. Speaking a dialect is no indication of deficit or inferiority; it is merely different. "I be good" for "I am good" is one example that, interestingly enough, can be traced back to a way of speaking centuries ago in England. Research has shown mixed results of the effects of the use of dialect or nonstandard English. Although some find a correlation between use of dialect and poor reading, others, such as Goodman and Buck (1973), found that the only disadvantage is one imposed by teachers and schools.[14] Rejecting a dialect as being improper can do much to undermine students' linguistic self-confidence. It is best to accept nonstandard English as it occurs and to present practice lessons in standard English to a group at regular intervals.

Cultural Meanings and Reading

When we read, the meaning of the text comes basically from our individual and cultural backgrounds.[15] For that reason, serious misunderstanding can take place when writer and readers represent different cultures. For example, in an English class a Chinese student might seem to be using first-person pronouns incorrectly, when using "we" instead of "I." To the Chinese, "we" means "I am not alone"—the Confucian concept of people as interdependent. Also, connotations of words in English are seldom the same as those of equivalent words in another language. For example, the German word *Freund* is not exactly the same as *friend*. *Freund* refers to a small, intimate group, involving quite different attitudes and mutual obligations than what Americans think of as "friends." Thus, the German student will have a different image and feeling when hearing or reading about friends.

Students must understand sound–symbol relationships, letter formations, spelling, punctuation, and capitalization to be considered literate in the English language. If they are not literate in their first language (L1), or if they have learned to read and write in a language such as Russian or Greek that does not use the Roman alphabet, they will need much practice. Arabs will have to practice writing from left to right instead of right to left; Chinese will have to learn to write alphabetically, not using ideographs, and to arrange words horizontally, not vertically.

Bilingualism and ESL Programs

When we speak of people as *bilingual,* we mean that they speak two languages. In practice, this may not mean they are equally proficient in both, as the term implies. For instance, some Mexican Americans whose mother tongue is Spanish and whose second language is English may have trouble understanding the nuances of English because of a more limited English vocabulary.

Thonis (1976) outlined conditions conductive to enhancing reading achievement of bilingual students.[16] These conditions are as follows:

1. Give more experience with oral language and concepts specific to the language used in school
2. Enhance self-concept, showing respect and empathy for differences
3. Establish fluency in listening and speaking (the natural way to learn) before imposing reading and writing in English

A number of programs have been developed for working with students for whom English is their second language:

TESOL: Teaching English to Speakers of Other Languages
TESL: Teaching English as a Second Language
TEFL: Teaching English as a Foreign Language

Those who do not have ready access to advice from an expert in one of these multicultural programs may still find help in a curriculum guide such as the one recently published by Washington State (*Reading Curriculum Guidelines K–12*, Division of Instructional Programs and Services, Office of the Superintendent of Public Instruction, Olympia, Washington, August 1988). In this guide, goals and learner outcomes are identical across grade bands, but instructional and teacher implications vary. Shown here is goal IV, grade band 10–12, on reading to understand diverse perspectives in a multicultural society.

Goal IV
The Student Reads to Understand the Diverse
Perspectives in a Multicultural Society.

1. **Learner outcome: The student reads to accept and affirm the uniqueness of self and others.**

   Instructional implications: The teacher will:

   - Encourage students to appreciate their own cultural identity through reading and writing.
   - Provide opportunities for students to demonstrate understanding of various multicultural perspectives.
   - Promote positive self-concepts by encouraging students to express and accept individual responses to the materials read.
   - Refrain from using "correct-answer" assessment strategies that promote the notion that there is only one correct answer to questions whose answer might depend upon the experiential background of the reader.
   - Present reading materials that affirm the uniqueness of individuals and avoid stereotyping.

2. **Learner outcome: The student appreciates and empathizes with other points of view about material being read.**

   Teacher implications: The teacher will:

   - Demonstrate the art of analyzing and appreciating what has been presented through various viewpoints.
   - Choose well-written material that meets students' needs and interests so that appreciation and empathy can be more readily demonstrated.

Goal IV *(Continued)*

- Encourage students to draw conclusions about their point of view compared to other points of view.
- Model reading/comparing materials with differing views about the same subject.

3. *Learner outcome:* **The student reads about diverse groups (ethnic, cultural, handicapped, age, and gender).**

   Instructional implications: The teacher will:

   - Provide appropriate materials about diverse groups.
   - Provide an environment reflecting an appreciation of the diversity of groups.
   - Extend students' understanding of text by inviting speakers from diverse groups to make presentations.
   - Encourage students to generate own material reflecting understanding of, and attitudes toward, diverse groups.

4. *Learner outcome:* **The student reads materials written by authors from diverse groups.**

   Instructional implications: The teacher will:

   - Provide materials written by authors representative of diverse groups.
   - Have students meet authors representative of diverse groups (e.g., "Authors in the Schools," Young Authors' Conferences).
   - Have students learn communication systems used by handicapped (e.g., sign and Braille).

5. *Learner outcome:* **The student responds to text written from diverse social, economic, and political perspectives.**

   Instructional implications: The teacher will:

   - Provide opportunities for students to read about current events in periodicals.
   - Provide opportunities for students to share points of view on social and political issues that affect their lives.
   - Encourage students to write about social/political issues and provide time for students to share writing with each other and/or with the community.
   - Encourage students to write and present simulations, plays, and dramatic sketches about political and social issues.
   - Provide students with experiences to generate interest in reading through guest speakers, choral reading, storytelling, role playing, drama.

Two Studies

Two studies of general interest in the area of cultural diversity follow. In the West and Southwest of the United States, Spanish-speakers are often referred to as *Chicanos* and English-speakers as *Anglos*. In a 1984 study, Rogers-Zegarra and Singer found that where Chicanos and Anglos were matched for general reading ability and had lived in a bicultural environment, Chicanos tended to perform as well on test-based reading comprehension as their Anglo peers.[17] Au and Jordan looked at culturally conditioned learning styles of Hawaiian children and found that when instruction in reading was altered to allow students to collaborate in discussion and interpretation of texts, there was dramatic improvement in both reading and verbal intellectual abilities.[18] These two studies have implications for teachers beyond the specific cultures studied.

PROBLEM READERS

Many complex, interwoven factors—physical, cognitive, affective, and experiential—are generally present in those secondary students who have problems mastering their school texts.

Physical Factors

Physical impeding factors include poor vision or hearing; poor general health, which can lead to sporadic attendance and lack of attentiveness; glandular deficiencies; and neurological impairment. Referral to community health care for those who cannot afford private care is essential.

Dyslexia is one condition that some authorities disregard, calling it a "garbage pail" term including any kind of problem with reading. As used here, however, the term *dyslexia* refers exclusively to severe reading problems in readers who have more than an adequate IQ and for whom there is no single obvious explanation for the problem. Dyslexic students tend to be bright, but without special help they may read extremely poorly or not at all.

In my many years of teaching reading, only two students personally stood out as being dyslexic. One was at the high school level, the other a senior at the university. Both students were exceptionally bright, with highly developed listening skills and memories. Here are their stories, as told in case studies. Perhaps they will help you perceive similar problems if and when you encounter them in your classes.

Case Studies in Dyslexia

Robert was a bright, pleasant-mannered, handsome high school junior when he first came to my reading lab. He maintained a B average although he could not read even first-grade-level material and, as I soon discovered, could not even copy words from a text. On the Wechsler Adult Intelligence Scale (WAIS) Robert had an IQ of 128, although on the block design in the performance section, he could not match the diagonal shapes nor even perceive the overall configuration of the blocks themselves. Robert's family had spent a small fortune over the years on tutors, all to no avail. His high grades were due to the fact that he had a tremendous listening capacity and long-term memory. As a case in point, he once reiterated an entire lecture almost verbatim. It was a matter of "once heard, never forgotten." Over the years, teachers had been willing to give him oral exams, in which he did exceedingly well. A noted neurologist took Robert's case as a study for no fee. His conclusion was that Robert had a neurological version of crossed wires and would never be capable of discerning patterns and print. It was recommended that he be allowed to use his other talents instead. With the pressure off from family and school, Robert sailed through his senior year and received a special high school certificate.

Sally (who has since changed her name several times) was my student a number of years later in a university reading class for potential and experienced secondary teachers. She planned to be a high school English teacher. Sally was very attractive, spoke in a well-modulated voice, and was an active, eager, and intelligent participant in class discussion. On the first essay exam I was surprised to note that she took much longer than anyone else to finish. In fact, there was practically nothing written—just a few sentences altogether. I gave her an F and wrote on her paper that I would like to see her in my office as soon as possible. After much hedging, she finally broke down and admitted her problem. It took her hours to read even a few pages, and writing was difficult because the normal way for her to write was backwards—an actual mirror image. Sally had survived the system because her tests had been, up to this point, primarily objective ones, and she had been able to get someone else to type and correct all her papers. She had a horror of anyone's finding out about her problem but acceded to my request that she get help through other university channels. She was thoroughly tested by the psychometrist in the guidance center, with the result that her disability, diagnosed as dyslexia, could mean special consideration from other faculty. A librarian who is also dyslexic tutored Sally over a period of time, discovering, among other things, that placing a tan-colored overlay on the white page with black print eased Sally's ability to distinguish the spaces between words. Sally can now process print much more rapidly, but she has decided not to try to teach English because she has a "lifetime of good reading" to catch up on first. It is noteworthy that many dyslexics have been successfully rehabilitated; dyslexia is not necessarily a lifelong disabling condition.

Cognitive Factors

Now let us look for a moment at cognitive factors that may impinge on students' reading ability. Reading is a cognitive act, which involves such processes as thinking, reasoning, problem solving, conceptualizing, recalling, associating, synthesizing, and evaluating. Those with limited intelligence may be reading and thinking as well as they can for their stages of development; thus, special remedial training may be wasted on such students. Many schools today place in remedial classes only those who have the capacity to benefit from special teaching.

Experiential Factors

When we consider experiential factors, we must realize that how well students read today depends in large measure on their language facility, their cultural and socioeconomic condition, their academic background, and their past reading experiences. We now realize the importance of ascertaining background knowledge. When there is a lack, we need to provide experiences that will fill in the gaps and ensure better comprehension of what is to be read.

Two Principles of Remedial Instruction

If, for some reason, you are assigned to a special reading class, here are some general principles to note for future references. (For those already serving in the role of remedial reading teacher, this will serve as a reminder.)

Young adults who have difficulty reading have a long history of feeling inadequate, guilty, stupid, and/or negative toward school. Many have developed a defeatist, "What's the use?" attitude. For this reason, they must be shown immediately that reading has many practical uses in everyday life, and materials must appear to them to be more adult than childish. These teenagers usually prefer newspapers, comic strips, record albums, menus, TV magazines, and drivers' manuals to workbook types of material. Nonreaders not only have to learn new skills but also must unlearn many misconceptions. Breaking bad habits and attitudes takes time. There is no quick fix, so patience is a necessity.

Any skill drill should be brief, supervised, with immediate feedback, and consistently reviewed. Just as in physical education, there is value in keeping score so that students can see their progress, even though it is in very small steps. Remedial students need a balance between a known routine and lengthy drill. Activities need to be brief and diverse, with practice in comprehending increasingly lengthy passages. There needs to be a time to listen, think, and discuss materials of some sophistication. Although these students cannot read at grade level, they should be exposed to thinking about mature concepts. This can be accomplished at times by reading to them. Developing comprehension means getting a proper balance between merely decoding words and, more important, thinking about the meaning of the message.[19]

Problem Readers in the Regular Class

With around 140 students a day, every secondary teacher will usually have a few culturally diverse, some remedial (those who cannot handle the regular class materials) and some gifted students who need an extra challenge. Early and Sawyer give us some good ideas that can be adapted to many achievement levels.[20]

1. Emphasize major concepts, not details, which are soon forgotten.
2. When possible, find special resources such as films or easier collateral reading on the subject.
3. Emphasize learning through listening, as everyone profits from becoming a better listener. Assigning listening tapes is one way to do this.
4. Keep in touch with the remedial teacher and any assigned tutors.
5. Preteach key vocabulary for every chapter or reading assignment required for the entire class.
6. Discuss interpretation of graphic aids in the text or other resources, asking questions that do not require previous reading of the text.
7. Allow needed time for disabled students to learn or practice a concept.
8. Adjust evaluation when possible to accommodate depressed reading and writing skills.
9. *Encourage, support,* and *challenge* remedial students to learn your subject matter, while accepting their limitations and seeking ways to help them.

Developmental Stages in Reading: Aid for Remedial Teachers

In order to best help our secondary study-readers, it is a good idea to have in mind the series of stages they have passed through to reach reading maturity. Remedial or second-language readers may need further instruction at earlier stages before they are asked to perform at the later stages.

Chall (1983) has proposed a theoretical multistage model to help us perceive the continuum from beginning to mature readers.[21] Of course, each stage is only approximate, with much possible overlapping. Using this as a checklist, you might wish to interview other teachers at varying grade levels to verify or modify the elements found within specific stages. This material is adapted with permission from *Stages of Reading Development* by J. S. Chall, copyright © 1983 by McGraw-Hill Publishing Company, New York.

Reading Stages

Stage 0: Birth to age 6 (prereading):	In a literate culture, the child accumulates knowledge about letters, words, and books.
Stage 1: Grades 1–2.5 (learning to read):	Instruction centers on decoding, associating written symbols with their corresponding sounds, alphabetic knowledge, and the purpose of letters.
Stage 2: Grades 2.5–4 (consolidation):	Consolidation of decoding and sight vocabulary skills, reading to confirm what is already known, using familiar content, high-frequency words, increasing fluency and automatic low-level processing. Word-by-word reading, common to stage 1, is indicative of reading difficulty by the end of stage 2.
Stage 3: Grades 4–8 (reading to learn):	This is a pivotal, transitional time in reading, when the emphasis shifts from decoding and confirmation of that decoding to comprehension of increasingly more complex material in a variety of disciplines. This stage requires more sophisticated language and cognition, as well as greater world knowledge. Reading must become reflective, with the reader accumulating many layers of facts to build upon, and noting fine details. Correctness and accuracy become important. Inability to reach this stage causes major problems in later content areas.
Stage 4: Grades 9–12 (toward reading maturity):	Readers grapple with multiplicity, comparing and contrasting a variety of viewpoints. They learn to detect irony and identify recurring themes. Rate of reading must be increasingly adaptable and effective in order to keep up with the multitude and variety of assignments. An important factor is being able to decide when to skim, scan, or focus intently while reading at a snail's pace. The facts and concepts acquired in stage 3 are the basic essential foundations for effective reading at stage 4.

| Stage 5: College, age 18 and above (reading maturity, constructive): | Reader can read in the degree and for whatever detail is needed to meet the purpose. They are selective, construct knowledge on a high level of abstraction and generality, and create their own truths. |

Remedial Readers and Metacognitive Deficiencies

Nine areas of metacognitive deficiencies are often found in low-achieving or remedial secondary readers.[22] (The list that follows is adapted with permission from "An Evaluation of the Role of Metacognitive Deficits and Learning Disabilities," by L. Baker, *Topics in Learning and Learning Disabilities*, 2, pp. 27–35, copyright © 1982 by Pro-Ed Journals.) *Metacognitive* awareness, as you may recall, is an awareness of what we do when we read, and the ability to select the most appropriate fix-up strategies when better comprehension is needed.

We need to assist these remedial readers in the following areas:

1. *Understand purposes of reading.* Poor readers may think of reading as merely decoding words or just a means to an end. They need to realize that the purpose of reading content material is to comprehend, gain information, retain it, and be able to retrieve it when necessary.

2. *Modify reading strategies for a variety of purposes.* Poor readers often do not adjust their rate or strategies to the purpose or task requirements at hand. They read everything at the same rate; if whatever strategy they use doesn't work, they have no notion of what or how to change. Their only purpose is to get through the material.

3. *Identify important information in a passage.* Poor readers often have trouble deciding on the relative importance of sections to the overall theme. They do not realize how parts of a text may aid them, and may have trouble summarizing what they do read.

4. *Recognize logical structure inherent in a passage.* Poor readers are not generally aware that texts often have a common structure. They do not recognize that illogical or disorganized texts are difficult to understand, nor can they articulate why these texts are difficult.

5. *Understand how new information relates to what is already known.* Poor readers can have trouble relating past knowledge and experience to what they are reading. They often do not evaluate print in terms of their own knowledge of the world.

6. *Attend to syntactic and semantic constraints.* Poor readers frequently do not recognize that their decoding errors are not syntactically (grammatically)

or semantically (meaningfully) congruent with the text, and thus they seldom alter what they have misread in order to make sense out of the passge.

7. *Evaluate text for clarity, completeness, and consistency.* Poor readers often cannot decide whether a text has missing information or whether it is difficult to understand. They may indicate that they did not understand ambiguous or inconsistent messages.

8. *Deal with failures to understand.* Poor readers generally do not know what strategies to use when they do not comprehend. For example, they may not reread, use a dictionary or context clues, or even ask for help.

9. *Decide how well material has been understood.* Poor readers are unable to judge when they have studied sufficiently and are ready to take a test. They cannot evaluate how correct their responses are to teachers' questions.

Each of these nine items is indicative of a problem that, once diagnosed, can be corrected. There are some interventions, to be described next, that can be applied to most problem readers.

Intervention Strategies

Repeated Readings
Chomsky used a repeated readings technique with students who had not learned automatic decoding skills.[23] Students listened individually to tapes of selections, while following along with the written text. They did this repeatedly until they could read the text with fluency on their own. Supplemental language games (word and sentence analysis) and independent writing were also used, which helped the students to become more active in interpreting the text. Repeated readings can also be done using the microcomputer, which gives immediate feedback to the reader and frees the teacher from this task.

Reciprocal Teaching
This cooperative technique, developed by Palincsar and Brown, has teachers and students taking turns leading a dialogue aimed at reconstructing the meaning of the text.[24] Four activities used are *questioning, clarifying, summarizing,* and *predicting.* Before the dialogue commences, everyone previews the strategies to be taught, and the teacher helps them to see how these strategies will be useful. Next, the title is given and students use their background information and knowledge to predict orally what they think will be learned. After the group reads the text section, the teacher leads the dialogue by asking questions and then summarizing what has been read.

Clarifications that are needed require readers to return to the text and reread or read ahead or ask further questions. Finally, when the group predicts what will happen in the text to be read, a new teacher or leader is appointed and the teacher acts then as coach. Students at all levels seem to enjoy playing the role of teacher.

Quick Tips for Helping Remedial Readers

The Far West Laboratory for Educational Research and Development offers further tips for classroom teachers who want to help students improve their reading.[25] Interview several other teachers in your area to find out which of these they already do and which they think are unnecessary.

_____ 1. Diagnose student's reading ability.

_____ 2. Determine text difficulty.

_____ 3. Select texts appropriate for student ability and concept to be developed.

_____ 4. Give direction and state a purpose for each reading assignment.

_____ 5. Build on student's background knowledge.

_____ 6. Teach critical vocabulary in context prior to reading.

_____ 7. Use visual aids, film strips, records, and so on to enhance background knowledge.

_____ 8. Limit length of assignments, remembering that it may take twice as long to do half the usual work.

_____ 9. Have important sections of text tape-recorded to be used by those who cannot read the text as it is.

_____ 10. Get easier books on the same subject from the curriculum librarian to augment gathering information.

_____ 11. Rewrite key sections when necessary.

_____ 12. Use students and resource people as helpers, using cooperative learning techniques.

_____ 13. At times, provide assignments not requiring the text.

_____ 14. Limit the amount of required reading as homework assignment.

<ul>
<li>_____ 15. Use classic comic books for motivation and for helping students see a story plot of an historical event.</li>
<li>_____ 16. Accept the fact that your own reading ability differs markedly from those of remedial students, so patience is important.</li>
</ul>

SUMMARY

Paying heed to affective concerns and individual differences of our students is vital to successful teaching and should underscore all that we try to do. Successful teachers want to capture their students' interests and motivate them to learn. Successful teachers have found ways to create in students positive feelings toward their subject. Those who read voluntarily for pleasure (ludic reading) usually have reached a level of reading maturity that allows them to focus on meanings, not the act of reading itself. They anticipate that reading will be pleasurable and are seldom disappointed. When students experience emotional problems in their lives, it is possible that bibliotherapy may help them by allowing them to see how others have handled similar problems.

Affective factors should be kept in mind for all students, from the gifted to the culturally diverse to the remedial or problem readers. Gifted students need to be challenged by exposure to the best writing of the ages. Culturally diverse students should become a part of cooperative pluralism whereby all students learn about "us" in an interrelated, connected perspective. Dialects should be accepted as a consistent variation of the English language, with no indication of deficit or inferiority.

Problem readers are generally assisted by a school reading specialist, but it is also probable that they will appear in classes throughout the school. Dyslexic students are rare but do exist. For those dealing with remedial readers, it can be helpful to refer to the developmental reading stages and to assess these students' metacognitive deficiencies.

NOTES

1. Dixie Lee Spiegal, *Reading for Pleasure: Guidelines* (Newark, DE: International Reading Association, 1981).
2. David Krathwohl, Benjamin Bloom, and Bertram Masia, *Taxonomy of Educational Objectives, Handbook II: Affective Domain* (New York: David McKay, 1964).
3. Robert Karlin, *Teaching Reading in High School*, 4th ed. (New York: Harper & Row, 1984), p. 12.

4. Robert G. Carlsen, *Books and the Teen-age Reader,* 2nd rev. ed. (New York: Bantam Books, 1980).

5. Margaret Early and Diane J. Sawyer, *Reading to Learn in Grades 5–12* (Orlando, FL: Harcourt Brace Jovanovich, 1984).

6. David L. Shepherd, *Comprehensive High School Reading Methods* (Columbus, OH: Charles E. Merrill, 1982), pp. 136–139.

7. V. Nell, "The Psychology of Reading for Pleasure: Needs and Gratification," *Reading Research Quarterly,* 18 (1988), 6–50.

8. William Bennett, "Important Works in the Humanities for Students," *Education Week,* 4 (1, September 5, 1984), L29.

9. Jeanette Plauche-Parker, *Instructional Strategies for Teaching the Gifted* (Needham Heights, MA: Allyn and Bacon, 1989).

10. John Goodlad, University of Washington, quoted in *Cooperative Pluralism: An Abstract* (Olympia, WA: Office of the Superintendent of Public Instruction).

11. John Goodlad, *A Place Called School: Prospects for the Future* (New York: McGraw-Hill, 1984).

12. Gina Cantoni-Harvey, *Content-Area Language Interaction: Approaches and Strategies* (Reading, MA: Addison-Wesley, 1987).

13. Ibid.

14. Kenneth S. Goodman and Catherine Buck, "Dialect Barriers to Reading Comprehension Revisited," *The Reading Teacher,* 27 (October 1973).

15. Cantoni-Harvey, *Content-Area Language Interaction.*

16. Eleanor Wall Thonis, *Literacy for American Spanish Speaking Children* (Newark, DE: International Reading Association, 1976).

17. Nancy Rogers-Zegarra and Harry Singer, "Anglo and Chicano Comprehension of Ethnic Stories," in Harry Singer and Robert Ruddell, eds., *Theoretical Models and Processes of Reading,* 3rd. ed. (Newark, DE: International Reading Association, 1984), pp. 611–617.

18. K. H. Au and C. Jordan, "Teaching Reading to Hawaiian Children: Finding a Culturally Appropriate Solution," in H. Trueba, G. P. Guthrie, and K. H. Au, eds., *Culture and the Bilingual Classroom: Studies in Classroom Ethnography* (Rowley, MA: Newbury House, 1981), pp. 139–152.

19. Margaret Early and Diane J. Sawyer, *Reading to Learn in Grades 5–12* (Orlando, FL: Harcourt Brace Jovanovich, 1984), pp. 216–217, 228.

20. Ibid., p. 237.

21. J. S. Chall, *Stages of Reading Development* (New York: McGraw-Hill, 1983).

22. L. Baker, "An Evaluation of the Role of Metacognitive Deficits and Learning Disabilities," *Topics in Learning and Learning Disabilities,* 2 (1982), 27–35.

23. C. Chomsky, "When You Still Can't Read in Third Grade: After Decoding, What?" in S. Jay Samuels, ed., *What Research Has to Say about Reading Instruction* (Newark, DE: International Reading Association, 1978).

24. A. S. Palincsar and A. L. Brown, "Reciprocal Teaching of Comprehension Fostering and Comprehension Monitoring Activities," *Cognition and Instruction,* 1 (1984), 117–175.

25. *58 Ways to Improve Student Reading* (Portland, OR: Far West Laboratory for Educational Research and Development, National Diffusion Network, 1981).

RECOMMENDED READINGS

Alexander, J. E., and Filler, R. C. *Attitudes and Reading.* Newark, DE: International Reading Association, 1976.

Appleton, N. *Cultural Pluralism in Education: Theoretical Functional.* New York: Longman, 1983.

Beyard-Tyler, K. C., and Sullivan, H. J. "Adolescent Reading Preferences for Type of Theme and Sex of Character." *Reading Research Quarterly,* 16 (1980), 105–120.

Brooks, C. K., ed. *Tapping Potential: English and Language Arts for the Black Learner.* Urbana, IL: National Council of Teachers of English, 1982.

Carter, B., and Harris, K. "What Junior High Students Like in Books." *Journal of Reading,* 26 (1982), 42–46.

Ching, D. *Reading and the Bilingual Child.* Newark, DE: International Reading Association, 1976.

Ciani, Alfred A., ed. *Motivating Reluctant Readers.* Newark, DE: International Reading Association, 1981.

DeBono, E. *Lateral Thinking: Creativity Step by Step.* New York: Harper & Row, 1970.

Donelson, Kenneth L., and Nilsen, Allen P. *Literature for Today's Young Adults.* Chicago: Scott, Foresman, 1981.

Elley, Warwick B., and Mangubhai, Frances. "The Impact of Reading on Second Language Learning." *Reading Research Quarterly,* 19 (1, Fall 1983), 53–67.

Elliott, Peggy G., and Kellner, Lesley L. Stein. "Reading Preferences of Urban and Suburban Secondary Students: Topics and Media." *Journal of Reading,* 23 (November 1979), 121–125.

Feldhusen, John, Van Tassel-Baska, Joyce, and Seelay, Key. *Excellence in Educating the Gifted.* Denver, CO: Love, 1989.

Freire, P. *Pedagogy of the Oppressed.* New York: Seabury, 1970.

Gentile, Lance M., and McMillan, Merna M. "Why Won't Teenagers Read?" *Journal of Reading,* 20 (May 1977).

Gonzales, Phillip C. "How to Begin Language Instruction for Non–English Speaking Students." *Language Arts,* 58 (February 1981), 175–180.

Grosjean, F. *Life with Two Languages: An Introduction to Bilingualism.* Cambridge, MA: Harvard University Press, 1982.

Haag, Enid. "Enriching Content Classrooms through Collateral Reading." In Marian J. Tonjes and Miles V. Zintz, *Teaching Reading/Thinking/Study Skills in Content Classrooms,* 2nd ed. Dubuque, IA: William C. Brown, 1987, pp. 324–363.

Haimowitz, Benjamin. "Motivating Reluctant Readers in Inner-City Classes." *Journal of Reading,* 21 (3, December 1977), 227–230.

Hiraga, M. "Senior High School Students' Reading Interests and Attitudes." *Science of Reading,* 17 (1973), 35–47.

Hughes, Billie J. "A Summer Reading List by Students for Students." *English Journal,* 70 (April 1981), 52–53.

Ignoffo, Matthew. "Improve Reading by Overcoming the Inner Critic." *Journal of Reading,* 31 (May 1988).

Keen, Dennis. "The Use of Traditional Reading Approaches with ESL Students." *Journal of Reading,* 27 (November 1983), 139–144.

Lamberg, Walter J. "Helping Reluctant Readers Help Themselves: Interest Inventories." *The English Journal,* 66 (8, November 1983), 139–144.

Le Sourd, Sandra J. "Using an Advance Organizer to Set the Schema for a Multicultural Lesson." *Journal of Reading,* 32 (October 1988), 12–18.

Lewis, R., and Doorlag, D. H. *Teaching Special Students in the Mainstream.* Columbus, OH: Charles E. Merrill, 1983.

Mace-Matluck, B. J. *Literacy Instruction in Bilingual Settings: A Synthesis of Current Research.* ERIC Document ED 222 079. Las Alamitos, CA: National Center for Bilingual Research, 1983.

Martin, Mavis, and Zintz, Miles. "Concerns about Comprehension of Children with Limited English Proficiency." *New Mexico Journal of Reading,* 5 (Fall 1984), 6–11.

Matthews, Dorothy, and the Committee to Revise High Interest–Easy Reading of the National Council of Teachers of English. *High Interest–Easy Reading: For Junior and Senior High School Students.* Urbana, IL: National Council of Teachers of English.

Nell, V. *Lost in a Book: The Psychology of Reading for Pleasure.* New Haven: Yale University Press, 1988.

Noland, Ronald G., and Craft, Lynda H. "Methods to Motivate the Reluctant Reader." *Journal of Reading,* 19 (February 1976), 387–391.

Pugh, Sharon L., and Fenelon, James. "Integrating Learning, Language, and Intercultural Skills for International Students." *Journal of Reading,* 31 (January 1988), 310–319.

Quandt, I. *Self-Concepts and Reading.* Newark, DE: International Reading Association, 1972.

Samuels, Barbara G. "Young Adults' Choices: Why Do Students 'Really Like' Particular Books?" *Journal of Reading,* 32 (May 1989), 714–719.

Sarkissian, Adele, ed. *High-Interest Books for Teens: A Guide to Book Reviews and Biographical Sources.* Detroit: Gale Research, 1981.

Shapiro, Jon E. *Using Literature and Poetry Affectively.* Newark, DE: International Reading Association, 1979.

Sims, R. *Shadow and Substance: Afro-American Experience in Contemporary Children's Fiction.* Urbana: IL: National Council of Teachers of English, 1982.

Spache, George D. *Good Reading for Poor Readers,* 9th ed. Champaign, IL: Garrard, 1974.

Steffenson, M. C., Joag, D., and Anderson, R. "A Cross-Cultural Perspective on Reading Comprehension." *Reading Research Quarterly,* 5 (1979), 10–29.

Stone, Nancy R. "Accentuate the Positive: Motivation and Reading for Secondary Students." *Journal of Reading,* 27 (May 1984), 684–690.

Taubenheim, B. W. "Erikson's Psychosocial Theory Applied to Adolescent Fiction: A Means for Adolescent Self-Clarification." *Journal of Reading,* 22 (March 1979), 517–522.

Thonis, E. *Teaching Reading to Non-English Speakers.* New York: Macmillan, 1976.

Tullock-Rhody, Regina, and Alexander, J. Estill. "A Scale for Assessing Attitudes toward Reading in Secondary Schools." *Journal of Reading,* 23 (April 1980), 609–614.

Turnbull, A. P., and Shulz, J. B. *Mainstreaming Handicapped Students: A Guide for the Classroom.* Boston: Allyn and Bacon, 1979.

Vorhous, R. "Strategies for Reading in a Second Language." *Journal of Reading,* 27 (5, February 1984), 412.

Wylie, R. S. *The Self-Concept: Theory and Research on Selected Topics.* Lincoln: University of Nebraska Press, 1979.

Zintz, Miles V. "A Rationale for Teaching Students with Limited English Proficiency." *American Reading Forum Yearbook* (1986), 1–5.

A SAMPLING OF BIBLIOTHERAPY REFERENCES
FOR TEACHERS

Agnes, Sister Mary, S.C. "Influence of Reading on the Racial Attitudes of Adolescent Girls." *Catholic Educational Review,* 45 (September 1947), 415–420.

Dreyer, Sharon Spredeman. *The Book Finder: A Guide to Children's Literature about the Needs and Problems of Youth, Aged 2–15.* 2 vols. Circle Pines, MN: American Guidance Service, 1981.

Edwards, Patricia, and Simpson, Linda. "Bibliotherapy: A Strategy for Communication between Parents and Their Children." *Journal of Reading,* 30 (November 1986), 110–118.

Heitzman, Kathleen A., and Heitzman, William Ray. "The Science of Bibliotherapy: A Critical Review of Research Findings." *Reading Improvement,* 12 (Summer 1975), 120–124.

International Reading Association. Bibliography #16. *Bibliotherapy: An Annotated Bibliography.* Newark, DE: International Reading Association, 1968.

Lindeman, Barbara, and Kling, Martin. "Bibliotherapy: Definitions, Uses and Studies." *Journal of School Psychology,* 7 (Spring 1968–1969), 36–41.

Manning, Diane Thompson, and Manning, Bernard. "Bibliotherapy for Children of Alcoholics." *Journal of Reading,* 27 (May 1984), 720–725.

Moore, David W., Moore, Sharon Arthur, and Readance, John E. "Understanding Characters' Reactions to Death." *Journal of Reading,* 26 (March 1983), 540–544.

Narang, Harbans L. "Bibliotherapy: A Review of the Research." *Saskatchewan Journal of Educational Research and Development,* 7 (Spring 1977), 5–12.

Newton, Eunice S. "Bibliotherapy in the Development of Minority Group Self-Concept." *Journal of Negro Education,* 38 (3, Summer 1969).

O'Bruba, William S., and Camplese, Donald A. "Beyond Bibliotherapy: Tell-A-Therapy." *Reading Horizons,* 20 (Fall 1979), 30–35.

Tillman, Chester E. "Bibliotherapy for Adolescents: An Annotated Research Review." *Journal of Reading,* 27 (May 1984), 713–719.

Winfred, Evelyn T. "Relevant Reading for Adolescents: Literature on Divorce." *Journal of Reading,* 26 (February 1983), 408–411.

Zaccaria, Joseph S., and Moses, Harold A. *Facilitating Human Development through Reading: The Use of Bibliotherapy in Teaching and Counseling.* Champaign, IL: Stipes, 1968.

Postorganizer 1
Thoughtful Reflection on Affective Concerns

Return to preorganizers 1 and 2 and reread your responses. What would you change? What stands out as most significant or meaningful to you? What would you like to share with others? Have you made a silent commitment to incorporate these ideas into your own teaching? If you are not certain, remember that change does not happen overnight. It is fine for now just to reflect and place this information in schema form into your long-term memory for later retrieval.

Postorganizer 2
Meeting Individual Differences

It is easy to pay lip service to the idea of meeting the individual differences of all your students in secondary classrooms. In groups of three to five, discuss, list, or summarize what you could do to assist the gifted, the culturally diverse, and the problem readers. After sharing results with the whole class, let your instructor help you to synthesize the best ideas and have them typed for a reference handout.

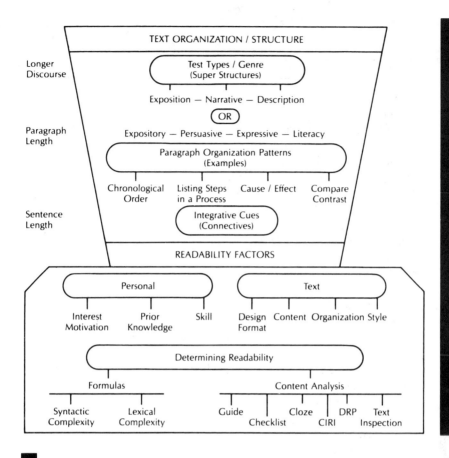

TEXT ORGANIZATION / STRUCTURE

Longer Discourse

Test Types / Genre
(Super Structures)

Exposition — Narrative — Description

OR

Expository — Persuasive — Expressive — Literacy

Paragraph Length

Paragraph Organization Patterns
(Examples)

Chronological Order | Listing Steps in a Process | Cause / Effect | Compare Contrast

Sentence Length

Integrative Cues
(Connectives)

READABILITY FACTORS

Personal

Interest Motivation | Prior Knowledge | Skill

Text

Design Format | Content | Organization | Style

Determining Readability

Formulas

Syntactic Complexity | Lexical Complexity

Content Analysis

Guide | Checklist | Cloze | CIRI | DRP | Text Inspection

3

The Text: Organizational Patterns and Readability Factors

CHAPTER OUTLINE

Preorganizers
Introduction
Text Organization/Structure
  Text Types/Genre or Superstructures
  Rhetoric's Place in Understanding Text Structures
  Paragraph Organizational Patterns
  Integrative Cues or Connectives
General Teaching Recommendations
  Teaching Organizational Patterns
  Characteristics for Text Selection Based on Goals
  Cause–Effect Training
Readability of Text
  Factors Contributing to Readability
  Cautions and Caveats
  Predicting Text Comprehensibility
  Measuring Word Recognition and Prior Knowledge
Formulas
  SMOG: Simple Measure of Gobbledygook
  Fry Readability Graph
Content Analysis of Texts
  Content Analysis Guide
  Checklists
  Perspective Readers Using Cloze or the CIRI
  Degrees of Reading Power (DRP)
  Text Inspection for Readability
  A Considerate Text
  Cloze or CIRI
Summary Recommendations
Postorganizers
Notes
Recommended Reading

COGNITIVE COMPETENCIES

1. Differentiate between text types, text structure, and organizational patterns.

2. Make a diagram showing factors and possible interrelationships of what makes a readable text.

3. Thinking of your own subject area, rank-order and defend the three most significant readability factors.

4. List the actual steps you will take in judging the adequacy of a potential text for your classes.

KEY TERMS

considerate text
content analysis guide
exposition, narrative, description
integrative cues
lexical complexity

nomograph
paragraph organization patterns
readability of text
syntactic complexity
text organization/structure

Preorganizer 1
Prereading Questions

Questions and declarative statements concerning tasks to be performed, often found at the end of chapters, should be read first in order to perceive important concepts and even possibly their relationships. You are behaving as a more active reader when you try to predict what the answers will be and, after reading, revise predictions where needed. Obviously, you are not expected to know all—or even any—of the answers now, but these will alert you to what is to come.

1. What are two basic kinds of text in terms of their overall structure?

   _____

2. Compare and contrast Just and Carpenter's text types to Hoskins's adaptation of Kinneavy's. State your preference and justify your choice.

   _____

   _____

3. What are the factors that make printed material difficult or easy to read? After making your list, how would you categorize them?

   _____

   _____

   _____

4. Critique the variety of ways that we measure the difficulty of print. Which would you use? _____

   _____

   _____

5. After defining the following terms, try to connect them in some way to show relationships.

   • Connectives or integrative cues _____

   • Content analysis _____

   • External text organization _____

   • Internal text organization _____

- Lexical complexity _____

- Readability formulas _____ ____

- Syntactic complexity _____

Preorganizer 2
Guesstimates

Before reading about the problems and promises of the notion of readability in the second half of this chapter, look first at the brief excerpts that follow. Take a guess and jot down what you think might be the readability level of each. If you revise your "guesstimate" after reading the chapter, remember to take into consideration all of the readability factors mentioned, not just those mentioned by existing formulas.

History Excerpt

> The historical beginnings of the United States commence in Asia many thousands of years ago, when Asian hunters initiated a migration to North America by transversing the Bering Strait and deciding to settle here. It is interesting to consider how even today Asian affairs have remained a remarkable concern of many American scholars, and indeed many others too.

English Excerpt

> **Sonnet Number 73 (Shakespeare)**
> *That time of year thou mayst in me behold*
> *When yellow leaves, or none, or few, do hang*
> *Upon those boughs which shake against the cold,*
> *Bare ruined choirs, where late the sweet birds sang . . .*

Science Excerpt

> There is one statement about living things that has not one exception, and that is that they will at some point die. Death implies life and living implies the possibility of dying. Although it is a recognized fact that not all organisms die of old age, nonetheless, all are subject to death.

3
The Text:
Organizational Patterns
and Readability Factors

INTRODUCTION

Conventional textbooks are, on the whole, the primary source of secondary school instruction. This is not really surprising when we consider their convenience and usefulness in conveying large amounts of information.

There are many factors that contribute to the ease or difficulty with which readers master these required texts. In this chapter we look at the qualities within the text itself, its organizational patterns, and its readability in terms of both readers and textual factors—what readers bring to the text and the text itself. We end with a variety of ways to measure readability and make instructional decisions about text appropriateness.

In a survey performed by Black in 1967, with approximately 250 million educational texts in existence at that time, it was concluded that on the average, students from the elementary through the high school years were expected to cope with a minimum of 32,000 text pages altogether.[1] For those going to college, another survey, in 1980, showed that 80 percent of university faculty required one text for their classes and 44 percent also used additional texts.[2]

Guthrie (1982) questions why, with so many texts in use today, we haven't developed a systematic, regular way to teach students how best to learn from them.[3] This is a good question, and one to which it is well worth giving thoughtful consideration.

TEXT ORGANIZATION/STRUCTURE

Successful readers are able to follow the author's structuring of ideas, how these ideas are tied together or related, and which ideas are more important than others. Often, the way chapters are designed—their format—will enable readers to perceive the structure. Meyer and Rice (1984) have found that knowledge of the ways texts are organized is a critical variable in both learning and remembering information from that text.[4]

Two basic kinds of *text structures*, then, are external and internal structures.

External organization is the overall design of the text—the format within chapters; the beginning and end of the text (preface, table of contents, references, appendix, index, and so on). Text chapters generally contain introductions and summaries, headings and subheadings, graphics, activities, and questions.

Internal organization is characterized by how ideas are related—whether they are superordinated or subordinated, whether they are central or peripheral, how cohesive they are, how they are tied together.

Text Types/Genre or Superstructures

There is a difference of opinion in the relevant literature as to how to categorize types of text. Just and Carpenter (1987) describe three text types: narrative, description, and exposition.[5] *Narrative* describes the occurrence of events over time, linked by a theme or sequence of causation (as in stories, novels, instructions, or histories). *Description* refers to a static situation in terms of its discernible physical features, as in a scene-setting paragraph within a novel, or to spatial layouts, and relative positions among objects and their shapes, colors, textures, or scents. *Exposition* logically describes related events, with the objective being to inform, explain, or persuade. It is found in educational texts, job-related reading, and printed news media.

Each of these three text types will often contain features of the other two. For instance, narratives and expositions usually include some description; however, the dominant genre of a text can still be easily ascertained.

Rhetoric's Place in Understanding Text Superstructures

Rhetoric (the study of elements used in literature and public speaking) can give us much information about text structure. In 1969 Kinneavy developed a schematic structure for classifying text types, this time into four modes—

expository, persuasive, literary, and inferential.[6] Hoskins (1986) adapted this theory for classroom teachers and changed inferential to expressive.[7]

1. *Expository:* The purpose is to explain concepts, to teach facts and information. There are three basic types of exposition: exploratory, informative, and scientific. In exploratory exposition, questions are raised, problems diagrammed, and definitions and solutions proposed. Informative writing includes text, news articles, reports, and summaries. Scientific writing includes both deductive and inductive proof.
2. *Persuasive:* The purpose of persuasive writing is to create a specific reaction in readers. The writing can be honest, or it can be biased and distorted.
3. *Expressive:* Here the attempt is to communicate the writer's own emotions, goals, and understandings.
4. *Literary:* Here, the emphasis is on the product and on giving entertainment or pleasure to readers.

Teaching these superstructures, as Hoskins labels them, helps readers readily identify the author's purpose. With that accomplished, the reader begins to control the text, rather than the text controlling the reader. The text becomes readers' own creation as they control and interpret it, perceiving the overall design.[8] Table 3.1 shows the four superstructures and specific examples within each category.

Paragraph Organizational Patterns

Paragraph organizational patterns can now be seen as patterns used within the superstructures of longer discourse.[9] When readers can recognize these patterns, they can both analyze the overall text organization and thus the organization of concepts.

Some important patterns are described next with brief, simplified examples:

1. *Chronological (or time) order:* Information is presented in the order in which it occurred, or a topic is traced so that readers should use this pattern to organize the information for later recall. Cue or signal words include *after, also, before, during, first, next, later, soon, second, until.*

At 4:00 P.M., Wednesday, July 16, 1969 Colonel Edwin Aldrin, Jr. USAF, with civilian astronaut, Neil Armstrong, landed on the moon's Sea of Tranquility. Several hours later Armstrong descended the ladder. As the first to set foot on the moon, he said, "One small step for man, one giant leap for mankind." Soon,

TABLE 3.1
Superstructure Examples

Expository	Persuasive[a]	Expressive	Literary
Exploratory			
Materials that:	Advertising	Diaries	Novels
Raise questions	Editorials	Journals	Short stories
Diagram problems	Letters	Personal narratives	Poetry
Propose defini-	Propaganda	Manifestos	Biography and
tions and	Political writing	Contracts	autobiography
solutions	Documents	Constitutions	Drama
	Legal opinions		Essays
	Speeches		
Informative			
Texts			
News articles			
Reports			
Summaries			
Scientific			
Deductive/			
inductive proofs			
Technical articles			
Treatises			

Source: Adapted from "Text Superstructures" by S. Hoskins, *Journal of Reading,* 29 (March 1986), pp. 538–543.
[a]A type of expository.

Aldrin joined him for a walk to collect rock samples. After a little over one half hour on the moon, they blasted off to rejoin their comrade, Lieutenant Colonel Michael Collins, in the Apollo spacecraft. On Thursday, July 24, they were home again on Earth.

2. *List steps in a process:* Facts, ideas, and information are listed in logical order or in order of importance. Readers here must decide on the relative importance of items. Cue or signal words include *one, first, next, finally, also,* and *too,* or this information can be summarized as follows:

1.
2.
3.
4.

3. *Compare and contrast:* This pattern points out likenesses and differences among concepts, events, facts, and people. It is often used to clarify points. Readers need to keep in mind the author's main idea and how the likenesses and differences illustrate it. Making lists is helpful. Cue or signal words include *although, but, despite, however, nevertheless, on the other hand, otherwise, similarly, in contrast, by comparison.*

Franklin Roosevelt and Harry Truman have both been described by some historians as two of our greatest presidents. However, the two men could not have been more unalike in terms of background, approach . . .

4. *Cause–effect (and effect–cause):* This pattern shows the effects or what occurred because of some fact, concept, or event, which helps readers see relationships among facts and ideas. Cue or signal words include *as a result, because, consequently, if, since, so, that, thus,* and *therefore.*

Travel can change and enrich our lives immeasurably. Why is that so? If nothing else, one thing to consider is that it can make us appreciate home more than ever before. Travel is stimulating—as anything new can be—whether it be the sights and sounds, the people, the food, or the customs. It involves, too, a bonus of giving three times the normal pleasure. One-third of the time we have the pleasure of reading and planning, one-third of the enjoyment is experiencing the travel, and one-third is reminiscing and sharing later with family and friends.

Other patterns that could be considered as separate include problem solving, question–answer, explanation of a concept or definition paragraph, classification, generalization, following directions, interpreting signs and symbols, and sequencing.

It is more important for most students to understand the overall concept of text organization than to be drilled on identifying specific patterns. However, remedial students may benefit from many experiences in which various types are pointed out. When students can follow the text organization, they will have improved their comprehension and retention.

Integrative Cues or Connectives

Texts contain many explicit cues to show relationships among ideas. When such cues are missing, readers will have to infer them, a more difficult task. ("It poured rain that morning; consequently, the picnic was postponed.") *Consequently* is a connective between sentences that helps to relate them explicitly to each other. If we leave out this connective, readers will have to infer the tie.[10]

Besides connectives, texts can explicitly show relations among events by stating the connection.

Several causes of the revolution included:

  a. Clergy upset by their loss of power
  b. Peasants suffering from near starvation
  c. Religious persecution

Other ways in which relationships can be shown include titles, subheadings, and high-level abstractions such as advance organizers or summary statements. Again, when not provided, these must be inferred.[11] Some common connectives and their relations are shown in Table 3.2.

Many writers combine patterns or write in such a way that patterns are not readily identifiable. For this reason, teachers need to guide students first to look for the crucial ideas with possible signal words, and second, to look for other important ideas to see if they are connected to the overall theme. Sometimes making a diagram on the board showing superordinate and subordinate ideas will clarify relationships for students. Alternatively, developing a cognitive map that shows connections among ideas in a variety of formats can be helpful.

Thus, patterns of organization give us logical connections among key ideas and help us to perceive the overall picture.

TABLE 3.2
Cues: Connectives and Relations

Connective	Relation
also, again, another, finally, furthermore, likewise, moreover, similarly, too	Another item in same series
afterwards, finally, later on, next, then	Another item in a time series
for instance, for example, specifically	An example or illustration of what has been said
accordingly, as a result, consequently, hence, then, therefore, thus, so	A consequence of what has already been said
in other words, that is to say, to put it differently	A restatement of what has been said
but, however, on the other hand, on the contrary	A statement opposing what has been said
granted, of course, to be sure, undoubtedly	A concession to an opposing view
all the same, even though, nevertheless, nonetheless, still	The original line of argument resuming after a concession
all in all, altogether, finally, in conclusion, the point is	A concluding item, or summary

Source: Adapted from Marcel Adam Just and Patricia A. Carpenter, *The Psychology of Reading and Language Comprehension.* Copyright © 1987 by Allyn and Bacon. Used with permission. Originally adapted from Cleanth Brooks and Robert P. Warren, *Modern Rhetoric,* 3rd ed., Table 3.3, pp. 37–38, copyright © 1970 by Harcourt Brace Jovanovich.

GENERAL TEACHING RECOMMENDATIONS

Positive results in teaching students to use knowledge of text structure and organizational patterns have been reported by Meyer, Brandt, and Bluth (1980).[12] Mateja and Wood (1982) propose that teachers should first model appropriate behaviors using a sample text, and follow this with a series of practice sessions that include further modeling, independent practice, and a systematic follow-up.[13] If this is done, the results for readers should be increased self-awareness, self-knowledge, and self-monitoring—especially when the strategies used consider their learning styles. Teachers need to show students the rules for text organization, give them a direct experience with a variety of texts, and finally show them the importance of using their background experience for learning.

Teaching Organizational Patterns

Early and Sawyer (1984) suggest some practical ways to teach students about text organizational patterns.[14] For slow learners and immature students, and to motivate other readers, teachers should present them with nonverbal devices that reinforce their recognition of the idea of patterns of organization—for example, one group of geometric patterns arranged logically and one group arranged haphazardly.

Another way to motivate readers is to present magazine illustrations showing groupings of objects such as sporting gear, musical instruments, or varieties of food, and then to ask students to group items and label them by central idea. A perennial favorite is to cut panels from popular comic strips like "Doonesbury" or "Prince Valiant," paste each segment on cardboard, and have students arrange them in a logical sequence. Magazine illustrations can also be used to show comparison/contrast (old versus new, urban versus rural). Having students locate these is a time-saver for teachers.

From pictures, we move to observation of topics, using similar sets of cards naming sports and games. For sports the pattern could be contrast (team–individual), ascending order (number of players), and so on. The table of contents is a good example of sequence, one that shows which patterns may predominate.

A more difficult task is to identify patterns in paragraphs and larger segments of text. Finding examples in their own text or working with a partner can enliven this activity for students. Another activity is to cut out samples from newspapers, give students labeled envelopes, and have them sort the samples. Once each envelope has several examples, have students number each one and decide which is the best example, justifying their choice.

Characteristics for Text Selection Based on Goals

Texts should be selected for use on the basis of learning goals. If the goal is *memory and recall*, Guthrie (1982) suggests that one linear text should be used as the sole source of information.[15] The readability should be appropriate; either the vocabulary should be already familiar or its meanings should be easily communicated; sentences and paragraphs should be coherent (flow and connect); and the length should be appropriate to readers' levels. In order to motivate reading here, the text should be aesthetically pleasing in design and language. Evidence of a variety of learning aids, such as graphics, questions, and summaries, and a pleasant style of writing are also important considerations.

Another goal might be *problem solving*, which would mean not having just one text that is read from front to back in sequence. Instead, you need a diversity of articles and materials with a hierarchical range from easy to difficult, including text chapters, encyclopedias, reference manuals, and specialized articles. Readability level does not matter, as information will be extracted as needed. Any class text used should contain a comprehensive information base with no constraints on length. Concise definitions with cross-referencing are important, as is easy access to principles, examples, and the like.

A third goal, *following directions*, is often underrated and yet is an important skill to have mastered, especially in an area like science, and later in many job situations. Guthrie found that texts meeting this goal have not been heavily researched. He suggested that characteristics for judging effectiveness might include: an easily located starting point; cues for sequencing the reading; readily available definitions for technical vocabulary, taking into account the potential readers' ability to carry out the operations; and signals that these operations have been completed.[16]

Cause–Effect Training

In a study of text patterns, their nature, and development of readers' awareness of these patterns, Horowitz (1985) summarized key components of cause–effect training.[17] Students were told they would be asked to respond to history essay questions following their training.

1. *Relate the cause–effect pattern to real life.* Provide examples of real-life cause–effect patterns and have students generate others—for example, chaining ("If you don't _____, you will _____, and that can lead you to _____, which will mean _____.")

2. *Study cause–effect relationships in history.* Historians show causes and

effects of historical events in hopes of shaping the future. Cause–effect study should be related to the discipline in which it is most commonly found.

3. *Mark and note-take.* Provide students with several passages of around seven hundred words in length drawn from secondary history texts. Have them underline causes with two lines, underline effects with one, and circle key or signal words. If cause–effect is only implied, they should make notes in the margin.

4. *Use visual representations.* Some readers remember visual patterns more easily than patterns of words. Cause–effect could be represented by two circles over two circles, with C standing for cause and E for effect,

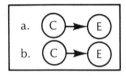

or they could be chained:

5. *Study macro (large) and micro (small) structures.* Provide simple examples of cause–effect within one sentence, then between two or more, then across paragraphs, and finally over whole chapters. Have students focus on microstructures (signal words, key vocabulary, subordinate ideas) and macrostructures or superordinate ideas (title, topic sentence, headings).

6. *Study patterns across topics and texts.* Have students practice recognizing and marking cause–effect relationships across three different passages on three topics drawn from their secondary texts.

Taking these categories into account, it was found that when a writing component was added, it significantly improved students' use of structures.[18] Students are then alerted at the start that because history is often organized with cause–effect structures, many essay questions will have this form. They are encouraged to develop a plan for answering those essay questions, to anticipate what could be asked, to comprehend the question thoroughly, to diagram the cause–effect relationship if needed, to diagram the relationship to be discussed, to use an outline of cause–effect relationships in the essay, and finally to use cause–effect topic sentences to organize their recalls. Having students generate their own practice questions and practice writing responses is important.

READABILITY OF TEXT

The next area of concern is how readable text materials are, taking into account not only factors inherent in the text itself but also those all-important personal factors readers bring to their reading. Printed materials vary greatly in their level of difficulty—their readability level. When we use the term *readable text*, we could actually be referring to any of these basic factors, all of which can affect the difficulty or ease with which material is read: internal or reader factors (interest, motivation, purpose, prior knowledge, and skill) and external or text factors (design, format, content, organization, and style). A readability formula is merely a predictive device intended to give a rough quantitative, objective estimate of reading difficulty. There should always be a distinction between predicting readable writing (which formulas are designed to do) and preparing or producing that writing.[19] Formulas were never intended to be "writeability" formulas, telling authors how to write.

Factors Contributing to Readability

In 1935 Gray and Leary wrote *What Makes a Book Readable;* it became a classic because of its comprehensive look at 228 text factors that could possibly contribute to readability.[20] Those text factors were classified under four headings:

1. Content (considered most important)
2. Style of expression and presentation (a close second)
3. Format (a distant third)
4. General factors of organization (least important)

Since then, most formula developers have usually omitted all but style because they were unable to measure the other factors successfully. Most of the more than thirty formulas available today look at style as a *syntactic* factor (sentence length) and a *lexical* factor (word length or frequency), both of which are easily measured.

However, as mentioned before, we have personal as well as textual factors to consider. Many consider personal factors the most crucial, but they are also relatively difficult and time-consuming to measure. They include reading skill, language facility, physical and mental capacity, prior knowledge, motivation, interest, relevance, and purpose—all very important to the reading act.

Text factors measured in most formulas look at syntactic complexity, which takes into account sentence length, writing style and sentence structure. The semantic factor—lexical complexity—looks at word difficulty in terms of word length or word frequency. It is assumed that easy words appear more frequently and have fewer syllables.

Many attempts have been and are still being made to broaden the base for readability formulas, as for example Carver's Rauding Scale (1975–1976).[21] But still, most formulas have not taken into consideration concept density (how many concepts are packed together); how many explanations, illustrations, or examples are given; and whether concepts are concrete or abstract. Also not taken into consideration are the overall organization patterns and text types discussed earlier in the chapter.

Cautions and Caveats

Even though readability formulas have been with us for many years, Klare points out that critics have questioned their validity since at least 1935.[22] In that year, Moore predicted that readers would "recoil from reading rewritten classics."[23] In 1953 Fitzgerald talked about "literature by slide rule";[24] McLaughlin warned in 1970 about "temptations of the Flesch" readability measure;[25] in 1981 Wagner told of "battling the Dale-Chall monster" (another much used formula);[26] and in 1982 Davison and Kantor gave us a case study of adaptations showing that readability formulas failed to define readable texts.[27]

Even more recently, these formulas have been sharply criticized, with some authorities suggesting that we cannot determine readability by formula at all. Davison (1984), for example, warns of the widespread abuse of formulas that were initially intended merely as evaluative tools for something already written.[28] Instead, they are being used by many writers and publishers to revise or write text by simplifying sentences and words, referred to today as the "dumbing down" of texts.

MaGinitie (1984) talks about readability as a solution that only adds to the problem.[29] He warns that using formulas to modify texts or to make decisions about their suitability can be harmful, preventing students from broadening their language experiences. On the other hand, he does acknowledge that from a practical perspective formulas have given us an objective basis for insisting that written information intended for the average citizen (e.g., insurance policies, army regulations, legal documents) be written in comprehensible or readable form.

It is noteworthy that readability scores should not be used to keep students from reading difficult texts when they wish to do so, but should serve only as a warning of possible dangers ahead that might require teacher intervention for maximum comprehension.

Fry (1987) in a rebuttal to critics about their use stated that approximately

40 percent of state and local school districts use formulas today as just one of the criteria for text selection.[30] Use of these formulas has also spread worldwide and has helped many. As long as we realize their limitations and use them appropriately, readability formulas will continue to have a place and serve a useful function in our world.

To the charge that formulas were causing the oversimplification of texts, Chall (1979) responded that it is teachers, not formulas, who are responsible for the trend toward easier texts, because they continue to request them from publishers.[31] She also pointed out that formulas can help us select harder as well as easier books.

Predicting Text Comprehensibility

For reading educators, an important recent understanding about readability has occurred because of a shift in emphasis from behaviorism to a cognitive approach to processing information. Whenever the reading level of material changes, our cognitive processing, or the way we deal with it, also changes. Skilled readers will have difficulty with simple material when they have no background knowledge to bring to it. On the other hand, unskilled readers who do not decode words accurately and automatically will also have difficulty with relatively easy material.

So it is what is inside the head that really counts. It is word recognition skill plus prior knowledge that facilitate text processing. When we view reading as a constructive process wherein experiences and attitudes are assimilated as we read, these come together to form cognitive structures called schemata. These schemata serve as a framework for storing and interpreting information implicit in the text.[32] For example, when we have a clear schemata for text organization, we can read many details about it and be able to categorize them properly for later recall. Without that schemata in our heads we would have to recall each item as a separate detail. (Refer back to Chapter 1 for a discussion of schemata.)

Measuring Word Recognition and Prior Knowledge

Both inside-the-head factors of word recognition and prior knowledge can be measured. There are three levels of word recognition: nonaccurate, accurate but not automatic, and accurate and automatic. When recognition is automatic, little effort is required, freeing readers to concentrate on meaning.

To measure word recognition, students can be asked to read a 150-word passage orally at their grade placement level as measured by readability formula and told to remember what they have read.

Scoring

1. Nonaccurate word recognition—less than 95 percent
2. Accurate but not automatic—above 95 percent in word recognition, but difficulty retelling
3. Accurate and automatic—above 95 percent word recognition and satisfactory retelling of the gist of the story

To measure knowledge of a text topic, a word association technique can be used, as described by Zakaluk, Samuels, and Taylor (1986).[33] A stimulus is chosen, which is a key word or phrase of the main idea of the topic. Students write as many words or ideas as possible in association with the key word or phrase. These authors suggest having a worksheet with the stimulus word printed at the start of each of twenty-five lines so that students will continue to use the original stimulus. Practice beforehand with an example, using a familiar topic, is recommended. Students should also be reminded, first, that no one is expected to fill all the spaces and, second, that they should keep key words in mind at all times, repeating them over and over as they write. Three minutes are allowed to complete the task. Responses are scored, giving one point for each reasonable idea unit up to a maximum of ten points. When items can be subsumed under a more general category, also written, one point goes to the general category item and one point total for all the subordinate items. When this occurs, it is assumed that students have begun to use words they have generated themselves rather than the initial stimulus word.

Outside-the-head factors, then, include use of a readability formula to judge the level of text, and adjunct comprehension aids such as objectives and study questions, which add to how easily the text can be comprehended. Aids highlight important information, which makes it possible to increase the depth of processing.

An example of a *nomograph* (a table using information from two sources to give information about a third area) is shown in Figure 3.1. There are three vertical lines, the left one standing for outside-the-head factors (text readability and adjunct aids), with readability ranging from first-grade through college level. The line on the right represents inside-the-head factors (knowledge of topic and word recognition skill). The center line shows the extent to which a reader can comprehend a particular text. Figure 3.1 shows a student reading a tenth-grade text that has adjunct aids, which lower the readability level by one-half point for each aid; the result then is a score of 9. The reader is considered to be automatic in word recognition (two

FIGURE 3.1
Application of the Nomograph for a Secondary-Level Text
for Tenth Grade

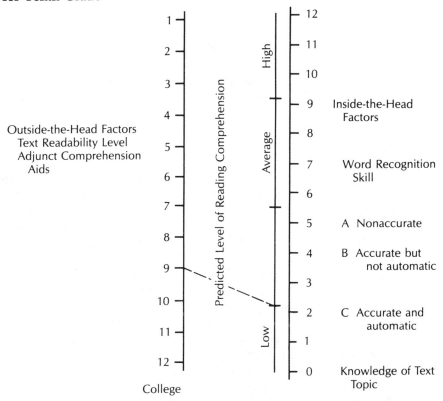

Source: From "A Simple Technique for Estimating Prior Knowledge: Word Association," by B. L. Zakaluk, S. J. Samuels, and B. Taylor, *Journal of Reading*, 30 (1986), pp. 56–60.

points) and has no prior knowledge (zero points). The combined inside-the-head score is therefore 2, and the predicted level of comprehension is low.[34]

FORMULAS

With this as background, it is now time to consider a few formulas. The best way to master what these formulas are actually measuring and not measuring is to practice using one or more. When you find one that fits your needs, stay with it for consistency. The following formulas can be useful rough estimates, which are easy to administer and have a high degree of reliability when used with more complex formulas such as the Dale-Chall.

SMOG: Simple Measure of Gobbledygook

SMOG, developed by M. C. Laughlin in 1969 for materials above the primary level, is based on the interrelationship of sentence length and the number of words with more than two syllables, as such words are often considered to be relatively difficult to read.[35]

To compute a SMOG score, follow these steps:

1. Count ten consecutive sentences near the beginning of the text, ten in the middle, and ten toward the end. Count as a sentence any string of words ending with a period, exclamation point, or question mark.
2. In the third group of sentences, count every word of three or more syllables. This includes any string of letters or numbers beginning and ending with a space or punctuation mark and in which you can distinguish at least three syllables when you read it aloud in context. When polysyllabic words are repeated, count each repetition.
3. Estimate to the nearest perfect square (a number multiplied by itself) the square root of the total number of polysyllabic words. For example, if the total count is 84, the nearest perfect square is 81 (9×9). When the count lies roughly between two perfect squares, choose the lower number. For example, if the count is 110, take the square root of 100 (10×10) rather than 121 (11×11).
4. Add 3 to the estimated square root to determine the readability level requiring 90 to 100 percent understanding, or the independent level. A SMOG score of 9 means that readers at a ninth-grade reading level should be able to handle the text independently, such as in homework. Recalling that the square root sign is $\sqrt{}$, the formula looks like this:

$$\text{SMOG} = \sqrt[3+]{\text{Number of words with 3 or more syllables in 30 sentences}}$$

Fry Readability Graph

In 1968 Fry developed a popular measure which has undergone some revision since that time. The formula and directions for its use can be found in Figure 3.2.[36]

FIGURE 3.2
Fry Readability Graph for Estimating Readability—Extended

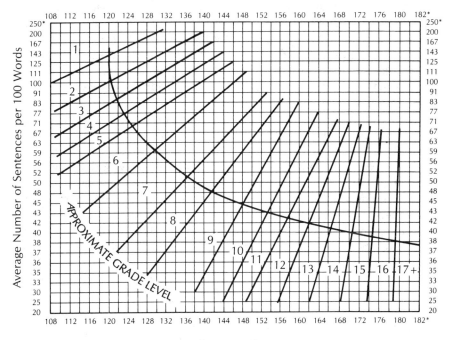

Average Number of Syllables per 100 Words

Expanded Directions for Working Readability Graph

1. Randomly select three (3) sample passages and count out exactly 100 words each, commencing with the beginning of a sentence. Do count proper nouns, initializations, and numerals.
2. Count the number of sentences in the hundred words, estimating the length of the fraction of the last sentence to the nearest one-tenth.
3. Count the total number of syllables in the hundred-word passage. If you don't have a hand counter available, an easy way is simply to put a mark above each syllable beyond the first one. Then, when you get to the end of the passage, count the number of marks and add 100. Small calculators can also be used as counters by pushing the numeral 1, and then pushing the + sign for each word or syllable when counting.
4. Enter graph with *average* sentence length and *average* number of syllables; plot a dot where the two lines intersect. The area where the dot is plotted will give you the approximate grade level.
5. If a great deal of variability is found in syllable count or sentence count, putting more samples into the average is desirable.
6. A *word* is defined as a group of symbols with a space on either side; thus, *Joe, IRA, 1945,* and & are each one word.
7. A *syllable* is defined as a phonetic syllable. Generally, there are as many syllables as vowel sounds. For example, *stopped* is one syllable, and *wanted* is two syllables. When counting syllables for numerals and initializations, count one syllable for each symbol. For example, *1945* is four syllables, *IRA* is three syllables, and & is one syllable.

Source: Edward Fry, "Fry's Readability Graph: Clarifications, Validity, and Extension to Level 17," *Journal of Reading,* 21 (1977), 242–252.

FOGINDEX for Microcomputers

Gross and Sadowski (1985) have suggested using the Gunning Fog Index, developed by Gunning (1952) in a microcomputer program that sidesteps some obstacles encountered in the past, such as software that required hardware with 48K RAM (random-access memory) and a hard disk drive.[37] The user-friendly—and free—program they have adapted uses 8K RAM (4.2K plus space for entering text) and does not require a hard disk drive. When the instruction screens are removed, the program requires only 6K RAM. It is reasonably accurate and does not require modification of the text when it is entered.

FOGINDEX does not have a reference list of familiar words built in, nor does it count syllables, but it does recognize the highest possible percentage of 3+ syllable words. There are no safeguards built in for incorrect use, and it has room for improvements by those with the RAM and the experience to make them. FOGINDEX does consistently grade material higher than other formulas, and this should be taken into account. Remember that formulas merely give us estimates. The program can be found in the *Journal of Reading*, 28 (April 1985), in an article by Phillip P. Gross and Karen Sadowski, "FOGINDEX—A Readability Formula Program for Microcomputers," p. 614.

CONTENT ANALYSIS OF TEXTS

Content Analysis Guide

Strahan and Herlihy (1985) give us a "Content Analysis Guide" that provides a systematic procedure for organizing ideas for guided instruction.[38] The following steps are adapted from their guide:

Step 1: Carefully read the chosen part of the text.
Step 2: Use boldface headings and subheadings or lead paragraphs to outline main topics and important details.
Step 3: Describe the organizational paragraph patterns (chronological, cause–effect, etc.).
Step 4: List key vocabulary and concept labels.
Step 5: Review outline and list, selecting key terms and ideas to emphasize in teaching.
Step 6: Group concepts and key vocabulary into clusters, labeling each and arranging in order of priority.

Step 7: Write a one-sentence generalization that organizes and summarizes the text selection.

Step 8: Write objectives describing what students will do to show understanding.

This analysis moves from facts to concepts to a generalization, making evaluative judgments and prioritizing information. The text is now a teacher aid rather than a dictator. Teachers going through this process will no longer tell their class to read Chapter 3 for a test on Friday or a discussion tomorrow, but instead will introduce objectives and goals so that students can better master their reading.

Checklists

A checklist approach is another way to determine how suitable a particular text will be. Marshall (1979) and Irwin and Davis (1980) have developed useful tools.[39] Marshall's checklist looks at main ideas, vocabulary, concepts, related ideas, referents and audience. Irwin and Davis look at *understandability,* or the relationships between the reader's conceptual experiential background and the text; concept development, syntax, irrelevant details; connectives that are implicit; resources; and readability level from a formula. Their checklist also looks at *learnability,* which includes organizational features, reinforcement activities, and motivational devices.

Prospective Readers Using Cloze or the CIRI

Another way to check the potential appropriateness of a text is to use readers themselves. This method takes into account the personal factors lacking in the above procedure. One simple way is to construct cloze tests on typical text areas. Another is to develop a CIRI (Content Informal Reading Inventory) for the text. Both of these devices may take into account motivation, interest, background knowledge, style, organization, and density of concepts. See Chapter 10 on assessment for complete descriptions of these tools.

DRP: Degrees of Reading Power

DRP units are reading levels. DRP is a criterion-referenced test that measures students' reading abilities at different levels of difficulty. At the same time, the district can purchase the Readability Report, which offers information on texts in terms of DRP units, so the match between reader and text can be made.[40] By measuring both at the same time it is hoped that a more accurate match will be found between reader and text. DRP units are based on cloze research conducted by John Bormuth.[41] Difficulty is measured by a cloze score, which is predicted from average word and sentence length and the percentage of easy words. A note of caution here is that Bormuth (1985) and Carver (1985) found that the DRP system overestimates the difficulty of easy material used with younger readers and also underestimates the difficulty of hard materials used with older readers. This is said to be in part the result of lack of background knowledge on the readers' part.[42]

Text Inspection for Readability

Plan to select your text using means other than just existing readability formulas. One tool you may use is a simple checklist such as the following, adapted from *Developing Readers and Writers in the Content Areas* by David W. Moore, Sharon Arthur Moore, Patricia M. Cunningham, and James W. Cunningham, copyright © 1986 by Longman Inc. (adapted with permission of Longman Publishing).[43]

_____ 1. *Vocabulary:* Are difficult words clarified by examples, visuals, context clues?

_____ 2. *Graphics:* Are they abundant, clear, and closely related to major concepts?

_____ 3. *Headings:* Do they cue readers to what the section will cover?

_____ 4. *Paragraphs:* Are they clearly written, with main ideas apparent?

_____ 5. *Transitions:* Are there good transitions between paragraphs, sections, and chapters?

_____ 6. *Introductory and review passages:* Do these help readers focus on what is important?

_____ 7. *Prior knowledge, interest, and motivation:* Does the material lend itself readily to developing students' connections with what they already know? Is it written in an interesting manner?

A Considerate Text

Thinking like a writer is another way to get students involved in analyzing the text. Anderson and Armbruster (1984) showed four decisions authors must make in writing a viable text that will get across their ideas to readers.[44] They called this a considerate text:

1. *Structure:* Writers select a pattern of text organization that best gets across the information for the given purpose. The structure should be readily apparent to the reader.
2. *Coherence:* Writers make logical connections from one idea to the next. Ideas are woven together smoothly.
3. *Unity:* Writers address one purpose at a time and do not distract readers with irrelevant information. Adjunct aids or excerpts are either boxed, indented, or in the appendix.
4. *Audience appropriateness:* Writers ascertain that the text fits the background knowledge of intended readers, yet also challenges them. Key concepts are defined.

SUMMARY RECOMMENDATIONS: CAUTIONS AND SUGGESTIONS

Some important cautions and suggestions for users of readability formulas today have been stated by Klare (1984).[45]

- Different formulas give different grade-level scores on the same piece of writing. For example, SMOG measures the independent reading level, whereas FRY measures the instructional level.
- After considering several existing formulas, pick one good one for your purposes, remembering that all formulas are merely rough screening devices and all scores are merely statements of probability.
- Since formula scores derive from counts of style difficulty, they become poorer predictors of difficulty at higher grade levels, where content becomes more important than style.
- Reconsider the purpose of the intended reading material, remembering that you may want to challenge your students, not just inform or entertain them.
- When using formula scores, also consider such reader aspects as motivation and prior knowledge. Otherwise formula scores may over- or underestimate difficulty.
- Do not rely on formulas alone when selecting reading materials; also use checklists, expert judges, and reliable consensus opinions.
- Keep formulas out of the writing process. If they are used for feedback, try this writing–rewriting cycle.
- Write first.
- Then apply formula.
- Revise if necessary.
- Apply formula again on revision.

Too often, when writers shorten sentences in order to bring down the readability level, they remove the cohesive tie (the connecting word) that ties two ideas together, thus making the reading in actuality more difficult, although the formula would show otherwise. For example, take the sentence, "Many people migrated to the new world *because* there were religious restrictions and high taxation." If you change this to "Many people migrated to the new world. There were religious restrictions and high taxation," the connection is lost, or must now be inferred by the reader. The word *because* is what makes the connection.

NOTES

1. H. Black, *The American School Book* (New York: Morrow, 1967).
2. Crossley Surveys, *The 1980 College Textbook Survey* (Washington, DC: Book Industry Study Group, 1980).
3. John T. Guthrie, "Aims and Features of Text," in Wayne Otto and Sandra White, eds., *Reading Expository Materials* (New York: Academic Press, 1982), p. 185.
4. B. J. F. Meyer and E. Rice, "The Structure of Text," in P. D. Pearson, ed., *Handbook of Reading Research* (New York: Longman, 1984), pp. 319–352.
5. Marcel Adam Just and Patricia A. Carpenter, *The Psychology of Reading and Language Comprehension* (Newton, MA: Allyn and Bacon, 1987), pp. 246–248.
6. James Kinneary, "The Basic Aims of Discourse," *College Composition and Communication,* 20 (December 1969), 297–304.
7. S. Hoskins, "Text Superstructures," *Journal of Reading,* 29 (March 1986), 538–543.
8. Ibid.
9. Ibid.
10. Just and Carpenter, *The Psychology of Reading,* pp. 250–251.
11. Ibid.
12. B. J. F. Meyer, D. M. Brandt, and G. J. Bluth, "Use of Top-Level Structure in Text: Key for Reading Comprehension in Ninth-Grade Students," *Reading Research Quarterly,* 16 (1980), 72–103.
13. John A. Mateja and Karen D. Wood, "Secondary Students' Knowledge of Textbook Metastructure," *Reading in the Disciplines,* Second Yearbook of the American Reading Forum, 1982, pp. 97–100.
14. Margaret Early and Diane J. Sawyer, *Reading to Learn in Grades 5 to 12* (New York: Harcourt Brace Jovanovich, 1984), p. 388.
15. Guthrie, "Aims and Features of Text," pp. 185–188.
16. Ibid.
17. Rosalind Horowitz, "Text Patterns: Part II," *Journal of Reading,* 28 (March 1985), 538.
18. Ibid.
19. George R. Klare, "Assessing Readability," *Reading Research Quarterly,* 10 (1974–1975), 62–103.
20. W. S. Gray and B. E. Leary, *What Makes a Book Readable* (Chicago: University of Chicago Press, 1935).

21. Ron Carver, "Measuring Prose Difficulty: The Rauding Scale," *Reading Research Quarterly*, 11 (1975–1976), 660–685.

22. Notes 22–26 were taken from George Klare, "Readability," in P. David Pearson, ed., *Handbook of Reading Research* (New York: Longman, 1984), pp. 682–684.

23. A. C. Moore, "Recoiling from Reading: A Consideration of the Thorndike Library," *Library Journal*, 60 (1935), 419–422. Cited in Klare, "Readability."

24. S. E. Fitzgerald, "Literature by Slide Rule," *Saturday Review*, February 14, 1953, pp. 15–16, 53–54. Cited in Klare, "Readability."

25. G. H. McLaughlin, "Temptations of the Flesch," unpublished paper, Communications Research Center, Syracuse University, 1970. Cited in Klare, "Readability."

26. B. J. Wagner, "Blood and Gore, Fens and Fears: Beowulf Battles the Dale-Chall Monster," *Reading Teacher*, 34 (1981), 502–510. Cited in Klare, "Readability."

27. A. Davison and R. M. Kantor, "On the Failure of Readability Formulas to Define Readable Texts: A Case Study from Adaptations," *Reading Research Quarterly*, 17 (1982), 187–209.

28. Alice Davison, "Readability—Appraising Text Difficulty," in Richard C. Anderson, Jean Osborn, and Robert J. Tierney, eds., *Learning to Read in American Schools: Basal Readers and Content Texts* (Hillsdale, NJ: Erlbaum, 1984), pp. 121–139.

29. Walter H. MacGinitie, "Readability as a Solution Adds to the Problem," in Richard C. Anderson, Jean Osborn, and Robert J. Tierney, eds., *Learning to Read in American Schools: Basal Readers and Content Texts* (Hillsdale, NJ: Erlbaum, 1984), p. 141.

30. Edward Fry, "The Varied Uses of Readability Measurement Today," *Journal of Reading*, 30 (January 1987), 339; A. Bridgeman, "Dumbing Down: The Cost of Aiming Low May Be High," *Education Week*, 4 (September 5, 1984), 39–40, 61.

31. Jeanne S. Chall, "Readability: In Search of Improvement," *Publisher's Weekly*, October 1979, pp. 40–41.

32. Beverly L. Zakaluk and S. Jay Samuels, "Toward a New Approach to Predicting Text Comprehensibility," in Beverly L. Zakaluk and S. Jay Samuels, eds., *Readability: Its Past, Present and Future* (Newark, DE: International Reading Association, 1988), pp. 121–144.

33. B. L. Zakaluk, S. J. Samuels, and B. Taylor, "A Simple Technique for Estimating Prior Knowledge: Word Association," *Journal of Reading*, 30 (1986), 56–60.

34. Ibid.

35. G. H. McLaughlin, "Smog Grading—A New Readability Formula," *Journal of Reading*, 12 (May 1969), 639–646.

36. Edward Fry, "A Readability Formula That Saves Time," *Journal of Reading*, 11 (April 1968), 513–516, 575–578.

37. Phillip P. Gross and Karen Sadowski, "FOGINDEX—A Readability Formula Program for Microcomputers," *Journal of Reading*, 28 (April 1985), 614.

38. David B. Strahan and John G. Herlihy, "A Model for Analyzing Textbook Content," *Journal of Reading*, 28 (February 1985), 438–443.

39. Nancy Marshall, "Readability and Comprehensibility," *Journal of Reading*, 22 (March 1979), 542–544; Judith Westphal Irwin and Carol A. Davis, "Assessing Readability: The Checklist Approach," *Journal of Reading*, 24 (November 1980), 124–130.

40. *Degrees of Reading Power: User's Manual* (New York: College Board, 1987–1988).

41. J. R. Bormuth, "Cloze Test Readability: Criterion Reference Scores," *Journal of Educational Measurement,* 5 (Fall 1968), 189–196.

42. John Bormuth, "A Response to 'Is the Degrees of Reading Power Test Valid or Invalid?'" *Journal of Reading,* 29 (October 1985), 42–47; Ronald P. Carver, "Measuring Readability Using DRP Units," *Journal of Reading Behavior,* 17 (1985), 304.

43. David Moore, Sharon Moore, Patricia Cunningham, and James Cunningham, *Developing Readers and Writers in the Content Areas: K–12* (New York: Longman, 1986), p. 164.

44. T. H. Anderson and B. B. Armbruster, "Content Area Textbooks," in Richard C. Anderson, Jean Osborn, and Robert J. Tierney, eds., *Learning to Read in American Schools: Basal Readers and Content Texts* (Hillsdale, NJ: Erlbaum, 1984), pp. 193–226.

45. Klare, "Readability," p. 730.

RECOMMENDED READINGS

Baldwin, R. S., and Kaufman, R. K. "A Concurrent Validity Study of the Raygor Readability Graph." *Journal of Reading,* 23 (1979), 148–153.

Beach, Richard, and Appleman, Deborah. "Reading Strategies for Expository and Literary Text Types." In Alan C. Purves and Olive Niles, eds., *Becoming Readers in a Complex Society.* Eighty-third Yearbook of the National Society for the Study of Education. Chicago: University of Chicago Press, 1984, pp. 115–143.

Bishop, R. L. "The Journalism Programs: Help for the Wary Writer." *Creative Computing,* 1 (1975), 28–30.

Brooks, C., and Warren, R. P. *Modern Rhetoric,* 3rd ed. New York: Harcourt, Brace and World, 1970, pp. 37–38.

Calfee, R., and Curley, R. "Structures of Prose in Content Areas." In J. Flood, ed., *Understanding Reading Comprehension.* Newark, DE: International Reading Association, 1984.

Carver, R. P. "Measuring Prose Difficulty Using the Rauding Scale." *Reading Research Quarterly,* 11 (1975–1976), 660–685.

Cheek, Martha Collins. "Reaction: Secondary Students' Knowledge of Textbook Metastructure." *Reading in the Disciplines.* Second Yearbook of the American Reading Forum, 1982, pp. 100–101.

Chance, Larry. "Use Cloze Encounters of the Readability Kind for Secondary School Students." *Journal of Reading,* 28 (May 1985), 690–693.

Dale, E., and Chall, J. S. "Formula for Predicting Readability." *Educational Research Bulletin,* 27 (1948), 11–20, 37–54.

Davison, A., Lutz, R., and Roalef, A. "Text Readability." *Proceedings of the March 1980 Conference Center for the Study of Reading,* Urbana, Illinois, 1981.

Dryer, Lois Goodman. "Readability and Responsibility." *Journal of Reading,* 27 (January 1984), 334–338.

Flesch, Rudolph. "A New Readability Yardstick." *Journal of Applied Psychology,* 32 (June 1948), 221–233.

Freebody, P., and Anderson, R. C. "Effects of Vocabulary Difficulty, Text Cohesion, and Schema Availability on Reading Comprehension." *Reading Research Quarterly,* 18 (1983), 277–305.

Harrison, Colin. *Readability in the Classroom.* Cambridge: Cambridge University Press, 1980.

Hartley, J., and Burnhill, P. "Understanding Instructional Text: Typography, Layout and Design." In J. A. Howe, ed., *Adult Learning: Psychological Research and Application.* London: J. A. Wiley and Sons, 1977.

Horowitz, Rosalind. "Text Patterns: Part I." *Journal of Reading,* 28 (February 1985), 448–454.

Horowitz, Rosalind. "Text Patterns: Part II." *Journal of Reading,* 28 (March 1985), 534–541.

Irwin, J. W., and Davis, C. A. "Assessing Readability: The Checklist Approach." *Journal of Reading,* 24 (1980), 124–130.

Jevitz, Lucille, and Meints, Donald W. "Be a Better Book Buyer: Guidelines for Textbook Evaluation." *Journal of Reading,* 22 (1979), 734–738.

Kincaid, J. P., Aagard, J. A., and O'Hara, J. W. *Development and Test of a Computer Readability Editing System (CRES).* TAEG Report No. 83. Orlando, FL: U.S. Navy Training Analysis and Evaluation Group, 1980.

Kintsch, W. "On Comprehending Stories." In M. A. Just and P. A. Carpenter, eds., *Cognitive Processes in Comprehension.* Hillsdale, NJ: Erlbaum, 1977.

Kretschmer, Joseph C. "Computerizing and Comparing the Rix Readability Index." *Journal of Reading,* 27 (March 1984), 490–499.

Singer, Harry. "The Seer Technique: A Non-Computational Procedure for Quickly Estimating Readability Level." *Journal of Reading Behavior,* 7 (1975), 255–267.

Smith, Nila B. "Patterns of Writing in Different Subject Areas." *Journal of Reading,* 7 (1964), 31–37.

Taylor, W. L. "Cloze Procedure: A New Tool for Measuring Readability." *Journalism Quarterly,* 30 (1953), 415–433.

Zakaluk, Beverly L., and Samuels, S. Jay, eds. *Readability: Its Past, Present and Future.* Newark, DE: International Reading Association, 1988.

Postorganizer 1
Your Summary

Textbook authors usually do the most difficult work for their readers by giving them a chapter summary. Instead, it is recommended here that you practice summarizing this chapter as you would ask your own students to do. In class, discuss the key concepts, how they tie together, what necessary facts should be attached to these concepts, and what the first step is. One suggestion would be to look back over Preorganizer 1, with introduction, headings, and subheadings, to get a retroactive overview. Summaries can be done individually or in pairs; class comparisons using the board or overhead projector should help refine this skill for any who might need it.

Postorganizer 2
For Practice

Three excerpts from books that can serve as practice exercises for running readability formulas, checklists, and the like can be found in Appendix 3. You might wish to consider all these excerpts as part of one anthology, so that you can get your average score by doing a sampling of all three excerpts. Note that at times reading an excerpt may make you want to get in touch with the story or book itself. You can easily transfer this idea to use with your own students, having them run readability formulas and check their rate on material that might also get them interested in reading further. In that case, you would want them to understand what your learning objective was in performance-based terms, specifying both the learning and the behavior that will demonstrate the learning.

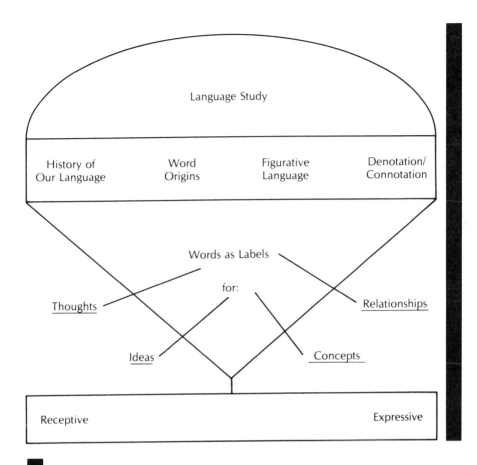

4

Vocabulary Concepts and Word Study

CHAPTER OUTLINE

Preorganizers
Introduction
  Are You Word-Sensitive?
  Are You an "I Want the Facts" Person?
Language Study
  Diachronic Linguistics
  Word Origins
  A Brief History of Our Language
  Changes in Sound Patterns and Meanings
  Amelioration and Pejoration
  Generalizations and Specializations
  Denotation and Connotation
  Figurative Language: Saying One Thing and Meaning Another
  Answers to Figurative Language Definitions
  Blending: Blends and Acronyms
  Mnemonics
Word Attack for Secondary Study-Reading
  The Need to Reteach CSSD in Secondary Classes
  Context—Taking an Educated Guess
  Structural Analysis: Unraveling Meaningful Word Segments
  Phonics: Sounds of Language
  The Dictionary—A Storehouse of Meanings, Etymologies,
    and Pronunciation
  Synonym Clustering Strategy Using a Dictionary or Thesaurus
Research-Based Recommendations for Teaching Vocabulary Activities
  Principles
  A Quick Checklist: What Teachers Can Do
General Teaching Strategies
  Semantic Feature Analysis (SFA)
  Open and Closed Word Sorts
  Magic Square: Find the Magic Number
  Magic Square: How Well Do You Know Literary Terms?
  Textual and Graphic Organizers as Preinstructional Strategies
  Modified Cloze Techniques
  Brainstorming as Concept Development
  Evaluating Vocabulary Development Strategies
Summary
Notes

Recommended Readings
Annotated Recommended Readings: Fun with Words
Special Dictionaries: A Sampling
Postorganizers

COGNITIVE COMPETENCIES

See the Learning Objectives in Preorganizer 1.

KEY TERMS

amelioration/pejoration
context clues
denotation/connotation
diachronic linguistics
figurative language

mnemonics
oxymorons
receptive/expressive vocabulary
structural analysis
thesaurus

Preorganizer 1
Learning Objectives for Vocabulary

After successfully completing this chapter, you will be able to do the following:

1. Explain to colleagues in writing (or orally) the values and limitations of including vocabulary development activities in secondary classrooms.
2. Describe in one concise written paragraph the general theory and principles of vocabulary/concept development.
3. Show appreciation of practical vocabulary strategies by such behaviors as voluntarily expressing your appreciation in class discussion, or opting to use one such strategy in a micro teaching situation or in your own classroom.
4. Select appropriate references for building your own professional library.

Remember to skim over these study-reading preorganizers before continuing to read. You and/or your instructor may select one or more appropriate ones to fit your individual needs.

Preorganizer 2
Interior Map

Follow these steps to create your interior map.

1. Study again the outline of topics found at the beginning of the chapter, thinking about how they might relate to each other and to the total notion of developmental secondary study reading.
2. Survey this chapter, noting major headings, graphics, and summary statement.
3. As you read this chapter, keep in mind key points and relationships among those points.
4. After you complete your reading, a postorganizer will ask you to draw a map showing key points and your interpretation of interrelationships of key terms.

After completing step 4, you should be ready to justify your thinking about organization of information, either in writing or in class discussion. No two interior maps will be exactly alike.

Vocabulary Concepts and Word Study

Preorganizer 3
Prediction Definition

Before reading this chapter, think of your own concept of what the term *vocabulary* entails. Write your prediction definition here for later reference.

_____

_____

_____

When you have completed this chapter, look back at your prediction definition and compare it to what you now know. Revise your initial definition here as needed. _____

_____

_____

_____

4
Vocabulary Concepts and Word Study

Those who think more deeply need words of larger meaning, those who are subtle thinkers look for more precise, discriminating words that speak for a specific shade of meaning. . . . Those who read and do not grow wiser seldom realize their own deficiencies. They complain of hard words and obscure sentences and ask why books are written which cannot be readily understood.

Paraphrase of Samuel Johnson, *The Idler and the Adventurer.* The Works of Samuel Johnson, Vol. 2, No. 70, copyright © 1963 by Yale University Press, New Haven, Connecticut. Used with permission.

INTRODUCTION

Word power is vitally important to comprehension, reading enjoyment, and school success. For reading to occur, readers need first to be able to identify words, and then to apply appropriate meanings to them. Readers need many opportunities to build concepts and perceive how words relate to each other conceptually. They also need to define words in a particular contextual setting. When many words are unknown, it takes the pleasure out of reading. When word study is taught in a dry, pedantic way (as is too often the case), many secondary and adult students are turned off to vocabulary study. This is sad because, if presented with gusto and enthusiasm, word study and language origins can be a never-ending, fascinating adventure.

Vocabulary can be defined here as a collection of words, or words and phrases, used by groups or individuals in a field of knowledge. Vocabulary must have meaning; otherwise it is merely a collection of empty, nonsensical sounds. Words are actually labels for thoughts, ideas, concepts, and relationships.

Are You Word-Sensitive?

Mature readers generally are word-sensitive. Some years ago, Wilfred Funk gave us a list of what he considered to be the ten most beautiful words in the English language. David Goldman then took those words and used them in a paragraph something like this to evoke imagery and possibly emotional involvement:

> The *golden* sun burst through the *dawn mist,* casting a *luminous* glow on the *tranquil* scene. As the *hush* was broken by the *melody* of church *chimes,* the *murmuring* of rustling leaves and the *lullaby* of a mother sparrow was heard trilling to her young.

Did you visualize and hear sounds as you read this? My list of the most beautiful words in the English language would also have to include *enchanting, exquisite, luscious,* and *soothing* as a start. When I shared this notion of beautiful words with my secondary classes, they got so involved in discussion and feelings of ownership of *their* most beautiful words that a natural outcome was a writing assignment in which *they* wanted to participate. Several volunteered to expand the assignment by making a list of the ten ugliest words (e.g., *grab, grunt, sneer, lecherous, ludicrous, infarct*).

This seemed to work equally well with all levels of developmental readers. With younger students, making up lists of what they called "snarl" words and "purr" words could be rewarding and fun. All this, then, was a way to get students to begin to think seriously about words.

Are You an "I Want the Facts" Person?

If so, you are anxious right now to get on with it—to learn more about factors behind vocabulary development. Some of these factors change over time.

1. *Ask yourself how large you think your present vocabulary is.* There are very roughly 500,000 words in the English language—that is, when you count different forms of the same word and obsolete words. They are all found in an unabridged dictionary such as the *Oxford English Dictionary.* Another 500,000 technical and scientific terms are not catalogued. Abridged dictionaries have approximately 100,000 different words. How many do you think you know?

On any given page of a dictionary, how many words are familiar to you? It has been said that the average adult has a vocabulary only one and a half times that of a child of ten. Of course, many adults are not college graduates, but what has happened to their questioning minds? Children are curious, and may learn on the average three new words a day. How many new words have you learned in the past week? Jot one down now for future reference:

_____.

What has turned off so many secondary and adult students to increasing their word knowledge? Could obsolete teaching techniques be one cause? One example of such a technique may trigger a memory. On Monday, or at the beginning of a unit, or before reading a chapter or story, the teacher put on the board a long list of words, in isolation. Your task, then, was to look up these words, define them, and use them in a sentence. Of course, you took the first meaning given in the dictionary, ignoring all the others. If these words were not used again soon, they were easily forgotten. Recall how negative you may have felt about having to do that assignment.

2. *Basically, we have two kinds of vocabulary, receptive and expressive.* Our receptive (taking-in) vocabularies include listening and reading, which are our largest. Our expressive (putting out) vocabularies include speaking and writing, which are more limited, with writing usually the smallest. For example, we may know the meaning of the word *redundant* when we hear it or see it in print, but we may rarely if ever use it when speaking or writing. We recognize the word when it is given to us but do not readily recall it ourselves.

3. *Vocabulary acquisition is interesting from a number of theoretical viewpoints.* First, there is a phenomenal growth of vocabulary by college age. The average college student is estimated to know approximately 40,000 to 50,000 words when encountered during reading. Typically, estimates are based on a process whereby readers are tested on a random sample of words selected from a word list or dictionary. Then the estimate is extrapolated to the entire body of words. For example, if a reader could define 50 percent of 200 words randomly selected from a 100,000-word dictionary, the estimate would be that the reader knew half the words in the dictionary (50,000 words). This procedure is just a reasonable starting point, which could bias the actual estimate of vocabulary size. Because estimates have varied widely, Just and Carpenter (1987) state that the most likely estimates are 5,000 (listening) words for first-graders and 50,000 for college students, at which point listening and reading vocabularies are about the same in size. The rate of vocabulary growth is about 2,700 to 3,000 words per year, or 7 or 8 new words a day. This suggests that rote memorization for acquiring all these meanings is unlikely. It is more likely that most vocabulary is acquired by inferring word meanings when reading or listening.[1]

4. *General types of words include these categories: general or standard, special, and technical. General* vocabulary includes common words with generally accepted meanings (e.g., *beginning, pleasant*). *Special* vocabulary words have a general meaning as well as a specialized meaning for a particular subject area (e.g., *root:* root of the matter, square root, root of a tree). This can be confusing to readers who encounter special words they think they already

know. *Technical* vocabulary includes those words that represent a specific concept applicable to a particular discipline (e.g., *photosynthesis, oxymoron, decimal*). Also, some technical terms will change meanings with a particular discipline (e.g., *square, prime, bank*). Kossack and Vigilante, in their taxonomy of mathematical vocabulary, include a category of word phrases whose combined whole is not equal to the sum of the meanings of the parts (e.g., *relative error, inferior vena cava*).[2]

5. *As a word comes into our vocabulary, it generally passes through at least three overlapping stages of understanding, from making one specific, literal association, to interpreting the word's function or use, and finally to conceptualizing or generalizing the word as part of a larger whole.* Forgan and Mangrum (1985) gave us a good example with the term *vote*. At the specific level, you would have a single association, such as "something that occurs during an election," or you might use the dictionary for one definition which you would memorize. At the second (functional) level, you would be able to describe the word in terms of its function: "a way of getting someone elected." In this case you might have used some interpretation and you could possible supply a synonym. At the highest level, conceptualizing or generalizing, you would understand most or all facets and uses of the term and be able to show how it fits into the big picture—in this case, how the vote is just one part of our complex democratic process of government.[3] At this point, look at the word you wrote down earlier that you have recently learned. At what level is your knowledge of that word? _____. Check the dictionary, if necessary, to be certain.

6. *Another way of looking at levels of knowing a word is to think of it in four stages.* You can use the following examples, of two made-up words and the word *serendipity*.
   a. *Pove, shug:* I never saw it or heard it before (these are actually nonsense words).
   b. *Serendipity:* I've seen it or heard it, but I'm not sure of its meaning.
   c. *Serendipity:* Ah, I can place it in a broad category. It has something to do with a pleasant feeling. It's a favorable word.
   d. *Serendipity:* I know it! I can define it with its shades of meaning. It means making fortunate discoveries by accident. It was coined by Horace Walpole after characters in a play, *The Three Princes of Serendip*, who made such discoveries. It was a serendipitous experience for them.

7. *Students for whom English is a second language can run into problems when they know only one meaning for a word and then meet it in a totally different context.* If they have learned the term *bank* as meaning a place that handles

money, it could be confusing to read "the bank of the river." They might picture a building by the river, or caches alongside for depositing money.

8. *Learning new words is, or should be, a dynamic, ongoing process throughout our lives, for when our words change, we change.* If I knew the extent and types of words you, the reader, have mastered, I would be able to describe the nature and quality of your life to date. Your vocabulary reflects what you have studied or read, what interests you have, where you have been, and all the subtle refinements of your mind. And, too, words are either building blocks or stumbling blocks to learning. Knowing their meanings is essential to comprehension. Having a sufficiently strong and diverse vocabulary is necessary not only for mastering secondary study-reading, but also for enjoying mature recreational reading. Therefore, there can be no greater service for our students, I believe, than to turn them on to vocabulary development. But first, *you* as teachers must be convinced of its importance.

Now that you have given a little thought to how you feel about words, and have considered some basic facts, it is time to look at language study, or how our words have changed through the ages.

LANGUAGE STUDY

Diachronic Linguistics

What is the meaning of diachronic linguistics? Using our knowledge of how structural analysis works, we may recall that *dia* means *through* (as in *diagram* or *diameter*) and that *chron* means *time* (as in *chronometer* and *chronological*). Thus, *diachronic* means "through time." Linguistics is the study of language, so we now know that *diachronic linguistics* is the study of language through time — its history and changes. Burmeister (1978) gives us some interesting facts and notions concerning word origins.[4]

Word Origins

New words come into our language when we coin and borrow from others. In *coining* new words, we may combine morphemes (meaningful word parts, as in *astronaut* and *television*), or we may *blend* the first part of one word with the last part of another (e.g., *smoke + fog = smog; breakfast + lunch = brunch; motor + hotel = motel; twist + whirl = twirl*), or we may create acronyms from the first letters of several words (e.g., UNESCO = United Nations Educational, Social, and Cultural Organization; *posh* = port out, starboard home; *snafu* = situation *n*ormal, *a*ll *f*ouled *u*p). Slang words come and go, but sometimes a few stay with us (e.g., *good buddy, antsville, zapped*). Slang expressions are fresh and picturesque when new but can soon become overused, stereotyped, and unimaginative (e.g., "Have a nice day").

We borrow from many languages. Students seem to enjoy guessing where certain words originated and are often surprised at the diversity of origins in our language. Table 4.1 shows a few examples.

A Brief History of Our Language

Our English language today is a descendant of the Germanic branch of the Indo-European family of languages. From this base, it changed to Anglo-Saxon (Old English), then to Middle English, and finally to the Modern English of today. In the fifth century A.D., tribes from the northwestern Continental fringe, who spoke a form of Low German, invaded and conquered

TABLE 4.1
Word Origins

Native American	*German*	*Persian*
pecan	otter	caravan
chipmunk	dollar	
toboggan	house	*Russian*
raccoon	wiener	sputnik
		sable
Arabic	*Greek*	babushka
candy	alphabet	
algebra	circus	*Scandinavian*
sugar	octopus	sister
	cryogenic	teeter totter
Australian		sky
kangaroo	*Hindi*	
boomerang	bungalow	*South America*
	shampoo	alpaca
Chinese	pajamas	
tea	jungle	*Spanish*
		tobacco
Eskimo	*Italian*	patio
kayak	cameo	potato
igloo	grotto	chocolate
	volcano	mosquito
French	piano	
pork	violin	*Turkish*
detail		coffee
humor	*Japanese*	yogurt
calendar	kimono	tulip
explore		
	Latin	
	calculus	
	column	

Classroom Activity: Word Origins

Using an unabridged dictionary, a special dictionary on etymologies, or any book on word origins (see the Recommended Readings at the end of this chapter for possible choices), find three words with interesting histories that you could include in a lesson with your own class. This may be done independently and handed in as a written assignment, or it can be done with a partner and discussed in class.

England. The dialects spoken by this handful of invaders became the basis of our language today. From roughly 450 to 1150 A.D., the English language was Anglo-Saxon (A.S.) or Old English (O.E.). Middle English (M.E.) can be dated only approximately between 1150 and 1475 A.D., with the first part a period of linguistic chaos among groups of separate dialects. By 1420, London English was becoming a standard for all of England, and Caxton sealed its acceptance by using it in his printed books. From 1476 to the present, we have what is called Modern English, which early on included rapid accretions of foreign words, particularly those coming from a Latin base. In the seventeenth century the settlement of the New England colonies by immigrants mainly from the southeastern section of England brought this type of English to America, where it formed the basis for the northeastern coastal American speech of today. From 1780 to the present, there has been what can be called a linguistic equilibrium; however, the development of the English phonemic system is still underway. Further change is inevitable.[5]

For more on this subject, see Appendix 4, "History of the English Dictionary."

Changes in Sound Patterns and Meaning

One change in the English language has been in the sound patterns of words, which has led to corresponding changes in spelling. English has undergone a "great vowel shift" from Old English to Middle English to Modern English. You can see this by comparing, for example, the original Chaucer with modern translations of the same passages. The consonant shift, often referred to as Grimm's law after the brothers Grimm, who described this change, is less complex. *Bh* became *b, dh* became *d, p* changed to *f (pater—father), d* changed to *t* or *th*.[6]

The original word *dent* was changed to *tooth* and *teeth*. We later borrowed the original cognate *dent* from the Latin to use in formal words such as *dental* and *dentist*. The original *gno* became *know*. From the Greek we now have *diagnosis, agnostic, prognosis*.

Today, as further evidence of change, we have begun to pronounce some three-syllable words as two syllables, omitting the middle vowel sound. For example, think about how you say these words: *poem, average, restaurant, omelet?* These words may eventually change their spelling to reflect the sound patterns.

Amelioration and Pejoration

Meaning changes include aspects such as amelioration and pejoration (elevation and lowering, respectively, of the meanings of words) and generalizations. Look at this list to see some of the changed meanings of words.

Amelioration	Pejoration
Minister once meant common servant.	*Lust* once meant pleasure, joy.
Nice once meant ignorant.	*Lewd* once meant unlearned.
Enthusiastic once meant fanatical.	*Pirate* once meant adventurer.
	Boy once meant imp.

Generalizations and Specializations

Starving once meant dying (today it is just one way of dying).
Girl once meant a young boy or girl.
Meat once meant any food.[7]
Shipping once meant only transporting by ship.

As we specialize, we become more precise in definitions. Instead of saying "a group of fish," we say *school*; for wolves, *pack*; for cattle, *herd*; for turtles, *glag*; for owls, *parliament*. Instead of saying *smell* or *scent* we say "aroma of coffee," "bouquet of wine," "fragrance of flowers."

Denotation and Connotation

Literal or scientific meanings of words are referred to as their *denotations*, whereas *connotations* are their interpretive, poetic, or emotional meanings. In the fields of science and mathematics, words have definite, precise meanings, generally agreed on throughout those disciplines. Denotative words are matter of fact and usually have only one meaning if used in these fields. For example, *biology* = the study of life; *square* = a four-sided figure with all sides equal. Note, however, that *square* may be used in other areas to mean a space in the center of a village, as in "village square" or in still another sense in the sentence "He squared off." Connotations are often found in literature, social studies, and newspaper reports. They are used to convince us of a certain point of view or to sway our feelings in some way. When you think of these terms, is your feeling about them positive or negative? — *square, red, lemon, liberal, republican, democrat, chicken.* What other words might you add to this list?

Figurative Language: Saying One Thing and Meaning Another

Figurative language includes not only the familiar rhetorical devices of irony, simile, metaphor, and euphemism, but also some more obscure devices (Ortony, 1985).[8] How many of these words can you readily define? How many have you never even *seen* before?

1. litotes _____

2. zeugma _____

3. synecdoche _____

4. metonymy _____

5. oxymoron _____

6. hyperbole _____

In each case these words stand for a figure of speech that says one thing and means another. If taken at face value, they may seem to be false, bizarre, or nonsensical. Is all the world really a stage? Is it actually raining cats and dogs? Is life not a bed of roses? (This last question is literally true as well as having a figurative meaning.)

More familiar terms include the following:

Simile: One thing is compared to another, dissimilar thing using *like* or *as* ("People, like columns of ants, moved along the path").
Metaphor: One thing is compared to another, different thing by being spoken of as if it were the other ("The fog was a curtain (blocking our view)"; "All the world's a stage").

Idiom: An accepted phrase or expression has a different meaning from the literal ("Let the cat out of the bag").

Euphemism: Auspicious or good words are used in place of those considered distasteful or offensive (to die = to pass away, pass on; janitor = maintenance superintendent; 80 years old = 80 years young; used car = preowned car; replacements in battle = reinforcements).

Figurative use of language is one of the most common ways in which we stretch language to suit our wish to communicate in a special way. It can be especially confusing to the English as a second language (ESL) learner.

Answers to Figurative Language Definitions

1. Something is expressed by a negation to the contrary—for example, "not a few" (many).
2. A simple modifier, usually a verb or adjective, applies to two or more words, with only one seeming to be logically connected ("The room was not light, but her fingers were").
3. A part or an individual is used for a whole or a class, or the reverse of this (*bread* for food, *army* for soldier).
4. The name of one thing is used for another thing associated with or suggested by it ("The White House has decided").
5. Opposite or contradictory terms are combined for effect (thunderous silence, beloved enemy, sweet sorrow, giant shrimp, good war, dictatorial democracy).
6. Exaggeration for effect, not meant to be taken literally ("He is as old as time").[9]

Blending: Blends and Acronyms

Blends are usually composed of the beginning part of one word and the ending of another, or the beginning part of one word plus another whole word (*brunch* = breakfast and lunch; *telecast* = television broadcast; *flurry* = flutter and hurry). On the other hand, acronyms are made up of first letters of several words (*posh* = port out starboard home; A.W.O.L. = away without leave). Students can compose their own blends, which others can attempt to unravel. For example, what are the following coined (newly minted) words?

vidiot
banalysis
synesthesia[10]

Class Activity: Oxymorons

Working in pairs, collect or create oxymorons (from the Greek *oxy* = sharp, *moron* = foolish). Have a contest to determine which pair created or collected the most, and most humorous, the most relevant, the most debatable, and so on. The following list should get you started:

- political scientist
- optimistic pessimist
- articulate brevity
- progressive regression
- absolute relativity
- still life
- elegant simplicity
- vast minority
- a definite "maybe"
- permanent change
- participating spectator
- jumbo shrimp[11]

We can also coin new words using a list of word parts as reference, and then define these new words. For example:

trans	*chron*	*itis*
across	time	inflammation

 Transchronitis: A disease occurring when a human travels by time machine

Mnemonics

Stories as mnemonic devices are another aid to helping students recall key terms. There are numerous sources for these, some of which are found in the references at the end of the chapter.

 Maverick: A Texas rancher in the 1800s, Old Sam Maverick, had such a soft heart that he refused to brand his cattle. This gave cattle rustlers a field day. They called his unmarked cattle "mavericks." Now we use this term for anyone who is different, not going the usual way.

Etiquette: French military orders were publicly posted on a piece of paper called an *etiquette*, which meant label, tag, or ticket. A gardener to the French court decided to use this idea and posted rules in the royal gardens to show people where they could walk. Visitors obeyed these "etiquettes" because it was the proper thing to do. That is why today we use the term *etiquette* to mean the proper thing to do in whatever situation.

WORD ATTACK FOR SECONDARY STUDY-READING

The Need to Reteach CSSD in Secondary Classes

Many adolescents with reading deficiencies have never mastered essential word attack skills taught in the elementary years. If asked, they may tell you that they try one way to figure out a new word, and if it doesn't work they just give up. It is possible, too, that elementary teachers, while doing a thorough job of teaching individual word attack skills, may not have emphasized to their students directly the need to try more than one skill on the basis of the problem at hand. Here are a few examples.

- Tim was an eleventh-grade student who could not alphabetize quickly or well enough to use the dictionary efficiently. He had forgotten about guide words and other aids, so he usually ignored unknown words. He never tried other approaches.
- Sue felt she must always look up unknown words and got discouraged because reading assignments took so much time.
- John, a visual learner, had always had trouble discriminating sounds, but because phonics had been overstressed he would try once to sound out a word and, when it made no sense, would give up.
- Marie thought the purpose of reading aloud was to sound good. Even when reading silently she said the words to herself without thinking about the meaning they conveyed.
- Sam tried merely to memorize his science words without looking at their structure and meaningful parts of words. He could sound the words out correctly, but he often confused terms that ended in the same way.

In each case (and you may think of other examples), these students were trying to get at new words and their meanings in inefficient and limited ways.

Let us look now at four ways to attack new words—context, structural analysis, sound (phonics), and dictionary (CSSD)—as combined methods of assisting these students. Overall, we should be saying to them: "Look, you were taught these skills and strategies at one time, but now we simply have to review them and decide when to put them together. First of all, try to figure out the word and its meaning from the context—the words around it, or how it fits into the sentence, and how it is used. It's all right to skip over an unknown word to finish the sentence or paragraph, and then come back and see if you can guess the meaning on the basis of what you are reading. We learn most of our words this way, through context. If context doesn't do it, don't give up, but try one of two things—either break the word into meaningful parts (structural analysis) and try to get at the meaning that way (*phon/eme—phone* is "sound," *eme* is "smallest unit of"), or try sounding it out (phonics) to see if it is a familiar word in your listening vocabulary (*plethora, pejorative*). Finally, if none of these approaches work, go to the dictionary to find the best meaning for the word as it is used here. This is a synthesizing of strategies. By stressing the variety of ways to attack an unknown word and then reviewing key aspects of each area with a follow-up practice, you should eventually notice a difference, not only in rate of comprehension but also in a more positive attitude toward the reading task."

It is important not to make the mistake one secondary reading teacher made while teaching in a black ghetto high school in California. She had decided (or had been taught) that word attack was the be-all and end-all of becoming a natural reader. In a large school where only a small percentage of students went on to higher education and over half the population were reading significantly below grade level, her voluntary reading laboratory was almost empty. As soon as students came to her for help, she tested them extensively and then set them to work on a series of dittoed syllabication exercises. They rarely lasted a week in her lab—and no wonder! Word attack skills, like other nitty-gritty skills, *should* be retaught and reviewed as needed, but just as this book allots only a small section of one chapter to them, so should your instructions be balanced with numerous other, more significant aspects of study-reading.

Context—Taking an Educated Guess

Most of us have increased our own vocabulary with almost unconscious effort by using context clues. We see a word several times while reading and eventually pick up the general meaning without looking the word up in the dictionary. In secondary schools we need to accelerate students' learning from context by helping them realize its value. At the same time, we must also warn them that context does not always give us the meaning we need and that our guesses should be checked with new context, meaning of word parts, or formal definitions. Native-born English speakers may more readily anticipate meanings through context than will those for whom English is a second language. Students who require assistance in using context clues must have multiple exposures to passages that contain such clues. For those readers who are not using context clues, direct modeling of the thought processes involved could be beneficial. They also need to be reminded to look for meaning farther along in the selection. Some types of clues are included in Table 4.2.

Do you know the word *gusle*? It is sometimes spelled *gusla*. Instead of turning to the dictionary right away, let us see if you can determine the meaning from context. We will do this in steps so that you can try to picture the word after each step.

TABLE 4.2
Context Clues

Type of Context Clue	Examples	
Synonym	*edifice*	A graceful building described as an historical edifice
Compare/contrast	*trundles*	Although called rapid transit it merely trundles along at twenty miles per hour, or, it does not speed—it trundles along.
Summary or examples	*frugality*	He was known for his frugality—never throwing anything away, saving tinfoil, string, empty bottles, etc.
Background experience	*conflagration*	Firefighters extinguished the conflagration in the rear cabin.
Definition or explanation	*speleologists*	A film about speleologists, men who explore caves, or, a speleologist is one who . . .
Reflection of a mood or situation	*obsequious*	In the genteel, upper-class atmosphere of the elegant and spacious dining room, gentlemen dined in style and comfort attended by obsequious waiters bent on pleasing them.
Familiar expression	*albeit*	Woolen mufflers, fur pieces, and protective hats, albeit with just a touch of ornamentation, are highly regarded for daily wear.
No safe clue (context may mislead or not reveal)	*antivivisection*	Many causes find champions in society. Earnest dowagers promote artists and antivivisection.
Punctuation	*phobias*	Phobias—irrational fears

Source: Adapted from "Context Clues" from *Reading to Learn in Grades 5 to 12* by Margaret Early and Diane J. Sawyer, p. 339, copyright © 1984 by Harcourt Brace Jovanovich, Inc., *reprinted by permission of the publisher.*

1. First, look at the word and try to pronounce it. Is it *gussle? goosel?* No, it is *gooselay* or *goosela.* (Perhaps that is the only clue you need, but I hope not, because then this exercise will have less personal meaning for you.)
2. Next, what happens when I say, "When I was traveling in Eastern Europe, I saw many gusles?" What do you now know about the word? It's a noun, it's concrete, there are many of them, and it has to do with something found in Eastern Europe.
3. The second sentence states, "In particular, I saw many men playing gusles." Now you can limit it to one of two things—it is either a game or a musical instrument.
4. "Normally, a gusle is used to accompany the chanting of folk epics." Ah, it's a musical instrument, but what kind? Percussion? Wind? String?
5. "Most gusles are made of wood covered with a sheepskin head, and have a single string; and a gusle is normally played with a bow." Now you should have a pretty clear picture of the word, and all of it comes from context. In linguistic terms, you have combined a set of features that eventually defined it for you.[12]

To show students the importance of punctuation in expressing meaning, it can be interesting to provide sentences that depend completely on where the punctuation is placed. Examples include:

1. *Woman without her man is nothing*
Woman—without her, man is nothing. This means, of course, that man is nothing without a woman. With a change in punctuation, however, the same sentence means that unless a woman has a man, *she* is nothing: *woman, without her man, is nothing.* Here is another example:

2. *Joshua said his brother was a thief*
How could this mean two different things? _____

_____

The following is a term in isolation that you may think you already know, but wait—look at the context before deciding.

Esquire: a. administrator   b. questioner   c. strong man
              d. horseback rider   e. gentleman

He was a king's esquire, which in those days meant working in the administrative department of the king's government. Having checked your answer, you should now realize more clearly the importance of context for older readers. And just as important, you will see why giving students long lists of words out of context is not a helpful teaching procedure.

Fun with a Simple Word

A few years ago a student shared this humorous look at the many meanings of one simple little word. It shows how all depends on context. You might want to use it with your own students to illustrate multiple meanings and context.

What's Up
(Author Unknown)

We've got a two-letter word we use constantly that may have more meanings than any other word. The word is *up*.

It's easy to understand *up* meaning toward the sky or toward the top of the list. But when we waken, why do we wake up? At a meeting why does the topic come up? Why do participants speak up and why are the officers up for election? Why is it up to the secretary to write up a report?

Often the little word isn't needed, but we use it anyway. We brighten up a room, we light up a cigar, polish up the silver, lock up the house and fix up the old car. At other times it has special meanings. People stir up trouble, line up for tickets, work up an appetite, think up excuses and get tied up in traffic. To be dressed is one thing—to be dressed up is special. It may be confusing but a drain must be opened up because it is stopped up. We open up a store in the morning and close it up at night. We seem to be all mixed up about *up*.

To be up on the proper use of *up*—look up the word in your dictionary. In one desk-sized dictionary *up* takes up half a page and lists definitions up to about fifty. If you are up to it, you might try building up a list of the many ways in which *up* is used. It will take up a lot of time, but if you don't give up you may wind up with a thousand!

Prediction through Context: Part A

A simple strategy suggested by Cunningham, Cunningham, and Arthur (1981) and illustrated by Readance, Bean, and Baldwin (1985) shows the importance of context in getting at meaning.[13] To illustrate, start by trying to define the following three words using only what you already know. Predict a definition for each.

1. carapace _____

2. nonsectarian _____

3. dispirited _____

If you were not able to come up readily with a definition, reading the following sentences with these three words in context may help.

1. "Without its *carapace*, the turtle would die from either his enemies or the weather." (Clue—your previous experience with turtles)
2. "Although she believed in God, she had a *nonsectarian* attitude toward religion." (Clue—comparing and contrasting belief versus formal religion)
3. "He presented the lesson in a dull, *dispirited* manner, which failed to stimulate or challenge." (Clue—describing a lackluster mood)

If these sentences helped, you were using context to get to meaning. Teaching prediction through context includes the following steps.

1. Select from students' reading unfamiliar or troublesome key words.
2. Write a sentence on the board or provide a handout for each word that contains clues to meaning, or use the sentence in the text if it contains clues.
3. Present words in isolation as was done here, and ask students to guess first at their meaning.
4. Tell students to read on to verify or revise their guesses, using the dictionary or glossary.

This simple activity teaches students to become more actively involved in using helpful processes to get at meaning rather than using rote memorization.

Prediction through Context: Part B

Another way to help readers become more independent in determining meanings of key words in a reading assignment is to model the process first by listing five to ten key terms on the board and pronouncing each one. (These selected key terms should be adequately defined in the context.) Students are then asked before reading to generate possible sentences containing each term. These sentences are written on the board verbatim and not discussed until after the reading. As students silently read the assignment, they are asked to determine the accuracy of their sentences and to make judgments. Inaccurate sentences are omitted or refined, and new sentences may be added. Finally, students record all approved sentences in their personal notebooks for future reference.

Preteaching terms (using the same list) by asking students to define or guess at definitions prior to reading is a powerful strategy. Students should provide a rationale for their guesses, and it can be expected that many will be wrong or even humorous. Without comment from teachers, the next step is to provide on the board an actual context for each word from the text. Students must again try to define or guess at appropriate meanings. After discussion of how context may help get at meaning, the last step would be to consult the glossary or dictionary for verification and comparison.

Classroom Activity: Context

The following classroom activity may help you see the overall importance of context. After reading this excerpt from Arnheim (1969),[14] summarize the message in one brief sentence and retitle it.

Context and the "Chaste"

The *protean* nature of word meanings becomes painfully evident when an inept teacher asks pupils to look up certain terms in the dictionary and then write sentences containing them. James Deese reports on the results a teacher of seventh-grade English obtained with the word "chaste." One student, finding that *chaste* meant "simple in design," wrote: "The amoeba is a chaste animal"; others, using the word as a synonym of "unstained" or "pure," wrote: "The milk was chaste" or "The plates were still chaste after much use." This attractive nonsense came about because the teacher forced his pupils to pick facets of a concept out of context. The words of the dictionary point to a random collection of such facets, and there is no way of using them correctly unless one knows the context in which they belong.

Source: Reprinted with permission from *Visual Thinking* by Rudolf Arnheim, Berkeley: University of California Press. Copyright © 1969 The Regents of the University of California.

Structural Analysis: Unraveling Meaningful Word Segments

Clues within words can sometimes help unravel meanings when external context clues do not help. Structural analysis, also referred to as morphemic analysis or morphological clues, is concerned with meaningful word parts, or *morphemes*. For example, if you know that *morph* means "meaning" and that *eme* comes from the Greek and means "smallest unit of," you can figure out that a *morpheme* is the smallest unit of meaning. If you know that *ology* means "the study of," then *morphology* must be the study of meaning. Now you can begin to transfer this knowledge to such words as phoneme, grapheme, phonology, and the like.

Morphemes can be either free or bound. A free morpheme is one that stands alone as a word, like *bed*. Sometimes two free morphemes are combined to make a compound word such as *bedroom* or *bookstore*. A bound morpheme is an affix to a word and by itself would not make a word. A bound morpheme must be affixed to a free morpheme, like the *s* in *beds* or the *dis* in *dislike*. Affixes include prefixes and suffixes, which are added to root words (free morphemes). Prefixes, attached to the beginning of a word, change its meaning (*un*common, *circum*navigate, *bi*section, *auto*biography). In the first example, *common* is the root word and *un* is the prefix, meaning *not*. On the other hand, suffixes, affixed to the end of a word, may change (1) the form (part of speech) such as *slow*, an adjective describing something, to *slowly*, an adverb telling how it is done; (2) the meaning (need*less*—without need); (3) the tense (*ed, ing*); (4) the number (*s* for plural); or (5) the degree (fast, faster, fastest). A suffix that changes the number, tense, or degree of a word is called an inflectional ending.

Spelling problems arising from adding suffixes to root words include the following: changing *y* to *i* when adding *ed (carry, carried)*; changing *f* to *v* for plural *(loaf, loaves)*, or doubling the final consonant before adding *ed (drop, dropped)*. Other spelling and pronunciation changes to root words when suffixes are added can be seen in these examples: *efficient—efficiency, require—requisition, vary—variety.*

According to Roe, Stoodt, and Burns (1983), of the 20,000 most commonly used words in our language, about 25 percent have prefixes, but fifteen prefixes make up over 80 percent of the total usage of all prefixes.[15] Those fifteen are certainly worth knowing, then. They are listed with their meanings here:

> *ab* (from)—*abnormal*
> *ad* (to)—*adhesion*
> *be*—*belittle*
> *com, con, co, col* (with)—*conjunction*
> *de* (from)—*decentralize*
> *dis, di* (apart)—*dissect*
> *en* (in)—*enact*
> *ex* (out)—*extract*
> *in, il, un, ir* (not)—*inadequate*
> *pre* (before)—*predict*
> *pro* (in front of)—*proceed*
> *re* (back)—*rebuttal*

sub (under)—*subway*
un (not)—*unpaid*

A majority of our words come from Latin and Greek. For example, *photo* comes from the Greek for "light"; *meter,* also from the Greek, means "measure." Now, if we know that *thermo* is heat and *graphic* can mean "pictorial," "written," or "printed," we can figure out the meanings of many words like *photographic* and *thermometer. Bio* means *life,* so a *biographer* is one who writes about life.

Secondary students who have been discouraged by long, unfamiliar multisyllabic words may become excited by the discovery that they can divide them into smaller meaningful parts and actually get at a general sort of meaning. When teaching or reviewing structural analysis, you might capture students' attention and interest by spreading out across the entire board the well-known term *antidisestablishmentarianism.* When asked to find the root, many fall into the trap of saying *establishment* before catching themselves. Place a box around the actual root, *establish,* and then ask for suffixes first, followed by prefixes. Place a slash dividing them. Next, talk about possible meanings of each affix and write the meaning under each. The example will look like this:

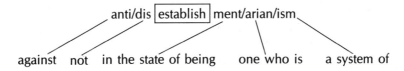

Remarking that this is truly an exaggerated example, I then read the definition as "a system of one who is in the process of being against not establishing." After a chuckle or two, we then arrive at "a system of those against separation or not establishing."

Homonyms/Homophones and Homographs
Using your knowledge of structural analysis, you might try defining these three terms when you know that *homo* = same, *phone* = sound, *graph* = writing. Look at Table 4.3 to clarify further any possible confusion among terms.

Phonics: Sounds of Language

The main reason for acquiring and refining word attack skills is to get at word meanings. Because our listening vocabulary may be more extensive

TABLE 4.3
Homonyms, Homophones, and Homographs

	Same	Different	Examples
Homonym	Sound and spelling	Meaning	*bank* (money) *bank* (river)
Homophone	Sound	Meaning and spelling	*New, knew, gnu*
Homograph	Spelling	Meaning and sound	*read* (present tense) *read* (past tense)

than our reading vocabulary, we may know a word's meaning if we hear it but cannot pronounce it correctly when we just see it in print. Phonic knowledge can help us get at word meaning only if we already know the meaning when we hear that word. Many older problem readers experience difficulty in this area.

Phonic analysis involves dividing words into basic sound elements and blending those sounds together to get a familiar spoken word. *A Dictionary of Related Terms* (Harris and Hodges, 1981) defines it as "an approach to the teaching of reading and spelling that stresses symbol–sound relationships, *especially in beginning reading instruction."* The last portion is emphasized here to alert you to the facts that reading and phonics are not synonymous and that phonics will play only a very small part in secondary study-reading. Many of you will breathe a sigh of relief at this news.

Although phonics at the secondary level is of minor importance, it should not be altogether ignored. Often, a simple reminder to struggling readers will be enough to give them a forgotten tool. Teachers looking for detailed coverage of phonics should refer to one of the excellent books in the field such as Rinsky's *Teaching Word Attack Skills* (1989) (see the Recommended Readings).

Having thus warned you that phonics will not be discussed here in depth, I would still like to share some aspects that some of my secondary students found to be helpful.

Even though there appear to be many exceptions to the rules in the English language, actually our language is approximately 80 percent regular. This means, then, that many of our words *can* be analyzed phonetically. Too often we have dwelt on the exceptions.

The major division in phonics is between consonants and vowels. Of the twenty-six letters of the alphabet, only five or six are vowels (*a, e, i, o, u,* and sometimes *y*), and the rest are consonants. Most consonants represent only one sound (the exceptions are *c*, *g*, *s*, and *x*), and these regular consonants are the single most important clues to unraveling word pronunciations. To see how little vowels give us as clues to words, look at the following sentence, written first without vowels and next without consonants.

1. Th_ sh_ _ _s _n th_ _th_ r f_ _t.
2. _ _e _ _oe i_ o_ _ _e o_ _e_ _oo_.
(The shoe is on the other foot.)

Although our vowels may have many different sounds depending on how they are combined in words with other letters (*bread, meat, heard, worm*) or depending on different dialects (*egg—aig, oil—earl, house—hoose, hockey—hawky*), there are still just two major divisions of frequent vowel sounds— the short sounds ă/ĕ/ĭ/ŏ/ŭ and the long sounds ā/ē/ī/ō/ū, with short sounds the most common. Short vowels appear in closed syllables that have a consonant on each side (*băt, rĕd, hŏt*) or in a syllable that ends with one or more consonants (*ăt, ăsh, ĭtch*).

Because short sounds appear most frequently, it is a good idea to try out the short sound first when attacking new words. As a crutch for those who still confuse the sounds, a simple chart may be referred to when needed. The short vowel appears at the beginning of the word, where it can be clearly heard, and then each short vowel appears in a closed syllable between the consonants *b* and *g*. The following illustration has been used successfully with secondary remedial readers. Starting with the very basic pictures, you or they can choose a content-specific word for each that will help them remember the short sound.

Short Vowel Sounds

a	apple		aspen, allegory
e	eskimo dog		Ecuador, esophagus
i	inchworm		iguana, India
o	ox		Oxford, octopus
u	umbrella		undercurrent, Uncle Sam

băg bĕg bĭg bŏg bŭg

The next most frequent vowel sounds are the long sounds, which say their own letter names $\bar{a}/\bar{e}/\bar{i}/\bar{o}/\bar{u}$ and are sometimes found in open syllables that end in a vowel (bī, bē) or even when two vowels appear together (mēat, ōak, cūte). They are consistent. When a word ends in silent e (not sounded), the vowel before it is long (sīze, hāte, rōbe).

The schwa sound is designated in a dictionary by an inverted e (e) which has the sound /uh/. It is an indistinct sound and is heard in a syllable that is not accented (stressed). In the word about, the accent is on the second syllable, "bout," and therefore the initial a has the schwa sound. Other examples include respirátion, féderal, corólla).

In terms of general pronunciation of words, look-alike words, if pronounced incorrectly, may give incorrect or confusing meaning to a passage. Students may benefit from a listing on the board of such words that appear in their text, especially if you point out the slight differences in spelling. A few examples follow.

decent	descent
ballot	ballet
quiet	quite
alloy	allure
except	accept
though	thorough

Also, mispronunciation of words can lead to spelling errors such as *artic* for the correct word *arctic*, *histry* for *history*, and *liberry* for *library*.

The Dictionary: A Storehouse of Meanings, Etymologies, and Pronunciation

By the time many students reach maturity, they have been turned off to the real and varied values of referring to a dictionary. If you ask them why this is so, they may tell you that being forced through the grades to look up definitions for long lists of words and then to use the words in sentences was a task they strongly disliked, and they forgot the meanings as soon as the task was completed. Inappropriate overuse of the dictionary is to blame here.

As a *final* step (*not* the first step) in attacking new words—when context, structural analysis and phonics fail—the logical move is to refer to the dictionary, glossary, or thesaurus. Students who have never adopted the dictionary habit will need to be reminded of the skills needed and shown the value through practice. Reminders that will help speed up the process of finding words include knowledge of alphabet placement and guide words.

Other necessary knowledge includes meanings of abbreviations; use of the pronunciation key; and, most important of all, how to select the meaning that best fits the context. Those students with spelling problems can be given a paperback word book that contains only a listing of the most common words in columns. Scanning the columns is an easy way to locate words. Also, if a teacher has a wide range of abilities in her class, it would be wise to consider collecting a number of dictionaries at different reading levels to help meet individual needs.

As Hayakawa so aptly reminded us a number of years ago, dictionaries are history books, not law books. New words come into our language and are added when they approach a certain frequency of use; they are deleted when they become obsolete (e.g., *poplollies, bellibones*). Current words, then, reflect usage as judged by a panel of experts.

Many students will be surprised to discover that other parts of the dictionary can make interesting and informative reading. For example, most regular-sized dictionaries have sections tracing the history of the English language and computer studies of how the most common words in print are determined. Perhaps you can add other contributions of today's dictionaries (or have students brainstorm usages).

"Slanguage"; Creating a Slang Dictionary for ESL Students
Connotations of words change over time. To an ESL learner, it can be confusing to know only the literal meaning of slang phrases and words like *out of sight, the pits, square,* or *outrageous.* As an enjoyable learning project for all students, you can have them make a current slang dictionary with definitions and illustrations. The realistic purpose might be to share the finished products with any ESL students in the school. Individual or group products could be combined and published.

The Thesaurus: Another Basic Tool
Whereas dictionaries give us meanings for given words, a thesaurus gives us words for given meanings—that is, synonyms and antonyms. This tool is essential for anyone who wishes to speak and write clearly, concisely, and effectively. The term *thesaurus* comes from Latin, where it meant "a storehouse of information." (Where do you suppose the word *dictionary* comes from? How would you find out?)

As mentioned earlier, a major problem for students is to find the best meaning of a word in the given context. *The Random House Thesaurus*, college edition (1984), alleviates this problem in a most practical way. Each entry and each different meaning for each entry begins with a sample sentence to help pinpoint exact shades of meaning. As an example, see the following entry for the word *abandon*, and then see Figure 4.1.

abandon   v   1 She abandoned her child on the doorstep of the church. Abandon ship! desert; forsake; leave; depart from; leave behind; withdraw from; evacuate; give up; quit; relinquish; jilt; run out on; let go; cast aside; turn one's back on; forswear; abdicate; renounce; repudiate   2 The scientist abandoned his research for lack of funds. discontinue; give up; drop; stop; cease; forgo; waive; discard; junk; wash one's hands of; get rid of; relinquish; forfeit; surrender; scrap
   —n   3 The Gypsies danced with abandon. unrestraint; freedom; immoderation; intemperance; recklessness; wantonness; impulsiveness; impetuosity; spontaneity; enthusiasm; gusto; elan; exuberance; spirit; dash; verve; ardor; animation
   Ant   1 claim; take; keep; hold; possess   2 continue; maintain; 3 restraint; control; caution; prudence; moderation; tameness; deliberation

Source: Reprinted with permission from *The Random House Thesaurus,* College Edition, edited by Jess Stern and Stuart Berg Flexner, copyright © 1984 by Random House, New York.

Synonym Clustering Strategy Using a Dictionary or Thesaurus

As Johnson and Pearson (1984) stated, working with synonyms is the most powerful tool for recognizing precise meanings of words.[16] A few years ago, on the basis of a creative writing technique, I developed an activity I call *synonym clustering.* Its purpose is to aid students in recognizing shades of meaning, clarifying misconceptions, and extending vocabulary through clustering of similar terms. This is especially useful when two or three terms such as *method, strategy,* and *approach* have been confused or used interchangeably but incorrectly. Take just one term, *spread,* and in looking it up you will note that it has eight different meanings, depending on context; the word *run* has twenty-eight sentences to show a wide variety of meanings.
   You might try this out with your class. Take a key word from the story or chapter and together proceed to diagram the clusters. Looking back again at the thesaurus entry for *abandon,* you might decide to cluster synonyms in three groups according to the three given meanings. Figure 4.1 shows how this might be diagrammed.
   Other ways to vary the process of clustering would be to have each group take one cluster and find synonyms for each synonym. Figure 4.2 shows how this might look. When groups share their diagrams, they can be asked how the synonyms in one cluster seem to be alike or different. Next, ask them to compare Cluster I with Cluster II. What is a general overall difference in meaning between the two verb synonyms? Next, these two clusters can be compared to the noun cluster. Finally, if you wish to continue, you could compare the antonyms for abandon—Cluster I: *claim, take, keep, hold, possess;* Cluster II: *continue, maintain;* Cluster III: *restraint, control, caution, prudence, moderation, tameness, deliberation.* Isn't it amazing how much vocabulary

FIGURE 4.1
Synonym Clusters for the Term *Abandon*

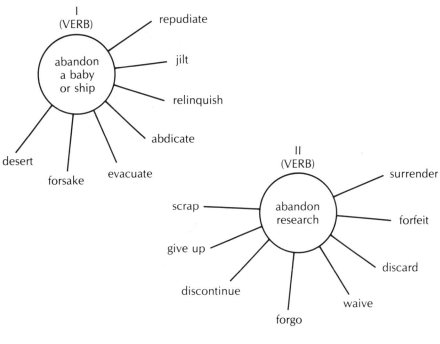

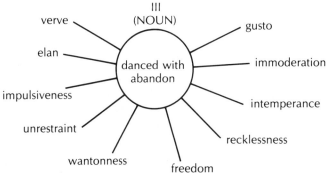

growth can be obtained with an in-depth look at just one word? This is not isolated, meaningless memorizing.

Fun with Definitions
Here is a sampling of definitions to get students started in collecting and composing their own.

1. *Adolescence*—derived from *adolescere* (Latin verb) meaning "to grow into maturity," a coming of age

FIGURE 4.2
One Cluster: Shades of Meaning

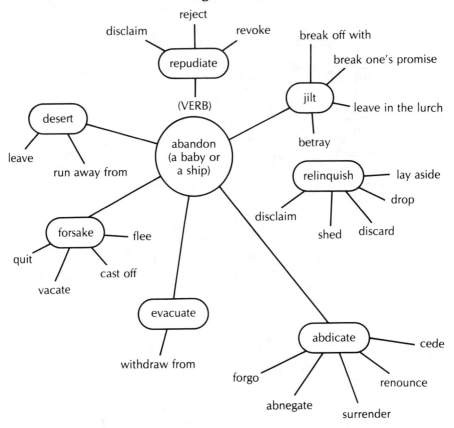

2. *Autobiography*—an unrivaled vehicle for telling the truth about other people (Philip Guedala)
3. *Cynic*—a man who knows the price of everything and the value of nothing (Oscar Wilde)
4. *History*—"a continuous process of interaction between the historian and his facts, an unending dialogue between the present and the past" (Edward Hallett Carr, *What Is History?* New York: Vintage Books, 1961, p. 35)
5. *Home*—the place where when you have to go there/they have to take you in (Robert Frost, "Death of the Hired Man")
6. *Radicalism*—the conservatism of tomorrow injected into the affairs of today (Ambrose Bierce)
7. *Slang*—a language that rolls up its sleeves, spits on its hands, and goes to work (Carl Sandburg)

8. *Time*—nature's way of making sure everything doesn't happen at once (Mike Mailway, "Coffee Break," *Seattle Post Intelligencer*, March 14, 1988).
9. *Liberty*—the right to do what the law permits
10. *Slave*—one who waits for someone else to free him

RESEARCH-BASED RECOMMENDATIONS FOR TEACHING VOCABULARY ACTIVITIES

Primary considerations for improving vocabulary development based on reviews of research have been espoused by such authorities as Stahl (1986); Robinson (1983); Shepherd (1982); and Manzo and Sherk (1971-1972).[17] As you make decisions concerning your own classroom vocabulary strategies, you might begin by referring for guidance to a few significant research-based principles and teaching recommendations.

Principles

1. *Wide reading:* Because we pick up many word meanings indirectly, in context while reading, it is wise to encourage outside recreational and collateral reading.
2. *Planned instruction:* In the classroom, planned instruction in vocabulary development can be superior to incidental teaching of terms when it is deliberately and innovatively built into regular course work, and can yield good learning return for the time spent.
3. *Fewer words often and in depth:* It is far better to teach fewer words in depth, and often, with all their shades of meaning, than to provide long lists asking for definitions and use in sentences.
4. *Deep processing:* Make more connections between the new and the known, first by associating the new to the old (e.g., use a word with its synonym, or a word in a single context); second, by applying this association to show understanding (e.g., classify with other words, find an antonym); and finally by creating a new written or oral product out of the association (e.g., restate the definition in your own words, compare to your own life experiences).[18]
5. *Contextual definitions:* Words should be given in context. Use them in a phrase, short sentence, paragraph, or graphic. Definitions must then conform to that context and may be taken from a dictionary,

glossary, or thesaurus, by using structural analysis or classification of terms.

6. *Coining new words:* Because we continue to coin new words, it is important to build in the habit of consistently increasing word knowledge.

A Quick Checklist: What Teachers Can Do

It would be interesting to check off the items your teachers did with you on a regular basis.

_____ Connect new words, defined with multiple meanings, to students' background knowledge and experience.

_____ Supply students with both definitions and examples in context, not bare lists of words.

_____ Discuss selected key vocabulary terms prior to reading and reinforce later through repetition and practice, using a variety of interesting modes and multiple exposures in different contexts.

_____ Create enthusiasm and be enthusiastic models; show personal interest in learning and using new words.

_____ Require students to be more specific, explain further, give appropriate examples.

_____ Avoid mindless skill drill, filling in blanks on worksheet.

_____ Reintroduce the dictionary and thesaurus as sources of interesting information.

_____ Build personal libraries of vocabulary references.

_____ Develop the idea that success in vocabulary development depends on each student's assuming responsibility for it.

GENERAL TEACHING STRATEGIES

Semantic Feature Analysis (SFA)

This strategy (Anders and Bos, 1986, p. 202)[19] can be used by secondary teachers of normal and learning-disabled students to enhance the vocabulary and concept knowledge needed for comprehension. It enables students to learn relationships between and among conceptual vocabulary and main ideas in the text. It was founded on schema theory, wherein ideas and concepts are related to each other in terms of levels of abstractness. The most abstract are called superordinate concepts; the most concrete are subordinate. This strategy helps students understand semantic relationships, or a hierarchy of words. It activates their prior knowledge and encourages them to relate personal experiences relevant to terms and concepts being discussed.

Step 1: Thoroughly read the assignment to be given to the students, to determine the main ideas.

Step 2: List in phrases or words the vocabulary related to each main idea.

Step 3: Examine the list to determine which words represent the biggest ideas—the superordinate concepts—followed by the words representing details relating to these main ideas—the subordinate concepts.

Step 4: Organize vocabulary into a relationship chart, with main idea terms for column headings across the top and minor terms listed down the side.

Step 5: Duplicate this chart for each student; also make an overhead transparency or large chart, or copy the chart on the board for class discussion.

Step 6: Distribute the chart before assigning the reading and briefly introduce the topic while defining each main idea and pointing to it. Encourage student participation here by asking for personal experiences or understanding.

Step 7: Introduce each subordinate concept by giving a simple definition.

Step 8: Lead the discussion to determine relationships between superordinate and subordinate terms, using a plus sign ($+$) for positive relationship, a minus sign ($-$) for negative relationship, a zero (0) for no relationship, and a question mark ($?$) for no consensus without getting further information.

Step 9: Fill in the chart through discussion and try to reach a consensus. Be sure to ask students why they reached a certain relationship rating.

Step 10: Have students read silently to confirm their predictions and to clarify uncertain ones.

Step 11: After reading, review the chart orally with students, changing anything necessary and reaching consensus on previously unknown relations.

This strategy involves your students actively in the learning process and enhances their reading comprehension. Building background experiences may also increase their interest in the topic at hand. Table 4.4 shows an example.

TABLE 4.4
Semantic Feature Analysis Chart

	Important Ideas			
	Right to Privacy	Need for Law and Order	Search with Search Warrant	Allowance of Evidence in Court
Important Vocabulary: 1. Search and seizure				
2. Absolute privacy				
3. Hot pursuit				
4. Evidence				
5. Exclusionary rule				
6. Stop-and-frisk				
7. Moving vehicle				
8. Plain view				

Source: Patricia L. Anders and Candace S. Bos, "Semantic Feature Analysis: An Interactive Strategy for Vocabulary Development and Text Comprehension," *Journal of Reading,* 29 (April 1986), 610–616.

Open and Closed Word Sorts

Using this strategy, students, in groups, sort out technical terms written on halved 3 × 5 cards. The words are to be grouped according to some shared feature of meaning. The easiest kind of word sort is a closed one, where labels are provided and the cards are placed under appropriate labels. This is a deductive thinking activity, which helps students study words closely and critically as they must classify under more general concepts. As an example, a closed sort might include labels such as *animal, vegetable,* and *mineral,* and a list of words like *zinc, arbutus, zucchini, wapiti,* and so on.

An open sort calls for inductive thinking with the possibility of divergent responses. No label or criterion for grouping is given. Instead, students must discover relationships for themselves from a list of terms and then justify the way they categorize them. For example, given a list of names of famous people, students might categorize them by such titles as field of endeavor, nationality, or cities and airports that have been named after them.

If your students have difficulty with this type of assignment, you might have them practice on more limited worksheets, which help them distinguish between superordinate and subordinate terms. Two examples follow, with one for you to try. (Doing this is better than just reading about it, for it checks your understanding and helps in retention and later recall.)

1. Circle the word in each column that includes the other words.

soldiers	(tone)
(armies)	humor
colonels	irony
officers	satire

2. Cross out the words in each column that does not belong. How are the remaining words then related? Label each column.

_____	_____	_____
oxymoron	senator	Dickens
metaphor	representative	Shakespeare
simile	governor	Tolkien
creativity	judge	Lewis
hyperbole	teacher	Twain

Magic Square: Find the Magic Number

Vacca and Vacca (1986) have described how to develop a magic square exercise that can be used in any subject area at any level.[20] Take an activity sheet and make two columns, one for terms and the other for definitions or distinguishing statements, such as examples. Direct students to do the following:

1. Match items with definitions, taking into consideration the letters signaling the terms and the numbers signaling the definitions.
2. Put the number of the definition in the proper space, shown by the letter of that term, in the magic square answer box.
3. If matchups are correct, they will form a magic square, in which the numerical total is the same for each row across and each column down. This total is the magic number.
4. Add up the rows and columns to check that you have the same number each time. If not, go back and reevaluate your answers.

Examples follow, with the magic number being 34.

Magic Square: How Well Do You Know Literary Terms?

The discussion in this section is from *Content Area Reading*, pp. 324–326, copyright © 1986 by Richard T. Vacca and Jo Anne L. Vacca, reprinted by permission of Scott, Foresman and Company.

Directions: Select from the numbered statements the best answer for each of the literary terms. Put the number in the proper space in the magic square box. The total of the numbers will be the same across each row and down each column (see Figure 4.3)

Literary Terms	*Statements*
A. point of view	1. Mental pictures within a story
B. symbolism	2. Events and happenings in a story
C. theme	3. The "when" and "where" of a story
D. mood	4. The overriding feeling in a work
E. plot	5. When something stands for something else
F. metaphor	6. An exaggeration of great proportions
G. structure	7. That which unifies a story as a whole
H. myth	8. Saying one thing but meaning another
I. setting	9. The central insight
J. simile	10. A comparison introduced by *as* or *like*
K. hyperbole	11. An implied comparison
L. allegory	12. Saying less, but meaning more
M. foreshadowing	13. Clues to future happenings
N. irony	14. A tale of human life told in supernatural proportions
O. understatement	15. When objects and characters are equated with meanings that lie outside the story
P. imagery	16. The vantage point from which everything is known or interpreted

Textual and Graphic Organizers as Preinstructional Strategies

We all have in our brains a structure or framework that reflects all of our previous meaningful learning. New material, to be meaningful and retained, must be associated in some way with that structure of prior knowledge. Along with the more common preinstructional strategies that try to lay the groundwork for processing new material, including pretests, objectives, previewing, and surveying, we have textual (written) and graphic (schematic) organizers. These can be especially helpful in building mental frameworks.

FIGURE 4.3
Answers and Combinations

Answer Box

A	B	C	D
E	F	G	H
I	J	K	L
M	N	O	P

Magic Number = _____

Model Magic Square Combinations

7	3	5
2	4	9
6	8	1

0* 15**

10	8	6
2	9	13
12	7	5

4* 24**

7	11	8
10	12	4
9	3	14

5* 26**

9	2	7
4	6	8
5	10	3

1* 18**

9	7	5
1	8	12
11	6	4

3* 21**

16	2	3	13
5	11	10	8
9	7	6	12
4	14	15	1

0* 34**

19	2	5	23	6
25	8	16	4	12
1	14	22	10	18
7	20	3	11	24
13	21	9	17	5

0* 65**

2	7	18	12
8	5	11	15
13	17	6	3
16	10	4	9

2* 39**

Source: From *Content Area Reading* by Richard T. Vacca and Jo Anne L. Vacca, pp. 324–326. Copyright © 1986 by Richard T. Vacca and Jo Anne L. Vacca. Reprinted by permission of Scott, Foresman and Company.
  *Foils needed in answer column.
  **Magic number.

Textual organizers are generally of two written types—expository, for unfamiliar material, and comparative, for familiar material that makes use of prior knowledge to make connections. For these to be effective, main concepts must be stated clearly and consisely so that category headings are provided under which new information can be placed. A good organizer is more general, comprehensive, and abstract than the material it introduces. No details or examples are included. It should eliminate the trap of getting bogged down in those seemingly unrelated details. These written organizers should be used only with difficult or complicated material.

Graphic organizers—visual aids that show hierarchical relationships among key concepts as an overview—have been used at the beginning of each chapter in this text. They are sometimes referred to as cognitive maps or structured overviews. To use a graphic organizer as a teaching device, briefly go over it with the class and remind them to refer back to it as they study-read to help keep things in perspective. The next phase is to ask students to develop their own graphic organizers. First, they must practice locating the key concepts, and then attempt to show interrelationships among them. Although this is far from an easy task, the payoff can be great.

Classroom Activity: Graphic Organizer

In small groups of no more than five people, select a previous chapter in this text and develop a different graphic organizer from the existing one, using only key terms and concepts. Be prepared to explain to the class your choices of the hierarchy, placement, and connections of items. Your goal is to improve on the existing graphic organizer in the text.

Modified Cloze Techniques

The term *cloze* stands for a procedure whereby every nth word (usually the fifth or seventh) is deleted in a selection of more than 250 words. The reader must restore 50 deleted words by carefully reading the remaining text and filling in the blanks with an exact word replacement. This serves as a readability measure of the fit between reader and text. (More on cloze will be found in Chapter 10 on assessment.)

In modified versions, using cloze for teaching rather than testing, teachers can be both playful and purposeful in deciding which words to delete, how many to delete, and the type of hints to give. Hints can include supplying the first letter, adapting the length of the deletion line to fit the length of the word, using _ _ _ _ (each dash standing for a letter), or placing all deleted words at the bottom of the page for selection. I like to put the answers in the left-hand column along the line where the words were removed; this column is then folded back until the student is ready to self-check. Two examples follow, one with every fifth word deleted and one with every seventh word deleted, each with different types of hints.

Excerpts from *The Art of Living*[21]
by John Gardner
p. 309

	FOLD BACK
I. So we did it.	
We ate by candlelight _____ in the	out
restaurant, old _____ Dellapicallo	man
at the end _____ the table leaning on	of
_____ elbows, no plate in _____	his, front
of him. Joe had _____ home.	gone
When he went _____ the door he	out
looked _____ than Angelina. I	smaller
was _____ for him . . .	sorry
II. He was the one who'd been right—sane	
and civilized from the beginning.	
But also his walk was oddly m_____	mechanical
and the way he shook his h_____ when	head
he looked back at us f_____ the door,	from
it was as if u_____ his hair he had	under
springs and g_____.	gears

Source: From *The Art of Living and Other Stories* by John Gardner. Copyright © 1981 by John Gardner. Reprinted by permission of Alfred A. Knopf, Inc.

Note that in each case the first sentence is left intact. The last sentence also would not contain deletions. Note, too, in the second example how the clue of giving the first letter helps, and how indicating the number of letters is another possible aid.

Classroom Activity: Cloze

Individually select an excerpt from a portion of the text already assigned and read. Develop a cloze on that section with 25 deletions. Do the same for a section of text not yet read. Exchange with a partner and compare results.

Brainstorming as Concept Development

To discover what a class as a whole knows about a subject or theme—their background knowledge—Taba (1962) suggested that teachers begin a unit by brainstorming.[22] First the class is asked a question, such as "What are the methods of transportation?" (for younger students) or "What is involved in career education?" (for more advanced ones). The class is reminded that in brainstorming all ideas are accepted. They should not praise or put down any response, and they do not have to raise hands but should call out responses as rapidly as possible. The teacher writes the responses on the board or on a long strip of butcher paper covering much of one wall (if it is a major concept). This is called the *list* step to concept development.

The second step—*group*—means asking students to group together several items on their list because they are alike in some way. As they do this, the teacher asks *the* important question, "Why?" "Why are they alike?" After this is discussed, the third step is to label each group on the basis of the reason given for the grouping. With a detailed, extensive list, group and label, her fourth step is to ask that they try to *subsume* some lists under other existing ones. This is an optional step.

Classroom Activity: Concept Development

Ask the class to brainstorm "uses of the dictionary" or "values of expository versus narrative writing" or some similar topic. Write responses on the board and proceed with grouping and labeling. Finish the activity by asking for three conclusions or generalizations students might make from this activity.

Evaluating Vocabulary Development Strategies

The following model for evaluating development strategies is one that teachers should consider carefully. There are 21 items for judging (Ruddell, 1986).[23]

Classroom Activity: Evaluating Vocabulary Strategies

Select one vocabulary strategy from this chapter and assess it in terms of Ruddell's criteria. By applying this to a concrete situation, you will have a better grasp of what it actually entails.

I. Reader environment
   A. *Textual features*

   _____ 1. Context is sufficient to define the concept.

   _____ 2. Text content is appropriate to experiential background of students.

   B. *Conversational features*

   _____ 1. Strategy provides for teacher–student interaction.

   _____ 2. Intent of interaction is to elicit, activate, and assess students' prior knowledge.

   C. *Instructional features*

   _____ 1. Strategy provides opportunity to establish clearly defined vocabulary product.

   _____ 2. Strategy sets students expectations and responsibilities related to product.

II. Knowledge use and control
   A. *Affective state*

   _____ 1. Goal direction and time expectation for instructional activity are clearly established for readers.

   B. *Cognitive state*

   _____ 1. Plan of action is established for readers.

   C. *Metacognitive state*

   _____ 1. Mental state for monitoring and evaluating is developed with special concern for awareness of what is not known.

D. *Text representation*

_____ 1. Students are encouraged to process meaning and be aware of need to revise earlier hypothesis about meaning.

III. Declarative and procedural
A. *Decoding*

_____ 1. Students are sensitive to mispronunciations which may activate inappropriate schema.

_____ 2. Readers are made aware of pronunciations that may cue word origin and provide meaning cue.

B. *Language and world knowledge—declarative*

_____ 1. Strategy provides chance for students to activate prior knowledge and schema related to word meaning.

C. *Language and world knowledge—procedural*

_____ 1. Strategy provides chance to activate and use procedures for developing understanding of new words.

IV. Reader product
A. *Comprehension*

_____ 1. Instructional strategy provides chance for students to understand instructional goal product—that is, learning and personal use of new words.

B. *Oral and written output*

_____ 1. Opportunity is provided to use new words and concepts in written and/or conversational form.

C. *Affective state change*

_____ 1. Strategy develops positive attitudes toward goal of independent vocabulary growth.

D. *Cognitive state change*

_____ 1. Strategy provides chance for students to develop plan or personalized strategy for continued independent vocabulary growth.

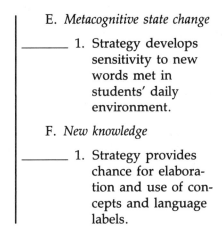

E. *Metacognitive state change*

_____ 1. Strategy develops sensitivity to new words met in students' daily environment.

F. *New knowledge*

_____ 1. Strategy provides chance for elaboration and use of concepts and language labels.

SUMMARY

Vocabulary development is a vital aspect of secondary study-reading, as it can be either a building block or a stumbling block to comprehending text. Sensitivity to words and ability to react to their impact are definite assets to secondary readers, as is awareness of how well we know words with their levels and shades of meaning. A brief look at language study shows us how words come into our language and have been changed over time in terms of spelling, sound, and meaning. Denotations and connotations of words include both literal and emotional meanings. Figures of speech are ways we stretch language to communicate in a special way. Word attack, including context, structural analysis, phonics, and dictionary skills, is an important area for review for those secondary students who did not master it in the elementary grades. A thesaurus should also be considered a valuable tool. In this chapter, underlying principles and teaching recommendations for decision making in selection of teaching strategies were given. A variety of teaching strategies to improve classroom vocabulary development were discussed, including those to be used both before and after reading. Deriving word meanings appropriate to the context is the heart of vocabulary development.

NOTES

1. Marcel Adam Just and Patricia A. Carpenter, *The Psychology of Reading and Language Comprehension* (Newton, MA: Allyn and Bacon, 1987), p. 103.

2. Sharon Kossack and N. Vigilante, "A Proposed Taxonomy of Mathematical Vocabulary," American Reading Forum *Yearbook,* 1983, pp. 60–63.

3. Harry Forgan and Charles Mangrum II, *Teaching Content Area Reading Skills* (Columbus, OH: Charles E. Merrill, 1985), p. 111.

4. Lou E. Burmeister, *Reading Strategies for Middle and Secondary School Teachers*, 2nd ed. (Reading, MA: Addison-Wesley, 1978), pp. 171–178.

5. Summarized from a number of dictionaries, including *The American Heritage Dictionary of the English Language* and *Webster's Collegiate Dictionary*.

6. Burmeister, *Reading Strategies*, p. 111.

7. Ibid.

8. Andrew Ortony, "Understanding Figurative Language," in P. David Pearson, ed., *Handbook of Reading Research* (New York: Longman, 1984), pp. 453–470.

9. Ibid.

10. Jeffrey C. Tonjes, "Fun with Words: Oxymorons and Creative Blending," unpublished paper, Albuquerque, New Mexico, 1986.

11. Ibid.

12. Owen Thomas, "Language and the Language Arts Teacher," in Martha King, Robert Emans, and Patricia J. Cianciolo, eds., *A Forum for Focus* (Urbana, IL: National Council of Teachers of English, 1973), pp. 108–109.

13. J. W. Cunningham, P. M. Cunningham, and S. V. Arthur, *Middle and Secondary School Reading* (New York: Longman, 1981); John E. Readance, Thomas W. Bean, and R. Scott Baldwin, *Content Area Reading: An Integrated Approach*, 2nd ed. (Dubuque, IA: Kendall/Hunt, 1985), pp. 98–99.

14. Rudolf Arnheim, *Visual Thinking* (Berkeley: University of California Press, 1969), p. 252.

15. Betty Roe, Barbara Stoodt, and Paul C. Burns, *Secondary School Reading Instruction: The Content Areas*, 2nd ed. (Boston: Houghton Mifflin, 1983), p. 58.

16. Dale Johnson and P. David Pearson, *Teaching Reading Vocabulary*, 2nd ed. (New York: Holt, Rinehart & Winston, 1984).

17. Steven A. Stahl, "Three Principles of Effective Vocabulary Instruction," *Journal of Reading*, 29 (April 1986), 662–668; H. Alan Robinson, *Teaching Reading, Writing and Study Strategies: The Content Areas* (Boston: Allyn and Bacon, 1983), pp. 115–131; David L. Shepherd, *Comprehensive High School Reading Methods*, 3rd ed. (Charles E. Merrill, 1982); A. V. Manzo and J. K. Sherk, "Some Generalizations and Strategies for Guiding Vocabulary Learning," *Journal of Reading Behavior*, 4 (Winter 1971–1972).

18. Stahl, "Three Principles," pp. 662–668.

19. Patricia L. Anders and Candace S. Bos, "Semantic Feature Analysis: An Interactive Strategy for Vocabulary Development and Text Comprehension," *Journal of Reading*, 29 (April 1986), 610–616.

20. Richard T. Vacca and Joanne L. Vacca, *Content Area Reading*, 2nd ed. (Boston: Little, Brown, 1986), pp. 324–326.

21. John Gardner, *The Art of Living and Other Stories* (New York: Knopf, 1981), p. 309.

22. Hilda Taba, *Curriculum Development: Theory and Practice* (New York: Harcourt, Brace and World, 1962).

23. Robert B. Ruddell, "Vocabulary Learning: A Process Model and Criteria for Evaluating Instructional Strategies," *Journal of Reading*, 29 (April 1986), 581–587.

RECOMMENDED READINGS

Anderson, Richard C., and Freebody, Peter. "Vocabulary Knowledge." In John Guthrie, ed., *Comprehension and Teaching: Research Reviews*. Newark, DE: International Reading Association, 1981, pp. 77–117.

Barrett, M. T., and Graves, M. F. "A Vocabulary Program for Junior High School Remedial Readers." *Journal of Reading*, 25 (1981), 146–150.

Bellows, Barbara. "Running Shoes Are to Jogging as Analogies Are to Creative/Critical Thinking." *Journal of Reading*, 23 (March 1980), 507–511.

Carr, Eileen. "The Vocabulary Overview Guide: A Metacognitive Strategy to Improve Vocabulary Comprehension and Retention." *Journal of Reading*, 21 (May 1985), 684–689.

Cunningham, Patricia M. "Decoding Polysyllabic Words: An Alternative Strategy." *Journal of Reading*, 21 (April 7, 1978), 608–614.

Dale, Edgar, O'Rourke, Joseph, and Bamman, Henry. *Techniques of Teaching Vocabulary*. Palo Alto, CA: Field Educational Publications, 1971.

Duffelmeyer, Frederick A., and Blakely, Barbara. "Developing Vocabulary through Dramatization." *Journal of Reading*, 23 (November 1979), 141–143.

Gipe, J. P. "Investigating Techniques for Teaching Word Meanings." *Reading Research Quarterly*, 14 (1978–1979), 624–644.

Graves, Michael F. "Selecting Vocabulary to Teach in the Intermediate and Secondary Grades." In James Flood, ed., *Promoting Reading Comprehension*. Newark, DE: International Reading Association, 1984.

Hayes, D. A., and Tierney, R. J. "Developing Readers' Knowledge through Analogy." *Reading Research Quarterly*, 17 (1982), 256–280.

Ignoffo, Mathew F. "The Thread of Thought: Analogies as a Vocabulary Building Method." *Journal of Reading*, 23 (March 1980), 519–521.

Jenkins, Joseph R., Stein, March L., and Wysocki, Katy. "Learning Vocabulary through Reading." *American Educational Research Journal*, 21 (1984), 667–687.

Johnson, Dale D., and Johnson, Bonnie Von Hoff. "Highlighting Vocabulary in Inferential Comprehension Instruction." *Journal of Reading*, 29 (April 1986), 622–625.

Johnson, Dale D., Toms-Bronowski, Susan, and Pittleman, Susan D. *An Investigation of the Trends in Vocabulary Research and the Effects of Prior Knowledge on Instructional Strategies for Vocabulary Acquisition*. Madison: Wisconsin Center for Education Research, University of Wisconsin, 1981.

Karahalios, S. M., Tonjes, M. J., and Towner, J. C. "Using Advance Organizers to Improve Comprehension of a Content Text." *Journal of Reading*, 22 (May 1979), 706–708.

Kaplan, E. M., and Tuchman, A. "Vocabulary Strategies Belong in the Hands of Learners." *Journal of Reading*, 24 (1980), 32–34.

Lee, Joyce W. "Increasing Comprehension through Use of Context Clue Categories." *Journal of Reading*, 22 (December 3, 1978), 259–262.

McCrum, Robert, Can, William, and MacNeil, Robert. *The Story of English*. New York: Viking Penguin, 1986.

Pany, Darlene, Jenkins, Joseph J., and Schreck, Janice. "Vocabulary Instruction: Effects on Word Knowledge and Reading Comprehension." *Learning Disability Quarterly*, 5 (1982), 202–215.

Piercy, Dorothy. *Reading Activities in Content Areas: An Ideabook for Middle and Secondary Schools,* 2nd ed. Boston: Allyn and Bacon, 1982.

Rinsky, Lee Ann. *Teaching Word Attack Skills,* 4th ed. Dubuque, IA: Gorsuch Scarisbrick, 1989.

Stahl, Norman A., Bozo, William G., and Simpson, Michele L. "Developing College Vocabulary: A Content Analysis of Instructional Materials." *Reading Research and Instruction: Journal of the College Reading Association,* 26 (Spring 1987), 203–221.

Stein, Jess and Flexner, Stuart Berg, eds. *The Random House Thesaurus,* College Edition. New York: Random House, 1984.

Stieglitz, E. L., and Steiglitz, V. S. "SAVOR — the Word to Reinforce Vocabulary in the Content Areas." *Journal of Reading,* 25 (1981), 46–51.

Thelen, Judith N. "Vocabulary Instruction and Meaningful Learning." *Journal of Reading,* 29 (April 1986), 603–609.

Tonjes, Marian J. "Using Advance Organizers to Enhance the Processing of Texts." In John Chapman, ed., *The Reader and the Text.* London: Heinemann Educational Texts, 1980.

ANNOTATED RECOMMENDED READINGS:
FUN WITH WORDS

Building your own resource library from among these, and learn more about words, language, and playing with words.

Augarde, Tony. *The Oxford Guide to Word Games.* New York: Oxford University Press, 1984. A collection of verbal ingenuity, this book is about all kinds of word play and games — from acrostics and crosswords to rebuses and tongue-twisters. It traces historical origins and describes how to play guessing games and verbal manipulation games. It uses copious examples, riddles, word squares, and so on.

Bowler, Peter. *The Superior Person's Book of Words.* Boston: Godine, 1985. A funny, useful, and at times elevating little book, which is supposed to help you amaze your friends, baffle your enemies, and write memos to end all discussion. Bowler shows us how to say it well with good, neglected, precise words for vocabulary exultation.

Brandreth, Gyles. *The Joy of Lex.* New York: William Morrow, 1980; and Brandreth, Gyles. *More Joy of Lex.* New York: William Morrow, 1982. A lighthearted celebration of our language, "a weird and wonderful world of words." These two books are all about how to have fun with many words. With humor throughout, these witty and informative books are laced with quizzes, games, and puzzles.

Espy, Willard R. *O Thou Improper, Thou Uncommon Noun.* Crown, 1978. Fifteen hundred words with origins in names of people and places. Espy enjoys digressing in the form of light verse, poetry, anecdotes, and asides — etymology at its best.

Freman, Morton S. *The Story behind the Word.* Philadelphia: ISI Press, 1985. Explores mysterious roots of words we take for granted and use or misuse daily. Because English absorbs words from a multitude of areas, our word origins are more amusing, surprising, or exciting than those of more homogeneous languages.

For example (p. 83), the word *cynic,* today a fault-finding critic, expecting the worst, originally applied to the highest degree of idealist—a case of pejoration. History of the word continues for three paragraphs.

Funk, Charles E. *Hog on Ice and Other Curious Expressions.* New York: Harper & Row, 1948; reissued 1985. Looks at origins of over four hundred curious expressions, such as "wild goose chase" or "a pig in a poke." Written with a combination of scholarship and humor, a must in everyone's personal library.

Funk, Wilfred, and Lewis, Norman. *Thirty Days to a More Powerful Vocabulary.* Pocket Books, 1975. How to make words your slaves, increase your language power, become a lively conversationalist, and impress others. Contains many challenging tests to check progress.

Parlett, David. *Botticelli and Beyond: Over 100 of the World's Best Word Games.* New York: Pantheon, 1981. A collection of traditional and all-new games from the casual and entertaining to the cunning and complex. Each game has suggestions for number of players, age, and level of difficulty, all designed for countless hours of fun and fascination.

Smith, Jack. *How to Win a Pullet Surprise.* New York: Franklin Watts, 1982. Smith had a syndicated column with the *Los Angeles Times* for many years. Here he takes a fresh and gleeful look at writing, reading, and conversation in our time. This is for anyone who loves words, enjoys humor, and cares about the English language.

SPECIAL DICTIONARIES: A SAMPLING

Asimov, Isaac. *Words of Science and the History behind Them.* Boston: Houghton Mifflin, 1959.

Bierce, Ambrose. *The Devil's Dictionary.* Owings Mills, MD: Stemmer House, 1978.

Boatner, Maxine Tull, and Gates, John Edward. *A Dictionary of American Idioms.* Woodbury, NY: Barron's Educational Services, 1975.

Burnams, Tom. *The Dictionary of Misinformation.* New York: Ballantine, 1975.

Cohen, J. M., and Cohen, M. J. *Dictionary of Modern Quotations,* 2nd ed. New York: Viking Penguin, 1980.

Crowley, Ellen T., and Thomas, Robert C. *Acronyms and Initialisms Dictionary.* Detroit: Gale Research, 1970.

Dictionary of American Regional English. Boston: Belknap Press, Division of Harvard University Press, 1985.

Evans, Bergen. *Dictionary of Mythology.* Lincoln, NE: Centennial Press, 1970.

Ferguson, Rosalind. *Dictionary of Proverbs.* New York: Penguin, 1983.

Green, Jonathan. *The Dictionary of Contemporary Slang.* London: Pan, 1984.

Greenhill, Eleanor S. *Dictionary of Art.* New York: Dell, 1974.

Harris, Theodore L., and Hodges, Richard E. *A Dictionary of Related Terms: Reading.* Newark, DE: International Reading Association, 1981.

Mager, N. H., and Mager, S. K. *The Morrow Book of New Words.* New York: William Morrow, 1982.

Morris, William, and Morris, Mary. *Dictionary of Word and Phrase Origins.* New York: Harper & Row, 1962, 1967, 1971.

Patridge, Eric. *Origins: A Short Etymological Dictionary of Modern English.* London: Routledge & Kegan Paul, 1958.

Pugh, Eric. *A Dictionary of Acronyms and Abbreviations.* Hamden, CT: Archon Books, 1970.

Reader's Digest Family Word Finder: A New Thesaurus of Synonyms and Antonyms in Dictionary Form. Pleasantville, NY: Readers' Digest, 1975.

Safire, William. *Safire's Political Dictionary.* New York: Random House, 1968, 1972, 1978.

Withycombe, E. G. *The Oxford Dictionary of English Christian Names.* New York: Oxford University Press, 1945, 1950, 1977, 1985.

Postorganizer 1
Mapping

Refer back to Preorganizer 1, Interior Map, where you were told that your final task would be to develop a map showing your interpretation of interrelationships of key concepts. To do this, you may wish to work with a partner or in a triad, starting with the essence, *vocabulary*, boxed in the middle of a blank page. After listing key terms found throughout the chapter, try building them into some pattern working out from the vocabulary box, for example:

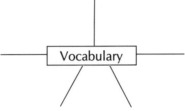

Postorganizer 2
Cinquains as Summaries

Summarize this chapter (or story or unit) succinctly by writing a cinquain.[24] You must agree with a partner on the topic and work together.
   Here are some examples of other students' summary cinquains:

Line 1—one-word title: study-reading
Line 2—two-word description: strategies, skills
Line 3—three words expressing action: reading to learn
Line 4—four words showing feeling for topic: crucial for all students
Line 5—one-word synonym restating essence: scholars!

Scholars
Studious, wise
Active, playful, deliberate
Our future rests here
Expert-learners

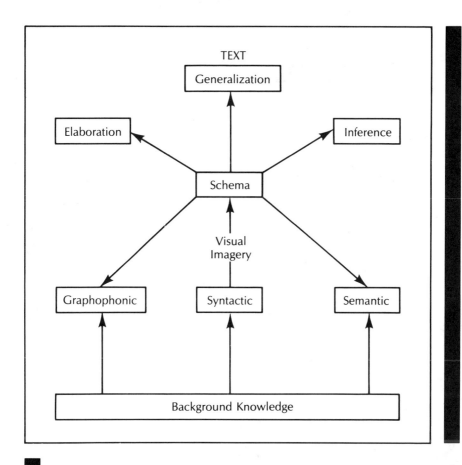

5

Expository
Comprehension

CHAPTER OUTLINE

Preorganizers
Introduction
Comprehension Processes
Information Systems
Anaphora or Anaphoric Relations
Schema Theory
Cognitive Processes
  Elaboration
  Generalization
  Inferences
Imaging or Visual Imagery
Main Ideas
  Main Ideas and Summarizing
  The "Aha—So What?" Test
Framework
  Reader Response
  Instructional Practices
Practice: Literal Comprehension Strategies
  Following Directions
  Categorizing
  Newspapers and Main Ideas
  Making Judgments
  Evaluating Technical Writing
  Drawing Supportable Conclusions
  Logic Activities
  Fact or Opinion
  Magazines for Metacognitive Practice
Questioning
  Facilitating Questioning Comprehension: Product and Process
  Taxonomies
  QARs
  Comprehension Questions for Assessment
  Frame Questions
  Pre-, During-, and After-Reading Questions
Summary: Looking Backward/Looking Forward
Notes
Recommended Readings
Postorganizers

COGNITIVE COMPETENCIES

1. Define *expository comprehension* in your own words.
2. Take a secondary text chapter and find three examples of anaphora that might cause a reader some difficulty in comprehension.
3. Describe the steps you would take to write a summary of the three cognitive processes found in this chapter.
4. Locate the most difficult section of this chapter for you and describe why it was more difficult than other sections.

KEY TERMS

anaphora
elaboration/generalization/
  inference
frame questions
graphophonic/syntactic/semantic

imaging (visual imagery)
product/process questions
QARs
schema theory

Preorganizer 1
Comprehending Comprehension

Do you agree with the following statements? Why or why not? Explain. Then summarize or rephrase each in your own words.

1. The most logical place for instruction in most reading and thinking strategies is in such subjects as social studies and science rather than in separate lessons about reading. The reason is that the strategies are useful mainly when the student is grappling with important but unfamiliar content.[1]

_____

_____

_____

2. We need to change the way we ask questions of students, the ways we have been teaching comprehension, and develop curriculum that treats comprehension and composition as similar processes.[2]

_____

_____

_____

3. Comprehending means building bridges between the new and the known. It is a dynamic interactive process of constructing meaning by combining existing knowledge with information presented in the text, within the context of the reading situation.[3]

_____

_____

_____

Preorganizer 2
Textual or Graphic Organizers

As you read this chapter, be thinking about creating a textual or graphic organizer for the next group of readers. Select one of the following and develop it with a partner after completing your reading.

_____ 1. List five generalizations that will cover all aspects. These will be superordinate learning statements under which you can subsume all details. Each will be a single sentence.

_____ 2. Write an explanatory textual advance organizer of the chapter of no more than 300 words which will be more general, comprehensive, and abstract than the text material itself.

_____ 3. Design a graphic organizer of the chapter that shows interrelationships among key concepts.

A discussion of these organizers was found in the previous chapter on vocabulary concept development.

5
Expository Comprehension

INTRODUCTION

A major avenue of learning is through reading. Yet, if we do not understand what we are reading, we cannot learn or remember it. Comprehending text is a major concern, then, of all teachers who use print materials
in the classroom.

In the past, comprehension has generally been taught as a series of
discrete levels and skills. Bloom's and later Barrett's taxonomies gave us levels
of thinking and comprehending from literal to evaluative to appreciative.[4]
(The Barrett taxonomy will be found in Chapter 6 and Appendix 1.)

Also, skill and drill practice was often held on such specific areas as finding the main idea of a brief passage or determining the sequence of events
in a story. These skill packages were seldom built around actual text material
and thus did not transfer readily to daily real-world reading task requirements. Also, elementary basal texts have contained little expository
writing, so exposure to informational or textual writing that explains things
has been minimal.

Lately, we have been rethinking our whole approach to the act of comprehending and looking closely at the covert processes involved and at ways
to help readers become more aware of their own reading processes, which
will lead them to become more independent learners. As we saw in Chapter
4, there are three major kinds of printed material: expository, descriptive,

and narrative. This chapter is concerned with the expository type, meaning textual material that seeks to explain. It is noteworthy that it is often difficult to separate comprehension from reading or cognition. Much overlap exists.

SHOE/JEFF MacNELLY

COMPREHENSION PROCESSES

From the writings and models of cognitive psychologists such as Kintsch and VanDijk (1978), and Just and Carpenter (1980), we can see that there are several comprehension processes that seem to occur at the same time.[5] Irwin (1986) has categorized them nicely. They are adapted here from Judith Westphal Irwin, *Teaching Reading Comprehension Processes*, copyright © 1986, pp. 2–7, 28–30, by permission of Prentice Hall, Englewood Cliffs, New Jersey.[6]

1. *Ability to group words into meaningful phrases (chunking):* This involves understanding the syntax of what is written. For example, in the sentence, "The azure skies were dotted with powder puffs of white clouds," readers would chunk the adjective *azure* with the noun *skies* because it describes the color of the skies, and *powder puffs* with *white* because they describe the clouds.

2. *Ability to choose which ideas to place into long-term memory:* Take as an example the sentence, "In the mid-sixteenth century, Henry VIII was

the major force behind the decision of many English people to abandon Catholicism." Budding historians already know that Henry VIII reigned during the sixteenth century, so they might decide that Henry VIII was the reason that many English chose to leave the Catholic church. Students of religion, tracing events, might focus on the approximate date of this religious exodus.

3. *Ability to make inferences and to elaborate between clauses and sentences so that they becomes a coherent whole:* In order to do this, readers must identify anaphora (referents) and infer such things as cause–effect or sequence. For example, "Stella drove the baby, Helen, to the doctor's office. She was ill." We infer that the second *she* refers to the child. We could have combined the two sentences using the word *because.*

4. *Ability to organize and synthesize single ideas into a summary statement:* In order to do this, readers must be able to select main ideas and summarize by disregarding unnecessary data.

5. *Ability to perceive and use the writer's organizational pattern in order to recall later what was stated:* For example, recognizing sequence of events as the organizational pattern will alert readers to think of first, second, next, last for key points.

6. *Ability to go beyond writers' intentions and form appropriate elaborations:* This can be in the form of making predictions about the future, forming mental images, or relating to past experiences.

7. *Ability to be consciously aware, monitor, and control thinking processes, often called metacognition:* This means knowing when and if we understand, and what to do about it when we do not. Readers have a number of strategies to select from and can adjust these accordingly. Examples include underlining, note-taking, previewing, rehearsing, reviewing, and rereading for inconsistencies or clarity.

By taking all these factors into consideration, we can define comprehension as the process by which readers understand and recall (in a selective manner) ideas in single sentences; understand or infer relationships between clauses and/or sentences; organize and synthesize ideas recalled, stating them in general terms; and go beyond writers' intentions to elaborate. Readers control and adjust these processes on the basis of their immediate goal. All processes occur almost simultaneously and are in constant interaction with each other.[7]

Read the following passage in order to note what comprehension processes you used:

Classroom Activity: Cartoon Exchange

Although painters may draw more respect, cartoonists get more laughs, even in Russia. The United States and Russia recently conducted a two-year exchange of more than two hundred cartoons, which were displayed across both countries with an opening-night video–phone hookup linking cartoonists here with those in Moscow. Humor is an area not especially explored, and this show has proved to be an extremely popular one.

When reading the foregoing, were you aware of:

_____ 1. Understanding ideas continued in each sentence?

_____ 2. Understanding how these ideas were connected?

_____ 3. Being able to organize or synthesize the information?

_____ 4. Elaborating on the passage on the basis of what you already know?

_____ 5. Being in control of your reading?

INFORMATION SYSTEMS

There are three information systems used when comprehending: *graphophonic, syntactic,* and *semantic.*[8] The discussion here is adapted with permission from "Unity in Reading" by Kenneth S. Goodman, in Alan S. Purves and Olive Niles, eds., *Becoming Readers in a Complex Society,* Eighty-third Yearbook of the National Society for the Study of Education, pp. 102–103, copyright © 1984 by The University of Chicago Press. *Grapho* means writing or letters and their combinations. *Phonic* means the sounds of letter combinations in alphabetic writing. Thus, we perceive the graphemes (written symbols) and attach sounds to them that will help us recognize words and meanings we already know. It is possible to sound out a combination of letters correctly without comprehending if there is no meaning attached to these letter combinations.

The syntax is the second system we use for comprehending. Grammar is mostly a matter of sentence structure or syntax. In the English language, sentence order is of prime importance, showing, for example, which nouns are subjects or objects. Look at these sentences:

Susan aced her opponent on her first serve.
The first serve to the opponent was aced by Susan.

Our grammatical system also takes into account affixes (bound morphemes), which indicate meaning, person, number, or tense in nouns and verbs (such as *pre, uni, ed, tion*), as well as function words, determiners, prepositions, and auxiliaries that have no lexical meaning but help create sentence patterns that can express unlimited meanings.

Not just a set of definable words, semantics, on the other hand, is the whole system by which our language represents highly complex personal and social meanings. We find subtle differences between the humorous and the serious, the sarcastic and straightforward, the profane and the profound—all within the text and the word meanings. A text is more than just a group of words and sentences. It has unity—it is both cohesive (bound together) and coherent (making sense). What one reader comprehends will differ from what another does, as meaning is created by each reader on the basis of what he already knows and the experiences he brings to bear on what he reads.

Readers select from these three systems as needed. They must then understand the alphabet and accompanying sounds, the syntax or grammar, and bring their own backgrounds to the overall concepts and meaning, the semantics. We may well wonder how we manage to do all these complex, interlocking things so easily and so well.

ANAPHORA OR ANAPHORIC RELATIONS

Research has indicated that relations between words where one word or phrase replaces another *(anaphora)* may cause problems with comprehension—for example, "Jason borrowed Ann's car. He got stopped by the police." Jason is the antecedent, the word being replaced by *he*. Besides replacing antecedents with personal pronouns, other types include *this, those, that, here, there, so, will,* and *have*. We can also substitute words using synonyms or more inclusive terms like "for these reasons" or "the latter." Also, the repetition of the word or phrase is sometimes only implied. "Someone has won the lottery. I would like to know who." Here, what is implied but not repeated is "won the lottery."

The distance between the relations and whether they are forward or backward relations can affect comprehension. When anaphoric relations are separated by at least a sentence it is more difficult to keep them in mind. It is also more difficult when the antecedent comes after the substituting term. An example of distance would be, "The party was a successful one from all standpoints. The food was delicious, the people congenial, and the decor stunning. It was talked about for weeks afterward." *It* stands for *party*. An example of an antecedent coming after the substituting term would be, "As they had believed and demonstrated over time, the voters acted accordingly." *They* is the antecedent for *voters*.[9]

In order to teach these relations, Baumann and Stevenson (1987) have suggested that we use an anaphoric cloze.[10] Readers, given several choices at first, must supply the referent or the antecedent. Later they would supply the correct word themselves. "The settlers were moving on.

_____ decided to try for greener pastures. The _____ were slow and cumbersome, but they provided shelter."

SCHEMA THEORY

A schema is a cognitive structure, an organization of what we know about an idea, concept, or thing. Rumelhart (1981) stated that it is an abstraction of reality.[11] The background knowledge we bring to a topic we are reading about is directly related to how well we comprehend and how motivated we are concerning that topic. Because schemata (the plural form of schema) are based on our individual experiences, each schema will be somewhat different. From experience we may have a schema for dining in a fine restaurant—what is involved in seating, ordering, tipping, and so on. This basic knowledge allows us to be comfortable entering a new restaurant, where it is even possible to adapt our schema when one of our expectations differs. With a text, our background knowledge helps us anticipate the author's ideas and predict what will occur next. By using our schema, we can organize and categorize the new material, comprehend and recall it. We have a framework into which we can place facts for later retrieval.

We also have a schema for different kinds of discourse. Expository discourse differs from the story grammar of literary discourse in a number of ways, which we will examine later. (Chapter 1 also discusses schema theory.)

There are a number of things teachers can do to help students use schemata effectively.

1. Prior to reading, build up and make connections with students' background knowledge, using some form of advance organizer: a discussion, lecture, speaker, field trip, or film.
2. Administer a pretest or brainstorm key concepts to discover what students already know and to help them tie the new to the known.
3. As an alternative, have students write everything they know about the topic first, or develop a graphic organizer in pairs.
4. Encourage students to see reading as something requiring meaning at all times.

5. Have students read the same information from two different sources, using magazines and other collateral reading.
6. Have students read the table of contents for the new chapter and analyze the logic of its structure.
7. At the same time that background knowledge is being enhanced, it is best to also build context-related vocabulary. This means teaching meanings that link concepts, not just asking for dictionary definitions, and ensuring multiple exposures and chances to use new terms.

COGNITIVE PROCESSES

Elaboration

McNeil (1987) describes the elaboration process as one form of deep processing, an embellishing of a text that is accomplished by drawing on background knowledge and experience, making inferences, paraphrasing, and relating what is read to our purpose for reading.[12] The discussion here is adapted with permission from *Reading Comprehension: New Directions for Classroom Practice* by John D. McNeil, copyright © 1987 by Scott, Foresman, and Company, Glenview, Illinois. Moffett and Wagner (1983) describe elaboration as the flowering of an idea, the unfolding of an object to be described in detail, a summary to be filled in, a statement to be exemplified, or a premise from which corollaries are to be deduced.[13]

Elaborations can clarify or show significance or relevance. In the sentence, "The frightened woman jumped into her car," the elaboration might be "to escape the attacker," which would be relevant; "to meet the attacker" would not.

Strategies for elaborating or embellishing text include making inferences that go beyond what is stated, using mental imagery, outlining, underlining, note-taking, and summarizing. These strategies may increase interest, draw attention to what is indeed relevant, and activate relevant reader schemata, allowing new information to be incorporated into a framework of past experiences. It is important that ideas singled out for elaboration are key ones; otherwise, comprehension results will be mixed.

Generalization

Generalization, the reverse of elaborating, is a process of selecting and rephrasing major ideas into concise statements that have just enough detail to be clear, but are not too wordy or filled with excessive details. A good generalization is one in which you can subsume many details to elaborate on it. The balance between too much and too little can be difficult for adults as well as for younger students. An overgeneralization might be, "There are many good comprehension strategies today." The opposite of an overgeneralization is also ineffective—for example, "Comprehension processes take into account all the processes inherent in them, from the ability to group words into meaningful phrases, to the ability to choose which ideas. . . ." The balance might be, "Numerous, effective comprehension processes such as ability to organize and synthesize may operate almost simultaneously." Subsumed under this would be a discussion of all the processes and how they relate to the general statement.

Inferences

The general strategy of making inferences or guessing is based on what is known already and what information is needed but not explicitly stated. This involves some risk taking, but success can build readers' self-confidence for making future logical inferences.

Elaborations made from inferences are important for several reasons. We are better able to see connections among sentences, we can better predict subsequent information, and we can better retain that information.

Three ways to make such inferences from reading were suggested by Carroll (1969):[14]

1. We can infer meaning from subtleties of expression, such as, "She was a duchess, but he was only a viscount."
2. We can draw inferences through reasoning something out, as in problem-solving situations. "If yesterday is two days after Sunday (Tuesday), and the day after tomorrow is the beginning of the weekend (Friday), what day is tomorrow? (Thursday)."
3. We can make inferences by bringing in our own background experiences to infer, for example, how historical figures might have felt under certain circumstances. "His eyes showed his feelings as he beheld his newborn son."

IMAGING OR VISUAL IMAGERY

Being able to visualize mental images when reading may help comprehension and recall as well as improving motivation. Using visual imagery, we activate our schemata, which in turn brings life to the print. We can visualize such things as historic events, characters, or solutions to situations. Readers can be asked to visualize and describe an alternative solution to a problem, a battle scene in history, a shoreline off Nova Scotia, a famous monarch, or the architecture of an ancient city. Obviously, the more we know, the better we can call up appropriate images. Teachers can assist students by providing concrete examples in the form of drawings, photographs, or films, and by allowing time in class for discussion of reactions to personal images. They can even ask students to draw their own images as part of a report or paper.

Aulls (1978) suggested a four-stage procedure to teach poor readers to use visual imagery.[15] First, students draw stick-figure cartoons to illustrate action in single sentences. Next, they identify details in pictures that become increasingly complex, and criticize their own cartoons in terms of how complete they are. Third, they draw cartoons for groups of sentences. Finally, they use images as an aid in answering difficult comprehension questions.

When instructing in visual imagery, teachers should also encourage students to describe odors, tastes, sounds, and tactile feelings. Involving more than one sense can be helpful in recalling information later. Students can also be taught specifically to form images of key words or concepts in a selection.

MAIN IDEAS

Discerning what are the main ideas in expository writing is important to overall comprehension. Cunningham and Moore (1986) have delineated nine main idea tasks (see Table 5.1). They selected a brief passage from Boning (1970) to use for examples. The passage is: "Some horses are said to become loco or insane from eating loco weed. They stagger around half blind and chew on tin cans or old bones . . . even barbed wire. Their joints get stiff, their coats become rough and soon death puts an end to their misery."[16]

TABLE 5.1
Nine Main Idea Tasks

Main Idea Tasks	Definitions
1. Gist	Summary of explicit content of a passage achieved by creating generalized statements that subsume specific information and then deleting that specific (and now redundant) information
2. Interpretation	Summary of possible or probable implicit content of a passage—for example, "Horses don't always know what's good for them."
3. Key word	Word or term labeling the most important single concept in a passage—for example, "horses"
4. Selective summary or diagram	Summary or diagram of explicit content of a passage, achieved by selecting and combining the most superordinate, important words and phrases (or synonyms for them) from a passage—for example, "Horses go crazy, get sick, and die after eating loco weed."

Main Idea Tasks	Definitions
5. Theme	Generalization about life, the world, or the universe that the passage as a whole develops, implies, or illustrates, but which is not topic- or key word–specific. For example, "Animal owners have a great responsibility for their charges."
6. Title	Given name of passage (not applicable here)
7. Topic	Phrase labeling subject of passage without revealing specific content from the passage. For example, "What happens when horses eat loco weed?"
8. Topic issue	Single word, term, or phrase labeling a conceptual context for the passage. For example, "dangerous plants"
9. Topic sentence/ thesis sentence	Single sentence in paragraph or passage that tells most completely what the paragraph or passage as a whole is about or what it states
10. Other	Any response that cannot be classified as one of the other main idea types, including all literal and critical responses

Source: Adapted from Cunningham and Moore (1986), pp. 1–17.

Main Ideas and Summarizing

If you stop to consider it, the skill of identifying main ideas is essentially a summarizing skill, which allows readers to reduce the amount of text information to a manageable size that can be readily recalled.[17] Low performers often have trouble deciding which points are major ideas and which are random details. To instruct students having difficulty in this area, certain steps are suggested. First, materials need to be simple enough so that students can focus on main ideas and not have to deal with other concerns. Brief passages of around 50 words or four to five sentences are good for a start. These are followed by a recognition task containing several different summary statements, only one of which is appropriate. One or more of the inappropriate statements should focus on details of the passage. Using pictures can also be helpful, as this gives readers time to examine them at length and decide on the critical features. A series of pictures depicting specific events and actions more closely approximates identification of the main idea in a text, as it requires students to progress from one context (picture) to another to decide on the main idea of the entire series. Students should then see that being able to identify main ideas requires that they identify, remember, and integrate information from one context to the next.

Low performers may need more immediate, systematic, and cumulative practice, with spaced review over time. This does not need to take up a large chunk of time. Also, after initial exercises, students' practice should be on the subject material they are expected to master.

Day (1980) developed five rules for summarizing, which should also help with deciding on main ideas:[18]

1. Delete all unnecessary or trivial information.
2. Delete redundant information.
3. Given a list of concepts, substitute a label only for those concepts.
4. Make use of topic sentences in the passage or chapter to be summarized.
5. Invent a summary sentence when none is provided in the passage.

Teacher-led practice in writing summary statements using these rules should help students decide on main ideas.

The "Aha—So What?" Test

Pearson and Johnson (1984) suggested using the intuitive "aha—so what?" test for determining main ideas in expository materials. If an idea seems to give some general rule or way of looking at the work, such as a generalization, meaningful conclusion, or rule about an event, type of event, or behavior, then the idea would receive an "aha" rating. If seemingly unimportant, it would receive a "so what?" rating. Teaching students to use this test may break them away from the belief that all print is equally meaningful. For it to be effective, students must first have sufficient prerequisite background information.[19]

FRAMEWORK

Reader Response

A school of criticism that has become increasingly popular in recent times is the study of reader responses, which can be considered an extension of schema theory.[20] Although there is diversity of opinion among scholars regarding the reader–text relationship, they do agree that meaning comes from interaction between the content and structure of the text and background knowledge of the reader; every reader is culturally, individually unique, so each may comprehend differently. Thus, instead of having only one correct interpretation of the text, it is more valid to examine readers' responses to that text and their logic or justification for their interpretations.

This theory of reader response gives us a useful framework to show readers that reading is not just getting correct answers to questions, nor is it just interpreting print personally. Instead, reading becomes a process of identifying, evaluating, assimilating, and accommodating a variety of text interpretations.

If you consider any typical secondary text chapter, it will call forth many perspectives or interpretations according to a point of view—that of the author, teacher, reader, classroom (expressed through discussion), and/or authority or critic found in a library assignment. Readers must then balance these various perspectives and use them to define or reexamine their own personal viewpoints.

The goal of using reader response is to make students aware that not only are their attitudes and opinions valid, but others' attitudes and opinions are valid, too. Truth is a point of view, and we must be open to considering others' interpretations in order to assimilate and accommodate ideas at variance with our own.

Instructional Practices

Six instrumental practices intended to accomplish this goal are suggested by Chase and Hynd (1987).[21]

1. Hold small- and large-group discussions to share interpretations and show reading as communication as well as individual reflection.
2. Provide a secure classroom environment that allows freedom of expression to assert points of view rather than merely extracting predetermined correct responses.
3. Provide multiple close readings of the text to search for and validate responses or interpretations.
4. Emphasize the fact that the ultimate purpose of reading is to use new information to help clarify personal positions.
5. Allow for both written and oral expression for responses and sharing of responses.
6. Use a wide variety of reading materials, varied in type, difficulty level, topic, and length.

PRACTICE: LITERAL COMPREHENSION STRATEGIES

Smith and Elliot (1986) have given us a number of good strategies.[22] The discussion here is adapted by permission of the publisher from *Reading Activities for Middle and Secondary Schools: A Handbook for Teachers,* 2nd edition,

Following Directions

Following directions is a skill that many secondary students have yet to master, as they may neglect to give full attention to the details given.

Here are some examples of the kind of exercises you might give students for practice.

1. Draw a vertical line of approximately three inches in length.
2. At the bottom of that line, draw an almost complete circle to the left and up, forming the letter C.
3. Starting at the top of the line, draw a backward S to the right of the line, crossing over to the left halfway down, and again to the right at the bottom of the line, finishing with an upward arc that ends in a downward slant next to the line and about one-third of the way to the bottom. The final product should resemble the musical treble clef.

You can adapt this notion to any subject. First, sketch the figure yourself, and then give directions as to how to draw it. It could be, for example, three geometric figures in juxtaposition, a piece of lab equipment, or a writer's book and pen.

Having students share their interpretations will help to show how differently we can interpret the same directions.

Categorizing

When we put things together because they are alike in some way, we categorize the items for easier retention and recall. We sort ideas and classify them into units, which could fall under the following systems:

1. Informative sequence
   Enumerative (1, 2, 3)
   Chronological (early, middle, late)
   Spatial (near, far)
   Narrative (around facts and ideas)
      cause–effect, question–answer, specific–generalization, example, conclusion, principle

2. Interrogative
   who, what, when, where, why
3. Language functions
   kinds of nouns, verbs, descriptive words
4. Appearance
   size, shape, weight, height, color, ornamentation
5. Function
   cutting, blowing, building, eating

For remedial students who have difficulty with abstract categorizing, provide them first with a box or bag of small items to sort into piles (e.g., buttons, paint store color chips, stones, items cut from catalogues). After they sort the items successfully, substitute cards with just words on each (e.g., *green button*).

Newspapers and Main Ideas

Identification of unstated main ideas is important but not always easily accomplished. One way to provide practice in this is to cut out paragraphs from the newspaper, number each (from 1 to 40 or as many as are in the class), paste the paragraphs to a sheet of paper, and hand out one to each student. Students then read the paragraph and write the main idea on their sheet by the number. They pass their paragraph to the next person in an understood rotation. Answers are then shared, followed by discussion.

Making Judgments

Analysis of written material is a complex skill and should be taught in a systematic way. When analyzing writing, we determine the writer's true purpose for writing it, the main idea, and the line of reasoning—all of this in order to catalogue the information, compare it with other experiences, or organize it for the purpose of making judgments.

Teachers can ask students questions such as the following:

1. Why do you think the author wrote this?
2. What evidence did you find to support your position?
3. Is there any evidence that the writer might have used exaggeration? Distortion? Overgeneralization or simplification? Faulty reasoning? Inaccurate sources? Propaganda techniques? If so, what is the evidence?

Evaluating Technical Writing

There exist both well-written and poorly written texts. Students need practice in deciding what makes for good technical writing. One way to do this is to divide the class into small groups, give each group a report, and ask them to develop criteria for evaluating it (such as simplicity, clarity, accuracy, and organization). Each group then evaluates the report based on the stated criteria and posts the results, which can be compared and contrasted with the other groups.

Drawing Supportable Conclusions

Find an article related to the subject under study, make copies for everyone to read, and ask students to draw three to four conclusions. These are written out, and partners exchange papers, marking each conclusion as to whether it is based on the evidence and whether it is correct, partially correct, or incorrect. Allow partners to discuss and defend their own conclusions with each other. Then have representative ones, agreed on in advance, written on the board for discussion.

Logic Activities

Students can create syllogisms which state authors' premises and conclusions.[23] Here are some examples:

Premises

1. Those people who have undesirable characteristics were prohibited from entering our country.
2. Some of our "new" immigrants had undesirable characteristics.

Conclusion
The new immigrants with undesirable characteristics were rejected.

Fact or Opinion

Another way of looking at the same information is to list facts and opinion statements in two columns.

Facts	Opinions
1. "Old" immigrants came from Britain, Scandinavia, Germany, and Holland.	1. "Old" immigrants are acceptable.
2. "New" immigrants come from Italy, Greece, and the Slavic countries.	2. "New" immigrants are not acceptable. They are ignorant, dirty, diseased, insane, and so on.

Magazines for Metacognitive Practice

Students, especially those with reading problems, need to become more aware of the processes and strategies they use when reading. Magazines offer many advantages for classroom use. There is a large variety of articles that can stimulate interest and motivate thoughtful discussion. Magazines can also provide background information and allow for practice of rate adaptability, metacognitive processes of self-awareness, and monitoring of reading behaviors.

Students can keep a journal of reactions and thoughts for each article they read. They might sort remarks into categories such as concentration, study-reading habits, adaptable rate, background knowledge of the subject, and interest level in the topic. Teachers should model and provide samples of journal entries. One entry might include comments about interest, concentration, rate, and trouble with vocabulary. A sample is shown here:

> The article _____(title)_____ was not very interesting. I got lost in all the statistics. As I was reading, I thought I had the main idea, but when I finished I realized I couldn't remember very much at all. Since the article was long and boring to me, I could feel myself going slower and slower. My concentration began to wander, and I didn't really care what was going to happen to me in 45 years! Besides, the vocabulary was difficult.[24]

By reading student journals, teachers can become aware of problems their students are facing and can thus suggest ways to improve their processing skills. This is a form of informal diagnosis.

Students must learn how to create interest in their own minds when it does not already exist. Doing a quick preview and asking, "What do I already know about this and how will it affect me or my family?" may call up background knowledge and help to personalize that information.

Next, to keep from losing concentration, students might refer to the following guidelines.

——————— 1. Stop immediately. Ask yourself, "Why?"

——————— 2. Are you getting too bogged down in details or statistics? Start again and continue reading for main concepts.

——————— 3. Is the article too long? If so, read it in sections with a brief break between sections.

——————— 4. Is the vocabulary too difficult? Try to figure out meanings in context or through the structure of the word. If this doesn't work, skim the article for unknown words and use the dictionary first before attempting to read it.

——————— 5. Is your rate becoming slower? Use a marker or your finger as guide and move down the page at a consistent rate, not looking back. Sit back and see what you can recall.

——————— 6. If possible, do not reread. Remember that the purpose of reading magazines differs from that of reading a text or novel. You do not have to recall every small detail.

——————— 7. Now, read for greater fluency, to capture main ideas and trends, and to practice becoming more proficient.[25]

An integrated approach rather than an isolated skills approach to teaching reading comprehension is a necessity. Teaching isolated skills gives students little to apply to reading when they are on their own. They need to develop reading fluency by processing connected discourse, reading actively, becoming aware of what is happening inside their heads as they read, recognizing when they do not understand, and then knowing what to do about it. Using magazines for practice is one way to achieve that fluency.

QUESTIONING

Facilitating Questioning Comprehension: Product and Process

Teachers tend to use mostly literal, trivial, factual questions to test how well students comprehend material. However, questions can be used for teaching, too. The distinction is between *product* and *process*. Rather than just finding out "who were the leading generals in the Civil War," we can ask process questions such as, "How would you go about finding out who. . . ." We should be using product questions for assessing, reviewing, and practicing comprehension, but we should use more process questions to help students begin to internalize how to comprehend. Table 5.2 shows some examples.

TABLE 5.2
Product versus Process Questions

Product Questions	Process Questions
1. What is the main idea?	1. How will you decide what the main idea is?
2. Why are they important to their economy?	2. What is the best way to read this for your purpose?
3. What is the meaning of the term _____?	3. How did you figure out what that term meant?
4. Do you think there will ever be another Nazi Germany?	4. What did you already know that led you to predict this would happen?
5. What are the major products of Argentina?	5. What specific words or phrases painted a picture in your mind? Describe your picture in words or in a drawing.
6. How would you assess the reign of Louis XIV as compared to that of Henry VIII?	6. What steps would you take to write a summary of this?
7. How would you develop your Utopia?	7. What part was difficult to understand? Why?
8. What three generalizations can you make concerning this topic?	8. What did you do to try to understand it better? Did it work? Why or why not?

Taxonomies

A number of taxonomies, such as Sanders (1968) and Barrett (1968), have been developed over the years to guide our questioning strategies and to lead us to ask more higher level questions.[26] For example, the Barrett Taxonomy of Comprehension includes the levels of recognition and recall, reorganization, inferential comprehension, evaluation, and appreciation, whereas Sanders's levels include memory, translation, interpretation, application, analysis, synthesis, and evaluation. (A complete copy of the Barrett Taxonomy is found in Appendix 1.) Raphael (1984) stated that these question taxonomies tend to treat questions as isolated units rather than as dependent on the text to which they refer.[27]

Pearson and Johnson (1984) suggested a different classification scheme.[28] Questions could be either *text explicit* (the answer appears directly in the text), *text implicit* (the answer requires integrating text information with what we already know), or *script implicit* (the answer comes from our knowledge base).

QARs

Following is an outline of procedures for using Question/Answer/ Relationships, or QARs, on the basis of Raphael's strategy.

1. *Right there (text explicit):* Readers find words used to create the question and examine the rest of the sentence to find the answer. The answer can be found in one sentence.
2. *Think and search (text implicit):* Readers look for an answer in the text, but the answer requires information from more than one sentence.
3. *Writer and me (text implicit):* Readers must look to their own background knowledge and tie it to what was read in the text for a correct response.
4. *On my own (script implicit):* Readers must find the answer in their own background knowledge.[29]

When teaching students these four strategies, it is important to work in groups, start with short examples, and give immediate feedback before moving to independent practice. Then, teachers should provide a transition from easy to difficult tasks.

Comprehension Questions for Assessment

Jones (1985) has presented a variety of materials to show how to recognize and respond to different questions.[30] Also, a taxonomy of questions in social studies texts has been developed by Armbruster et al. (1983).[31] Eight types of questions are:

1. Time (when)
2. Location (where)
3. Quantity (how much, how many)
4. Name (who, whose)
5. Concept identification (what, which)
6. Explanation (why, how)
7. Description (what is)
8. Comparison (compare/contrast, how did X change?)

For each category of question, there is a type of information given in the question and the pattern of ideas needed in the response. For example, a "why conflict" question (a subcategory of #6, explanation) requires readers to identify goals and actions of the parties in the conflict, with the question giving the definition of the conflict: "Why was there trouble between the colonists and the Indians?" Now, to explain the conflict fully, the reader must explain how whatever the colonists did interfered with the Indians' goals and vice versa.

Frame Questions

From this information, we can see that once students analyze a question to find key information, the next step is to organize their answers. Jones describes a recent concept of frames, developed by Armbruster and Anderson (1984).[32] *Frame questions* are key sets of questions fundamental to understanding a given discipline. For example, a typical frame underlying many narrative texts is called *goal-action-outcome*. We can use this frame to understand the behavior of a story character or a group action in a historical narrative. Key questions in this frame would be: "What were the goals of this group?" "What actions were needed to achieve those goals?" "What was the result or outcome of those actions?" (From literary narrative might be added: "What problems did this group have in reaching its goals?" "How did the group respond internally?")

Pre-, During-, and After-Reading Questions

When you plan the questions you will ask students, it is also a good idea to think about triggering prior knowledge and helping them set purposes for reading. These should be broad questions. Questions for reading could be in the form of a study guide, and you might focus on process questions to help students be more aware of their study reading behaviors as they read. After they read, teachers should consider a wide variety of questions leading to analysis, synthesis, and evaluation of what has been read.

SUMMARY: LOOKING BACKWARD/ LOOKING FORWARD

In this chapter on comprehending expository text, a number of important considerations for all teachers have been discussed, as well as a number of processes that occur during comprehension of information: processes used during the act of comprehending, anaphoric concerns, schema theory and reader response. Numerous teaching and questioning strategies were outlined.

In Chapter 6, on literary comprehension, we will be discussing narrative and descriptive text, and examining the important notions of metacognitive script and glossing. These are two powerful comprehension tools, which can actually be used with any kind of text.

NOTES

1. R. C. Anderson, E. H. Niebert, J. A. Scott, and L. Wilkinson, eds. *Becoming a Nation of Readers*, Report of the Commission on Reading, Contract No. 400-83-0057 (Washington, DC: National Institute of Education, 1985).

2. P. David Pearson, "Changing the Face of Reading Comprehension Instruction," *The Reading Teacher*, 38 (1985), 724–738.

3. D. Cook, ed., *A Guide for Curriculum Planning Reading* (Madison: Wisconsin Department of Public Instruction, 1986).

4. Benjamin S. Bloom et al., *Taxonomy of Educational Objectives, Handbook I: Cognitive Domain* (New York: Longman, 1956); and Thomas Barrett, "Taxonomy of Cognitive and Affective Dimensions of Reading Comprehension," discussed in "What Is Reading? Some Current Concepts," by Theodore Clymer, in *Innovation and Change in Reading Instruction*, edited by Helen M. Robinson, Sixty-seventh Yearbook of the National Society for the Study of Education, Part II, 1968, pp. 1–30.

5. W. Kintsch and T. A. Van Dijk, "Toward a Model of Text Comprehension and Production," *Psychological Review*, 85 (1978), 363–394; and M. A. Just and P. A. Carpenter, "A Theory of Reading from Eye Fixations to Comprehension," *Psychological Review*, 87 (1980), 329–354.

6. Judith Westphal Irwin, *Teaching Reading Comprehension Processes* (Englewood Cliffs, NJ: Prentice-Hall, 1986), pp. 2–7.

7. Ibid.

8. Kenneth S. Goodman, "Unity in Reading," in Alan S. Purves and Olive Niles, eds., *Becoming Readers in a Complex Society*, Eighty-third Yearbook of the National Society for the Study of Education (Chicago: University of Chicago Press, 1984), pp. 102–103.

9. Irwin, *Teaching Reading Comprehension Processes*, pp.28–30.

10. J. Baumann and J. Stevenson, "Teaching Students to Comprehend Anaphoric Relations," in J. W. Irwin, ed., *Understanding and Teaching Cohesion Comprehension* (Newark, DE: International Reading Association, 1987).

11. David Rumelhart, "Schemata: The Building Blocks of Cognition," in John Guthrie, ed., *Comprehension and Teaching: Research Reviews* (Newark, DE: International Reading Association, 1981), pp. 3–26.

12. John D. McNeil, *Reading Comprehension: New Directions for Classroom Practice* (Glenview, IL: Scott, Foresman, 1987), pp. 3–4.

13. James Moffett and Betty Jane Wagner, *Student-Centered Language Arts and Reading K–13: A Handbook for Teachers*, 3rd ed. (Boston: Houghton Mifflin, 1983).

14. John B. Carroll, "From Comprehension to Inference," in Malcolm Douglas, ed., *Thirty-third Yearbook, Claremont Reading Conference* (Claremont, CA: Claremont Graduate School, 1969).

15. Mark Aulls, *Development of Remedial Reading in the Middle Grades* (Boston: Allyn and Bacon, 1978).

16. James W. Cunningham and David W. Moore, "The Confused World of Main Idea," in James F. Baumann, ed., *Teaching Main Idea Comprehension* (Newark, DE: International Reading Association, 1986).

17. Edward J. Kameenui, "Main Idea Instruction for Low Performers: A Direct Instruction Analysis," in James F. Baumann, ed., *Teaching Main Idea Comprehension* (Newark, DE: International Reading Association, 1986).

18. J. D. Day, "Teaching Summarization Skills: A Comparison of Training Methods," unpublished doctoral dissertation, University of Illinois, 1980.

19. P. D. Pearson and D. Johnson, *Teaching Reading Comprehension* (New York: Holt, Rinehart and Winston, 1984).

20. Nancy D. Chase and Cynthia R. Hynd, "Reader Response: An Alternative Way to Teach Students to Think about Test," *Journal of Reading*, 30 (March 1987), 530–540.

21. Ibid.

22. Carl B. Smith and Peggy G. Elliot, *Reading Activities for Middle and Secondary Schools: A Handbook for Teachers*, 2nd ed. (New York: Teachers' College Press, 1986), pp. 117–118, 178.

23. Betty Roe, Barbara Stoodt, and Paul Burns, *Secondary School Reading Instruction: The Content Areas*, 3rd ed. (Boston: Houghton, Mifflin, 1987), p. 114.

24. Sherrie L. Nist, Kate Kirby, and Annice Ritter, "Teaching Comprehension Processes Using Magazines, Paperback Novels, and Content Area Texts," *Journal of Reading*, 27 (December 1983), 253–261.

25. Ibid.

26. Richard J. Smith and Thomas C. Barrett, *Teaching Reading in the Middle Grades*, 2nd ed. (Reading, MA: Addison-Wesley, 1979), pp. 63–66; and Benjamin Bloom, ed., *Taxonomy of Educational Objectives: Cognitive Domain* (New York: David McKay, 1956), pp. 201–207.

27. T. E. Raphael, "Teaching Learners about Sources of Information for Answering Comprehension Questions," *Journal of Reading*, 27 (January 1984), 303–311.

28. P. David Pearson and Dale Johnson, *Teaching Reading Comprehension* (New York: Holt, Rinehart and Winston, 1984).

29. Raphael, "Teaching Learners," pp. 303–311.

30. Beau Fly Jones, "Response Instruction," in Theodore Ham and Eric Cooper, eds., *Reading, Thinking and Concept Development: Strategies for the Classrooms* (New York: College Entrance Examination Board, 1985), pp. 105–130.

31. B. B. Armbruster et al., *What Did You Mean by That Question? A Taxonomy of American History Questions*, Reading Education Report No. 308 (Urbana: University of Illinois, Center for the Study of Reading, 1983).

32. Jones, "Response Instruction," pp. 105–130; B. B. Armbruster and T. H. Anderson, "Content Area Textbooks," in R. C. Anderson, J. Osborn, and R. J. Tierney, eds., *Learning to Read in American Schools: Basal Readers and Content Texts* (Hillsdale, NJ: Erlbaum, 1984); and Armbruster et al., *What Did You Mean by That Question.*

RECOMMENDED READINGS

Anderson, Richard C., and Pichert, John W. "Recall of Previously Unrecallable Information Following a Shift in Perspective," *Journal of Verbal Learning and Verbal Behavior*, 17 (1978), 1–12.

Armbruster, B. B., and Anderson, T. H. "Content Area Textbooks." In R. C. Anderson, J. Osborn, and R. J. Tierney, eds., *Learning to Read in American Schools: Basal Readers and Content Texts*. Hillsdale, NJ: Erlbaum, 1984.

Ausubel, D. P. "In Defense of Advance Organizers: A Reply to the Critics." *Review of Educational Research*, 48 (1978), 251–257.

Baumann, James F. "The Direct Instruction of Main Idea Comprehension Ability." In James F. Baumann, ed., *Teaching Main Idea Comprehension*. Newark, DE: International Reading Association, 1986, pp. 133–178.

Campione, J. C., and Armbruster, B. B. "Acquiring Information from Texts: An Analysis of Four Approaches." In J. Segal, S. Chipman, and R. Galser, eds., *Thinking and Learning Skills: Relating Instruction to Research*. Hillsdale, NJ: Erlbaum, 1985, pp. 317–359.

Chapman, John J. *Reading Development and Cohesion*. London: Heinemann Education Books, 1983.

Christenburg, Leila, and Kelly, Patricia P. *Questioning: A Path to Critical Thinking*. Urbana, IL: National Council of Teachers of English, 1982.

Cunningham, J. W. "Generating Interactions between Schemata and Text." In J. A. Niles and L. A. Harris, eds., *New Inquiries in Reading Research and Instruction*, Thirty-first Yearbook of the National Reading Conference. Blacksburg: Virginia Polytechnic Institute and State University, 1982, pp. 42–47.

Halliday, M., and Hasen, R. *Cohesion in English*. London: Longman, 1976.

Hare, Victoria Chou, and Bingham, Adelaide Bates. "Teaching Students Main Idea Comprehension: Alternatives to Repeated Exposures." In James F. Baumann, ed., *Teaching Main Idea Comprehension*. Newark, DE: International Reading Association, 1986, pp. 179–194.

Hare, V. C., and Borchardt, K. M. "Direct Instruction of Summarization Skills." *Reading Research Quarterly*, 20 (1984), 62–78.

Johnson, Dale D. "Developing Comprehension of Anaphoric Relationships." In Theodore Harris and Eric Cooper, eds., *Reading, Thinking and Concept Development: Strategies for the Classroom*. New York: College Entrance Examination Board, 1985, pp. 33–49.

Johnston, William R., "Light on Heteronyms." *Journal of Reading*, 31 (March 1988), 570–573.

Kent, Carolyn. "A Linguist Compares Narrative and Expository Prose." *Journal of Reading*, 28 (December 1984), 232–236.

McGee, L. M. "Awareness of Text Structure: Effects on Children's Recall of Expository Text." *Reading Research Quarterly*, 17 (1982), 581–590.

New Directions in Reading Instruction. An International Reading Association Gertrude Whipple Professional Development Project. Newark, DE: International Reading Association, 1988, p. 17.

Pearson, P. D., "Changing the Face of Reading Comprehension Instruction." *Reading Teacher*, 38 (1985), 724–738.

Winograd, P. N. "Strategic Difficulties in Summarizing Text." *Reading Research Quarterly*, 19 (1984), 404–425.

Postorganizer 1
Comprehending Comprehension

Refer back to Preorganizer 2 and select the task you prefer, working with a partner. These can be shared later on an overhead projector or on butcher paper or the chalkboard.

Postorganizer 2
Developing Questions

This is an excellent time to compose and collect your own series of generic and specific question types at various levels of thought and explicitness for later reference. Develop a series of product questions that might be used for assessment, and also process ones to teach your students. Exchange questions with your partner and actually answer each others' questions.

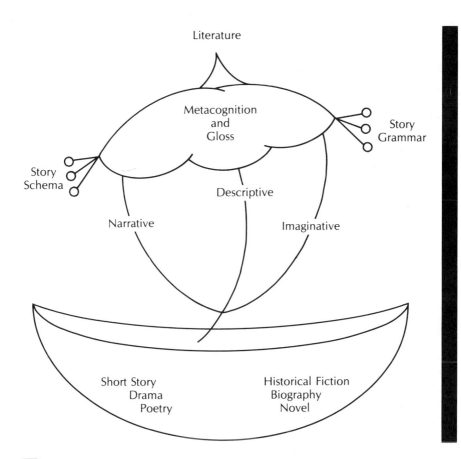

6

Literary Comprehension

CHAPTER OUTLINE

Preorganizers
Introduction
Expository versus Narrative Text
   Narrative, Descriptive, Imaginary
   Story Schemas and Story Grammars
   Rules for Reading Imaginative Literature
Teaching Literary Comprehension
   Purposes
   Language Arts Skills
   Barrett's Taxonomy
Reading for Adolescents
   Secondary Stages and Levels
   The Novel for Adolescents/Young Adults
General Aids for Teaching
   Questions for Summarizing Narrative
   Rhetorical Devices for Identifying Authors
   Reaction Guides to Readings
   Taxonomy of Responses to Literature
   Using Charts to Enhance Literary Comprehension
   Better Questions for Response Journals
Teaching Poetry Lessons
   Poetry: Using the Maze Technique
   Taxonomy of Literary Understanding and Skills
Activities to Expand Readers' Background Knowledge
   Before Reading
   After Reading
   Readers' Theater Scripts
Metacognition
   Metacognition and Reading
   Metacognitive Script
   Metacognitive Monitoring and Awareness
   Checklist of Awareness of Reading Behaviors
Sustained Silent Reading
Shakespeare as It Could be Taught
Glossing as an Adjunct Aid
Summary
Notes
Recommended Readings
Postorganizers

Literary Comprehension

COGNITIVE COMPETENCIES

1. *List* the strategies you use for enhancing your comprehension and retention of information, especially as it relates to literary comprehension.

2. *Describe* key differences between narrative, descriptive, and expository text.

3. *Summarize* what is meant by story grammar in literary comprehension, comparing likenesses and differences with schema theory.

4. Using Barrett's taxonomy, *develop* questions at each level, given one literary work.

5. After examining Moffett and Wagner's characteristics, kinds of reading, and levels, *conclude* what is most useful to you in your subject.

6. *Evaluate* the comparative worth of metacognitive scripts or glosses for aiding students' comprehension in your class.

KEY TERMS

Barrett's taxonomy
gloss
metacognitive script
narrative, descriptive, imaginary
readers' theater

response journals
rhetorical devices
story grammar/story schema
sustained silent reading (SSR)

Preorganizer 1
Metacognitive Scipt

As you read this chapter for the first time, try to be aware of your own study-reading processes. What do you tie to past experience? What do you do when you come to unfamiliar terms? What strategies do you use for enhancing your comprehension and retention of information? Jot these down as they occur. After reading, develop a brief metacognitive script of your inner thoughts—for example, "I'm not an English major so why should I read this chapter? Hm, maybe I can tie this to collateral reading in my history class. . . . What's this? I'd better reread this to see what I missed. *Genre*—I *should* know the definition—let's see if I can pick it up from the context . . ."

1

Preorganizers are intended to serve as a readiness activity to get readers prepared to be actively involved and thinking about the reading to come.

Preorganizer 2
Gloss

Note that part of this chapter has marginal notations, which act as a silent teacher to explain processes (not just facts and definitions). The gloss should be referred to by readers only when needed. After reading this chapter, however, you should return to the beginning and read the glosses. These may serve as models for you in developing a gloss in class with a partner for your own students. For that reason, the glosses here are the kind you could use with your lower level readers. (See the section on "Glossing as an Adjunct Aid" later in this chapter for a more complete explanation of gloss.)

Literary Comprehension

6
Literary
Comprehension

2 The title gives the focus for this chapter. We have looked at the expository comprehension in the last chapter. It will help to compare the two types.

The nineteenth-century critic Matthew Arnold said that literature was the best that has been thought and has been said in the world; literature is writing known for its universal appeal and beauty.

INTRODUCTION

Literary comprehension, or comprehension of descriptive, narrative, and imaginary prose, occurs most often in English classrooms, but it does have a place in the other disciplines too, especially in the area of collateral reading for a particular subject, such as biographies of scientists, mathematicians or famous people in history.

In the last chapter, we looked at the compre-

3 Here is a definition and a reason for reading this chapter. Always pay close attention to paragraphs like this introduction, as they may help you understand and enhance your motivation.

hension of expository writing. There we were concerned mainly with informative abstract ideas, concepts, logical processes, or directions. Comprehending literary discourse is quite a different matter. When we read a poem, for example, we may respond directly and actively to whatever the verbal symbols (words) stir up in us. As Rosenblatt (1968) said so well, there is an electric charge between the text and the reader, and it is this live circuit that we call the literary expeience.[1] "Literature is, first of all, this sensing, feeling, thinking, this ordering and organizing of image, idea and emotion in relation to a text. The texture and structure of the reader's experience in relation to the text becomes for him the poem, the story, or the play."[2]

EXPOSITORY VERSUS NARRATIVE TEXT

Let us look for a moment at basic differences between expository and literary text. Table 6.1 shows some of these differences.

Narrative, Descriptive, Imaginary

A narrative describes a number of events occurring over time and linked by a theme or cause. Narratives can vary in how they describe events. For example, we can use flashbacks, which describe events out of their natural order. Narratives also can vary in terms of the roles the narrator plays, ranging from active to neutral. When we comprehend narratives, we fill in the gaps in a chain relating to the events described, and we do this by inference.[3]

Descriptive discourse attempts to show in words a stationary, perceptual scene, usually a visual one. As Brewer (1980) states, typical descriptive passages can be represented by a picture, typical narratives by a motion picture, and exposition only by some abstract form such as a logical notation.[4]

Descriptions generally occur in scene-setting paragraphs and are most often visual, although other senses can be depicted. Descriptions give information about spatial arrangements, shape, color, and texture. Prior knowledge aids our comprehension of descriptions by allowing us to fill in

TABLE 6.1
Differences between Narrative and Expository Text

	Narrative	Expository	
Person	First or third	Not necessary	
Orientation	Agent/actor	Subject matter	
Time	Series of events accomplished within a time frame, related by cause or theme	No temporal focus	**4** Tables and figures give us much information in a condensed form, so should be studied, not ignored.
Linkage	Chronological	Logical	
Language	Use metaphors, multiple meanings	Explicit, unambiguous	
Major aims	Entertain, provide aesthetic experience	Explain, inform, persuade	
Thinking	Must do own thinking about an experience in order to learn	Try to understand writer's thinking	

the gaps and elaborate on them. Many times we picture a character or setting in our mind's eye in such a way that it goes with the author's actual description. Both narrative and descriptive types of discourse often occur in imaginary literature.

Literary writing, then, is a body of writing that includes our beliefs, experiences, values, and aspirations; our legends, myths, and creative imaginations.

Story Schemas and Story Grammars

An important aspect of comprehending fiction is our familiarity with the genre—the story components, the purpose of each, and their relationships to each other.[5] The knowledge we extract about the typical story structure is called a story schema, or mental framework containing slots with labels for each story component—for example, *setting:* an Eastern European country; *goal:* character(s) want to get to the United States; *complication:* the Eastern European country's government refuses the character(s) permission to leave; *resolution:* a solution is found, and the character(s) are allowed to make the journey.

Story grammars, on the other hand, are slightly different. Like schemata, they are also frameworks with slots representing the story's structural components. But they differ in that they also denote the hierarchical relations among the components more directly. In other words, they describe basic parts of a story and how these fit together. The composition of a story is indicated by labels such as *episode* and *setting*. In simple stories, the episode introduces some of the characters (protagonists) and the setting of the story. The episodes may have an initiating event, an internal response, an attempt, a consequence, and a reaction.[6] The theme involves us in interpreting what the story means. Nezworski, Stein, and Trabasso (1982) illustrated this well in a simple story that was purposely written to conform to the frameworks or grammars.[7] It is reprinted with permission from "Story Grammar" by T. Nezworski, N. L. Stein, and T. Trebasso, *Journal of Verbal Learning and Verbal Behavior,* Vol. 21, p. 197, copyright © 1982 by Academic Press.

Setting: There once was an old woman who
   lived in a forest.

Initiating event: One hot day, while wandering
   through the forest, she discovered a tiger's   **5**
   cave.

Internal response: She had always wanted a
   tiger's whisker, so she decided to try to get
   one.

Here we have an example to help us apply the idea of a story grammar. After

Attempt: She returned with a bowl of raw meat, which she placed in front of the cave, and then began to sing softly.

Consequence: Hearing the music, the tiger came out and ate the meat. While he ate, the old lady pulled out one whisker and then scampered home.

Reaction: She was very happy because her trick had worked, she had her whisker, and she was safe at home.

> reading it through once, it is important to go back, focus on each descriptor (e.g., setting), and check to see if you can recall the story example for each.

Although story grammars may generally apply more to simple stories than to complex narratives such as novels and short stories, some of the latter do have a consistent enough structure to use for comprehension and retrieval.

It is important to remember that most texts cannot be totally expository, narrative, or descriptive, but will be a mix of two or all three types. For example, narratives and expositions usually have some description, and expositions and narratives can include elements of each.[8]

Rules for Reading Imaginative Literature

According to Adler and Van Doren (1972), there are three groups of rules for reading what they call imaginative literature (novels, short stories, plays, and poetry).[9] They are reprinted by permission of Simon & Schuster, Inc., from Mortimer J. Adler and Charles Van Doren, *How to Read a Book*, p. 246. Copyright © 1940, 1967 by Mortimer J. Adler. Copyright © 1972 by Mortimer J. Adler and Charles Van Doren.

> **6** Whenever we see something like "three groups of rules," we should read them through once slowly and then return to recite to ourselves the basic rules, omitting the examples and explanations. When reviewing the rules, we should then try to recall the discussion, examples, and explanation.

1. We must discover the unity and the partial/whole structure by:
   a. Classifying fiction according to its kind (e.g., a play differs from a novel in that it usually is narrated entirely by speeches and actions; a lyric generally portrays a single emotional experience, whereas novels and plays are more complex.
   b. Grasping the unity of the whole work. The unity of a story is always in the plot, not in a proposition or argument as is found in exposition.

    c. Reducing the whole to its simplest unity. The parts of fiction are the steps the writer takes to develop the plot. To know the structure of a narrative, it is necessary to know where it begins (which may not be at the beginning of the story) and what the crises are that lead to the climax with its aftermath. In exposition the subparts can usually be read independently, but that is not true of chapters in a novel.

2. We must decide on interpretive rules for fiction by:
    a. Getting acquainted with details of episodes, incidents, and characters—their thoughts, feelings, and actions.
    b. Finding the connections that vitalize the elements of fiction. "Become comfortable in this imaginary world; know it as if we were observers on the scene; become a member of its population, willing to befriend its characters, and able to participate in its happenings by sympathetic insight, as we would do in the actions and sufferings of a friend."[10]
    c. Following the characters through their actions and adventures. The setting or scene is a *static* connection, the unraveling of the plot is a *dynamic* connection. Even in poetry there is at least one character—the speaker of the lyric.

3. We must determine the critical rules for fiction by:
    a. Fully appreciating what the writer has attempted to have us experience before criticizing. We agree or disagree, we either like it or we do not. We critique according to its beauty, the pleasure it gives us.
    b. Criticizing with justification of our reactions, pointing to whatever aspects in the writing caused those reactions.

TEACHING LITERARY COMPREHENSION

Purposes

When we think about teaching literary comprehension, we need to consider the main purposes for the variety of genres and also the numerous processes of literature. It is helpful to make explicit to students certain purposes. The following list shows possible purposes for reading:

- *Story:* To enjoy the plot, characters, setting; to become a part of the story

- *Drama:* To interpret the conversations of the characters as well as their actions; to become a part of the drama
- *Poetry:* To determine the writer's ideas, emotions, moods, or imagery; to appreciate the beauty and implied meanings, to find others' words that say how we feel
- *Biography:* To follow the chronological facts and reach conclusions concerning the biographer; to better understand key historical figures and current celebrities
- *Historical fiction/fictionalized history:* To assist in visualization of the life and times of a particular place and eras

The processes of literature include: talking and writing about it, interpreting what the writer is saying and being able to defend that interpretation, applying learnings from one piece to another, relating distinct elements of a piece to the whole, evaluating writing using specific criteria, discriminating among genres and authors, valuing the relevance to one's own life, and creating responses through art, music, poetry, prose, dance, dramatics, and pantomime.[11]

Language Arts Skills

Students need to know and understand the central role of language in mastering their subject matter. Shepherd (1982) has delineated communication and thinking skills in language arts that show similarities among speaking, listening, reading, and writing (see Table 6.2).[12]

Barrett's Taxonomy

In an unpublished paper, Thomas Barrett identified two misconceptions teachers face when teaching comprehension: that comprehension is a single unitary skill, and that comprehension has so many separate skills as to be unmanageable.[13] To simplify matters, Barrett developed a taxonomy or hierarchy, which he divided into five major areas or levels: literal, reorganization, inferential, evaluation, and appreciation. Within each category he gave examples of specific types of tasks in the form of purposes.

This taxonomy may be found in its entirety in Appendix 1. It lends itself especially to comprehending literary works and combines the affective with the cognitive in its final and highest category of appreciation. Teachers will find it useful for developing a variety of questions and purposes for reading.

It is important to note, however, that there is often an overlap among categories, and sometimes what appears to be a more difficult question is

TABLE 6.2
Similarities among Language Arts Skills

Speak (do)	*Listen* (receive)	*Read* (receive)	*Write* (do)
1. Knows word sounds	1. Recognizes word sounds	1. Knows word structure, meaning, clues, sound clues	1. Knows how to spell, use affixes
2. Knows words meanings	2. Knows word meanings used	2. Knows word meanings	2. Knows words to express a specific thought
3. Understands how to form various sentence patterns and how to express meaning through them	3. Understands how to get thought from sentence patterns used	3. Understands how to get thought from sentence patterns used	3. Understands how to formulate sentence patterns, express meaning through them

Source: Adapted with permission of the author from *Comprehensive High School Reading Methods* by David L. Shepherd (Columbus, OH: Charles E. Merrill, 1982), pp. 136–139.

actually not so because it was explicitly stated in the text. Also, no taxonomy can take into account the crucial aspect of readers' background knowledge.

READING FOR ADOLESCENTS

Secondary Stages and Levels

Moffett and Wagner (1983) have developed a comprehensive listing of characteristics and kinds of reading for all ages.[14] The secondary stages and levels are shown here, starting with stage 3. The listings are reprinted here with permission from *Student-Centered Language Arts and Reading, K–13: A Handbook for Teachers,* 3rd edition, by James Moffett and Betty Jane Wagner, copyright © 1976 by Houghton Mifflin Company. Stages gives us characteristics, and the levels list the kinds of reading materials.

Stage 3 (initial adolescence, ages 12–16 on):
- Vacillates between lingering dependence on adults and real independence, recreating the Terrible Two's; behavior may be self-contradictory or irrational.
- Attaches tightly to peer group and follows its rules, treads delicately between those rules and compliance with adult demands.

Stage 4 (adulthood—only some reach this stage in high school):
- Continues to value peer group, but group coincides more closely to the general adult public.
- Reaches full physical growth.
- Focus is on career and/or mate selection.
- Has full mental capacity but is limited by early conditioning and by inexperience as an adult.

Levels 3 and 4 (12–adult):

- Diaries—true and fictional
- Letters—true and fictional
- Autobiography—true and fictional
- Memoirs—true and fictional
- Biographies—true and fictional
- Chronicles—true and fictional
- Charts and graphs
- Maps
- Advertisements
- Dictionaries
- Information
- Eyewitness reports
- Third-person reports
- Informal essays of reflection
- Formal essays of generalization
- Transcripts
- Proverbs
- Fables
- Legends
- Parables
- Song
- Narrative poetry
- Sonnets
- Theater, mime, and puppet scripts
- Radio scripts
- Film and television
- Adventure stories
- Sports stories
- Mystery stories
- Science fiction
- Humorous stories
- Jokes
- Limericks
- Comics
- Riddles
- Brain teasers
- Codes
- Signs
- Captioned photos
- Readers' theater scripts
- Dialogues and monologues
- Myths
- Epigrams and sayings
- Ballads
- Lyrics

The Novel for Adolescents/Young Adults

An important phenomenon in secondary education programs over the past twenty years or so has been the increased use of the genre of the novel specifically for adolescents, which portrays young adults in a realistic fashion and is written intentionally for that age group. This genre evolved from the junior novels of the 1940s and 1950s, which often revolved around such episodes as middle-class summer romances. Many of today's novels deal more realistically with teenage problems across the socioeconomic strata, and there now exist examples from all types of writing.

The adolescent novel is less difficult to read than the adult novel and is intended to bridge the gap between children's books and those written for adults.[15]

Popular authors in this category include Judy Blume, who appeals to young adolescents; Lois Duncan, who has been successful in capturing the imagination of those teens interested in the occult, mystery, and young romance (many of her teen novels are based on actual experiences with her five children); and Norma Klein, who creates teenagers in her writing who are intelligent, independent, and introspective, and does so with humor and warmth. Samples of their writing include:

Judy Blume:
Are You There, God? It's Me, Margaret
Blubber
Deenie
Otherwise Known as Sheila the Great
Lois Duncan:
The Twisted Window
Locked in Time
The Third Eye
Stranger with My Face
Killing Mr. Griffin
Norma Klein:
Breaking Up
Mom, the Wolfman and Me
Taking Sides
It's Not What You'd Expect

One of the best collectors of poems for young people today is Paul Janec. His poetry anthologies are published by Bradbury Press. They include:

Don't Forget to Fly: A Cycle of Modern Poems, 1981
Going Over to Your Place: Poems for Each Other, 1987
Strings: A Gathering of Family Poems, 1984
Pocket Poems, 1985
Poetspeak: In Their Words, about Their Work, 1983
Postcard Poems: A Collection of Poems for Sharing, 1979

A sample list of adult books adolescents have enjoyed over the past few years is also included here. You may wish to conduct a survey and compile your own list of current and choice books for your student population.

Armstrong, William, *Sounder*
Asimov, Isaac, *Fantastic Voyage*
Brown, Dee, *Bury My Heart at Wounded Knee*
Carson, Rachel, *Silent Spring*
Clarke, Arthur, *2001: A Space Odyssey*
Herriot, James, *All Creatures Great and Small*
Heller, Joseph, *Catch 22*
Kesey, Ken, *One Flew Over the Cuckoo's Nest*
Ludlum, Robert, *The Bourne Identity*, and others
Michener, James, *Hawaii, Chesapeake, Texas*, and others
Uris, Leon, *Exodus*, and others
Vonnegut, Kurt, *Cat's Cradle*, and others

Reviews of current adult literature can be found in the *Journal of Reading*. A listing for the year is found in the May issue.

GENERAL AIDS FOR TEACHING

Questions for Summarizing Narrative

Singer and Donlan (1982, pp. 166–187) developed a series of questions that follow a story's organization and suggest ways to summarize and reconstruct.[16] These are adapted here with permission.

1. *Leading character:*
   • Who is it?
   • What action does the character initiate?
   • What did you learn about the character from his actions?
2. *Goal:*
   • What is the leading character striving toward?
   • What did you learn about the character from the nature of the goal?
   • What courses of action does the character take to reach the goal?
   • What did you learn about the character from the courses of action taken?
3. *Obstacle:*
   • What is the first/last obstacle the character meets?
   • How does the character deal with it?

- How does the character alter the goal because of this obstacle?
- What did you learn about the character when or if the goal was altered?

4. *Outcome:*
   - Does the character reach the original or revised goal?
   - If successful, what was most helpful—forces within or outside the character's control?
   - If unsuccessful, what hindered most—forces within or outside the character's control?

5. *Theme:*
   - What does this story basically show? (A struggle with self? nature? other people?)

Rhetorical Devices for Identifying Authors

McNeil (1987) describes some rhetorical devices that serve as communication lines between the author and the reader. These have been referred to as "stories within stories." This embedding can be the way an implied author introduces the text supposedly written by a renowned historian. It can also be in the form of drama, parts of books within a text, or letters.[17]

Other rhetorical devices include direct author commentary ("I will next show you . . ."), irony, an unrecognized narrator (not a participant in the story), and the engaged author (narration in the first person and separate from the implied author). Finally, immersion is a device whereby the reader enters directly into the story.

Reaction Guides to Readings

Instead of merely asking questions of students, a guide that outlines tasks can be helpful (Moore et al., 1986).[18] An example of such a guide follows:

Composition Guide for Reporting on Readings

Select and complete one task listed under each category.

Character
1. Write a letter to a family member or friend or an actor. Describe how the person to whom you are writing is like or unlike one character in the story.

---

2. Think of yourself as becoming one of the characters in the story. Write a letter to *Dear Abby* to get advice on coping with the major problem you face. Write her response to your letter.

Plot
1. Produce a calendar of events reflecting the story line. Divide this among hours, days, weeks, months, or years. Illustrate your calendar.
2. Write a diary that might have been kept by one of the characters. Chronicle the event in that character's life and what you suppose his or her reaction would be.

Setting
1. Pretend that this story is being turned into a mini-series on television. Describe in detail five locations where five different scenes could be filmed.
2. You have been made responsible for obtaining props for a stage production of your story. Describe five props essential for this production, and justify their use.

Theme
1. Describe one insight a main character gained by the end of the story.
2. Describe how another story you have read made the same point as this one or a similar point.

Other
1. Write an outline for a new story paralleling the one just read.
2. Write a new ending for the story.

Taxonomy of Responses to Literature

Developed over a 10-year span, this taxonomy by Hillocks and Ludlow (1984) requires the high level of thinking necessary to elicit thoughtful responses from students in an essay format.[19] It is adapted by permission of the publisher from "A Taxonomy of Responses to Literature" by George Hillocks and Larry H. Ludlow, *American Education Research Journal*, Spring 1984, copyright © 1984 by the American Educational Research Association.

Level 1 — Basic stated information: These are literal facts essential to the working of the story.

Level 2 — Key details: These occur at important points in the plot and bear some causal relationship to what happens.

Level 3 — Stated relationships: These are explicitly described in the text and often relate to characters and events in a causal fashion.

Level 4 — Simple implied relationships: These are stated relationships among events and people, for which the causes must be inferred.

Level 5 — Complex implied relationships: These relationships include many details to be coped with simultaneously.

Level 6 — Author's generalizations: These are abstract statements illustrating fundamental perceptions of the human condition.

Level 7 — Structural generalizations: These explain how parts of the writing operate together to achieve certain effects. They often relate the nature of the characters to the plot structure and require an explanation.

Using Charts to Enhance Literary Comprehension

The charts in Table 6.3 can help students perceive the structure of key ideas in narratives, and also compare and analyze character traits. When students fill in the boxes themselves and discuss the reasons for their choices, they will have a better grasp and will be able to retrieve key notions from their reading. Before assigning the reading, display the chart(s) on the board and discuss each category with the class, using examples of past, similar, and familiar readings. Explain how what is to be read may match these parts. Provide the usual background information, develop vocabulary and concepts, and state a purpose for the silent reading.

After reading, ask for volunteers to describe what they have read and put key ideas on the board. Encourage thinking aloud. Have other students select one idea on the board, place it in a category, and tell why it fits into that category. When the chart is completed, have students summarize key thoughts and draw conclusions.

Better Questions for Response Journals

Using response journals is a good way to help readers react more thoughtfully to what they have been reading. To help them in those responses, it is a good idea to provide them with questions to use as a guide. Examples follow.

TABLE 6.3
Charts to Enhance Literary Comprehension

A. Structure of Ideas

Setting	Characters	Plot (Goal, Attempt, Conflict, Consequence)	Resolution

B. Similarities and Differences in Character Traits

Greg	Luciano	Ana
brave	cheerful	honest
gloomy	friendly	brave
impatient	cowardly	modest
loving	irresponsible	patient
suspicious	destructive	cheerful

C. Analyzing Character Traits through Reasons for Actions

Character	Action	Reason	Traits
Jerry	Leaves John's glove at scene of crime	Wants to pin his crime on John	tricky, devious
Police inspector	Sees glove, assumes John is the culprit	Wants the easy way out	lazy, unimaginative

Characters

1. Which characters did you like best or dislike the most? Why?
2. What character reminds you of someone you already know? Describe.
3. If you could choose to be any character in this work, who would it be? Explain.
4. What qualities of a character would you like to develop within yourself? Why? How does the character show you these qualities?

Your General Attitude

5. What kind of feelings did you have after reading a few paragraphs? After finishing? Did your feelings change? Explain.
6. Did you like this book? Why or why not?
7. What incidents or ideas reminded you of something in your own life?
8. What parts were confusing to you, if any? Why do you think they were confusing?
9. What opinion is being expressed by the writer? How do you know? Do you agree or disagree? Why?
10. Is the title appropriate or significant? Explain.
11. If you could change the ending of this story, how would you change it? Why?
12. Did you feel that there was more to tell in this book? If so, what do you think might happen next?

TEACHING POETRY LESSONS

On the basis of an extensive review of the literature, Shapiro (1985) has put together criterion statements and procedures for effective instruction in poetry.[20]

1. *Poetry should be presented in meaningful context.* It should be preceded by experiences that stimulate interest and promote involvement, although these need not be lengthy or elaborate. The teacher may help relate students' personal experiences to poems, provide questions to guide listening, introduce key words or phrases (not in drill form), or discuss the relationship of one poem to another poem, story, or event.

2. *Poetry should be orally interpreted by the teacher.* Because poetry as a form of literature expresses feelings, thoughts, and experiences by using concentrated, condensed language, it is often more difficult to read than prose. Rather than allowing readers to get bogged down in decoding or phrasing demands, it is recommended that poetry be read aloud to students. This means preparing ahead of time for oral interpretations, so that the teacher is able to combine the elements of "sound and sense" and internalize the full meaning before interpreting to others. When students read poetry to themselves, they should be encouraged to subvocalize in order to feel and hear the effects of the sounds of words.

3. *Poetry instruction should encourage active participation.* This will only be achieved satisfactorily when an atmosphere of acceptance is created in the classroom. Small-group, teacher-guided instruction gives the greatest

opportunity for student interaction, dialogue, and evaluative responses. In this way students can relate their responses to those of their peers without feeling vulnerable or compelled to verbalize.

4. *Poetry instruction should be an exploration of feelings, thoughts and ideas.* The teaching and learning of poetry should be an aesthetic experience, with emphasis on contemplation of the poem rather than on analysis of the text. The main purpose of discussion should be to provoke thought, not merely to check on comprehension or teach poetic techniques. Poetic understanding is extended when students are encouraged to relate poetry to their own experiential background. Overanalysis interferes with experiencing poetry. When mechanics are taught, they should be taught inductively, by having students generalize from exposure to many examples. This should occur only after meaningful experience with content.

5. *Poetry appreciation should be extended by providing opportunities to share the poetic experiences in interesting and meaningful ways.* Follow-up activities such as poetry writing, art, choral speaking, dramatics, and music will enhance student involvement. Writing serves as an extension of reading, helping students express inner feelings, encouraging self-awareness, and developing unique expressive ideas. This means avoiding the assignment of writing with a predetermined topic, which may be perceived as an academic rather than a creative endeavor. Using these various activities to relate poetry to other art forms can enrich student experiences while showing them that art, music, poetry, and dramatics are all interrelated.

Poetry: Using the Maze Technique

Prose means words in their best order, while *poetry* means the *best* words in the best order (McKenna, 1981).[21] The maze technique (Guthrie, 1974) is a good way to show students the poetic suitability of various words.[22] It involves placing selected words amid vertical arrays of distractors:

$$\text{The lengthy} \begin{cases} \text{flowers} \\ \text{delightful} \\ \text{shadows} \end{cases} \text{fell over the garden at sunset.}$$

The original word *shadows* must be selected from the distractors, *flowers*, which is the same part of speech, and *delightful*, which is semantically unacceptable.

When the distractors are all correct both semantically and syntactically, however, this is a much different task:

$$\text{The long light} \left\{ \begin{array}{l} \text{reflects} \\ \text{shakes across the lake. (Tennyson)} \\ \text{gleams} \end{array} \right.$$

Here, the one-syllable word is metrically appropriate. Also, one of the two distractors forms an internal rhyme (*shakes—lake*). As well as teaching rhyme and meter, the maze method can also be used to teach assonance, onomatopoeia, and plays on words.

Maze can be a powerful resource in teaching poetry because it underscores the importance of word selection, isolates elements of versification, stimulates discussion, encourages critical thinking, and provides a link between preassessment and instruction—all with great simplicity.

Taxonomy of Literary Understanding and Skills

When we look at poetry instruction objectives, we must consider sensory appeal, where readers are asked to choose words that best convey odor, feel, or sound; objectives that create similes or metaphors; those that personify words or create rhymes, alliteration, or assonance; and onomatopoeic words.

ACTIVITIES TO EXPAND READERS' BACKGROUND KNOWLEDGE

There are numerous things teachers can do to alert students to what they already know and to help them personalize reading.[23]

Before Reading

- Discuss experiences students may have had or concepts they may have learned that are connected or similar in some way to the topic.
- Preread a selected passage and ask students to predict what will occur next.
- Have available collateral reading on related topics.
- Select key words and ask students to free associate, recording responses around each word on the board.
- Select key words in context and tie them to students' past experiences.
- Use maps to pinpoint the location of stories or historical places.

- Assign certain students to be resident experts, changing experts with each chapter or unit.
- Use simulations like "you are there" scenarios to let students experience first-hand what they will be reading about.
- At all times, tie new information to what is already known.
- Ask: Have you ever felt that way? What questions would you ask? How would you compare this to _____?
- Have half the group or class adopt one point of view, the rest the opposite point of view.
- Ask them to visualize and draw a quick sketch, to be revised after reading if necessary.
- Display information in chart form.
- Ask students to be ready to act as tour guides through the text.

After Reading

- Ask chosen class experts to prepare a test. Ask others to help evaluate how apt the questions are for the text read.
- Have students fill in empty slots on charts with what they have learned.
- Help students see through discussion how the pieces fit together and form a whole.
- Ask pairs or triads of students to make five generalizations or select five main ideas from the reading.
- Encourage students to bring to class from home informational material related to what has been read.
- Have groups develop short stories into readers' theater scripts.

Readers' Theater Scripts

Readers' theater is an excellent means for developing oral interpretation, analysis, synthesis, and general study-reading and -writing skills. Although many scripts are already available for secondary students, it is beneficial, after experiencing one, for students to develop their own scripts. As with the use of scripts for the radio, this dramatization activity requires no memorizing of lines, no scenery, props, or costumes. Some high school classes have developed scripts based on well-known fairytales to deliver to young children.

METACOGNITION

Metacognition has now come of age. Although we have been interested in it for years, we did not label it as such. As early as 1917, the notion that comprehension is an active, constructive process was stated by Thorndike, who suggested that problems in comprehension might arise when readers do not treat the ideas they encounter in reading as merely provisional. If they did, readers would be able to inspect and welcome ideas or reflect on them as they read. Thorndike also stated that poor readers who need to say words in their heads without thinking about what the words mean are not testing their own understanding.

Metacognition has two parts: (1) reading for meaning (which can be called comprehension monitoring) and (2) reading to remember (which requires knowledge of selecting appropriate strategies, tasks, and goals).

General comprehension failures are influenced by the following:

1. Lack of sufficient knowledge about a topic, which limits the reader's ability to interpret the text because he has no appropriate schema with which to do so.
2. Failure of the author to provide enough clues to suggest an appropriate schema, or failure to convey ideas clearly.
3. Low reading ability, because poor readers consistently misinterpret the text or "understand" the text but not the author's intent. Such poor readers do not realize that their comprehension is faulty. Good readers who are unable to construct a coherent interpretation are, by contrast, more likely to try to clarify their understanding in such a situation.
4. Reading what the author intended without considering alternative viewpoints; believing whatever is read unquestioningly and uncritically.

Metacognition, or comprehension monitoring by sophisticated readers, is seldom a conscious experience. Brown (1980) states that skilled readers can be said to be operating with a lazy processor, as most skills are on automatic pilot. When a comprehension failure occurs, it triggers these skills, and the reader slows down to allow for extra processing of the problem area. These debugging devices and strategies take time and effort.[24]

To stretch the point a bit and use some visual imagery, think of a train running smoothly and rapidly down a straight, level track. All lights have been green, and the correct switches have been thrown. Now suddenly the engineer realizes that he has missed a switchover, that he is no longer on the main track but is heading off on a tangent from his goal on a trunk line. He immediately slows the train to a grinding halt and then advances slowly as he checks for a way to rejoin the main track. If this is not possible, he must painstakingly backtrack to the missed switchover, analyze the situation, and probe for reasons that this occurred so it won't happen again, especially when a wrong track could mean a head-on collision. An unobservant engineer might well continue on the wrong track until confronted with the irrefutable evidence (e.g., a station sign) that he is misdirected. He is less likely to be able to explain what happened than is the engineer who retraced his steps and analyzed the situation. Readers get off the track, too. When they do, it is important that they realize it in time and have some idea of how to correct the situation efficiently.

Metacognition and Reading

The process of learning from written materials is incredibly complex.[25] There are four major aspects to consider, each with a large variety of subtopics:

1. The task itself, or end point (exercise, test, report, problem solving, experiment).
2. The nature of the reading material (narrative, exposition, directions, graphics).
3. The characteristics of the readers (their prior knowledge, background experiences, abilities, interest, motivation).
4. The learner activities (their tactics and strategies for successful learning).

As mentioned earlier, the term *metacognition* refers to a high-level process and has a two-pronged definition. First, it relates to our knowledge of our own cognition, our abilities and the variety of strategies we use to meet the task demands of the text. Second, it relates to the self-regulatory mechanisms we use while reading, including planning our next move, checking the effectiveness of the strategies we use, monitoring, testing, revising, and evaluating.[26]

Unfortunately, many students are not taught how to become active readers in control of their own destinies. They are not told why, when, where, and how to use a strategy, but are just given the *what*—the facts—without understanding their application. As a result, most students are dependent learners.

Metacognitive Script

Using a metacognitive script (a process of thinking aloud) we can begin to help students see what mature readers do when reading. Students have a copy of the text in front of them so they can follow along. One of the areas with which we can help them overtly is knowing what the task demands. Reading a script of our inner thoughts, we could say something like, "I'm going to be expected to write a reaction to this story, so I had better pay attention to my thoughts and feelings as I read. I might even need to take a few notes as I go." Next, we might point out the nature of the writing. "Let's see, this short story should fit into what I already know about story schemas and story grammar. I think I'll use one of our chart forms as I go along to fill in the pieces."

To activate prior knowledge, interests, and so forth about the topic, we could continue: "Now, let me think for a minute, what do I already know about this (locale, time in history, problem, etc.)? Ah yes, I know a friend who has had to deal with a similar problem. Maybe the solution here might help her. I can remember my trip to that part of the country. . . ."

Now, reading aloud the actual short story with the students following along in their own copies, we could make interspersed remarks such as, "I need to have a clearer image of this main character, how he looks and what his traits are. Besides being tall and strong, I think I'll have him look a bit like _____. When he behaves this way, it makes me think he is being a bit too daring. . . . Now I'm not really understanding the point of this part, so I had better stop right here and look back to see how it might be related to what I just read. No, that didn't help, I'll just continue and make a mental note to clear it up after the reading. . . . Here's a word I should know—I'll read to the end of the sentence to see if the context helps me. No, not really. Can I break it up into meaningful parts? No. I'll have to resort to the glossary after I read. I'll just jot it down now so I won't forget."

Metacognitive Monitoring and Awareness

Platt (1987) has put together handy examples for metacognitive monitoring and awareness. Table 6.4 on metacognitive monitoring is adapted from her list.[27]

Checklist of Awareness of Reading Behaviors

Students should check appropriate items as to their own reading behaviors.

1. Distracted:
   - Mind wanders, daydreams
   - Has trouble concentrating
   - Responds to noise or quiet

TABLE 6.4
Metacognitive Monitoring

1. To focus on details	Names, quotes, places, facts, noting similarities, differences, distinguishing between twins
2. To tie to previous experience	Think about how own experiences compare, relate new to known
3. To adjust rate	Snail's pace to skimming
4. To read with emotion	Note feelings about readings (surprise, fear, anxiety, disbelief, skepticism, curiosity, interest, empathy, appreciation)
5. To read for gist	Main idea, skip details, generalities
6. To reread	Check understanding, enjoy description, ponder significance
7. To interpret graphics	Connect ideas to text
8. To formulate questions	Figure out question writer is trying to answer
9. To review	Think back to key point, go over significance, repeat or recite information to oneself, take notes
10. To concentrate/attend	Keep mind on meaning, read carefully and thoughtfully
11. To remember/memorize	Decide what must be recalled, go over and over to memorize

Source: Adapted from "The Metacognitive Performance of College Students in Reading: Implications for Instruction" by Jennifer J. Platt, in *Changing Conceptions of Reading: Literacy Learning Instruction,* Seventh Yearbook of the American Reading Forum (1987), pp. 56–58.

2. Reason for rereading:
   - Doesn't understand message
   - Doesn't understand words, sentences, or paragraphs
   - Eyes regress automatically
3. Comprehending
   - Knowing content or not
   - Understanding meaning or not
4. Personalizing:
   - Empathizing with the character or situation
   - Associating with past experiences
   - Becoming emotionaliy involved with the content

5. Reading habits:
   • Word by word, not by thought units
   • Same rate regardless of purpose
   • Subvocalizing

SUSTAINED SILENT READING

We have accomplished little if we teach our students how to read but not how to value reading. It is also true that we improve our reading by reading. A total school program of sustained silent reading (SSR) can do much for students who are unmotivated or need more easy practice in reading. Take, for example, a local high school in the Northwest that inaugurated a total school reading program three days a week for 30 minutes. Everyone, from administrators and teachers to students and kitchen staff, stopped at the bell, picked up a recreational reading book (not a magazine or newspaper), and read without interruption.

To get this program started, the staff collected old books and paperbacks over the summer and sorted them for distribution to different content-area classrooms. Thus, every room had a backup of recreational books for those students who forgot to bring one with them.

The rules for SSR are simple. Everyone does it. There are no interruptions, no walking around. Full-length books are used. No questions are asked. There is no accountability for later recall, and everyone should find something he or she enjoys reading. Sessions may last around 20 minutes of uninterrupted silent reading. Try it, it really does work!

SHAKESPEARE AS IT COULD BE TAUGHT

Rosenfeld (1987), a humanities teacher, described a successful program in bringing to life not only the Elizabethan period, but also Shakespeare's poetry and plays.[28] Together with a colleague, she planned and executed a student-centered learning program that included films, music, art projects, reading, writing and a few minilectures. The discussion here is adapted with permission from "An Elizabethan Interlude: A Course for Middle Schoolers" by Judith B. Rosenfeld, *English Journal*, December 1989, copyright © by The National Council of Teachers of English.

As a prelude to reading Shakespeare, the teachers used the following materials with their classes:

1. Elizabeth Marie Pope, *The Perilous Gard* (New York: Ace, 1986). A Newbery Honor Book. A rich source for studying language arts and literature with a lead-in to *A Midsummer Night's Dream*.

2. C. Walter Hodges, *The Battlement Garden: Britain from the War of the Roses to the Age of Shakespeare* (New York: Clarion, 1980). For a historical setting.
3. Barbara Holdridge, ed., *Under the Greenwood Tree: Poems of Shakespeare for the Young* (Owings Hill, MD: Stemmor House, 1986). This is a poetry collection ingeniously arranged according to the "seven stages of man."
4. Leon Garfield, *Shakespeare Stories* (New York: Schocken, 1983). Beautifully told prose versions of twelve plays.
5. Films:
   a. *Lady Jane:* On Elizabethan life and Lady Jane, viewing the period through the lives of two teenage lovers; giving readers a knowledge of costume, travel, food, and religion
   b. Zeffirelli's *Romeo and Juliet:* A beautiful and poignant film
   c. *Elizabeth, the Cub,* with Glenda Jackson: To learn about politics and the royal succession
   d. Short films about the Globe Theatre and Shakespeare's life
   e. *The Invention of the Adolescent:* Comparing young people's lives then and now
   f. *McCauley's Castle:* From the book by David McCauley

Students were asked what they wanted to know about Elizabeth I, Shakespeare, England in the sixteenth century, and the Age of Exploration and Discovery. Students then researched their chosen topic in the library to prepare an oral report for the class. At the same time they read together the "All the World's a Stage" selection. In triads they discussed what they thought Shakespeare was saying and designed a class presentation, miming, or a choral or individual reading.

The next day, Sonnet 29, "When in disgrace with fortune and men's eyes" was read. Students wrote telegrams of the basic message of the sonnet to someone they knew in ten words or fewer on yellow paper with black felt pens. Each day, half the period was spent working in the library. By the second week, reports were given. A local actor came and presented a reading and an enactment of scenes from *Macbeth* ("Is this a dagger that I see before me . . .")

They then read the "Winter's Poem" from *Love's Labour Lost,* and wrote their own winter poems, using borders found in the artwork of the Stemmer book illustrations. Next came *The Perilous Gard,* and here they learned the "Ballad of Tam Lin," a tale of daring, described in the book. After locating the complete ballad, they wrote as a class "The Ballad of the Perilous Gard" in the same style. They also wrote journal entries for two characters in *The Perilous Gard,* and drew pictures of their interpretation of the castle and the underworld. The novel was taught by bringing the readers into the book and the characters and ideas into the students' lives. This was done by discussing how it feels to be falsely accused, what it is like for people who always win, and what weak points, if any, such people have.

For fifteen minutes a day, the teachers lectured from Hodge's book on farming, the church, and Henry VIII's manipulations of the world.

On Valentine's Day the classes read the *Romeo and Juliet* poetry in *Under the Greenwood Tree* as well as Garfield's prose version of the play. The students made valentines using Shakespeare's love poetry and using glitter, doilies, colorful pens, and markers.

Next came the line-by-line reading of *A Midsummer Night's Dream,* acting out the mismatch of lovers. Students voiced in their own words the complaints of Lysander, Hermia, and Demetrius. They enjoyed the fun of rephrasing the lines in modern vernacular. Halfway through the reading of the play, there was a ten-minute in-class writing assignment. Each student wrote freely about love and how love was represented in the play. After sharing these ideas orally, they wrote a paper on Shakespeare's view of love as represented in the play.

After they attended a production of *Love's Labour Lost* at a nearby university, the point was made again that Shakespeare is best when seen and acted, which is what the playwright intended, of course.

A final activity was an evening of sharing, "An Elizabethan Interlude," which took six to seven periods of planning. Recipes were located, masks created, and a group dance learned. One class became characters in a "wax museum" to present information they had gathered. The other class became doctors, teachers, or scientists and talked about their learning. Some presented dramatic readings, and others sang and danced to Elizabethan music, accompanied by students playing instruments. They began with Sonnet 18, "Shall I compare thee to a summer's day?" and ended with Puck's apology.

Students' evaluation of their learning experiences was most positive. There had been no memorizing, no scanning, no testing of dates—just language, ideas, total involvement. (As a footnote, my student typist remarked to me when she finished reading the rough draft of this section that she wished her own English teachers had made Shakespeare so fascinating and dynamic.)

GLOSSING AS AN ADJUNCT AID

The process of *glossing,* often referred to as *marginal gloss,* is similar in many ways to metacognitive script, but the differences make it another valuable study-reading tool.

In metacognitive script, we share with the class, orally and informally, our inner thoughts, miscues, predictions, and strategies. Gloss, on the other hand, is more formal, written as an adjunct aid to be used only when students need it to become more independent, successful readers. Gloss can also be a handy permanent record for future reference.

The original glossses were in the form of illustrations found in the margins of ancient manuscripts. Later gloss became a form of study guide, often printed in a different color, to define terms, give background information, tell readers something, or merely ask them questions.

Otto and associates (1981) developed the notion that gloss could serve as a silent teacher, explaining processes and showing readers which strategies to use and why.[29] Glosses can be written in several stages: model (demonstrate), develop (practice), and internalize and fade.

The first stage is the most difficult to construct because it teaches *how* rather than just telling students to do something. In the model gloss stage, reasons are given. The idea is always that what we explain here will transfer later. If a question is asked at this stage, it is answered immediately.

The second stage develops and allows the practice of strategies or skills taught in stage 1. For example, if a main idea is to be located in the second stage, readers can be referred back to a specific numbered bracket that explains it for them.

In the final stage, internalizing and fading, only brief reminders are given. The idea throughout is to be developing independent learners.

Table 6.5 shows a sample gloss of the poem "We Wear the Mask" by Paul Lawrence Dunbar. Note that the text is on the left side, which means the gloss sheet will be slipped under the page just to the center line and will be lined up with the top and bottom of the text page, so that the brackets enclose the exact portion of the text to be processed. Brackets are numbered consecutively throughout the work or chapter.

To use gloss with your students, first decide your content goals or what is important for them to learn. Next, think about their ability to handle the material. What skills and strategies will they need? Skim-read the material to note difficult areas, key concepts, special vocabulary, and the like. Then decide what skills, strategies, and processes you can help them with. At this point you are ready to gloss.

Remember that gloss is a crutch and should be removed when it is no longer needed. Perhaps only one chapter, one story, or one poem will be glossed. After students have used this tool, they will benefit from working in small groups to produce a gloss for future students.

SUMMARY

Comprehending descriptive, narrative, and imaginary prose, although it occurs most often in English classes, can also be a part of other subject areas

TABLE 6.5
Model Gloss (Step One)

Poem (text)	Gloss of Poem
We Wear the Mask by Paul Lawrence Dunbar	**1** *Mask* is a symbol here. We can tell this as we read on, that we do not literally wear a cloth mask. We pick up this meaning from the context of the rest of the poem.

We wear the mask
  that grins and lies
It hides our cheeks
  and shades our eyes—
	2 Who are *we*? You might speculate that *we* stands for people trying to hide something—their faces or feelings.

This debt we pay to human guile With torn and bleeding hearts we smile	**3** *Guile* means trickery here. If you cannot determine meaning from the context here, it would be necessary to look it up in the glossary or dictionary.
And mouth with myriad subtleties	**4** *Mouth* and *myriad* are examples of alliteration, each starting with the letter *m*. Alliteration sometimes helps to emphasize something.
Why should the world be over-wise in counting all our tears and sighs? Nay, let them see us while we wear the mask.	**5** We can learn much about those who hide feelings, such as their possible motivations for doing so. Haven't you hidden some feelings at times when you were afraid and didn't want anyone to know it, or sad and didn't want to cry in public? Think about how you felt and try to empathize with the author
We smile, but O great Christ, our cries To thee from tortured souls arise. We sing, but oh, the clay is vile. Beneath our feet, and long the miles, But let the world dream otherwise, We wear the mask.	**6** *Vile* means extremely unpleasant—which you might pick up again from the context here. When you see a new word, try to figure out first what you think it means.

Source: "We Wear the Mask" by Paul Lawrence Dunbar, from *The Complete Poems of Paul Lawrence Dunbar.* Copyright © 1913 by Dodd, Mead.

Something to ponder: In terms of background, the poet is black. How might this affect the meaning here? We might decide that he is speaking mostly for the downtrodden, particularly the blacks of the era in which Dunbar lived. This is why it is often important to know about the poet's life, as it may help you to read between the lines.

when collateral reading is required for enrichment. It is important when reading fiction to be familiar with the genre—the story components, purposes, and interrelationships—called a story schema. Story grammars, like schemata, are frameworks, but here they show direct relationships among parts, how each fits together with the others. Barrett developed a taxonomy of reading comprehension based on Bloom, in which appreciation is added as the highest level. Reading for adolescents/young adults is influenced by a variety of characteristics at different age groups. General aids for teaching include questions for summarizing narrative, rhetorical devices for identifying authors, reaction guides, the use of charts and taxonomies, response journals, the teaching of poetry and Shakespeare, the expansion of background knowledge, and readers' theater. Metacognitive script and glossing were also described.

NOTES

1. Louise M. Rosenblatt, "A Way of Happening," *Educational Record*, 49 (1968), 339–346.

2. Ibid., p. 341.

3. Mortimer J. Adler and Charles Von Doren, *How to Read a Book*, 2nd ed. (New York: Simon and Schuster, 1972), p. 246.

4. William F. Brewer, "Literary Theory, Rhetoric, and Stylistics: Implications for Psychology," in Rand J. Spiro, Bertram C. Bruce, and William F. Brewer, eds., *Theoretical Issues in Reading Comprehension* (Hillsdale, NJ: Erlbaum, 1980), p. 224.

5. Marcel Just and Patricia Carpenter, *The Psychology of Reading and Language Comprehension* (Newton, MA: Allyn and Bcon, 1987), pp. 227–235.

6. Ibid., p. 232.

7. T. Nezworski, N. L. Stein, and T. Trabasso, "Story Structure versus Content in Children's Recall," *Journal of Verbal Learning and Verbal Behavior*, 21 (1982), 197.

8. Just and Carpenter, *Psychology of Reading*, p. 246.

9. Adler and Van Doren, *How to Read a Book*, p. 208.

10. Ibid., p. 211.

11. C. Cooper and A. Purves, *A Guide to Evaluation* (Lexington, MA: Ginn and Company, 1973).

12. David L. Shepherd, *Comprehensive High School Reading Methods*, 3rd ed. (Columbus, OH: Charles E. Merrill, 1982).

13. Theodore Clymer, "What Is Reading? Some Current Concepts" in Helen Robinson, ed., *Innovation and Change in Reading Instruction*, Sixty-seventh Yearbook of the National Society for the Study of Education, Part II, Vol. 67 (Chicago: University of Chicago Press, 1968, pp. 19–23).

14. James Moffett and Betty Jane Wagner, *Student-Centered Language Arts and Reading K–13: A Handbook for Teachers*, 3rd ed. (Boston: Houghton Mifflin, 1983).

15. Richard Beach and Deborah Appleman, "Reading Strategies for Expository and Literary Text Types," in Alan C. Purves and Olive Niles, eds., *Becoming Readers in a Complex Society*, Eighty-third Yearbook of the National Society for the Study of Education (Chicago: University of Chicago Press, 1984), pp. 115–143.

16. Harry Singer and Dan Donlan, "Active Comprehension: Problem-Solving Schema with Question Generation for Comprehension of Complex Short Stories," *Reading Research Quarterly*, 17 (1982), 166–187.

17. John D. McNeil, *Reading Comprehension: New Directions for Classroom Practice*, 2nd ed. (Glenview, IL: Scott, Foresman, 1987).

18. David Moore, Sharon Moore, James Cunningham, and Patricia Cunningham, *Developing Readers and Writers in the Content Areas: K–12* (New York: Longman, 1986).

19. George Hillocks, Jr., and Larry H. Ludlow, "A Taxonomy of Skills in Reading and Interpreting Fiction," *American Educational Research Journal*, 21 (Spring 1984), 7–24.

20. Sheila Shapiro, "An Analysis of Poetry Teaching Procedures in Sixth-Grade Basal Manuals," *Reading Research Quarterly*, 3 (Spring 1985), 368–381.

21. Michael C. McKenna. "A Modified Maze Approach to Teaching Poetry," *Journal of Reading*, 24 (February 1981), 391.

22. John T. Guthrie et al., "The Maze Technique to Assess, Monitor Reading Comprehension," *The Reading Teacher*, 28 (November 1974), 161–168.

23. Robert J. Tierney et al., "The Metcalf Project: A Teacher-Researcher Collaboration," in S. Jay Samuels and P. David Pearson, eds., *Programs: Principles and Case Studies* (Newark, DE: International Reading Association, 1988), pp. 206–226.

24. Ann L. Brown, "Metacognitive Development and Reading," in Rand J. Spiro, Bertram C. Bruce, and William F. Brewer, eds., *Theoretical Issues in Reading Comprehension* (Hillsdale, NJ: Lawrence Erlbaum, 1980), pp. 453–481.

25. Bonnie B. Armbruster and Ann L. Brown, "Learning from Reading: The Role of Metacognition," in Richard C. Anderson, Jean Osborn, and Robert J. Tierney, eds., *Learning to Read in American Schools* (Hillsdale, NY: Erlbaum, 1984), p. 273.

26. Ibid., p. 274.

27. Jennifer J. Platt, "The Metacognitive Performance of College Students in Reading: Implications for Instruction," in *Changing Conceptions of Reading: Literacy Learning Instruction*, Seventh Yearbook of the American Reading Forum (Sarasota, FL: American Reading Forum, 1987), pp. 56–58.

28. Judith B. Rosenfeld, "An Elizabethan Interlude: A Course for Middle Schoolers," *English Journal*, 76 (December 1987), 49–51.

29. Wayne Otto et al., *A Technique for Improving and Understanding of Expository Text: Gloss, Part I. Part II, Examples of Gloss Notation* (Madison, WI: Research Development Center for Individualized Schooling, 1981).

RECOMMENDED READINGS

Andrews, L. "Responses to Literature: In Tennis the Serve Is Crucial." *English Journal*, 63 (2, February 1974), 44–46.

Applebee, Arthur N. *The Child's Concept of Story, Ages Two to Seventeen*. Chicago: University of Chicago Press, 1978.

Bruce, Bertram. "Stories within Stories." *Language Arts*, 58 (November–December 1981), 931–935.

Carey, Robert F. "The Reader, the Text, the Response: Literary Theory and Reading Research." *English Quarterly*, 18 (Fall 1985), 17–23.

Cline, Ruth K. J., and Kretke, George L. "An Evaluation of Long-Term SSR in the Junior High School." *Journal of Reading*, 23 (March 1980), 503–506.

Devine, T. "Poetry in the English Class." *Connecticut English Journal*, 70 (1, January 1981), 39–45.

Dilworth, C. "The Reader as Poet: A Strategy for Creative Reading." *English Journal*, 66 (1977), 43–47.

Fillion, B. "Reading as Inquiry: An Approach to Literature Learning." *English Journal*, 70 (1, 1981), 39–45.

Gambrell, Linda B., and Bales, Ruby J. "Mental Imagery and the Comprehension-Monitoring Performance of Fourth and Fifth Grade Poor Readers." *Reading Research Quarterly*, 21 (Fall 1986), 454–464.

Giesen, C., and Peeck, J. "Effects of Imagery Instruction on Reading and Retaining a Literary Text." *Journal of Mental Imagery*, 2 (1984), 79–90.

Harris, Raymond. *Best Selling Chapters: Fifteen Novels for Teaching Literature and Developing Comprehension*. Providence, RI: Jamestown Publishers, 1979.

Lindberg, Barbara. "Teaching Literature: The Process Approach." *Journal of Reading*, 31 (May 1988), 734–735.

Mandler, J. M., and Johnson, N. S. "Remembrance of Things Parsed: Story Structure and Recall." *Cognitive Psychology,* 9 (1977), 111–151.

Marshall, Nancy. "Using Story Grammar to Assess Reading Comprehension." *The Reading Teacher,* 36 (March 1983), 616–620.

McKenna, Michael C. "A Modified Maze Approach to Teaching Poetry." *Journal of Reading,* 24 (February 1981), 391–394.

Minton, Marilyn Joy. "The Effect of Sustained Silent Reading upon Comprehension and Attitudes among Ninth Graders." *Journal of Reading,* 23 (March 1980), 498–502.

Pairio, A. "The Mind's Eye in Arts and Science." *Poetics,* 12 (1983), 1–18.

Pearson, P. David, and Johnson, Dale D. *Teaching Reading Comprehension.* New York: Holt, Rinehart and Winston, 1978.

Peters, E. E., and Levin, J. R. "Effects of a Mnemonic Imagery Strategy on Good and Poor Readers' Prose Recall." *Reading Research Quarterly,* 21 (1986), 161–178.

Phillips, T. "Poetry in the Junior High School." *English in Education,* 5 (1971), 51–62.

Probst, Robert. "Transactional Theory in the Teaching of Literature." *Journal of Reading,* 31 (January 1988), 378–381.

Richgels, D. J., and Hansen, R. "Gloss: Helping Students Apply Both Skills and Strategies in Reading Content Texts." *Journal of Reading,* 27 (1984), 312–317.

Richgels, D. J., and Mateja, J. A. "Gloss II: Integrating Content and Process for Independence." *Journal of Reading,* 27, 424–431.

Rosenblatt, Louise M. *The Reader, the Text, the Poem: The Transactional Theory of the Literary Work.* Carbondale: Southern Illinois University Press, 1978.

Sadoski, M. "The Natural Use of Imagery in Story Comprehension and Recall: Replication and Extension." *Reading Research Quarterly,* 20 (1985), 658–667.

Tonjes, Marian J. "Metacognitive Modeling and Glossing: Two Powerful Ways to Teach Self-Responsibility." In Christine Anderson, ed., *Reading: The ABC's and Beyond.* London: Macmillan, 1988.

Webb, Agnes. "Transactions with Literary Texts: Conversations in Classrooms." *English Journal,* 71 (March 1982), 56–60.

Postorganizer 1
Creative Elaboration or Evaluation of the Chapter

Reading literary works and reacting to them should be a pleasurable activity for all. Think about key aspects of this chapter, such as story grammar, the reading of imaginative literature, novels for adolescents, reaction guides, and the like. Select one area and be creative in elaborating on it or evaluating it, using other means than just reporting to get your point across. For instance, you might construct an artistic presentation, a collage, a dramatization, a musical, a poem, or a game. Be ready to share these at a later time designated by your instructor. The idea is to have fun and at the same time to be creative.

Postorganizer 2
Evaluating Novels

Select a novel for adolescents and a familiar adult novel. Using Barrett's taxonomy outline and the full description in the appendix, evaluate each novel and compare and contrast findings. How are they alike? How different?

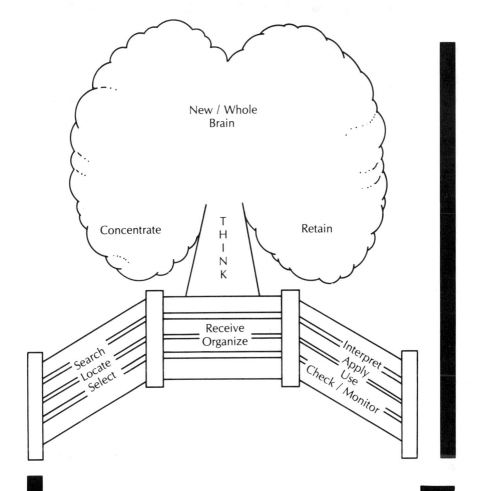

New / Whole
Brain

Concentrate

T
H
I
N
K

Retain

Receive
Organize

Search
Locate
Select

Interpret
Apply
Use
Check / Monitor

7

Study-Learning:
Part I

CHAPTER OUTLINE

Preorganizers
Introduction
Definitions and Distinctions
  Study-Reading
  Study-Learning
  Study-Monitoring
Scope and Sequence Outline for Study-Learning
Study-Learning Foundations: The Brain
  "New" Brain Theory
  Whole-Brain Activities and Learning Styles
  Brain-Compatible Learning
  Brain Growth Spurts
  Brain Aerobics
  A Future Forecast of Brain Language
Concentration and Retention
  Short-Term versus Long-Term Memory
  Mnemonic Devices
  What We Can Learn from History
  Memorizing Today: Some Personal Reminscences
  Super-Learning
Skills and Strategies Framework with Activities
  I. Search and Locate Information, Select Appropriate Resources
  II. Receive and Organize Information
  III. Interpret/Apply/Use/Check Information
Summary for Part I
Notes
Recommended Readings for Chapters 7 and 8

COGNITIVE COMPETENCIES

1. *Summarize* the total concept of study-learning in one paragraph.

2. *Develop* mini lesson plans in your subject that are based on brain-compatible and super-learning.

3. *Create* several mnemonic devices to assist students in your subject.

4. *Write* a five-minute lecture for students on using book parts in their text.

5. *Compare* two kinds of outlines given in terms of applicability to your subject.

KEY TERMS

learning styles
mnemonic devices
"new" brain theory/brain
   language, whole brain
scope and sequence for study-
   learning

short-term/long-term memory
study-reading/study-learning/
   study-monitoring
super learning

Preorganizer 1
Summaries

a. Decide before reading that you will be able to summarize this chapter in your own words. Try to limit your summary to one brief paragraph consisting of generalizations.

b. As an alternative to a written summary, decide before reading that you will be able to summarize major points by drawing a graphic or cognitive map showing relationships. This should differ from the one at the beginning of the chapter. (See Chapter 5 for further explanation of mapping.)

c. Discuss your rough draft of either a or b with a partner and combine ideas into a final draft. Tape this to the board for whole-class comparison and discussion, or make one master cognitive map to display during discussion.

Preorganizer 2
Experiment with Background Baroque

Before starting to read this chapter, put on a tape or record of Baroque music, such as Bach, which has a definite mathematical slow beat of about one beat per second (similar to a heartbeat at rest). Do not use rock music. Keep the music soft enough to serve as background to eliminate other possible auditory distractions. As you come to key points, stop and recite them to the beat of the music. Review the chapter to try to ascertain if you have remembered more than usual.

Preorganizer 3
Study-Learning Checklist

Before reading this chapter, check what you actually do now when studying for retention and retrieval. After reading, check those items that you plan to do in the future. This checklist or a similar one may be useful to your students. It is intended to help you tie in the information in this chapter you are about to read with your own background knowledge.

The checklist is adapted from Bernice Jensen Bragstad and Sharyn Mueller Stumpf, *A Guidebook for Teaching Study Skills and Motivation*, 2nd edition, p. 237, copyright © 1987 by Allyn and Bacon. Used with permission.[1]

Study-Learning Checklist

Before reading this chapter   *After reading it*
When studying do you:

_____   1. Seriously try to become interested in the topic?   _____

_____   2. Consciously intend to remember the information?   _____

_____   3. Feel confident you will remember?   _____

_____   4. Give your undivided attention to the reading?   _____

_____   5. Keep an open mind to new ideas?   _____

_____   6. Look for the way ideas are organized, using   _____
                  headings, summaries, and so on?

_____   7. Make sure that you accurately understand the   _____
                  material in the first place?

_____   8. Recite key points from memory (quiz yourself)   _____
                  immediately after reading a section?

_____   9. Review class notes and reading at least once a   _____
                  week?

_____   10. Use several ways to reinforce study learning   _____
                  such as note-taking, discussing with peers, or
                  reciting aloud?

_____   11. Relate what you are learning to what you already   _____
                  know?

_____   12. Use mnemonics to memorize and recall lists of   _____
                  items?

_____   13. Alternate studying similar kinds of subjects to   _____
                  avoid interference and forgetting? (e.g., Spanish
                  and French or French and math)

_____   14. Keep learning at peak levels by taking short   _____
                  breaks every 40 or 50 minutes?

_____   15. Organize your study time effectively for max-   _____
                  imum efficiency?

_____   16. Continually adapt your rate according to your   _____
                  purpose and text difficulty?

_____ 17. Outline a paper before writing and write from _____
your outline?

_____ 18. Write rough drafts of all research papers and _____
reports?

_____ 19. Seek out criticism of rough drafts for _____
improvement?

_____ 20. Use classical (Baroque) music or no music as _____
background when studying?

_____ 21. Use good test preparation techniques? _____

_____ 22. Consciously evaluate your own learning as you _____
go?

7
Study-Learning:
Part I

INTRODUCTION

Secondary students who have already developed good study habits will learn more and spend less time studying. From the intermediate grades on, students are required to do much study-reading as well as study-learning. Yet unfortunately, they are often not taught directly how best to accomplish this. In study-reading they should be acquiring information through careful reading of expository or literary text. On the other hand, in study-learning they need to concentrate on organizing, retaining, and retrieving needed information, not just acquiring it.

Thomas and Moorman (1983) discuss why study-reading and -learning skills are not regularly taught. They blame first of all those commercial reading programs that either neglect direct teaching of these skills or fail to teach for transfer to real-life learning tasks.[2] Overburdened elementary school teachers may hope that secondary teachers will deal with this, whereas secondary teachers may well assume their students have already been taught how to read and study in order to learn. It is a classic Catch-22 situation.

DEFINITIONS AND DISTINCTIONS

The underpinnings of becoming educated include the ability to read, think, study, and monitor what we are engaged in.

Study-Reading

This includes comprehension monitoring of difficulty levels and potential problems, interpreting words, discerning text organization, following written directions, adapting rate to purpose, and creating interest. It could be argued that some reading generally takes place in the category of study-learning, so these divisions are sometimes arbitrary.

Study-Learning

This includes thinking/learning skills and strategies that enhance the ability to search, locate, and select appropriate information; receive and organize it; and interpret, apply, use, and check it (see Table 7.1).

In actual practice, we generally move back and forth between categories—sometimes almost simultaneously—searching, locating, and selecting sources; receiving—orally or in writing—needed information; organizing and interpreting it (or vice versa); referring to directions, monitoring our own understanding and retention; adapting our rate, using good time management; and producing a final product to evaluate how well we have done, which may be in the form of a test, written or oral report, or paper.

Study-Monitoring

Study-monitoring is similar to comprehension monitoring (watching how well we are understanding). However, study-monitoring requires a split or double focus.[3] This means attending to the material itself in order to learn it, while at the same time checking to see whether the mental operations we select are indeed producing the desired learning. It is a process of

TABLE 7.1
A Sample Comparison of Study-Reading and Study-Learning Skills

Study-Reading Skills	Study-Learning Skills
Monitor comprehension.	Monitor study.
Interpret words in context.	Locate information.
Discern text organizational patterns.	Organize information in writing.
Follow directions.	Interpret graphics.
Use general study-reading/learning strategies.	Use general study-reading/learning strategies.

comprehending plus learning. We must not only concentrate on main ideas while reading or listening but also select and use a tactic to induce learning and then evaluate the effectiveness of the tactic we selected.

SCOPE AND SEQUENCE OUTLINE FOR STUDY-LEARNING

A scope and sequence outline for study-learning skills and strategies follows. You may find it helpful to use this as a reference point to refer back to when reading about each item.

 I. *Search* and *locate* information, *select* appropriate sources:
   A. Alphabetical order
   B. Book parts
   C. General and specific references
   D. School library
 II. *Receive* and *organize* information:
   A. Listen
   B. Outline—formal and informal
   C. Note-take and summarize—lectures and text
III. *Interpret/apply/use/check/monitor* information:
   A. Interpret graphics
   B. Use time management
   C. Prepare for and take tests
   D. Write research papers, reports
   E. Participate in speech-making, discussions, debates
   F. Select and practice general study-learning strategies

After a brief discussion of theoretical foundations for study-learning, which includes how the mind works, new brain theory, concentration and retention, and super-learning, we will look more closely at each item on this scope and sequence outline.

STUDY-LEARNING FOUNDATIONS: THE BRAIN

"New" Brain Theory

We have heard much in the last few years about the left brain and the right brain, brain-compatible teaching and learning, and even brain language. In 1977 Ornstein listed aspects of the left and right hemispheres of the brain (see Table 7.2).[4]

TABLE 7.2
Specialized Halves of the Brain in Most Right-Handed People

Left Hemisphere	versus	Right Hemisphere
Intellectual		Intuitive
Analytic		Synthetic
Linear		Holistic
Verbal		Nonverbal
Sequential		Simultaneous
Temporal		Spatial
Digital		Analogical
Explicit		Implicit
Literal		Metaphorical

Source: Reprinted with permission from *The Psychology of Consciousness,* 2nd edition, by Robert Ornstein (New York: Harcourt Brace Jovanovich, 1977).

A simple and enjoyable test for determining left or right "brain-ness" is to close your eyes and fold your hands. If you naturally put your right thumb *over* your left then you are said to be right brained and vice versa. One way should feel very *un*natural!

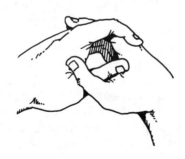

Recently, however, considerable doubt has been cast on the practice of delegating all knowledge to only one hemisphere of the brain.[5] Cherry and Cherry (1985) reported in the *New York Times* that recent neuroscientific advances have come about because of the plethora of information on how mental processing occurs.[6] Now we seem to have moved toward the notion of appealing to the whole brain.[7] In the past, schools have been noted for relying mainly on so-called left-brain types of skills—verbal, analytical, and reductionist—as opposed to right-brain activities—holistic thinking, intuition, visual imagery, and synthesis. According to Gray (1980), functions of the brain complement and temper each other and are not independent.[8] We should be combining aspects of both into our classroom learning activities.

Whole-Brain Activities and Learning Styles

It has also been suggested by Luvass-Briggs (1984) that we can facilitate learning by considering whole-brain activities and cognitive learning styles.[9] According to McCarthy (1980), there are four equally valuable learning styles.[10] If we use the mnemonic device of acronyms for recalling lists, these learning styles can be remembered as ACID: (1) analytic (2) commonsense, (3) innovative, and (4) dynamic. Which is your basic style?

Examples of activities that tie in the whole brain with these varied learning styles include the following:

1. *Visual imagery:* While the teacher reads aloud a descriptive passage containing some unknown words, students are told to imagine the person, place, or thing. When they have a clear mental picture, they describe their image to the class and speculate from descriptions of unfamiliar words.

2. *Pictorial representations:* After working on a list of unknown words in context (in a phrase or sentence) divide the class into small groups and distribute magazines such as *National Geographic, Time,* and *Good Housekeeping.* The students' task is to find pictures representing their words; then have the class guess which word on the list each picture represents.

3. *Photographs and paintings:* From magazines such as *Life, Town and Country, Travel and Leisure,* or *Country,* make photocopies of pictures and photographs. In small groups, students determine the main idea and make inferences based on each picture.

4. *Dramatization:* Select one or two words to be acted out in pantomime, skit, or charades. When they have been guessed correctly, brainstorm possible synonyms.

5. *Cognitive mapping:* After reading a chapter or article, students discuss main ideas and supporting details, which may then be listed on the board. Groups use large sheets of paper and markers to construct a cognitive map or graphic organizer of these main points and details. These maps are then hung on the wall and compared for accuracy, wholeness, likenesses, and differences. Maps may be playful—for example, drawn in the shape of the topic (see the section on comprehension of expository material for further information).

Brain-Compatible Learning

Hart (1975) defines *learning* as "the accommodation of facts to what is already known."[11] He believes that the brain is held together by a program structure—mostly conscious—and is capable of carrying on a large amount of program structuring simultaneously. For example, we do not consciously think about how to put on our clothes or drive to the store; it's an automatic process. The process of learning today's lesson may well depend much more often on the student's total previously stored experiences than on how the teacher presents information.

According to Hart (1978), then, brain-compatible learning involves these factors:

1. Every brain is aggressive and unique in searching, demanding, and accepting only what it needs now to make sense out of the reality of the environment.
2. Much of the brain is devoted to language activity, so students need to talk a great deal.
3. Students also need to move around, talk to other students, explore possibilities, and work on projects.
4. Each brain processes its innumerable complex programs in different ways and admits only what it decides to. Remember that teachers may be teaching a concept, but students are teaching themselves something else, possibly unrelated.
5. The neocortex, which is the newest part of the human brain and encompasses five-sixths of the whole brain, does not function well under threat or pressure. It would be well for teachers to ponder this when accepting failure from students. Could teachers have behaved differently so that students would experience success?
6. The brain operates as a computer does, by programs or schemata (established sequences), not by precision but by great, vague approximations. It has little use for step-by-step-logic.

From this we might say that learning means active experiencing, with all its ramifications. Hart also says that we should not be overly concerned that every student appear to be paying attention all the time. Students may have eight to ten or more structures making connections in their brain at one time and therefore may be able to also keep up with what the teacher is saying.[12]

Brain Growth Spurts

Epstein (1978) formulated the theory of growth spurts, periods of time when actual brain growth spurts occur (ages 2 to 4, 6 to 8, 10 to 12, and 14 to

16+).[13] The intervening times are spent integrating previously learned material. During ages 10–12, girls are supposed to experience considerable brain growth, while some boys' brains grow much less. During the 14–16+ growth spurt, boys are said to make considerably more gains than girls. Epstein believed that learning accelerated during these growth spurts. This theory has been disputed by some other authorities, but it still bears considering.

Goodlad (1984) proposes a redesigned continuum for our curriculum based on our knowledge of growth spurts, Piaget's stages of cognitive development, and physical changes of puberty.[14] Ages 4 to 7 would be the primary phase (preschool through grade 3). Ages 8 to 11 would be the elementary phase (grades 4–8). Ages 12 to 15 would be the secondary phase (grades 9–12). This has interesting implications for the way we now divide up our schools and for how we might rethink that division.

Brain Aerobics

Dudley Lynch (1986) discussed what he called "brain aerobics" or the ultimate human exercise for producing an always-young brain.[15] The secondary school and college years are none too soon to be thinking about how to put these ideas into practice.

1. *Practice future forecasting.* This puts to work your forward-thinking frontal lobes. (Predict what will happen next in a novel, or forecast what might have happened if the South had won the U.S. Civil War.)

2. *Go into action.* When your body goes into action, so does your brain's limbic system, where powerful chemical controllers of emotions originate (perhaps physical warmups prior to exams).

3. *Learn another language.* This process puts new "muscle tone" in the language centers of the brain's left hemisphere. Language learning actually should be started in first grade or earlier, when it is most natural.

4. *Prime your mind.* Visualize a task before doing it to exercise your right brain hemisphere's visualizing apparatus. (Have students visualize the battle, the walk through the woods, and so on.)

5. *Become sensitive to stimuli usually ignored.* This exercises your reticular activating system, allowing you to be conscious of some things while remaining unconscious of others. (What odor is it, how does it feel to the touch, what is going on next door?)

6. *Locate new routes to familiar places.* A creative process of finding a new way allows the old "animal brain" to cooperate with the newer human cerebral cortex (mapping alternative routes).

7. *Deal directly with change.* Defending unpopular ideas exercises the oldest, least adaptive brain structures, which interfere with ways we deal with our changing world (e.g., debating on the opposite side from your actual beliefs).

8. *Grow addicted to mental challenges.* Doing crossword puzzles and manual spatial skill games puts the chemical and electrical mechanisms of the brain through their paces. (These activities can be used for extra credit or when assigned tasks are completed early.)

A healthy, challenged brain never stops learning, and we might well strive to instill this willingness to keep learning in all our students.

A Future Forecast of Brain Language

Fortier (1983) describes how reading may be taught in the future. Two major research fields that may influence the teaching of reading are artificial intelligence and neuroscience, both of which explore still unknown dimensions of the brain. The symbiosis of people and computers is beginning to

"Hagar the Horrible" by Dik Browne, December 14, 1986. Reprinted with special permission of King Features Syndicate, Inc.

help scientists understand the brain's cognitive functioning. For example, we now know that reading aloud simultaneously activates seven discrete cortical regions, whereas reading silently activates only five areas. This gives us an idea of how accurately we are beginning to pinpoint activities in the deepest parts of the brain.

Fortier also suggests that humans may develop a "brain language to rule all language activities, which will involve gaining direct access to the brain's network, words may be replaced by electrical signals which will not require eyes to see information. In the future, basic skills may have to be taught only once, as we learn how to impress knowledge permanently on the brain."[16] The notion of communicating through brain language is certainly an intriguing one, possibly even a bit frightening in its implications.

CONCENTRATION AND RETENTION

When we really concentrate, we are focusing so strongly that we block out the rest of the world around us. Concentration means sustained attention, demanding a mental set or attitude and a determination to allow nothing to interfere with the learning task at hand. It demands active involvement and alertness with a positive attitude toward the material being studied.[17]

Retention here means organizing and storing information comprehended in such a way as to be able to recall it when needed (organize, store, retrieve).

Short-Term versus Long-Term Memory

Background information is essential to comprehension because we search back through what we know in order to make sense of the new information we encounter. Our background information is connected to memory storage and retrieval. The two aspects of memory are called short-term and long-term. Short-term memory, or *working memory*, holds information temporarily until it is processed into long-term memory or is erased in order to make room for new incoming information.[18] Short-term memory has a limited capacity and lasts only very briefly, whereas long-term or *permanent* memory has an infinite capacity for storing all our past knowledge and experience in a highly organized way. Long-term memory has one limitation: It is relatively slow in processing new information, depending on how meaningful that new information is to us.

As we all can attest, it is possible to concentrate and understand material read or heard at the time, and then promptly forget it. When reading a novel for pleasure or relaxation, for example, we can follow the plot and characters with no problem as we read, but later, if suddenly called on unexpectedly to share detailed information on this novel, we might be hard pressed to do so. Thus, we concentrate on a learning task, making sure we comprehend it, but we must take other steps to ensure retention. Several ways to do this are included in the mnemonic device CAPS:

1. *Categorizing:* Placing the information into a larger framework, making connections to what we already know
2. *Applying:* By making a model, map, or project
3. *Personalizing:* Associating any new information with our own personal experiences, such as connecting a particular adjective to someone we know
4. *Self-reciting:* Using all sensory channels through repetition silently and aloud, mnemonics (like CAPS), and the like[19]

Mnemonic Devices

As just shown, an effective learning technique for memorizing names, dates, places, and miscellaneous terms is to use mnemonic devices (acronyms like CAPS, rhymes, mental imagery). (Mnemonics in the form of acronyms are scattered throughout this text.) Whenever material to be memorized has little inherent structure, it is more difficult to retain. These devices are not intended to deepen understanding, only to assist retention. Some involve formal or mental images. One technique involves using successive locations in a familiar territory, such as the school layout. If ten items are to be recalled, each is placed mentally in a different location. Then you mentally walk through the school collecting them one by one. Because the school is familiar, this is used as the device to organize random items. Another technique means imagining an interaction between each item and a well-known list of words or items in a rhyme, "One is a bun, two is a shoe, three a tree. . . ." The first item is imagined to be interacting with a bun, the second with a pair of shoes, and so forth—the sillier the better.[20]

Rhymes and songs are also useful for recalling facts:

> *Thirty days hath September*
> *April, June, and November*
> *All the rest have thirty-one*
> > *Except February alone*
> *Which has twenty-eight days clear*
> *And twenty-nine in each leap year.*

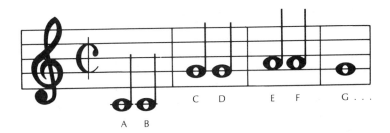

For recalling letters of the alphabet, the alphabet song as shown here has helped many youngsters. Other examples include acronyms, which use the first letter of each word:

RADAR: Radio detecting and ranging
RSVP: Respondez s'il vous plaît (reply if you please)
NATO: North Atlantic Treaty Organization

Students of beginning music were taught that the lines in the staff, EGBDF, might be remembered as: "Every good boy deserves fudge" or "does fine," and the spaces as FACE. In the past, some remedial teachers tried to help poor spellers spell *geography* and *arithmetic* by showing how the first letter in each word of the following sentence spells the subject; *George Ellen's old grandmother rode a pig home yesterday. A rat in the house might eat the ice cream.* Older students having trouble with particular words might profit from trying this. As another example, some years ago, when the president's cabinet had ten members, students used the acronym *St. Wapniacl*, to remember the different departments: *S*tate, *T*reasury, and so on. (MURDER as an acronym will appear later in this chapter.)

One caution—when mastering mnemonic devices is more difficult than just learning the material, then it is advisable to avoid mnemonics.

The Russian psychologist Smirnov (1973) discussed ways to aid concentration and retention that can serve as a model for students.[21] The acronym "GRIPP it" is used here for easier recall of his main points, using the first letter of each term:

Group thoughts
Relate to background knowledge
Image—use imagery
Paraphrase in your own words
Ponder significance

We all tend to lack concentration when any of the following conditions prevail:

1. We are anxious as a result of procrastinating.
2. We allow our minds to wander, thinking of one thing and then another—we have a conflict of interests or desires.
3. We study without breaks over long periods, such as two to three hours at a time.[22]
4. We are distracted by outside noises.

To concentrate more effectively, we need to know *why* we are doing the assignment, *what* to do, and *how* to do it. Teachers should check to assure that the why, what, and how are adequately covered and comprehended by all.

We forget rapidly unless we see meaning and make connections; therefore, new information needs to be linked to what we already know. When we teach students about retaining and retrieving information, we should caution that memorizing is only a step toward building our memory banks. When we organize the information properly, these banks can then be used to facilitate new learning.

What We Can Learn from History

There was a time in history when so few people could either read or write that memory was an essential commodity. In those early days, a useful *aide-memoire* was rhyme. For example, French merchants used a poem made up of 137 rhyming couplets that contained all the rules of commercial arithmetic, because writing materials were costly and rare. A trained memory was also a necessity for scholars. University students could repeat 100 lines of text shouted to them only once by their teachers. (Imagine that happening in a class today!)

The major mnemonic reference work of the Middle Ages, called *Ad Herennium,* provided a technique for recalling vast amounts of information by means of "memory theaters." Material to be remembered was conceived of as a familiar location, such as all or part of a building with the interior elements easily differentiated. If too large an area was chosen, recall would suffer; if too small, the separate details would be too close together; if too bright it would blind, if too dark, it would obscure. The various locations were thought of as being around thirty feet apart to isolate sections of the material. After this preparation of the memory theater, the memorizer would take a mental walk through the building to ensure that it was logical and easily recallable. The material to be memorized took the form of strong mental images representing the elements to be remembered. These could be humorous, bloody, unusual, gaudy, and so forth. Each image acted as an agent of memory and would trigger several components of the material. Stored images could also relate to single words, phrases, or entire arguments. Onomatopoeia, the use of words that sound like the action they describe, also helped. When printing spread throughout the world, learning became increasingly text-oriented, so the memory theater fell into disuse. Likewise, prose became more prevalent as the mnemonic value of poetry became less important. As we changed from the old mnemonic ways of recall and the collective memory of the community, the development of printing isolated us in a way, yet still left us capable of sharing vicariously in a bigger world (adapted from *The Day the Universe Changed* by James Burke, copyright © 1985 by London Writers Ltd., by permission of Little, Brown and Company).[23]

Memorizing Today: Some Personal Reminiscences

Many schools appear to have strayed from requiring students to memorize poetry or prose. We need to stop and ask ourselves if we are actually cheating our students of a lifetime of enjoyment, as well as denying them valuable practice in memory training. For example, as I walked through England's Lake District for the first time, I was enraptured with the scenery. Suddenly, seemingly out of nowhere, came the words of Wordsworth's poem:

> *I wandered lonely as a cloud*
> *That floats on high o'er Vales and Hills*
> *When all at once I saw a crowd,*
> *A host of golden daffodils;*

He had said it so much better than I could ever do.

Also from personal experience, I was on a coastal steamer to the North Cape of Norway when, in order to get my "diploma" showing I had crossed the Arctic Circle, I was required to sing a song with four German passengers who spoke little English. Thank heaven for that high school music teacher and the German version of "Silent Night," even though it was August.

Finally, I did not appreciate it at the time when my senior high English teacher, Miss Jackson, required that all of us memorize and recite 150 lines of *Macbeth*. But some forty years later they are still with me and have made the viewing at Stratford of *Macbeth* a special joy as I sit there silently mouthing the words along with the actors.

Super-Learning

As described earlier, variables affecting comprehension include the reader, the text, and the context—the setting, time, place, and so forth. One aspect of setting, auditory background, refers to the type and intensity of the aural stimulation.[24] Research has shown that extraneous noise can distract from and limit concentration and can inhibit general performance.[25] On the other hand, some researchers have found that certain types of classical music, used as background, facilitate reading comprehension, creative writing, and art in many students. Soft, slow classical music has been found to relax learners, eliminate distractions, and stimulate creativity and reasoning.[26]

An exploratory study by Millikin and Henk (1985) looked at effects of three types of background music on comprehension of students in grades 4 through 8. Classical music outperformed rock music or no music, giving consistently higher mean scores.[27]

Ostrander and Schroeder (1979) in their book *Super Learning*, describe the science of "suggestology," which has gained acceptance with some educators.[28] For example, Prichard and Taylor (1976) reported that 90 percent of remedial students in a 16-week suggestology treatment gained one or more years in both oral and silent reading. Prichard and Taylor described super-learning as dealing with your PQ (potential quotient), not your IQ (intelligence quotient). This music memory method involves relaxing first to the slow movements of Baroque music without distracting noises in order to get rid of tensions—music such as Bach, which has a steady beat of about one beat per second. This is said to calm the body and release the mind. Then the idea is to listen to a slow-paced lecture on tape or read aloud to the beat of the music. This is supposed to place information more readily into long-term memory.[29]

SKILLS AND STRATEGIES FRAMEWORK WITH ACTIVITIES

Now that we have considered some theoretical, underlying concerns, it is time to turn to specific study-learning skills and strategies. You may wish to refer back to the scope and sequence outline at the first part of the chapter for a total review.

I. Search and Locate Information, Select Appropriate Sources

This first category includes alphabetical order, book parts, general and specific references, and the school library.

A. *Alphabetical order or sequence:* This is the most basic skill required to locate information in a dictionary or reference book. Many remedial tenth-graders, when asked to alphabetize beyond the first letter, found the task so difficult and time-consuming that they noted that they would have given up on their own. A few short speed drills should suffice to remind most students of how to use this skill efficiently.

B. *Book parts:* Textbooks contain many elements to assist readers. Unfortunately, too often they are ignored. Even at the college level, many students admit that they just read the assigned pages. At the beginning of a term it is helpful to take a few minutes of class time with the new text to remind students of the importance of each part.

1. *Title page:* This tells us the subject, author(s), and publisher; indicates what the book is about and who the author(s) are
2. *Copyright:* Usually at the back of the title page, this tells us how up-to-date the information is and – if more than one edition – how well received the text has been. Generally, when two books are compared for validity, the newest copyright is judged to be the more accurate. Considering new discoveries in science, for example, this will likely be true. But for a history text dealing with past time, we must not be hasty in deciding who is the best authority.
3. *Table of contents:* This is a complete outline, a map of the domain of the text, showing main categories and some subcategories. It can serve as a mental framework when reading and should be looked at carefully before starting the first chapter.
4. *Preface:* The preface gives the authors' purposes for writing, their philosophy or bias, and possibly some suggestions for how to get the most out of the text. It may be wise for teachers and students to read parts of prefaces together or at least to discuss the contents in class.
5. *Appendixes:* These contain interesting supplementary material to enrich what was stated in the body of the text.
6. *Glossary:* These include technical terminology with meanings specific to the subject matter of the text. This can be less confusing than the regular dictionary with its multiple meanings.
7. *Index:* This is an alphabetical listing of specific subjects and authors, with page numbers for rapid location within the text. Learning how to search in the index by cross-referencing is important. If students look for a word in the index and it is not there, they must think of what synonym or what larger category of words might encompass it. For example, if "Mississippi (River)" is not there, look for "river" to see if different rivers are listed. The name of the author who wrote about a concept may be in the author index.
8. *Bibliography or references:* This is a complete record of works of other authors used as references for the text.
9. *Recommended readings:* These are particularly useful for those students

who wish to delve more deeply into aspects of the subject or who need to get a better grasp by reading another's explanation.

10. *Questions and suggested activities:* These are usually found at the end of each chapter. Students who read the questions before reading the chapter will have a type of *advance organizer* in their minds, a framework into which the details can be placed. Suggested activities should serve as enrichment.[30] (See Chapter 5 on comprehension of expository material for further information on advanced organizers.)

C. *General and specific references:*

1. *Dictionary and thesaurus:* These are excellent tools for developing vocabulary. Dictionaries go from words to meanings, whereas a thesaurus takes meanings and provides many synonyms for each meaning. (See the section in Chapter 4 for more detail.)

2. *Encyclopedias:* These are often used as a first resource for investigating a topic. From there it is possible to move on to specialized or specific encyclopedias, atlases, indexes, yearbooks, and almanacs.

3. *School libraries and media centers:* These are vital to student research and enjoyment. The school librarian or media director will help your class make effective use of the library or resource center. Setting up a schedule with librarians early in the school term is necessary and is much appreciated.

4. *Providing collateral reading material:* This refers to material for enhancing students' understanding of history. If they read fiction about the time period they are studying, it may come alive for them. For example, *The Witch of Blackbird Pond* was a Newbery Prize winner that could be read by middle school students when the text covers the topic of the Salem witch trials. (For a great deal of help with uses of collateral reading, see Chapter 11 of Tonjes and Zintz.[31])

II. Receive and Organize Information

A. *Listening* is still a fairly neglected area in language arts, and yet we receive much information through our auditory channels. Remembering what we hear is usually more difficult than remembering what we have read because it is not as easy to relisten as it is to reread. In lecture situations, the first thing to do is to tune in to what the speaker is saying. Teachers need to remind themselves to wait until they have complete attention before starting to lecture or explain. Listening can be considered, in learning situations, to be allied to note-taking. Listeners need to make mental decisions about what to jot down for later, more detailed mental recall. Practice in listening can be provided by slowly reading a short text selection, having students listen without writing and then take a mock (practice) quiz on what they have heard. Discussion of which are the main thoughts and which are the supporting details is as essential here as it is in reading comprehension. Students should also be reminded of any faulty habits in listening that need to be overcome. These include faking attention, letting the mind wander, or tuning out, listening without a clear purpose or questioning frame of mind, getting mired in inessential details, or allowing the speaker's characteristics to distract from the message.

B. *Outlining and summarizing*, like listening skills, are helpful to good note-taking, whether from lectures or reading. Formal outlines, though introduced around the fourth grade, need to be reexplained and practiced throughout the secondary grades. Outlining is similar to summarizing in that both require analyzing what is most important, or the key points. Outlining consists of a hierarchical structure of different categories that relate in some way to one another. Outlining, writing main points, and summarizing all form a framework that is useful for later retrieval. Learning is improved by acquiring an outline before or immediately after reading. Anderson and Armbruster (1984) analyzed research and discussed common study techniques of underlining, outlining, summarizing, and note-taking.[32] They stated that although the research to that date had not confirmed the benefit of these techniques, this might well be because we have mostly ignored the influence of reader knowledge or beliefs about the task at hand. We have not considered whether comprehension during study time matches later retrieval processes in order to perform the task. Outlining is time-consuming and requires thinking through logical relationships and then representing those meanings in an alternative form. We should be aware that it is possible to use the format of an outline while processing the information only superficially. Summarizing is most likely to be effective if readers receive instruction on how to compose summaries. It is just as important that the task they are asked to perform should reflect the kind of processing used in summary writing. If, for example, the task is for detailed knowledge, summaries would be inappropriate, as they best serve main ideas.[33]

Examples of two kinds of notations used for outlines follow. The first kind is the most familiar to most of us.

I. Main idea or topic
   A. Subtopic
      1. Supporting detail
      2. Supporting detail
         a. Explanatory detail

          (1) Further support
          (2) Further support
       b. Explanatory detail
   A. Subtopic
II. Main idea or topic
   A. Subtopic
      1. Supporting detail
      2. Supporting detail
   B. Subtopic

Sometimes text headings lend themselves to good outlines:

I. Center heading
   A. Free-standing heading
      1. Indented, boldface heading
         a. Main idea of paragraph
           (1) Supporting detail

The second kind of notation for outlining may be easier to construct but may have a more cluttered appearance:

1.0 Center heading
1.1 Free-standing heading
1.1.1 Indented boldface heading
1.1.1.1 Main idea of paragraph
1.1.1.1.1 Supporting detail
2.0 Center heading

   C. *Teaching outlining skills:* Teaching students how to outline includes having them first look over the whole selection, then read carefully each label and topic sentence to determine its relative importance. For those still having difficulty, it is wise to return to simple examples and procedures. Short paragraphs can be used where students must determine the topic sentence, then give supporting details. Next, provide students with a complete outline of a topic in the text and have them work in pairs, comparing the outline to the text. Encourage questions and discussion. The next step is to give them a partially filled-in outline of a text section and have them complete it with a partner. Next, give them only the letters or numbers to be filled in. The final step is to have them create their own outline for comparison.

   In a handy little monograph titled *How to Study in High School,* Snider (1983) suggests that when outlining a reading assignment before class, you leave space after each section for class notes to be added relating to the topic.[34] A sentence outline, then, is really like a summary of main ideas in paragraph form, where each statement may contain a main idea.

D. *Summarizing,* as noted previously, is an important skill, which forces students to identify and organize essential information and to integrate the reading and writing processes. When writing a summary, it is sometimes beneficial to begin with the text conclusion and work backward to locate key points leading to that conclusion. Many students have trouble noting text organization and developing subordinate and superordinate ideas in expository composition. Taylor (1986) developed a hierarchical summarizing that directs attention to the way ideas are organized and is supposed to improve recall of text.[35] The six steps, with teacher assistance, include:

a. Previewing a short segment of three to five pages
b. Developing a skeleton outline by writing Roman numerals for each subheading, capital letters for subsections, and numbers for details
c. Reading and outlining the segment
d. Writing a summary
e. Generating a main idea statement for the whole segment
f. Listing key supporting details

Before moving to the next segment, students write a topic sentence by the Roman numeral for the segment just completed. In the left margin they write key phrases, drawing lines to corresponding subsections.

Key phrases   I. Main heading
      A. Subheading
        (details)
civil rights   B. Subheading
        (details)
      C. Subheading
      D. _____
Great Society   E. _____
programs   F. _____

Students will benefit even more if they are required to write about what they learned from these procedures. Writing a paragraph discussing main points with one or two supporting details may help them to internalize the process.

E. *Studying and orally retelling:* Students study their material, reviewing summary information and distinguishing among topic sentences for sections, key phrases connecting subheadings, main ideas, and supporting details. The final step is oral retelling of their learnings to partners who look at the summary to cue them to parts they have forgotten. *Mapping* in graphic form is an informal way to outline or summarize material and can bring out creativity and diversity. Originally developed by Hanf (1971), it involves first identifying the main idea or concept and placing it in the center of the paper to build around it.[36] Drawing a shape around the topic to represent what it stands for (e.g., a dollar sign for a school budget, a book cover for a novel) can enliven the task. From four to seven major supporting categories are determined and are drawn around the central figure. The final step is to attach details to each supporting category. The map then becomes a graphic summary. An example can be seen in Figure 7.1.

F. *Note-taking from lectures and texts:* Note-taking is a difficult skill requiring students to process deeply what they hear or read. Often students

FIGURE 7.1
Creative Outlining or Mapping

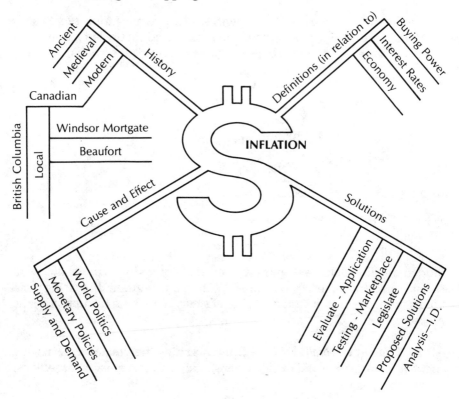

believe they are taking notes, when in fact they are actually not recording information efficiently or for ease of later recall. When listening to a lecture or reading a text, students must do so with a purpose, interpreting, analyzing, and synthesizing at the same time they are writing or reading. Because of its complexity, note-taking should be practiced frequently as a skill, and notes should be handed in periodically for teacher or peer critique but not for a grade.

A handout like the example seen in Table 7.3 for student reference is also helpful and can be duplicated. One way to give guided practice is to give a brief lecture to your students, telling them that they may use their notes for the quiz. Another way is to provide them with a notes facilitator—an outline of the lecture or chapter to be filled in as they listen or read (see REAP later in the chapter for an example). Aiken, Thomas, and Sheenum (1975) suggest that spaced note-taking can improve recall of lectures. Lectures can be broken into segments with spaced intervals of silence lasting several minutes, allowing time for students to take notes and ponder their significance.[37]

III. Interpret/Apply/Use/Check Information

These third and final aspects of study-learning are concerned with time spent preparing for and taking tests, writing research papers and reports, giving speeches and participating in discussions, interpreting graphical literacy, using general study-learning strategies, and evaluating metacognitively.

TABLE 7.3
Good Note-Taking

Good notes can save a great deal of time and effort and are vital when reviewing for a test. In order to take good notes:

1. When listening, tune in right away to the speaker and have a questioning frame of mind.
2. When reading, skim first to get an overview and try to sort out the key points and jot down phrases rather than complete sentences.
3. Have some type of shorthand abbreviations for content-related words that recur frequently.
4. Leave a wide margin on the left to use later for inserting key words for each section.
5. Leave spaces for filling in details later.
6. Make notes that are clear and organized.
7. When reading, it is better to summarize information without using the author's words.
8. Underline or box notes that are most important for later referral.
9. If, in a lecture, the outline is written on the board ahead of time, copy it immediately, leaving spaces to fill in while listening.
10. Review notes from the previous lecture or chapter as a bridge to the new material.

A. *Time management—Purposeful use of time:* How best to budget time is a concern for most people. This budgeting process is often referred to as *time management,* and it means overcoming a common tendency to procrastinate. Managing time involves advance planning of what is to be done and then setting priorities for accomplishing specified tasks.

Starting with a daily schedule and noting all the changes made will lead to a more realistic plan in the future. To make a workable schedule, it is good to have students keep track of how their time is spent for one week, including sleeping, eating, working, commuting, and the like, noting how much time is not accounted for each day. With that as a base, students initiate their individual plan by first listing only the essential tasks, and then those that might be accomplished (see Table 7.4.) A follow-up discussion concerning their choices and priorities may assist them with better time management in the future.

B. *A metacognitive note-taking strategy:* In order for students to become independent learners, deciding for themselves the relative worth of text material, they must become metacognitively aware. They need solid study-learning techniques as well as knowledge to control their own learning. Lindquist-Sandmann (1987) recommends using a model she developed that incorporates the four variables of metacognition: text characteristics, the task, strategies for accomplishing the task, and learners' characteristics of interest and ability.[38]

At first she provided students with a model in the form of study guides for each chapter, with kinds of questions she felt were important. She discussed their importance and provided background before assigning them to read. Then, as the students read, she shifted to student notes only and took away all former props. Students were tested on the material read, using only their own notes as reference. The discussion following this test was important in helping them see how well they had selected key points that would have assisted them in answering the test questions. They judged and assessed themselves. Discussion followed on the structure of the text, noting such tools as subheadings, summaries, and italics. The purpose here was to elicit from students how much of the text structure they used consciously. When discussing the task, students had trouble accepting that although their notes could not be "wrong," there were alternatives that authorities thought to be stronger. Strategy and learner characteristics were discussed last, as these may well be painfully personal. Here students examined how they created their own note-taking strategies and reached their decisions.

C. *Conditions for study-learning:* Students should keep in mind that certain study conditions will increase the efficiency of their use of time (see Table 7.5 for some suggestions).

TABLE 7.4
Sample Time Management Chart: How Do You Spend Your Time?

	Monday	Tuesday	Wednesday	Thursday	Friday	Saturday	Sunday
6:00 A.M.							
7:00							
8:00							
9:00							
10:00							
11:00							
12:00 noon							
1:00 P.M.							
2:00							
3:00							
4:00							
5:00							
6:00							
7:00							
8:00							
9:00							
10:00							
11:00							
12:00 midnight							

   D. *Preparing for and taking tests:* Teachers need to share information with their students on how to be test-wise. Being test-wise means having long-term study strategies as well as immediate ones when taking a test. These are not related directly to knowledge of the subject. Long-term strategies include learning as much as possible in advance about what type of test it will be, finding out the kinds of questions that will be asked, and having examples or samples of those questions. Working with a partner to try to predict questions that will appear on the test is another possible long-term strategy.

TABLE 7.5
Good Study Conditions

1. Find a quiet spot with few distractions and set it up as a personal study center, gathering needed tools and materials ahead of time.
2. Try to plan definite times each day for studying, based on other commitments and your own mental prime time (when you are not too fatigued or lethargic from having just eaten, or still only half awake).
3. Allow a specified amount of time for each assignment and try to keep to that schedule. Tackle the hardest one first when your mind is keenest.
4. Take a brief break of 5 to 10 minutes each hour for mental refreshment (50-minute classes do that automatically for students).
5. Start studying each assignment by doing a quick review of the previous material in order to tie the new to the known.
6. Allow a short time at the end of each assignment to recite, review, and reflect.
7. Review weekly to cut down on time needed to study just before a test.
8. To avoid interference or confusion, study subjects consecutively that are quite different (e.g., not French followed by Spanish, but French followed by math).

As the teacher, you should share with students the following points: Cramming right before a test can cause needless test anxiety; it is better to get a good night's sleep so your mind is fresh and to eat a good breakfast for mental energy. Arrive early if possible and relax before starting. When the test is handed out, skim over the entire test, noting the type of information and the weighting of potential points for specific questions. Read questions carefully and budget time appropriately, allowing at least five minutes to recheck answers.

  E. *Test types:*

  1. *Essay tests* can be difficult for some students because they must recall information and use good writing skills and organization. Noting key words is important here. Some examples include the following.[39]

Essay Word	Meaning
compare	Point out similarities and differences
contrast	Point out differences
critique	Summarize, evaluate
enumerate	Name one at a time
evaluate	Judge the merit of
illustrate	Explain with examples
justify	Give reasons for
summarize	Give brief version of key points
trace	Tell the history or development from earliest to most recent times

"Can we hurry up and get to the test? My short-term memory is better than my long-term memory."

Bill Hoest, "Laugh Parade," *Parade Magazine,* January 20, 1985, p. 16, used with permission.

Budgeting time is essential in an essay exam in order to give full treatment to each question. Students should try to answer each question, trying never to leave any completely blank for no possible credit. They should give a full answer, using the terminology of the subject, and should be careful of punctuation, capitalization, spelling, grammar, and general neatness. If one question requires a complex, lengthy answer, students should take a few minutes to outline first. Let them know that poor organization of thoughts, illegibility, or carelessness can irritate the test grader.

2. *Multiple choice:* Following directions carefully is vital here, as is budgeting time. Students might make a small mark next to difficult or unclear questions and return to them after completing the test. They should realize that it is always good to guess instead of leaving any blank, unless there is a penalty stated for guessing wrong. With difficult questions, they should eliminate choices that are obviously wrong or silly until there is a 50–50 chance of getting the correct answer. Sometimes the answer to one question appears in the stem of another question, and sometimes a stem does not match grammatically, which generally means it is wrong. When two alternatives

seem equally correct, they should choose the longest, which is more likely to be right. As a last resort, they may select an option that is neither first nor last.

3. *True–false:* Remind students to read all directions carefully, budget their time, and always guess if they do not know the answer. When any part of a statement is false, the whole question should be considered false. Students should watch out for absolute words like *always* or *never,* which often mean an answer is wrong. Long statements are often more likely to be true. Generally, teachers ask straightforward questions, so students should not try to argue or reason with possible exceptions. Tell them to move along rapidly, leaving time at the end to reread. Finally, they should stay with a first hunch rather than changing an answer later when they are still unsure, as first hunches tend to be right more often than not.

4. *Matching:* Whenever you ask students to match answers in one column with those in the second one, the second column of possible answers should always have several choices, to keep them from using the process of elimination. Tell students to read all choices first.

5. *Completion/fill in the blank:* Here you are asking students to complete a sentence or fill in the blank for key concepts or terms. This requires that they know exactly what to fill in and is useful when you want to find out details rather than main ideas.

F. *Writing research papers and reports:* This important study-learning skill requires application and is an effective way to assist students in grasping, learning, and using course content. Writing involves both form (mechanics) and content (organized concepts and facts). Writing a research paper or report requires utilizing a variety of skills. These include locating sources, selecting key information, organizing according to purposes, interpreting, and expressing information appropriately.

After locating appropriate sources in the library, teachers can guide students in organizing and selecting ideas by having general discussions concerning the purpose of the paper. Are they comparing and contrasting? Identifying and describing? Analyzing and evaluating? Sometimes it is helpful to have them write in one sentence "who, what, where, when, why, and how" to clarify their own thinking.

When they have read over their collected notes, it is important that students develop some form of outline to organize the data into a coherent form. If an outline is developed prior to gathering references, it will need to be checked for expansion, deletions, and changes in emphasis before writing. The outline is used as the guide to writing the first rough draft. When that is completed by a designated date, it is helpful to have peer or small-group critiques. Letting the draft rest for a few days allows students to return to it with fresh perception. When major changes need to be made, a second rough draft is helpful. Before writing the final draft, they should read the paper carefully to check form and flow. Using a checklist helps students evaluate their own work and saves much teacher time. The final draft should also be proofread for typographical errors or omissions before it is handed in. Students can learn skills in cooperation and planning if two or three students work together on reports and papers.

Two things that help students stay on track are a time line with due dates for each major step of the process, and a reference sheet or writing tips to which they can refer as needed. If they are held accountable for having their reference notes and outlines checked, for example, they will not be able to procrastinate unduly. Writing tips can be concerned with what is: (1) a good introduction (i.e., purpose statement, any limits, importance of topic), (2) an adequate body (i.e., accomplishes purpose, has supporting details for main ideas, documents facts), (3) an appropriate conclusion or summary (i.e., states how the purpose was accomplished, uses generalizations of major points stated in the body).

G. *Speeches, debates, discussions:* Study-learning also involves speaking formally or informally. It is interesting to note that scholars in ancient times were afraid that, if reading and writing became too popular, speaking and active dialogue would fall into disuse. Because they require active involvement, speeches, debates, and discussions should be an integral part of classroom learning.

1. *Speeches:* Students need practice in overcoming shyness or nervousness when presenting material to a group or class. Before requiring a set speech, it is helpful to have many small-group discussions, giving a specific task or topic to each member. Putting all reticent students in one group may force each one of them to do more talking. Writing full-sentence outlines helps in recall during the actual performance as it means less ad-libbing for the anxious speaker.
2. *Debates:* Informal class debates on current topics of interest to secondary students can also alleviate fears. When it comes time for formal debates or speeches, help students practice with each other, using detailed notes at first, moving finally to note cards and outlines.
3. *Discussion:* New teachers are often amazed, even horrified, when their seemingly well-planned discussion periods fall flat. Of course, students need to have taken the time to read the material, but other recommendations may also help. Instead of just assigning a reading and telling the class they will be discussing it, try being more specific. For example, "Tomorrow, be ready to discuss the key points and implications in Chapter 6. I expect everyone to participate. You may

refer to your text and notes as references during our discussion." Now students should know exactly what is expected of them and realize they cannot sit back and let a few people carry the ball.

Before holding the first class discussion, establish a discussion critique. For example, should hands be raised before speaking? How should disagreements be handled? Who should summarize? After each discussion period, allow time for self-evaluation and constructive peer criticism. Assigning specific tasks to individuals at various difficulty levels also improves the discussion atmosphere. A list on the board will help.

Normal speeches and debates require much advance planning and practice. Encourage use of the board and other audiovisual aids. Keeping to time limits also takes practice. Using a kitchen timer will keep everyone on their toes. Audiences walk away from a speech with only three or four main points. Therefore, it is better to illustrate and emphasize a few things rather than to overload with facts.

H. *Graphic literacy: A picture worth 1,000 words:* Fry (1981) has given us an important handle for perceiving, interpreting, and using graphics. He defines graphic literacy as the ability to read, comprehend, and draw five main types of graphs (linear, quantitative, spatial, pictorial, and hypothetical). His taxonomy shows the larger scope and potential for developing and using the right brain, which is global, meaning that parts of anything have meaning only through their relationship with the whole.[40]

A major reason for using graphs is that they often communicate meaning or information more quickly and concisely than words, by packing much information into a small space. In today's world we find them widely used in textbooks, newspapers, magazines, and computer software, as well as on television.

Assessing graphic comprehension through questioning is similar to reading comprehension questioning: What is the main idea? Supporting details? Purpose? How are details interrelated? What are the meanings of new words (symbols)?

The types of graphs making up graphical literacy are given in Table 7.6. In order to enhance learning, all types of illustrations must be clear, uncluttered, and not redundant, but should add to the power of the message and should highlight key concepts and interrelationships. Graphics should make the information more concrete than abstract words alone and thus easier for learners to interpret, organize and retrieve.[41]

1. *Graphic Information Lesson (GIL).* Reinking (1986) recommends a model-type lesson to increase students' awareness and use of graphic aids, in order to make them thinkers, not just readers. The model is supposed to heighten interest and help students move beyond the literal level.

TABLE 7.6
Graphical Literacy

Type	Purpose	Examples
1. Linear	Sequential data	Time line, flow chart, genealogy
2. Quantitative	Numerical data	Frequency polygon, bar graph, pie graph
3. Spatial	Area and location—two- or three-dimensional	Road map, floor plan, building elevation, contour map
4. Pictorial	Visual concepts—from realistic to abstract	Photograph, schematic drawings, cartoon, abstract representing something (e.g., row of cars)
5. Hypothetical	Interrelationships of ideas— conceptual and verbal	Theoretical model of reading, semantic mapping, sentence diagram

Stage 1: Students determine what graphic information appears in a particular text and how it relates to the printed information.

Stage 2: Teachers present accurate examples invented by them to be either consistent or purposely inconsistent with the text information. Individually or in groups, determine which examples are believable or not, based on their own background information and that found in the text. Lively debates may ensue. The purpose here is to have students synthesize the information learned and use it to evaluate graphics.

Stage 3: Give closure by allowing students to work independently with text and graphic aids. They might create pseudographics to be shared with the class, defend their choice of the most important or relevant aid, or critique the author's use of such aids.[42]

SUMMARY FOR PART I

In this first of two chapters on study-learning, distinctions have been made between study-reading, study-learning, and study-monitoring. The scope and sequence for the entire topic of study-learning includes three phases: (1) search and locate information, and select appropriate resources; (2) receive and organize information; and (3) interpret, apply, use, check, and monitor information. Foundations for study-learning include a look at how our brain works and the problems of concentration and retention.

Because study-learning has been divided into two chapters, the postorganizers will be found at the end of the next chapter, "Study-Learning, Part II."

NOTES

1. Bernice Bragstadt and Sharyn Stumpf, *A Guidebook for Teaching Study Skills and Motivation*, 2nd ed. (Newton, MA: Allyn and Bacon, 1987), p. 239.

2. K. T. Thomas and G. Moorman, *Designing Reading Programs* (Dubuque, IA: Kendall-Hunt, 1983), pp. 135–136.

3. E. Q. Locke, *A Guide to Effective Study* (New York: Springer, 1975), p. 126.

4. Robert Ornstein, *The Psychology of Consciousness* (New York: Harcourt Brace Jovanovich, 1977).

5. Barbara Z. Presseisen, "Thinking Skills: Meanings and Models," in Arthur L. Costa, ed., *Developing Minds: A Resource Book for Teaching Thinking* (Alexandria, VA: Association for Supervision and Curriculum Development, 1985), p. 20.

6. Laurence Cherry and Rona Cherry, "Another Way of Looking at the Brain," *New York Times Magazine*, June 9, 1985, Section 6, pp. 56–57, 108–111, 116, 120.

7. Linda Luvass-Briggs, "Some 'Whole Brain' Activities for the Community College Reading Class," *Journal of Reading*, 27 (April 1984), 664–647.

8. Ester Cappon Gray, "Brain Hemispheres and Thinking Styles," *The Clearing House*, 54 (November 1980), 127–32.

9. Luvass-Briggs, "Some 'Whole Brain' Activities," pp. 644–647.

10. Bernice McCarthy, *The 4MAT System: Teaching to Learning Styles with Right/Left Mode Techniques* (Oakbrook, IL: Exel, 1980).

11. Leslie Hart, *How the Brain Works* (New York: Basic Books, 1975), p. 198.

12. Leslie Hart, "The New Brain Concept of Learning," *Phi Delta Kappan*, 59 (February 1978), 396.

13. Herman Epstein, "Growth Spurts During Brain Development: Implications for Educational Policy," in J. Chall, ed., *Education and the Brain* (Chicago: National Society for the Study of Education, 1978).

14. John I. Goodlad, *A Place Called School: Prospects for the Future* (New York: McGraw-Hill, 1984).

15. Dudley Lynch, "Brain Aerobics," *Modern Maturity* (June–July 1986).

16. Giles Fortier, "Reading in the Future: The Brain Language, or How to Read without the Eyes," *Journal of Reading*, 27 (November 27, 1983), 164–168.

17. Dorothy Rubin, *Teaching Reading and Study Skills in Content Areas* (New York: Holt, Rinehart and Winston, CBS College Publishing, 1983), pp. 106–107.

18. C. J. Brainerd, "Working-Memory Systems and Cognitive Development," in C. J. Brainerd, ed., *Recent Advances in Cognitive Development Theory* (New York: Springer-Verlag, 1983).

19. Kenneth G. Graham and H. Alan Robinson, *Study Skills Handbook: A Guide for All Teachers* (Newark, DE: International Reading Association, 1984), pp. 100–101.

20. Marcia A. Just and Patricia A. Carpenter, *The Psychology of Reading and Language Comprehension* (Newton, MA: Allyn and Bacon, 1987), pp. 406–407.

21. A. A. Smirnov, *Problems of the Psychology of Memory* (New York: Plenum Press, 1973).

22. Bragstadt and Stumpf, *Guidebook for Teaching Study Skills*, p. 29.

23. James Burke, *The Day the Universe Changed* (Boston: Little, Brown, 1985), pp. 98–123.

24. Colleen N. Millikin and William A. Henk, "Using Music as a Background for Reading: An Exploratory Study," *Journal of Reading*, 28 (January 1985), 353–358.

25. Francis P. Robinson, *Effective Study* (New York: Harper & Row, 1970).

26. Sheila Ostrander and Lynn Schroeder, with Nancy Ostrander, *Super Learning* (New York: Dell, 1979); and Gail Cohen Taylor, "Music in Language Arts Instruction," *Language Arts*, 58 (March 1980): 363–368.

27. Millikin and Henk, "Using Music."

28. Ostrander and Schroeder, *Super Learning*, Chapter 4, pp. 62–76.

29. Allyn Prichard and Jean Taylor, "Adapting the Lozanov Method for Remedial Reading Instruction," *Journal of Suggestive-Accelerative Learning and Teaching*, 1 (Summer 1976), 110.

30. Marian J. Tonjes and Miles V. Zintz, *Teaching Reading/Thinking/Study Skills in Content Classrooms*, 2nd ed. (Dubuque, IA: William C. Brown, 1987), pp. 212–214.

31. Ibid., pp. 323–360.

32. Thomas H. Anderson and Bonnie B. Armbruster, "Studying," in P. David Pearson, ed., *Handbook of Reading Research* (New York: Longman, 1984), pp. 657–680.

33. Ibid.

34. Joan Snider, *How to Study in High School* (Providence, RI: Jamestown, 1983), p. 29.

35. Barbara M. Taylor, "A Summarizing Strategy to Improve Middle Grade Students' Reading and Writing Skills." in Ernest Dishner, Thomas Bean, John Readence, and David Moore, eds., *Reading in the Content Areas: Improving Classroom Instruction*, 2nd ed. (Dubuque, IA: Kendall/Hunt, 1986), pp. 274–278.

36. Buckley M. Hanf, "Mapping: A Technique for Translating Reading into Thinking," *Journal of Reading*, 14 (January 1971), 224–230, 270.

37. E. G. Aiken, G. S. Thomas, and W. A. Sheenum, "Memory for a Lecture: Effects of Notes, Lecture Rate and Informational Density," *Journal of Educational Psychology*, 67 (1975), 280–286.

38. Alexa Lindquist-Sandmann, "A Metacognitive Strategy and High School Students: Working Together," *Journal of Reading*, 30 (January 1987), 326–332.

39. John Readence, Thomas Bean, and Mark Baldwin, *Content Area Reading: An Integrated Approach* (Dubuque, IA: Kendall/Hunt, 1985).

40. Edward Fry, "Graphical Literacy," *Journal of Reading*, 24 (February 1981), 383–390.

41. Ibid.

42. David Reinking, "Integrating Graphic Aids into Content Area Instruction: The Graphic Information Lesson," *Journal of Reading*, 30 (November 1986), 146–151.

RECOMMENDED READINGS
FOR CHAPTERS 7 AND 8

Anderson, Thomas H., and Armbruster, Bonnie B. "Studying." In P. David Pearson, ed., *Handbook of Reading Research*. New York: Longman, 1984, pp. 657–680.

Armbruster, Bonnie, and Anderson, Richard C. "Research Synthesis on Study Skills." *Educational Leadership*, 19 (November 1981), 154–156.

Beers, Penny G. "Accelerated Reading for High School Students." *Journal of Reading*, 29 (January 1986), 311–315.

Bower, G. H. "A Selective Review of Organizational Factors in Memory." In E. Tulving and W. Donaldson, eds., *Organization and Memory*. New York: Academic Press, 1972.

Bragstadt, B. J., and Stumpf, S. M. *A Guidebook for Teaching Study Skills and Motivation*, 2nd ed. Boston: Allyn and Bacon, 1982.

Brieve, F. "Time is Money." *Phi Delta Kappan*, 59 (December 1977), 282.

Brown, Ann L., Bransford, John D., Ferrara, Roberta A., and Campione, Joseph C. *Learning, Remembering and Understanding*. Technical Report No. 244. Urbana: University of Illinois, 1982.

Carver, Ronald P. "Optimal Rate of Reading Prose." *Reading Research Quarterly*, 18 (1982), 56–88.

Christen, William L., and Searfoss, Lyndon W. "Placing Learning and Study Strategies in the Classroom." In Ernest Dishner et al., eds., *Reading in the Content Areas: Improving Classroom Instruction*, 2nd ed. Dubuque, IA: Kendall/Hunt, 1986, pp. 299–307.

Cooke, Jane Kita, and Haipt, Mildred. *Thinking with the Whole Brain: An Integrative Teaching/Learning Model K–8*. Washington, DC: National Education Association, 1986.

Dimond, Stuart. *Introducing Neuropsychology: The Study of Brain and Mind*. Springfield, IL: Charles C Thomas, 1978.

Gilling, Dick, and Brightwell, Robin. *The Human Brain*. London: Orbis, 1982.

Hoffman, Steve. "Using Student Journals to Teach Study Skills." *Journal of Reading*, 26 (January 1983), 344–347.

Hubel, David. "The Brain." *Scientific American*, 241 (September 1979), 45–53.

Karlin, Robert. *Teaching Reading in High School: Improving Reading in the Content Areas*, 4th ed. New York: Harper & Row, 1984.

McAndrew, D. A. "Underlining and Notetaking: Some Suggestions from Research." *Journal of Reading*, 27 (1983), 103–108.

Olshavsky, Jill. "Reading as Problem Solving: An Investigation of Strategies." *Reading Research Quarterly*, 12 (1976–1977), 654–674.

Ostrander, Sheila, and Schroeder, Lynn, with Ostrander, Nancy. *Super Learning*. New York: Dell, 1979.

Pauk, Walter. "Notetaking: More Bad Advice Exploded." *Reading World*, 18 (1979), 300–303.

Resnick, Lauren B. *Education and Learning to Think*. Pittsburgh, PA: Learning Research and Development Center, University of Pittsburgh, 1985.

Reynolds, R. E., Staniford, S. N., and Anderson, R. C. "Distribution of Reading Time When Questions Are Asked about a Restricted Category of Text Information." *Journal of Educational Psychology*, 71 (1979), 183–190.

Schuster, Donald H. "Introduction to the Lozano Method." *Journal of Suggestive-Accelerative Learning and Teaching*, 1 (Winter 1976), 278–293.

Sheikh, Anees A., and Sheikh, Katharina S. *Imagery in Education: Imagery in the Educational Process*. Farmingdale, NY: Baywood, 1985.

Sherman, T. M., and Wildman, T. M. *Proven Strategies for Successful Test Taking*. Columbus, OH: Charles Merrill, 1982.

Simpson, Michele L. "The Status of Study Strategy Instruction: Implications for Classroom Teachers." *Journal of Reading,* 28, 2, (November 1984), 136–142.

Smith, Anthony. *The Mind.* New York: Viking Press, 1984.

Tonjes, Marian J. "Selected Instructional Strategies for Promoting Content Reading and Study Skills." In A. Hendry, ed., *Teaching Reading: The Key Issues.* London: Heinemann Educational Books, 1981, pp. 97–106.

Ulrich, Anna L. "Brain Growth: Implications for the Future." *New Mexico Journal of Reading,* 4 (Spring 1984), 7–10.

Wood, E., and Middleton, D. "A Study of Assisted Problem-Solving." *British Journal of Psychology,* 66 (1975), 181–191.

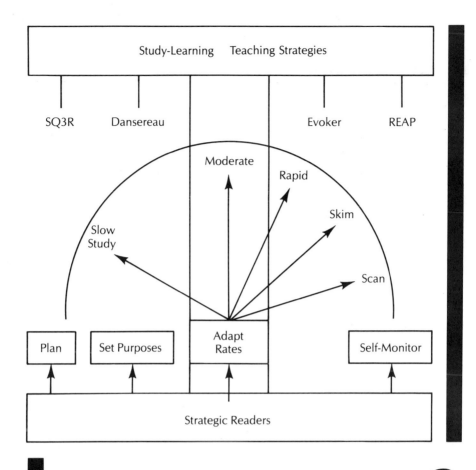

8

Study-Learning: Part II

CHAPTER OUTLINE

Preorganizers
Introduction
General Teaching Strategies
  SQ3R: The Original
  The Dansereau Learning Strategy System for Retaining Information
  Other Strategies
Considerations When Teaching Study-Learning Strategies
Overcoming Grading Problems
Rate
  Rate's Place in Strategic Reading
  Adaptable Rates
  Comprehension and Rate
  Eye Movements
  Paradoxes and Reasons for Slow Rates
  Success Secrets
  Practice Finding Your Own Rates
  Research on Rate With Superior Readers
Summary
Postorganizers

COGNITIVE COMPETENCIES

Also see the Cognitive Competencies in Chapter 7, "Study-Learning: Part I."

1. *Plan* to become more adaptable in the rates in which you read by keeping a two-week record of type of material read and overall rates.

2. *Select* one of the four general teaching strategies to try out yourself on another assignment, with the end product being a mini-plan to teach it to your students.

3. *Critique* the section on grading problems after discussing potential problems with two other practicing teachers.

4. *Summarize* how you will assist your students with *needed* study-learning strategies.

KEY TERMS

adaptable rates
Dansereau's learning strategy
  system
Evoker
holistic grading

REAP
rubrics
SQ3R
saccadic sweep
strategic reading

Preorganizer 1
Review of Cognitive Competencies in Chapter 7, Part I

From reading and studying in the previous chapter, you should now be able to:

1. Define and make distinctions among the terms *study-reading, study-learning,* and *study-monitoring.*

2. Describe in general terms the scope and sequence for study-learning.

3. Summarize key points concerning the brain's role in study-learning.

4. React personally to the discussion on concentration and retention, citing some examples from your own experiences.

5. Select and describe one useful skill or strategy from each of the three major study-learning areas, stating why it is personally relevant to you.

8
Study-Learning: Part II

INTRODUCTION

In "Study-Learning: Part II," we will be looking at general teaching strategies, considering why students lack mature strategies for independent learning, and considering rate of reading. A general summary for "Study-Learning, Part I" and "Part II" concludes this chapter.

GENERAL TEACHING STRATEGIES

The following are four general teaching strategies for study-learning. These include SQ3R, Dansereau's Learning Strategy System, Evoker, and REAP.

SQ3R: The Original

Francis Robinson's Survey-Question-Read-Recite-Review (SQ3R) (1946) is the precursor of all study-learning strategies today.[1] As a secondary teacher, he was determined to help his students become better learners, so he started with teaching them the first three steps: surveying the chapter, turning subheadings into questions, and reading to answer their own questions. His students improved measurably, but Robinson still was not satisfied, so he added the last two steps: reciting after each subsection to check retention, and finally reviewing the entire chapter. His students showed even more improvement following all five steps (see Table 8.1 for more details of each step).

With its success, then, why has not SQ3R become an integral part of our curriculum from the early grades on? There are several possible answers to that question, which could well apply to *any* study-learning strategy.

1. Teachers may *not* have emphasized adequate practice on real-life materials.
2. Time-consuming study-learning strategies may not always be needed, especially on easy, familiar material.
3. Some parts of the strategy might be used as necessary, but not always all parts.

Students, then, should be taught to adapt what they need at the time according to the purpose and difficulty of the material.

TABLE 8.1
SQ3R: A Study Strategy That Works

Steps	Purpose	Tasks
1. Survey	To get an overall sense of the assignment, a map of the domain, an organization or framework	Skim or preview the chapter by first reading the introduction and summary, reading just the subtitles, examining all graphics, and reading the questions at the end of the chapter. *Check:* You should be able to talk about the chapter in general terms as to what it will cover.
2. Question	To set purposes for reading, and to aid concentration	Turn each subheading into your own question; revise questions when not adequate.
3. Read	To find answers to questions posed, to focus on main ideas and not get bogged down in unnecessary details	Read only to the end of that section to answer your question; while reading, note how the paragraphs are organized to help later recall.
4. Recite	To aid and check retention immediately and fill in gaps	Before moving on to the next section, check yourself by covering your notes or text pages and reciting from memory the steps or the gist of the section. Then look back to see what was missed.
5. Review	To renew what was learned, to tie new learning into old, to set information into long-term memory, to self-evaluate the adequacy of learning	Before starting this assignment, review major subheadings of the previous chapter. After completing the entire chapter, review all subheadings to recheck main ideas.

The Dansereau Learning Strategy System for Retaining Information

More than forty years after SQ3R was initiated, a program was developed by Dansereau and colleagues, intended primarily for improving information retention.[2] Their program contains three groups of strategies: (1) improving initial comprehension and retention, (2) using and retrieving information, and (3) support strategies for monitoring when and how to study. Figure 8.1 shows each with the attendant processes. The first group resembles SQ3R except that it teaches specific techniques for each part of the general strategy rather than leaving it up to readers to do independently. Note that the second group of processes differs in only one aspect, *detail* rather than *digest*.[3]

FIGURE 8.1
Dansereau's Learning Strategy System

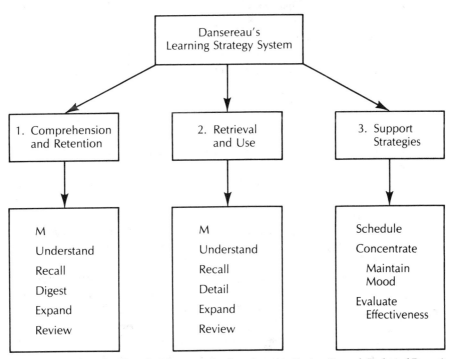

Source: Adapted and used with permission from *Learning Strategy Research* Technical Report) by D. F. Dansereau, Fort Worth: Texas Christian University, 1983, Figure 1, p. 52.

Three main types of strategies in Dansereau's system include: initial comprehension, with names making up the acronym for first-degree MURDER (without the M); retrieving and using information with names forming the acronym for second-degree MURDER; and support strategies, which are used to control and monitor study processes.

Students have one hour to study the text using the strategy being taught. About five days later they are given a variety of test types for feedback as to the success of the strategy.

Group I. Comprehension and Retention (First-Degree MURDER)
Using the acronym MURDER, this strategy is intended to be independent of the reading purpose or goal and is also intended to improve the level of understanding of the text. The letters for the first group stand for the following:

M–
Understand the material.
Recall the material.
Digest the material through organization and elaboration.
Expand knowledge by making elaborative inferences.
Review mistakes and inadequacies revealed by the test.

Group II. Use the Information (Second-Degree MURDER)
The purpose in Group II is to try to organize, store, and plan how to retrieve information according to the learning purpose. Here, the D in MURDER stands for detailing main ideas. The strategies in second-degree MURDER are directed toward a particular kind of test or text.

Group III. Support Strategies
Three components in Group III include:

1. *Planning and scheduling:* Keep a diary and study schedule (alter when needed).
2. *Managing concentration:* Maintain a relaxed mood, give self-motivating sermons about studying, decrease study aversion through some types of behavior therapy.
3. *Monitoring effectiveness of study:* Use feedback from tests to decide how effective study is and modify behavior as necessary.

In this program, students are taught a specific technique for better recall, such as networking. They write main ideas in outline form, showing properties and interrelationships, and form mental images (visual imagery) of main ideas and connections. Networking is similar to developing cognitive maps or to mapping, but it is more specific in terms of specifying different kinds of links. The six links or relationships in networking are:

1. *Part of* (a toe is part of a foot). *Key words:* portion of, segment, a part of

2. *Type of* (an Irish terrier is a kind of dog). *Key words:* example of, a type or kind of
3. *Causal* (mist causes dampness). *Key words:* causes, leads to
4. *Analogy* (a pet kitten can behave like a little child). *Key words:* is like, corresponds to, is similar to, can be like
5. *Characteristic property* (garbage usually has a bad smell). *Key words:* is a feature of, has
6. *Indicator* (swelling in cheeks may indicate mumps). *Key words:* indicate, is proof of, supports[4]

Although there are other relationships among text information types, just the act of awareness and thinking about these may help readers process the text.

Other Strategies

Numerous other strategies have evolved over the years. A few are mentioned briefly here.

Evoker
Pauk (1963) developed a study strategy to be used especially with prose, poetry, and drama for *close* reading. The steps are explore, vocabulary, orally read, key ideas, evaluate, and recapitulate.

Explore: Read the entire selection silently to get an overall feeling for the message.
Vocabulary: Note key words, look up necessary words, unfamiliar places, events, people mentioned.
Orally read: Read aloud with expression.
Key ideas: Locate to see the author's organization. What's the main idea or theme?
Evaluate: Evaluate key words and sentences as to how they contribute to the development of key ideas.
Recapitulate: Reread the selection.[5]

REAP
Eanet and Manzo (1976) created a strategy intended to improve reading, thinking, and writing skills which they called REAP. This stands for:

1. *Read:* To find out author's message
2. *Encode:* Translate message into own language (paraphrase)
3. *Annotate:* Write the message in one of several annotation forms:

a. *Summary annotations:* Brief restatements of author's main ideas and relationships between them.
b. *Thesis annotations:* State main premise or theme.
c. *Question annotation:* Question(s) readers feel the author is answering in the selection.
d. *Heuristic annotation:* Take quotations from selection that suggest essence and stimulate responses.
e. *Critical annotation:* Includes statement of author's thesis and statement of reaction to thesis, with defense or justification of that reaction.
f. *Intention annotation:* States author's purpose as understood by reader.
g. *Motivation annotation:* Speculate about probable motives of writer.
h. *Probe annotations:* Emphasize verification, consequences, and alternatives.
i. *Personal view:* Annotations—answer the question "How do personal experiences, views, and feelings stack up against the thesis or main idea?"
j. *Inventive annotations:* Take a creative approach, drawing from other contexts or synthesizing ideas.
4. *Ponder:* Think about the significance of the author's message and discuss with others.[6]

See Table 8.2 for an example of a notes facilitator for REAP that students can use when taking notes from the teacher's lecture on REAP.

CONSIDERATIONS WHEN TEACHING STUDY-LEARNING STRATEGIES

Simpson (1984) discusses reasons that students lack mature strategies necessary for independent learning. Either they have not been taught study skills, or they cannot regulate the skills they have been taught, or they do not think to apply them.

Partially adequate strategies by themselves would include the following:

1. Reading slowly
2. Underlining or marking text while reading
3. Rereading whole chapters numerous times
4. Memorizing by rote

The danger is that once habits are formed, students may be reluctant to replace these with more mature strategies, such as interacting with text,

TABLE 8.2
REAP: Using a Notes Facilitator

Eanet and Manzo (1976) developed a strategy for improving reading/writing/study skills based on the idea that we need to process information and organize it so that it is useful to ourselves and others. Use the existing spaces to take notes as we talk about each aspect.

Steps
  R (read)
  E (encode)
  A (annotate)
  P (ponder)

Types of annotations (samples)
  1. Summary
  2. Thesis
  3. Questions

Steps for teaching students to write summary annotations:
  1. Recognize and define
  2. Discriminate
  3. Model
  4. Practice

Source: From Marian J. Tonjes and Miles V. Zintz, *Teaching Reading/Thinking/Study Skills in Content Classrooms*, 2nd ed., p. 257. Copyright © 1987 Wm. C. Brown Publishers, Dubuque, Iowa. All Rights Reserved. Reprinted by permission.

elaborating underlying meaning, previewing, selectively annotating and underlining, or note-taking, which are more demanding tasks. Students may well have some type of study skill instruction during their school years, but it is generally "not sufficient or sophisticated enough to show them how to become more active readers, or those who attend, interact, reconstruct, and elaborate upon the text meaning as it relates to a specified learning task."[7]

If readers are to self-regulate their learning, they must be able to plan activities prior to comprehending a problem. They must know how to monitor, revise, and evaluate outcomes as to how effective they have been in terms of the task and purpose involved.

Instead of using a generic approach to study strategies, it is possible to teach students to regulate their own learning strategy. Instruction in how to regulate learning should include the following:

1. Simple, explicit, basic steps for the strategy
2. Frequent modeling or demonstration of the strategy in which the teacher performs the steps with the students
3. Guided instruction with immediate feedback to move students toward independence in judging the effectiveness of their learning
4. Spaced practice with a variety of texts and tasks.

In this way students will learn better how to transfer or apply the strategy to new tasks as they arise.[8]

Assisting students with study-learning strategies should involve several actions by the administration and teacher committees.

1. Form a district-wide committee of teachers in a variety of levels and content fields to examine:
   a. Which study strategies are being taught already and are most used by the students
   b. The relevance of these strategies to curriculum purposes
   c. Whether these strategies are taught in a realistic setting, emphasizing transfer of learning
2. Present methodology to see if students are being taught to think and learn independently. Direct instructions should include the following:
   a. *Explicit rules* for how to do something (e.g., how to summarize)
   b. *Verbal modeling* (a metacognitive script) of the type of thinking they need to go through when applying rules to a specific task. (This helps them to see the why, when, where, and how.)
   c. *Guided practice* in using their own self-regulatory skills. (For example, give checklists to students to complete as they work independently, with questions such as "Did you check the chart on page 72?" and guideposts or reminders such as "Don't forget to read the summary as an overview before reading the chapter." A gloss or "teacher looking over the shoulder" is helpful here. See Chapter 5 for more details on gloss.)
3. Help teachers in grades 4 to 8 to better understand the relationship between learning to read and reading to learn. Reading instruction should do more than teach students how to read stories, but should be balanced with expository materials.
4. Involve all secondary teachers in teaching study strategies appropriate to their own subject area—for example, note-taking across the curriculum, SQ3R in science or social studies.[9]

OVERCOMING GRADING PROBLEMS

Pearce (1983) recommends several ways to ease teachers' burden of grading many papers, including some type of holistic grading, rubrics, checklists, teacher-selective evaluation, and student involvement in evaluation.

1. In *holistic grading,* teachers decide which major traits are desired,

such as accurate and adequate content on the topic, and coherent presentation. This allows concentration on these aspects of the content without excessive concern for form or other problems at this point. Brief written comments and questions on these selected traits give formative feedback to students. Questions should challenge them to problem-solve and encourage interaction rather than put them down. Instead of writing "This is unclear," ask, "What further evidence can you give to convince me?" or "What is another way you might state this?"

2. *Rubrics* are summary lists of traits to be written about, as well as characteristics of good to poor papers, providing students a guideline and teachers a framework for evaluating efficiently. For example, "a high-quality paper would contain an overview of the topic, a defining statement, at least one other approach, good organization, and so on." This, then, is a rubric.

3. With a *checklist* of general features desired, each paper is read rapidly and then rated for each feature (for example, see Table 8.3.[10] Note too that Chapter 9 deals exclusively with study-writing concerns.)

Teachers can do selective evaluation early, on a rotating basis, with only a portion of the papers evaluated by the teacher each time. Involving students in the evaluation process is also a realistic time-saver. Students can self-evaluate or work in pairs, evaluating each other's rough drafts. In peer evaluation, give them guidance and structure by asking them to respond in the following order: (1) What are the best aspects of the paper? (2) What might be added? (3) What helpful changes can you suggest? Eventually students can use the rubric or checklist independently. Small groups can also be used either for initial evaluation of drafts or merely for interaction with the course material.

Students must learn ways to give both negative and constructive

TABLE 8.3
Checklist of Quality of Writing

	Excellent	Good	Fair	Poor	N/A[a]
1. Topic definition					
2. Main points covered					
3. Generalizations supported					
4. Logical development of ideas					
5. Clarity of writing					
6. Personal interpretation					
7. Summary statement					
8. Spelling, punctuation, grammar					

[a]N/A = not applicable.

criticism. Many may identify only negative things unless teachers point the way by saying such things as "I like this," "This is O.K. but doesn't help," or "You need to check this further." Students should be reminded that any evaluation should start by pointing out the good things before identifying the negative. We build people up in order for them to accept criticism more easily.

Another type of grading sheet follows in Table 8.4.

RATE

Rate's Place in Strategic Reading

Being a strategic reader involves planning, setting a purpose, adapting rate, self-monitoring while reading, and then reflecting on the message. There are certain things teachers can do to help all students become more strategic.

TABLE 8.4
Final Grade Sheet

Final Grade Sheet	Excellent 5	Good 4	Fair 3	Poor 2	Nonexistent 1
1. Correct form (spelling, grammar, punctuation)					
2. Correct bibliography, references form					
3. Organization of paper (i.e., topics build toward a logical conclusion)					
4. Originality (individual thought, not copied)					
5. Documented support when needed					
6. Accomplishes purpose explained in introduction					
7. Accurate presentation of material					
8. Conclusion ties paper together					
9. Overall appearance (neatness, proper manuscript form)					

10. General comments: _____

_____

_____

Source: Adapted with permission from *A Guidebook for Teaching Study Skills and Motivation*, 2nd ed., by Bernice Bragstadt and Sharyn Stumpf, copyright © 1987 by Allyn and Bacon, Newton, Massachusetts, p. 381.

First, tell students directly to plan how they will read a variety of materials, from magazines or newspapers to directions in texts and novels. Next, have them think about why they are reading the material. To what use will they put this reading? This helps to set the purpose. If they skim over the material first, they will be able to decide how to adapt their rates on the basis of their purpose and how difficult the material appears to them. As they read, they should be self-monitoring to determine how well they are comprehending. Later, they can reflect on the meaning. Let us look now at the concept of adaptable rates as one part of being a strategic reader.

Adaptable Rates

Four types of rates can be readily differentiated:

1. *Study rate, 250 words per minute (wpm) or less:* Slow, careful reading when the purpose is to obtain clear comprehension and retention of difficult words, concepts, details, and material

2. *Moderate rate, 250–350 wpm:* Normal or average rate when the purpose is overall comprehension and material is not too difficult, using assignments, literature, magazines, or newspapers

3. *Rapid rate, 350–800 wpm:* Fast rate for general comprehension of easy fiction, easy newspaper or magazine articles, correspondence, review of study material

4. *Reference rate or skimming or scanning, 800+ wpm:* Searching for information used for reviewing or overviewing, looking through the text to select appropriate information or scanning topics in an index, specific details, numbers, and so on; often means omitting large segments of material to get to the gist

It is noteworthy that faster is not necessarily better; in fact, it is often detrimental. The idea is to have a variety of rates and to adapt them as we read, moving from the snail's pace (study rate) all the way to skimming and scanning (reference rate). Table 8.5 shows an example of how we might adapt our rates within a given text chapter.

Thus, we adapt our rates to our purpose for reading and to the level of difficulty of the material. Skimming the chapter first as a preview gives us a mental framework into which we can eventually fill in pertinent details as we read, and we can actually increase our moderate rate.

TABLE 8.5
Adapting Rate within a Text Chapter

Part	Purpose	Rate
Overview	Organization/structure	Reference (skim)
Introduction	General idea	Rapid
First paragraphs in a section	Understand thoroughly what the section is about and how each part relates to the whole	Study
Description	Enjoy the imagery	Study
Whole chapter	Understand main ideas with supporting details	Moderate
Summary	Review important points	Study

Exercise on Rate Adaptability

To apply your knowledge, and recalling that rates depend on a given purpose and text difficulty—in terms of style, concept density, background knowledge, and subject interest—decide at what rate(s) you would read the following and what your purpose would be:

Rate   *Purpose*

_____ An article on preparing income taxes   _____

_____ A scientific article in a popular magazine   _____

_____ An essay on today's philosophy of education   _____

_____ A poem by Robert Frost   _____

_____ A gourmet recipe for preparing trout   _____

_____ A love story or a sports story   _____

_____ A historical novel   _____

_____ A text chapter   _____

_____ A Shakespearean sonnet   _____

_____ The history of the decline of the Roman Empire _____

_____ A mathematics problem   _____

It would be interesting to discuss and compare your responses with your group in class, taking into account that because of individual differences you may wish to agree to disagree. A historian might find the last item easy reading because of background knowledge, while the same might be said for the English major when reading a sonnet.

Comprehension and Rate

Because rate is only as good as the comprehension level we need to obtain, it is important to test our understanding and recall without looking back. If we took a ten-question quiz on the material and missed four questions, our comprehension would only be 60 percent, which might mean we needed to slow down and read again. Words per minute (wpm) is merely a raw score and should always be tied to the level of comprehension. One way to test comprehension of a newspaper article in a general way is to try to recall five of the seven main ideas in a seven-paragraph article.

Eye Movements

We have eye movement cameras that can record actual eye movements of good and poor readers. A beginning or remedial reader's eye movements are very different from those of the accomplished reader. As the eyes move across the line, taking in groups of words, this is called *saccadic sweep*. When the eyes stop (a *fixation*), this is the only time psychologists believe we see the print clearly and think about the message. To test this notion, if you move your head very quickly from side to side you will only see a blur. Every fixation then takes in approximately three or four words. Figure 8.2 shows a variety of saccadic sweeps and fixations, which are shown as dots. Think of a race course as you look at the sweeps. If that was the road, how much longer would it take the race driver to reach the goal?

When we read slowly, our minds wander at times. This may be because we can *think* at about 1,200 words per minute, and if we are reading at only 200, we are not using our brains to their capacity.

To check your own eye–voice span, try reading aloud to a friend at night and have him turn off the light without warning. The number of words you can say after the lights are out is your eye–voice span; it shows how far ahead your eyes were from your speaking voice. Teachers may need to practice taking in a line at a time so that they can monitor the class while reading to them.

FIGURE 8.2
Eye Movement Patterns

1. A beginning reader fixating on each word or part of a word:

—sweep

2. A remedial reader who regresses often:

3. A mature reader with a return sweep to the next line:

Paradoxes and Reasons for Slow Rates

Bragstadt and Stumpf (1987) talk about reading paradoxes that cover undesirable factors causing slow reading. These same factors may well be desirable when careful study-reading is needed. These include the following:

1. *Regression:* Returning too often to reread a segment can be nonproductive, but if we don't comprehend, we do need to go over the material as many times as it takes to figure it out.

2. *Subvocalizing:* Talking to ourselves, saying each word silently in our heads, will keep the rate down to the speed of normal speech (220–240 wpm) but, again, is necessary when material is difficult for us.

3. *Thought units:* Reading phrases rather than individual words generally assists comprehension, but there are times when every word carries significant meaning and should be attended to.

4. *Main ideas:* When the purpose is just to get the key thoughts, locating

topic sentences and skimming or eliminating supporting details may be worthwhile. For study-reading, however, it is necessary to look at these supporting arguments, how facts fit, and how examples relate in order to decide if the argument is valid and what the total picture is. Reflecting on the reading is important for in-depth study.[11]

There are numerous reasons that students read more slowly than they should or could. It may be just habit—being in a rut and not being conscious of alternative rates. Readers may lack specific purpose or motivation; they may have trouble concentrating or may possess habits that interfere with a more rapid rate: regressing, constantly talking to themselves—either by moving lips or by using inner speech—or reading word by word rather than in thought units.

Success Secrets

Realizing possibilities, pushing, practicing, keeping purposes in mind, skimming first, and getting rid of interfering habits when they are not needed are the basic ways to increase reading rate when it is desirable to do so. Knowing that you can do it as others have gets you past the first barrier. Pushing yourself to read faster helps you get out of your comfortable rut. Recognizing any habits you have maintained regularly that are not now needed except with difficult material is the first step toward breaking those habits. Keeping a purpose in mind helps you maintain focus and keeps your mind from wandering. Skimming first gives you an overall map to which details can be attached.

Practice Finding Your Own Rates

The formula for finding your words per minute (wpm) rate is straightforward. Your effective rate—how fast you read material with adequate comprehension—is easily determined if you are using a workbook with questions and answers. If not, you will have to estimate.

Raw score: $\dfrac{\text{Number of words read}}{\text{Number of seconds read}} \times 60 = \text{wpm}$

or

$\dfrac{\text{Number of words read}}{\text{Number of minutes read}} = \text{wpm}$

Effective Rate: wpm × comprehension % = ER (effective rate)

Here is an example of a workbook rate and comprehension check taken from a graded series of essays from easy to college-level. The ten comprehension questions are divided between straight recall of facts and a broader understanding of ideas. Answers will be found at the end of the chapter. For further checks on your rate in wpm, see Appendix 3, where you have three choices of excerpts with the words already counted for you.

When workbooks are not readily available, word counting can be estimated accurately enough for present purposes by measuring ten lines of a typical page. To get the average number of words per line, count the number of words in the ten lines selected and divide by ten (move the decimal point one place to the left). Next, count the number of lines on a page to get the average number of lines per page. Multiply the number of words per line by the number of lines per page to get the average number of words per page. Once this is done on a particular text, it will not have to be repeated.

To determine how much time it takes to read a segment, use a second hand on the clock or a stopwatch, writing down the beginning and ending times. Or decide on a specific amount of time to read, such as five minutes, and set the kitchen timer. Then count the number of lines or pages read when the timer goes off.

Research on Rate with Superior Readers

Carver (1985) asked how good those readers are whom we call "superior." Using four different ways of determining rate, he measured superior readers' rates at between 300 and 600 words per minute, not including the comprehension factor. They tended also to show superior comprehension and intellectual ability. There was no evidence in his study that they had an exceptional ability to skim. Instead, they seemed to get more of the gist the more time they had to read the material. Looking at their ability to comprehend eighth-grade-level material, he found it unreasonable to expect more than 75 percent of the material to be comprehended at rates higher than 600 wpm. When they were given books to read, he found strong evidence that recall of important details was in proportion to the amount of time they were given for reading. When readers do what is called speed reading, they are actually skimming, omitting large segments of text, picking up key thoughts only.[12]

40. Sorting out the facts

Reading time _____

Comprehension score _____

Words per minute _____

Effective rate _____

Insurance, whether it be health, car, or life, is protection for an individual and his family against risk.

Good health is one of the most valuable things in life, but good health does not remain the same throughout life. By having enough health insurance, one can largely be relieved of the risk of financial disaster from a long-term illness.

It is often very hard to sort out the facts and obtain the kind of health insurance one seeks because health insurance contracts are detailed and are not easy to understand. By considering carefully the following items, one will be likely to get the essential items in his health insurance plan.

What are the types of expenses that are covered by the policy? Every policy covers certain kinds of expenses. These expenses will be subject to certain conditions. Hospital indemnity, which is one of the simplest forms of health insurance, will pay only a fixed amount during hospitalization. If one receives outpatient treatment, he probably will collect nothing.

How much will the policy pay? The glowing ads give the top payments possible, but few policy holders receive the top payment. To be safe about what the policy does and does not cover, one should get a copy of the actual policy and study it.

When the ad for a health insurance plan says, "Up to $20,800 extra cash when you're in the hospital" and "Get $100 tax free each week," one should stop and do some thinking and figuring. To collect the $20,800 at the benefit rate of $100, one would have to be hospitalized for four years!

Not considering maternity, mental, and tuberculosis cases, only fifteen out of 100 people are hospitalized during any one year. The average hospital stay is eight days. Those with the highest hospitalization rate stay an average of 12 days.

There are other methods designed to limit payments. These might include deductibles, copayment provisions requiring the payment of some of the expenses, and the specified amount allotted for various kinds of operations.

One should always find out what the limits and restrictions are in any policy. If one is paying $50 per day for his room, plus drugs, X-rays, and operating room expense, and the indemnity policy pays $14 a day, he is going to be left with the remainder of the hospitalization expense. [389 words]

Source: Reprinted with permission from *Timed Readings,* Book 8, by Edward Spargo and Glenn R. Williston, copyright © 1980 by Jamestown Publishers, Providence, Rhode Island, pp. 93–94.

Selection 40: Recalling Facts without Looking Back

1. The average hospital stay is
   ☐ a. four days   ☐ b. eight days   ☐ c. fourteen days
2. The health insurance policy mentioned by the author pays $100
   ☐ a. per day   ☐ b. per week   ☐ c. per month
3. Collecting $21,000 in hospital benefits might require a stay of
   ☐ a. one year   ☐ b. four years   ☐ c. eight years
4. How many people out of every 100 are hospitalized in the United States annually?
   ☐ a. five   ☐ b. ten   ☐ c. fifteen
5. One of the least complicated forms of insurance is
   ☐ a. term life insurance
   ☐ b. hospital indemnity
   ☐ c. collision coverage

Selection 40: Understanding Ideas

6. According to the author, hospital indemnity insurance
   ☐ a. will not pay for hospital outpatient treatment
   ☐ b. will not pay for broken bones
   ☐ c. will not pay for minor surgery
7. The reader can infer that
   ☐ a. most insurance plans do not pay maternity benefits
   ☐ b. tuberculosis is still a serious illness
   ☐ c. cancer claims more lives than any other illness
8. The author implies that
   ☐ a. insurance advertisements are often deceiving
   ☐ b. many insurance companies bill customers on the first of the month
   ☐ c. people over seventy years of age cannot buy life insurance
9. Daily rates for a hospital room sometimes include the cost of
   ☐ a. ambulance service   ☐ b. drugs   ☐ c. television rentals
10. Many health insurance policies
    ☐ a. become void after ten years of payments
    ☐ b. can be canceled after a claim is paid
    ☐ c. do not pay the full cost of a hospital room

NOTES

1. Francis P. Robinson, *Effective Study* (New York: Harper & Brothers, 1946, 1961).

2. D. F. Dansereau, "The Development of a Learning Strategy Curriculum," in H. F. O'Neil, Jr., ed., *Learning Strategies* (New York: Academic Press, 1978).

3. Ibid.

4. C. D. Holley, et al., "Evaluation of a Hierarchical Mapping Technique as an Aid to Prose Processing," *Contemporary Educational Psychology*, 4, 227–237. In M. A. Just and P. A. Carpenter, eds., *The Psychology of Reading and Language Comprehension* (Newton, MA: Allyn and Bacon, 1987), p. 414.

5. Walter Pauk, "Evoker," *The Reading Teacher* (November 1963).

6. M. Eanet and A. Manzo, "REAP: A Strategy for Improving Reading/Writing/Study Skills," *Journal of Reading*, 19 (1976), 647–652.

7. Michele L. Simpson, "The Status of Study Strategy Instruction: Implications for Classroom Teachers," *Journal of Reading*, 28 (2, November 1984).

8. Bonnie Armbruster and Richard C. Anderson, "Research Synthesis on Study Skills," *Educational Leadership*, 19 (November 1981), 154–156.

9. Simpson, "Status of Study Strategy Instruction," pp. 140–141.

10. Daniel L. Pearce, "Guidelines for the Use and Evaluation of Writing in Content Classrooms," *Journal of Reading*, 27 (December 1983), 212–218.

11. Bernice Bragstadt and Sharyn Stumpf, *A Guidebook for Teaching Study Skills and Motivation*, 2nd ed. (Newton, MA: Allyn and Bacon, 1987), p. 345.

12. Ronald P. Carver, "How Good are Some of the World's Best Readers?" *Reading Research Quarterly*, 20 (Summer 1985), 389–419.

RECOMMENDED READINGS
FOR CHAPTERS 7 AND 8

Anderson, Thomas H., and Armbruster, Bonnie B. "Studying." In P. David Pearson, ed., *Handbook of Reading Research*. New York: Longman, 1984, pp. 657–680.

Armbruster, Bonnie, and Anderson, Richard C. "Research Synthesis on Study Skills." *Educational Leadership*, 19 (November 1981), 154–156.

Beers, Penny G. "Accelerated Reading for High School Students." *Journal of Reading*, 29 (January 1986), 311–315.

Bower, G. H. "A Selective Review of Organizational Factors in Memory." In E. Tulving and W. Donaldson, eds., *Organization and Memory*. New York: Academic Press, 1972.

Bragstadt, B. J., and Stumpf, S. M. *A Guidebook for Teaching Study Skills and Motivation*, 2nd ed. Boston: Allyn and Bacon, 1982.

Brieve, F. "Time is Money." *Phi Delta Kappan*, 59 (December 1977), 282.

Brown, Ann L., Bransford, John D., Ferrara, Roberta A., and Campione, Joseph C. *Learning, Remembering and Understanding*. Technical Report No. 244. Urbana: University of Illinois, 1982.

Carver, Ronald P. "Optimal Rate of Reading Prose." *Reading Research Quarterly,* 18 (1982), 56–88.

Christen, William L., and Searfoss, Lyndon W. "Placing Learning and Study Strategies in the Classroom." In Ernest Dishner et al., eds., *Reading in the Content Areas: Improving Classroom Instruction,* 2nd ed. Dubuque, IA: Kendall/Hunt, 1986, pp. 299–307.

Cooke, Jane Kita, and Haipt, Mildred. *Thinking with the Whole Brain: An Integrative Teaching/Learning Model K–8.* Washington, DC: National Education Association, 1986.

Dimond, Stuart. *Introducing Neuropsychology: The Study of Brain and Mind.* Springfield, IL: Charles C Thomas, 1978.

Gilling, Dick, and Brightwell, Robin. *The Human Brain.* London: Orbis, 1982.

Hoffman, Steve. "Using Student Journals to Teach Study Skills." *Journal of Reading,* 26 (January 1983), 344–347.

Hubel, David. "The Brain." *Scientific American,* 241 (September 1979), 45–53.

Karlin, Robert. *Teaching Reading in High School: Improving Reading in the Content Areas,* 4th ed. New York: Harper & Row, 1984.

McAndrew, D. A. "Underlining and Notetaking: Some Suggestions from Research." *Journal of Reading,* 27 (1983), 103–108.

Olshavsky, Jill. "Reading as Problem Solving: An Investigation of Strategies." *Reading Research Quarterly,* 12 (1976–1977), 654–674.

Ostrander, Sheila, and Schroeder, Lynn, with Ostrander, Nancy. *Super Learning.* New York: Dell, 1979.

Pauk, Walter. "Notetaking: More Bad Advice Exploded." *Reading World,* 18 (1979), 300–303.

Resnick, Lauren B. *Education and Learning to Think.* Pittsburgh, PA: Learning Research and Development Center, University of Pittsburgh, 1985.

Reynolds, R. E., Staniford, S. N., and Anderson, R. C. "Distribution of Reading Time When Questions Are Asked about a Restricted Category of Text Information." *Journal of Educational Psychology,* 71 (1979), 183–190.

Schuster, Donald H. "Introduction to the Lozano Method." *Journal of Suggestive-Accelerative Learning and Teaching,* 1 (Winter 1976), 278–293.

Sheikh, Anees A., and Sheikh, Katharina S. *Imagery in Education: Imagery in the Educational Process.* Farmingdale, NY: Baywood, 1985.

Sherman, T. M., and Wildman, T. M. *Proven Strategies for Successful Test Taking.* Columbus, OH: Charles Merrill, 1982.

Simpson, Michele L. "The Status of Study Strategy Instruction: Implications for Classroom Teachers." *Journal of Reading,* 28, (2, November 1984), 136–142.

Smith, Anthony. *The Mind.* New York: Viking Press, 1984.

Tonjes, Marian J. "Selected Instructional Strategies for Promoting Content Reading and Study Skills." In A. Hendry, ed., *Teaching Reading: The Key Issues.* London: Heinemann Educational Books, 1981, pp. 97–106.

Ulrich, Anna L. "Brain Growth: Implications for the Future." *New Mexico Journal of Reading,* 4 (Spring 1984), 7–10.

Wood, E., and Middleton, D. "A Study of Assisted Problem-Solving." *British Journal of Psychology,* 66 (1975), 181–191.

Postorganizer 1
Summary of Study-Learning

Study-learning involves all the processes of locating, organizing, comprehending, retaining, and retrieving needed information. More specifically, it involves efficient searching; locating and selecting appropriate sources; receiving and organizing the information for later retrieval; and then interpreting, applying, using, and monitoring it. Study-learning strategies and considerations should be based on how the brain best processes information, the variety of student learning styles, and recognition of the differences between long- and short-term memory. Knowing ways to memorize is also important to study-learning. Having a repertoire of skills and strategies to use is beneficial to the study-learner. While study-reading, rate should be adaptable to the purpose and difficulty of the material.

Postorganizer 2
FGS (Focus, Generalization, Significance)

1. *Focus:* Retitle this chapter taking everything into account and using only synonyms for each existing word. _____

   _____

2. *Generalization:* What is one general cognitive learning statement that would cover one segment of this chapter? _____

   _____

3. *Significance:* What information was personally significant to you, and

   why? _____

   _____

Answers to Selection 40, page 278

1. b
2. b
3. b
4. c
5. b
6. a
7. b
8. a
9. b
10. c

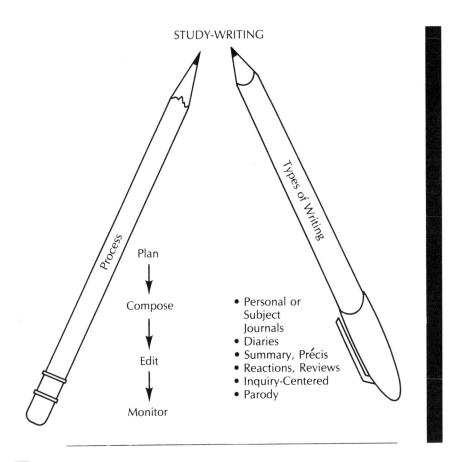

Process

Plan

↓

Compose

↓

Edit

↓

Monitor

Types of Writing

• Personal or
  Subject
  Journals
• Diaries
• Summary, Précis
• Reactions, Reviews
• Inquiry-Centered
• Parody

9

Study-Writing

CHAPTER OUTLINE

Preorganizers
Introduction
Reading Like a Writer: Similarities between Study-Reading and
    Study-Writing
  Roles for Readers and Writers
  The Role of Study-Writing in Secondary Classrooms
  Importance and Purposes of Readable Writing
  Kinds of Study-Writing
Types of Productive Writing Activities
  The Personal Journal or Diary
  The Subject or Learning Journal
  Summary or Précis Writing
  Reactions or Reviews
  Parody
  Exercises for Remedial Students
  Inquiry-Centered Writing
Study-Writing Strategies
  Story Impressions
  Basic Writing Competency
  PORPE
Grading Papers: The Role of Writing Teachers
Workshops
  Writing Workshop Procedures
  A Process Approach Workshop for Composing
  A Writing In-Service Workshop
  Materials for Writing and Publishing
Sample List of Publications Accepting Student Work
Summary
Notes
Recommended Readings
Postorganizer

COGNITIVE COMPETENCIES

1. Compare and contrast study-writing to study-reading.

2. Describe how study-writing will fit into the daily plans and procedures of your own classroom.

3. Critique Moffett's belief that we learn to write by writing, and his warnings about materials used today to teach writing.

4. Select one productive writing activity and justify its merits for your subject.

KEY TERMS

discourse
inquiry-centered writing
"hot" cognition
parody
personal journal

PORPE
précis writing
story impressions
subject journal

Preorganizer 1
Thinking about Writing and Writers

1. You will be given a maximum of 10 minutes in class to write several paragraphs about the importance to you of the major products of Peru. Be ready to share this writing with the class (or group) for their critique. State your reactions now to this type of assignment in the space provided here. _____

_____

_____

2. Make a list of three things of great interest to you in your own subject area that you would enjoy talking about or writing about later in class.

_____ / _____ / _____

3. If you were able to become a famous writer, who might be your favorite model?

_____ James Michener	_____ Agatha Christie
_____ William Shakespeare	_____ Ralph Waldo Emerson
_____ Charles Dickens	_____ Arnold Toynbee
_____ René Descartes	_____ Paul Lawrence Dunbar
_____ Thomas Hardy	_____ Anya Seton
_____ Mark Twain	_____ Ray Bradbury
_____ Edgar Allan Poe	_____ Danielle Steele
_____ Brontë Sisters	_____ Victoria Holt
_____ Beatrice Potter	_____ Robert Frost
_____ Steven King	_____ Charles Darwin
_____ Daphne DuMaurier	_____ Leonardo Da Vinci
_____ William Wordsworth	_____ J. R. Tolkien
_____ Robert Ludlum	_____ Frances Parkinson Keyes
_____ Isaac Asimov	_____ Paolo Freire
_____ C. S. Lewis	_____ Other (Name)

Study-Writing

What is it about their writing that you would wish to emulate?

_____

4. Predict here what you think are some similarities between the processes of reading and writing?

Reading   *Writing*

a. _____   _____

b. _____   _____

c. _____   _____

Preorganizer 2
An Expository Advance Organizer

Study-writing, one of our most important instructional means, includes all the concerns for teaching relevant writing skills and strategies in secondary classrooms across the curriculum. It can be compared to study-reading as the other side of the same coin, as both reading and writing are concerned with planning, composing, editing, and monitoring. In general, students have insufficient opportunity for practicing extended writing, which is one of the best ways to improve. A variety of writing forms can be used to make an assignment more interesting, and we must take into account the role of emotions in writing tasks. Different types of productive writing activities also help us to meet our teaching goals and objectives. A large variety of strategies, sources, and materials exist for the improvement of study writing.

"Peanuts" ° by Charles Schultz, reprinted from the *Seattle Times*, Sunday, March 20, 1988. © 1988 United Feature Syndicate, Inc.

Study-Writing

9
Study-Writing

READING LIKE A WRITER: SIMILARITIES BETWEEN STUDY-READING AND STUDY-WRITING

Study-reading and study-writing are closely related abilities, both requiring knowledge of language and background experiences for success. They are processes of negotiating meanings between reader and writer throughout a text. Pearson and Tierney (1984) describe reading as an event in which thoughtful readers behave like composers. Essential roles of both thoughtful readers and writers would include planner, composer, editor, and monitor, with all four roles meshing interactively. The following section is adapted from "On Becoming a Thoughtful Reader" by P. D. Pearson and R. J. Tierney, in *Becoming Readers in a Complex Society*, the Eighty-third Yearbook of the National Society for the Study of Education.[1]

Roles for Readers and Writers

Role 1: Planners have purpose, use background knowledge, predict, question, align. Planners set purposes, think about their background knowledge of the topic, predict what will be said, and ask questions about what the text might address. This can be compared to what writers do when they begin to write. Most high school students spend little time researching or considering topics before, during, and after reading, but instead read their texts once over lightly, not pausing to reflect, refer to other sources, or consider what they already know about what they are reading.

As planners, readers should align themselves with respect to the writer and the text, deciding what position to take. For example, they may wish to identify with a character in a narrative, to become an eyewitness to a historical account, to side with or battle with the writer of a persuasive text. All this can have a powerful effect on understanding and later recall for the reader.

Role 2: Composers monitor and create. During reading, readers must constantly monitor what the reading the writer has composed really means. This is based on their goals and predictions and on the questions they have asked. Because the text is merely a blueprint for meaning, readers must create their own mental picture, their model of meaning, always striving for coherence, to make things fit. At times this may mean filling in gaps, using their own predictions and imagination.

Role 3: Editors pause, rethink, revise. As readers create satisfactory models, they go beyond the planning and composing to the role of editor, forming small to wholesale revisions. To have control over their own models of meaning, readers must approach the text with the same thoughtful reflection that good writers use as they revise. They may reread, annotate with reactions, and question. Many secondary students approach the text for the purpose of memorizing for a test, reading either superficially or laboriously, item by item, without making appropriate connections among concepts.

Role 4: Monitors examine the balance of power. Thoughtful readers look at the print and its messages and decide the relative importance of the roles of planner, composer, and editor. They think about when to call up one of these roles for action or revision. Monitors decide when everything is completed, having met established criteria as well as they can.[2]

The Role of Study-Writing in Secondary Classrooms

Study-writing has been shown to improve thinking, learning, and reading. Study-writing is a process used in most classrooms, but often without much direct instruction as to how best to perform the task, or much allowance for practice in extended writing. The exception, of course, is in English classrooms, but English teachers should not be asked to carry the total burden. In a major study of writing across the curriculum, Applebee (1984) found that a majority of secondary classrooms only require writing for taking notes and writing short answers to study questions or tests.[3] If students were given more opportunity for extending their writing beyond a paragraph, the act of composing could help them better comprehend and see relationships among ideas, as well as to perceive the organization of these ideas. As most writers know, there is no better way to master a body of knowledge than to have to write about it. There is a real satisfaction, too, in saying something in print that you wish to say, and being able to say it in the most effective way.

We need to rethink the role of writing in assisting students' overall learning. Some of the techniques described later in this chapter will show possible ways to incorporate writing across the curriculum.

Importance and Purposes of Readable Writing

Writing is one of the most important instructional tools available to us. We use it to communicate, to argue, to explain or instruct, and to link past to future. There appears to be a consensus among scholars and practitioners alike that writing is a tool that makes possible a variety of expressive activities, including writing to participate in the community (e.g., setting rules in the classroom), knowing ourselves and others (e.g., diaries), or occupying our free time communicating with others (e.g., letters). Writing is also a way to demonstrate academic competence and to express our thoughts creatively.[4]

Kinds of Study-Writing

There are two kinds of study-writing—discourse and nondiscourse. Discourse, which is what concerns us here, is connected, extended writing and includes anything from brief encyclopedia entries to complete texts, both literary and expository. Nondiscourse material includes directions, tables, lists, and the like.

Looking at discourse alone, we can divide it into several categories: (1) materials intended primarily for general instructional purposes such as texts and articles; (2) programmed instructional materials; and (3) scientific, technical, nonfiction, and literary (all text that is not written deliberately for instructional use).

Table 9.1 shows some of the kinds of writing that could be incorporated into a classroom to give variety, motivation, and personal interest to assignments. History teachers might, for example, select written advertisements of a particular era, biographical sketches of famous people, confessions of historical villains, or diaries of royalty—to name a few. Table 9.1, then, shows the variety of discourse possible.

TABLE 9.1
Writing Forms Reference

advertisements	monographs
anecdotes	newspaper stories
aphorisms	observation papers
applications	pamphlets
autobiographies	petitions
ballads	photo essays
biographical sketches	plays
broadsides	poetry
cartoons	policy papers
children's story and verse	posters
commercials	predictions and prophecies
confessions	profiles
dialogues	propaganda
diaries	reminiscences
directions (how to)	requests
dramatic monologues	research
editorials	resumes
fantasy	reviews
fiction	riddles
films	satires
flyers	science notes
graffiti	sketches
historical "You Are There" scenarios	slide tape//slide show scripts
imitations of other writers	sound tapes
interviews	stories
jokes	story problems
journals	stream of consciousness
letters	summaries
light essays	telegrams
magazines	TV scripts
memos	thumbnail sketches
metaphors	written debates

"Hot" Cognition

It has been said that writing and emotions can be closely intertwined. Brand (1987) talked about a new cognition for written language, a "hot" one, which refers to cognition that is affected by feelings. She believes that the writing process has become overrationalized, that composing is generally seen today as sequential, deliberate, goal-directed—all with machinelike objectivity.[5] However, the very act of writing can lower anxiety and increase positive responses.

When we write or read, we bring to the act all of our past history of experiences. Connected to this are our feelings about how competent we are in performing the task and whether our feelings about writing are positive or negative. As Brand puts it, "It is in cognition that ideas make sense. But it is in emotion that this sense finds value."[6]

Learn to Write by Writing

Many of us are aware that some of our students lack the ability to compose effectively. They have trouble defending or supporting their ideas. When they do write, their work tends to be superficial, stilted, or too abstract. Such students may not have had enough exposure and practice in thinking and writing. The tests they take may be mostly objective tests (easily scored) and study worksheets, which generally require few connected sentences. With overloaded classes a usual condition, teachers tend not to assign long papers that would require hours of reading, correcting, and grading.

Moffett (1983) warns that much of the material used to teach writing today might well be in texts for teachers, but it is not helping students learn to write by writing.[7] Such materials being used with students include the following:

1. *Advice:* The cookbook type of "how to do it" lists all the pointers. Students try to remember them all as they write, which can actually inhibit productive thought.
2. *Definitions and explanations:* Students are asked to memorize generalities for tests, which again may lead them to do only what the book (the teacher) says.
3. *Workbook exercises:* Students are asked to do something with dummy sentences or paragraphs, such as "underline the word . . ." "make a single sentence out of. . . ." Words, sentences, or paragraphs, Moffett warns, are not building blocks or bricks that can be learned and manipulated separately.
4. *Brief writing models:* Samples to be read and referred to as models of good writing might better be read in their entirety.

Thinking back to your own secondary classes, how many of these materials were commonplace in your school? How much opportunity did you have to learn to write by writing?

TYPES OF PRODUCTIVE WRITING ACTIVITIES

There are numerous productive extended writing activities that can be used to meet a variety of goals and objectives. Among these are personal journals or diaries, subject or learning journals, summary or précis writing, reactions or reviews, and inquiry-centered writing.

The Personal Journal or Diary

By keeping a personal journal or diary, students can learn more about themselves. This may help their writing fluency and give them insights into their own ways of thinking, as well as the thinking of others.

In a developmental reading program in an Albuquerque high school remedial class, students were required to keep a personal journal for nine weeks. The minimum requirement was one notebook-sized page, written fully on both sides, to be turned in each Friday. If anything was too personal to be read by the teacher, students could write in red ink at the top of the page that this was a private matter. Because no corrections of spelling, grammar, organization, or anything else were made, there was no extra burden on the teachers, but teachers could note specific problem areas for future lessons. Some students actually became "hooked on writing." One student wrote out his anger and rage concerning what he felt was unfair treatment by another teacher and requested that it not be read. Later, after his rage had dissipated, he brought the journal back for the reading teacher to see. He admitted that the journal process had been therapeutic, a way of acting out without actually doing something disruptive or destructive.

The Subject or Learning Journal

The subject or learning journal is simply a special kind of notebook, but it is more informal and personal than class notes because it requires that students react and express their own thoughts about selected aspects of the subject matter. It also serves as a form of review and provides an opportunity to answer questions about material posed by either the teacher or the text. Teachers can respond to the students' answers either personally or in oral statements to the class. Because this is still informal expository writing, study or learning journals help teachers see how students are processing information. In large classes, this is a productive communication device whereby students may also ask questions on unclear points that they preferred not to ask in class. Personal reactions help students to ponder the significance of the material, relate the information to their own lives, and internalize it. They will discover that writing in these journals acts as a natural review process and is more meaningful than merely reviewing for a test.

Summary or Précis Writing

Research into texts has shown that summary writing helps students comprehend, retain, and later recall significant information. Summaries or précis are concise statements of essentials. Specific ways to teach summarizing can be found in Chapter 8, "Study-Learning, Part II."

In an honors American literature class, the teacher brought in a selection of magazines that featured excellent writing. Students chose a short article and spent thirty minutes reading it carefully, taking notes on the content. Then, using only the notes, they rewrote the article, imitating as closely as possible the language and style of the original. Although the students found this challenging, they also enjoyed the practice and became more interested in observing how successful writers write. As the next step in applying what they had learned from this activity, they were asked to write a précis on in-class content.

Reactions or Reviews

Another way for students to improve their thinking and writing is to have them become critics, noting how professionals handle the basic writing elements of setting, plot, character, dialogue, and style. Farrington (1986) has given us some student guidelines for writing reactions or reviews, which are adapted here from "You Be the Judge: Writing Book Reviews" by Jan Farrington, *Writing*, April 8, 1986, pp. 3–11. Special permission granted by *Writing* magazine, published by Field Publications, copyright © 1986 by Field Publications.[8]

1. If possible, read the entire work at one sitting. Try to relate to what is occurring and identify with a character—become a part of the story or history.
2. In order to be fair in judging, find some good points first, before you give any negative statements. Finish with a statement of how the work might be useful or with a summary of your overall reactions.
3. If you are reading a novel, be patient—remember that it sometimes takes a while to sort out all the characters and what is actually occurring.
4. Do not judge imaginative literature such as science fiction as being unrealistic. It is true if its internal reality brings the experience to life for the reader.
5. As a critic, decide how well writers of literature have handled the setting, plot, and character, or how writers of text handled sequence, organization, and clarity of ideas.
6. The way writers use words, phrases, and language in general may give clues to the theme or pattern. Words may have many levels of meaning.

7. Critics should always be ready to defend their positions with specific statements or examples.
8. Turn to other references when additional information is needed for better understanding (e.g., recent works with similar themes on the same subject).
9. While reading, jot down notes on any specific passages that might be useful for later reference in the review.
10. In a story, never disclose the plot or the ending because readers of the review may wish to read the story later.

In one high school, a teacher had her American literature honors class students read period American novels in pairs, two students to one novel. Then they reviewed the novel in front of the class using "Sneak Previews" and "At the Movies"–style formats. The teacher provided the students with the criteria to be used in the review (e.g., length, characters, story line, suspense, description, theme). If students found the book boring, they had to explain why. This review procedure worked so well that an advanced British literature class did the same and presented the reviews to slower classes to help students choose novels they would enjoy on the basis of peer opinions.

Science and mathematics teachers can also pair students to read biographies of their mentors, science fiction, and the like.

Parody

Another productive writing activity is parody which imitates the characteristic style of another's work and treats it in a nonsensical manner, such as a caricature. Students first read a good parody as a model. Then, in groups of varying sizes, they write and produce their own parodies of favorite (or least favorite) selections in literature, historical figures, or periods. They can produce a play, puppet show, radio program, videotape, or simply a written parody. What they learn is that *good* parody requires a thorough understanding of the content, style, and structure of the piece, period, or person they are trying to spoof. In this way, students analyze writing without seeing it as a chore and, at the same time, learn a lot about the nature of humor and staging. For further feedback, the whole class can critique the parodies following presentation.

Exercises for Remedial Students

There are a variety of exercises that can be used with students who find writing difficult and frightening. Completion of one-sentence, provocative

"If . . ." phrases; creating poems by combining nouns, verbs, and adjectives in set orders; drawing concrete poems; creating one-line metaphors and similes—these are just a few examples. Keeping exercises short (from a single sentence to one paragraph) and encouraging both unusual and humorous expression helps students to see not only that it is possible for them to write, but that there is no mystery to the process. Once they build some confidence, they can work on longer pieces.

A useful tool for working with both persuasive and expository writing has been explained by Brueggeman (1986). Her model teaches the process of writing reactions to editorials and includes four phases: teaching, guided practice, independent practice, and critical analysis.[9]

Phase I: Teaching

- Choose a controversial topic in the school or local paper.
- Ask students how they feel about the issue and list responses on the board or overhead. This is a brainstorming phase, and no judgments are made as to the worth of ideas.
- Together categorize responses, such as: (1) experiences, (2) pro, (3) con, (4) feelings or attitudes, and (5) importance of the topic.
- After students skim the editorial for the gist, have them read it to find the main viewpoint. Then ask the class to discuss what is important to that viewpoint.
- Have the class write a summary statement for this editorial and, with the teacher, discuss the issue. Encourage opposing points of view. List reactions under the labels "pro" and "con" and have students give reasons for their viewpoints.
- Ask the class to create a composite reaction beginning with a position statement. List several reasons for this position. Later, this time-consuming first phase can pay dividends.

Phase II: Independent Practice
Give students a selection of topics ranging from serious to humorous from which to choose. They proceed individually through the same steps that they did as a whole class. After the summary statement is written, topic groups are formed to reach consensus on a group summary statement. Students then write reactions individually.

Phase III: Guided Practice
This means that students form their own positions without group support. Topic groups are then formed to share completed products and to identify opposing viewpoints and how they can be supported. Following these

discussions, students add a paragraph describing an alternative point of view with possible support. This phase can be expanded to include the rest of the school by using a hall bulletin board for the best products.

Phase IV: Analyzing Selections
After several weeks of practice, Phase IV could be accomplished more quickly than the earlier phases. After all the practice in writing reactions, students should be able to analyze persuasion selections from the author's point of view and give a rationale to support the author's position.

Inquiry-Centered Writing

Inquiry-centered writing can benefit students by helping them better comprehend and synthesize what they have been learning. The important thing is to strike a balance between student self-reliance and guidance by the teacher. There needs to be enough structure so that students have a problem to focus on, yet freedom to pursue their ideas. They will need access to reference materials and constructive feedback when sharing results.[10]

Inquiry may start with questions that have been raised by students about a particular topic under study. Teachers can guide the inquiry by asking such questions as "What can we learn from . . .?" "How can we find out?" "Which is best?" "What does it mean to you?" This may help students realize what they already know or do not yet know about the topic.

Students are then asked to make predictions about what they might find. Next they locate and select appropriate materials. Teachers guide them in their search for information and ask helping questions as to how they are coming along and what kind of help they need.

Having gathered their information, students will select the form of writing for the report—essay, story, case history, editorial, or the like. When the information is organized, students write a rough draft and then continue through the cycle of editing, revising, rewriting, and publishing.

STUDY-WRITING STRATEGIES

Story Impressions

McGinley and Denner (1987) describe a study-writing strategy that combines reading with writing and helps students activate what they already know from their reading.[11] The idea of story impressions differs from the usual kinds of previews in that it does not divulge large amounts of plot. Instead, it uses key words to help build an anticipatory model or blueprint before reading. As the story is read, readers either confirm, deny, or modify predictions.

First, readers who have been given only fragments of the actual content are asked to predict events to be read. The fragments are used as clues to be turned into the readers' own story before reading. Less able readers may now begin to see reading as a drafting and composing process. For example, take the well-known story "The Tell-Tale Heart," by Edgar Allen Poe. Clue words are selected from the story and given in sequence, with arrows showing clue order. Here McGinley and Denner suggest a murder scheme ending in a confession (Figure 9.1).

To introduce this to a class for the first time, McGinley and Denner suggest several steps:

1. "Today we will be writing what we think this story *could* be about."
2. "Here are some clues to use in writing our version. When finished writing we will read the story to see if the author had similar ideas." (This may be done orally and on the board as a whole-class activity, or individually, depending on the ability of the class.)
3. Discuss similarities and differences, emphasizing that a close match is not important—only writing a logical story is.

In order to develop a set of story impressions, teachers must first read through the story and select words that designate characters, setting, and key plot elements. They need to use words directly from the story with a maximum of three words per clue, and limit clues to 10 to 15 or fewer for a short story or chapter, around 20 for a novel. They then arrange clues vertically with arrows.

Students enjoy writing stories based on impressions. Connecting clues can help them see both reading and writing as composing processes. By composing their own stories, they may be motivated to attend more closely to the actual reading of the author's version.[12] Best of all, once they have the process down pat, they may enjoy developing their own story impressions for other students to use.

Basic Writing Competency

It is a common misconception that there is just one simplified, standard form to be used as a model for good writing, and that once students learn that form, they will automatically become better writers. This misconception, if pursued, can lead to student ennui, and bored students are an old enemy of educators. Instead, Hoffman (1987) suggests that in obtaining true

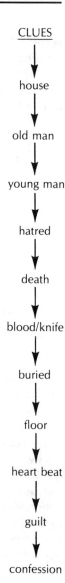

FIGURE 9.1
An Example of Key Words

Source: From "Story Impressions: A Prereading/Writing Activity" by William J. McGinley and Peter R. Denner, *Journal of Reading*, 31 (December 1987), pp. 248–252. Used with permission.

competency in basic writing, we must have creative choice and also we must be aware of who our audience will be. He suggests that we not teach a grammatical principle or technique of style without explaining clearly how it will help writing competency. Students do want to know why something is good and why it works. For example, we know that long sentences can help smooth the flow of writing so that it actually reads more like natural speech (even though readability formulas say otherwise).[13]

Railroad Ramble and Double Exposure are two writing strategies that show how to combine a series of subjects, verbs, and objects and how to splice together two points of view. Each uses visual images connected to photography. In the first, Railroad Ramble, modifying phrases are taught through a process involving telescoping sentences. Commas represent zoom lenses, and the sentence's frame of reference is moved even closer to the subject of the sentence. With Double Exposure, it is possible to take two essays on the same subject that have different styles and points of view and splice them together. The specific (truthful) point of view interrupts the general (official) point of view after every few paragraphs or pages and can be set apart by underlining or boxing in.[14] Herman Wouk used a similar technique in *Winds of War* by inserting an occasional chapter written from the point of view of a German general, who gave another impression of the wartime events occurring in the regular story. In the film *Annie Hall*, Woody Allen juxtaposed dialogue and subtitles. The dialogue represented the official pose, the subtitles the characters' truthful desires, secrets, and insecurities.

PORPE

PORPE (Predict, Organize, Rehearse, Practice, Evaluate) was developed by Simpson (1986) as an independent learning strategy for planning, monitoring, and judging. It requires that students act as effective readers — aware and in control of their own cognitive processes (metacognition) while study-reading. First, students predict potential essay questions, ones that will guide them in their study. Next they organize key ideas in their own words, using their own structure and methods for organizing. Then they rehearse (review) these key ideas and practice recalling writing tasks they assigned themselves that required analytical thinking. Finally, they evaluate their written product on the basis of the criteria of completeness, appropriateness, and accuracy in relation to the essay question they predicted in the first place.[15]

GRADING PAPERS: THE ROLE OF WRITING TEACHERS

Recently, researchers have been looking more carefully into the role of teachers of writing and their approach to this teaching. For example, Krest (1987) examined research in teaching writing over the past fifteen years and found evidence that the current approach is not as effective as it could be.[16] One reason is that it is not based on how people learn best, nor is it flexible in taking into account various learning styles. The current widely used approach has teachers serving as active judges and editors, and students as passive learners and imitators. This approach focuses more on correctness, style of writing, and organization of ideas than on creativity, individual development, and expression of new ideas.

As we rethink and redefine the role of writing teachers today, we might well decide that we ought to be helping students recognize their own strengths and then work on particular weaknesses, a few at a time. Our goal is to help our students become more confident, purposeful writers as they practice, not just to produce perfect products each time.

There are numerous principles of good writing that should be considered in small segments, as part of a developmental process. Reigstad and McAndrews (1984) have suggested that teachers read papers for a few (one to three) specifically chosen skills each time.[17] These might include writing mechanics, spelling, style, sentence structure, organization, main ideas, or supporting details. Selecting a few areas to focus on means that students are not overwhelmed and can then readily use comments for practice when revising. Peer editors and peer graders may also be given specific tasks to critique, while ignoring other writing deficiencies. Just before the final copy, peer graders may be used by replacing names with numbers on papers and posting papers around the room. With a checklist, peer graders walk around the room and rate each paper, using their own coded number by each rating. The teacher tallies these and returns papers with ratings to each writer, thus giving them constructive feedback for reworking needed areas.

An important principle of evaluation is to comment on strengths first in order to build up confidence before giving constructive criticism. Saving general comments until the end of the paper allows us to follow this principle. Any paper that is returned covered with red penciled corrections does not have a constructive effect and can be discouraging.

A few other tips for teachers include the following:

1. Writing teachers often keep folders on each student's drafts and revisions, giving a grade not only for the final paper but also for the effort and improvement shown.
2. Computers in the classroom can assist in checking style, mechanics, and spelling.
3. Brief individual conferences at the rough draft stage can be more efficient and effective than elaborate written comments.

Writing-intensive classes are always labor-intensive and thus should have a limited enrollment. When that is impossible, however, some of the ideas given here may help relieve the writing teacher's burden.

WORKSHOPS

Writing Workshop Procedures

Students need to know what to expect when enrolling in a writing-intensive class or workshop. One way to accomplish this is described by Atwell (1987), who first distributes two lists to the class that outline both student and teacher roles.[18] These lists can also be shared with parents.

Student's role: You will:

1. Come to class each day with your daily writing folder, keeping in it all drafts of work in progress. This folder will be the text for this class.
2. Write and complete some writing every day.
3. Make a daily plan for writing in class and at home.
4. Write about topics that interest you.
5. Take risks, try new techniques, new kinds of writing, topics, and skills.
6. Draft your prose writing in paragraphs.
7. Number and date every draft. This is important.
8. Self-edit final drafts in a pen or pencil of a different color.
9. Maintain the skills list (to be handed out in class) and use it as a guide in editing and proofreading.
10. Make final copies legible and correct, and use appropriate margins.
11. Monitor your own writing, noting what works and what does not.
12. Listen to and question other writers' work, giving helpful, thoughtful responses.
13. Do nothing to distract yourself or others from writing in class.
14. Try to maintain a positive attitude at all times.
15. Discover what writing can do for you!

Teacher's role: I will:

1. Keep track of what you are writing, where you are, and what you might need.
2. Grade your writing four times a year based on your effort, growth, and final drafts.
3. Write and finish some pieces every day.

---

4. Prepare and present mini-lessons based on what I see you need to know next. (*Example:* I will provide you with a sheet of proofreading marks you can use.)
5. Help you locate topics and materials you are interested in pursuing.
6. Provide a safe, predictable environment where you feel free to take risks as a writer.
7. Organize this room to meet individual writers' needs.
8. Help you learn editing and proofreading skills.
9. Be your final editor.
10. Give you opportunities to publish your writing.
11. Photocopy finished pieces you choose as examples of your best work to date.
12. Provide any writing materials you need.
13. Listen to you and respond to your writing by asking thoughtful, helpful questions and keeping a record of what happens in our individual conferences.
14. Try to maintain a positive attitude at all times.
15. Help you discover what writing can do for you!

Source: Reproduced and adapted with permission from *In the Middle* by Nancie Atwell (Boynton-Cook, Portsmouth, NH, 1987), copyright © 1987 by Heinemann Educational Books, Inc., pp. 125, 131.

Atwell's book *In the Middle* (1987) is an excellent, detailed reference for study writing. A few other tips include some given on helping students in the revising process. Teachers should show the use of carets (^) for inserting a new word or phrase; arrows to connect with empty spaces, margins, or the back of the sheet; asterisks (*) for inserting large chunks of material; and "spider legs"—strips of paper with new material stapled to the rough draft in the appropriate spot. Remind students that cutting and taping to reorganize information saves having to rewrite it. On rough notes and drafts, students can circle sections in different-colored inks, one color for each different topic.[19]

A Process Approach Workshop for Composing

Ferris and Snyder (1986) have specified a four-stage approach when conducting a workshop for composing.[20]

Stage One: Prewriting
Use the language experience approach to improve thinking processes and assist in deciding on a topic. In other words, help students develop

thoughts and language through some shared experiences. Examples include brainstorming, clustering ideas in a graphic form, practicing using analogies, free-associating activities, games, role playing, class journals, films, records, and literary models examined for variety of styles.

Stage Two: Writing Rough Drafts
Having decided on a topic during or following the prewriting stage, students write rough drafts containing some thoughts they developed during stage 1. They organize their ideas by writing passages of varied lengths and using appropriate formats. They try to adjust their style and tone to their intended audience.

Stage Three: Revising
In this stage, students try to reformulate their ideas for clarity of tone or style. They use the technique of sentence combining, connecting thoughts with key words like *because* or *but* to show relationships between and among ideas. They also proofread for typographical errors.

Stage Four: Presenting or Publishing
Finally, the polished paper is presented to the class and teacher for evaluative comments. Some works are published in a class newspaper or school magazine, or on bulletin boards.[21]

A Writing In-Service Workshop

A fascinating account of a successful in-service workshop on writing for teachers is described by Neilsen (1986). Much of what he details could be adapted to a writing-intensive secondary classroom.[22]

The workshop started off with an activity in which everyone was asked to write a page about "The Environmental Impact of Off-shore Drilling in Nova Scotia," deliberately chosen as a topic not likely to be well known or of much direct concern or interest to the group at hand. Telling the group that they would be given ten minutes, the instructor just sat and watched them write.

After ten minutes, participants exchanged papers, made several written suggestions for improvement, and then returned the paper to the partner. They were told that it would be discussed later. Immediately moving to the next activity, they made a list of three things that interested them and that they felt comfortable talking about. They shared with a partner, chose one of the topics, and began again to write for twenty minutes, having been told not to worry about mechanics, just to get down their ideas as a beginning. The instructor did the same, joining one of the groups to write.

When the time was up, they shared with a partner by reading their own piece aloud. Listeners responded by giving some positive feedback about something they liked, asking questions such as why a particular topic was chosen, or asking for more information.

The instructor then discussed with them the first activity, explaining how it made writing difficult, and asked for their reactions to the second activity. From this discussion, participants developed guidelines as a group for promoting writing in their classes. Instead of just being told, these workshop participants had ownership in the whole process because they had experienced the bad as well as the good and then had been allowed to contribute to the guidelines.

The guidelines developed by a group might resemble the following:

1. Students must be allowed to choose their own topics, revise, and decide whether or not to publish.
2. They need *time* to write (e.g., three thirty-minute blocks per week).
3. Teachers should model the process and write and share with their students.
4. It is important initially to emphasize ideas, not mechanics.
5. Feedback should be supportive, constructive, and encouraging, and teachers should offer advice when asked.[23]

As Graves (1983) advises, creative writing involves, first, organizing the classroom for writing, bringing in collections of motivating materials, and creating a supportive environment; next, allowing students to select topics from their own lists of things they would like to write about; and then modeling writing for them by taking them through the stages step by step. These stages include planning (first draft, composing, developing a topic), revising or editing (examining both content and organization of ideas, choice of words, and mechanics), and finally publishing (sharing a polished final piece).[24]

Materials for Writing and Publishing

A detailed list is provided here for reference:

1. *Variety of paper:* Size, weight, color, texture; lined, construction, ditto, colored, graph, index cards, oak tag, Post-It notes, and so on
2. *Variety of writing implements:* Size, color, style; regular and colored pencils, ballpoint and roller ball pens, crayons, markers, manuscript pens, watercolors, poster paints, brushes
3. *General equipment and supplies:* Erasers for ink and pencil, opaquing

liquid, staplers and staple removers, scissors, transparent and masking tape, paper clips and fasteners, rubber cement, white glue and paste, paper punches, rulers, yardstick, rubber bands, thumb tacks, clipboards, rubber date stamp and pad, book display racks, tape recorder and blank tapes, overhead projector, transparencies, markers

4. *Publishing:* Cardboard, wallpaper, vinyl adhesive letters, lettering stencils, needles and dental floss, bookbinding tape, awls, book press, glue, paste, typewriter, word processor, printer

5. *Resource and reference materials:* Dictionaries, Spellex spellers (from Curriculum Associates, Inc.), usage handbooks, models of standard formats for letters, classroom references, variety of literature samples, magazines, card file of professional publications featuring students' writing

6. *Materials for organizing writing:* File folders or portfolios—two or more per student:

   a. Daily folders containing student lists of topics already written about, list of potential topics, lists of editing skills the writer has taught

   b. Permanent folders to hold all drafts of written work filed in chronological order and notes from quarterly evaluation conferences. File cabinet or divided boxes for storing folders.

   c. Teacher's records—weekly class status check sheet; conference log; trays or boxes for writing ready for editing, publishing, or photocopying[25]

Sample List of Publications Accepting Student Work

Action, Scholastic, Inc.
730 Broadway
New York, NY 10003
(ages 12–14)

English Journal
1111 Kenyon Road
Urbana, IL 61801
(annual "Spring Poetry Festival")

Cobblestone
20 Grove Street
Peterborough, NH 03458
(ages 8–14)

Hanging Loose
231 Wyckoff Street
Brooklyn, NY 11217
(ages 14–18)

Co-Ed Magazine
Your Space
50 West 44th Street
New York, NY 10036
(poetry page)

Just About Me
Ensio Industries
247 Marlee Avenue, Suite 206
Toronto, Ontario, Canada M6B, 4B8
(ages 12–19, girls only

Merlyn's Pen
P.O. Box 716
East Greenwich, RI 02818
(grades 7–10, all types of writing)

Purple Cow
Suite 315, Lates Center
110 E. Andrews Drive, N.E.
Atlanta, GA 30305
(ages 12–18, nonfiction)

Scholastic Scope Magazine
50 West 44th Street
New York, NY 10036
(grades 7–12, "student writing" or
"mini-mysteries" written for
adolescents reading at 4th to 6th
grade level)

Scholastic Voice Magazine
50 West 44th Street
New York, NY 10036
(grades 7–12, emphasis on grades
8–10, poems and stories under 500
words, "Your Turn")

Seventeen
850 Third Avenue
New York, NY 10022
(ages 13–21)

Stone Soup
Box 83
Santa Cruz, CA 95063
(ages up to 15; all student work, including stories, essays, poetry, art
work and photographs)

The Sunshine News
Canada Sunshine Publishing, Ltd.
465 King Street, East, #14A
Toronto, Ontario, Canada M5A 1L6
(ages 14–17)

Teenage Magazine
217 Jackson Street
P.O. Box 948
Lowell, MA 01853
(ages 14–19)

Voice
Scholastic, Inc.
730 Broadway
New York, NY 10003
(ages 12–18)

SUMMARY

Writing as a process is an important consideration for most classrooms. Writing-intensive courses should be as prevalent in science and history classes, for example, as they are in English classes. The term *writing-intensive* does not mean just requiring a great deal of written work from students. Instead, it implies the process delineated in this chapter, a process of rough drafts, feedback, and revision, with instructor assistance along the way as needed. Study-writing, like study-reading, is crucial to the education of our young people today. Becoming a better writer can have a positive effect on reading comprehension or study-reading.

NOTES

1. P. D. Pearson and R. J. Tierney, "On Becoming a Thoughtful Reader: Learning to Read Like a Writer," in A. C. Purves and O. S. Niles, eds., *Becoming Readers in a Complex Society*, Eighty-third Yearbook of the National Society for the Study of Education (Chicago: University of Chicago Press, 1984), pp. 144–173.

2. Ibid.

3. A. N. Applebee, *Writing in the Secondary School: English and Content Areas* (Urbana, IL: National Council of Teachers of English, 1984).

4. Susan Florio, Christopher M. Clark, et al. "The Environment of Instruction: The Forms and Functions of Writing in a Teacher-Developed Curriculum," in Gerald Duffy, Laura Roehler, and Jana Mason, eds., *Comprehension and Instruction: Perspectives and Suggestions* (New York: Longman, 1984) pp. 104–115.

5. Alice G. Brand, "Hot Cognition: Emotions and Writing Literacy," in *Changing Concepts of Reading: Literacy Learning Instruction*, Seventh Yearbook of the American Reading Forum (1987), pp. 22–31.

6. Ibid.

7. James Moffett, *Teaching the Universe of Discourse* (Boston: Houghton Mifflin, 1983).

8. Jan Farrington, "You Be the Judge: Writing Book Reviews," *Writing*, April 8, 1986, pp. 3–11.

9. Martha A. Brueggeman, "Read First, Analyze Second: Using Editorials to Teach the Writing Process," *Journal of Reading*, 30 (December 1986), 234–239.

10. R. T. Vacca and J. L. Vacca, *Content Area Reading*, 2nd ed. (Boston: Little, Brown, 1986), pp. 221–223.

11. William J. McGinley and Peter R. Denner, "Story Impressions: A Prereading/Writing Activity," *Journal of Reading*, 31 (December 1987), 248–252.

12. Ibid.

13. Gary Hoffman, "Toward Literate Writing: Back to Basics but Not Back to Boring," *Curriculum Review*, 27 (September–October 1987), 33–39.

14. Ibid.

15. Michele L. Simpson, "PORPE: A Writing Strategy for Studying and Learning in Content Areas," *Journal of Reading*, 29 (February 1986), 407–414.

16. Margie Krest, "Time on My Hands: Handling the Paper Load," *English Journal*, 76 (December 1987), 37–42.

17. Thomas J. Reigstad and Donald A. McAndrews, *Training Tutors for Writing Conferences* (Urbana, IL: National Council of Teachers of English, 1984).

18. Nancie Atwell, *In the Middle: Writing, Reading and Learning with Adolescents* (Portsmouth, NH: Boynton/Cook, 1987), p. 125.

19. Ibid., p. 131.

20. Judith Ann Ferris and Gerry Snyder, "Writing as an Influence on Reading," *Journal of Reading*, 29 (May 1986), 751–756.

21. Ibid.

22. Allan R. Neilsen, "Knowing by Doing: An Active Approach to Writing Inservice," *Journal of Reading*, 29 (May 1986), 724–728.

23. Ibid.

24. Donald Graves, *Writing: Teachers and Children at Work* (Portsmouth, NH: Heinemann Educational Books, 1983).

25. Atwell, *In the Middle*, pp. 263–267.

RECOMMENDED READINGS

Aldridge, Ann. "Inspiration from the Past: Using Historical Documents to Stimulate Student Writing," *English Journal*, 69 (September 1980), 44–47.

Applegate, Arthur N. *Writing in the Secondary School: English and Content Areas*. Urbana, IL: National Council of Teachers of English, 1981.

Cooper, Charles R. "Holistic Evaluation of Writing." In Charles R. Cooper and Lee Odell, eds., *Evaluating Writing: Describing, Measuring, Judging*. Urbana, IL: Council of Teachers of English, 1977, p. 3.

Daniels, Harvey, and Zemelman, Steven. *A Writing Project: Training Teachers of Composition from Kindergarten to College*. Portsmouth, NH: Heineman Educational Books, 1983.

Draper, Virginia. "Writing to Assist Learning in *All* Subject Areas." In Gerald Camp, ed., *Teaching Writing: Essays from the Bay Area Writing Project*. Portsmouth, NH: Boynton/Cook, 1983.

Early, Margaret, and Sawyer, Diane. *Reading to Learn in Grades 5 to 12*. New York: Harcourt Brace Jovanovich, 1984.

Emig, Janet, "Writing as a Mode of Learning." *College Composition and Communication*, 28 (May 1977), 122–129.

Frager, Alan M. "Content Area Writing: Are You Teaching or Testing?" *Journal of Reading*, 29 (October 1985), 58–62.

Fulwiler, Tobey. "Journals across the Disciplines." *English Journal*, 69 (December 1980), 14–19.

Kintsch, W., and VanDijk, T. "Toward a Model of Text Comprehension and Production." *Psychological Review*, 85 (1978), 363–394.

Kirby, Dan, and Liner, Tom. *Inside Out: Developmental Strategies for Teaching Writing*. Rochelle Park, NJ: Hayden, 1980.

Knoblauch, C. H., and Brannon, Lil. "Writing as Learning through the Curriculum." *College English*, 45 (September 1983), 465–474.

Langer, Judith A. "Where Problems Start: The Effects of Available Information on Responses to School Writing Tasks." *Research in the Teaching of English*, 18 (February 1984), 27–44.

Lehr, Fran. "Writing as Learning in the Content Areas." *English Journal*, 69 (November 1980), 23–25.

Moffet, James. *Teaching the Universe of Discourse*. Boston: Houghton Mifflin, 1983.

Myers, Kris L. "Twenty (Better) Questions." *English Journal*, 77 (January 1988), 64–65.

Myers, J. *Writing across the Curriculum*. Bloomington, IN: Phi Delta Kappa, 1984.

Powell, J. L., and Brand, A. G. "The Development of an Emotions Scale for Writers." *Educational and Psychological Measurement*. ERIC Document Reproduction Service No. ED 268-152, 1986.

Roe, Betty D., Stoodt, Barbara, and Burns, Paul. *Secondary School Reading Instruction: The Content Areas*, 3rd ed. Boston: Houghton Mifflin, 1987.

Rosenblatt, L. M. *The Reader, the Text, the Poem.* Edwardsville: Southern Illinois University Press, 1978.

Rubin, Dorothy. *Teaching Reading and Study Skills in Content Areas.* New York: CBS College Publishing, 1983.

Santa, Carol Minnick, Dailey, Susan C., and Nelson, Marylin. "Free Response and Opinion Proof: A Reading and Writing Strategy for Middle Grade and Secondary Teachers." *Journal of Reading,* 28 (January 1985), 346–352.

Smith, Frank. "Reading like a Writer." *Language Arts,* 60 (May 1963), 558–567.

Stein, Nancy L. "Knowledge and Process in the Acquisition of Writing Skills." In Ernst Rothkopf, ed., *Review of Research in Education.* Washington, DC: American Educational Research Association, 1986, pp. 225–258.

Stewig, John Warren. *Read to Write,* 2nd ed. New York: Holt: Rinehart and Winston, 1980.

Strunk, William, Jr., and White, E. B. *The Elements of Style,* 2nd ed. New York: Macmillan, 1972.

Tchudi, S., and Yates, J. *Teaching Writing in the Content Areas: Senior High School.* Washington, DC: National Education Association, 1983.

Tierney, R. J. and Leys, M. *What Is the Value Connecting Reading and Writing?* Reading Education Report No. 55. Urbana: University of Illinois, Center for the Study of Reading, 1984.

Tierney, R. J., and Pearson, P. David. "Towards a Composing Model of Reading." *Language Arts,* 60 (May 1983), 568–580.

Zinsser, William. *On Writing Well,* 2nd ed. New York: Harper and Row, 1980.

Postorganizer
Writing a Mini Lecture

Look back now at Preorganizer 1, item 2, where you listed three things of great interest to you in your own subject area that you would enjoy talking about or writing about. Select one and develop a rough first draft of a mini-lecture you would share with your class. Then look back at pertinent areas in this chapter and, with a partner, go through the steps needed to develop a polished piece you would be willing to share or publish.

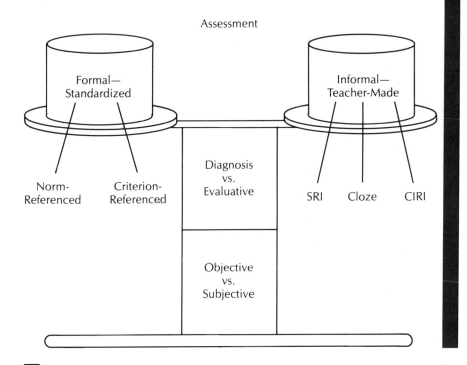

Assessment

Formal—
Standardized

Informal—
Teacher-Made

Norm-
Referenced

Criterion-
Referenced

Diagnosis
vs.
Evaluative

SRI

Cloze

CIRI

Objective
vs.
Subjective

10

Assessment Procedures

CHAPTER OUTLINE

Preorganizers
Introduction
Formal Testing: Standardized Tests
  Norm-Referenced Tests
  Criterion-Referenced Tests
  Minimum Competency Testing
  Aptitude Tests
  Selected Standardized Assessment Instruments
Specific Diagnostic Instruments
  Miscue Analysis: A Qualitative Assessment
  Quick-Score Achievement Test
  Reading Style Inventory
Informal Tests: Levels of Reading Proficiency
The Content IRI or CIRI
  Construction
  Administration and Scoring
A Secondary Inventory for Reading/English Teachers
The Cloze Procedure
PreP: The Prereading Plan
Test Questions
  Creating Test Questions
  Types of Test Questions
  Levels of Questions
Inconsiderate Texts and Future Inventories
  Inconsiderate Text Sample
  Warnings
  Pressure Pattern
  Glossary
Glossary for Assessment
Summary
Notes
Recommended Readings
Postorganizers

COGNITIVE COMPETENCIES

1. *Differentiate* in column form the various types of assessment devices discussed here.

2. *Design* your own reading assessment program.

3. *Construct* questions on one topic in your subject for each level of the cognitive domain.

4. *Appraise,* with reasons given, the relative merits of formal versus informal measures.

KEY TERMS

cloze procedure
Content IRI (CIRI)
criterion-referenced tests
inconsiderate text
miscue analysis
norm-referenced tests

PreP
Quick Score Achievement Test
  (Q-SAT)
Reading Style Inventory (RSI)
Secondary Inventory (SI)

Preorganizer 1
Checklist as a Diagnostic Instrument

The following checklist for secondary readers can be worded so that individuals fill it out themselves, or it may serve as a teacher observation checklist. Try filling it out before reading the chapter in order to self-assess your own study-reading behaviors.

Observation/Checklist for Readers' Study-Reading Behavior

While reading I am able to:

	3 Usually	2 Sometimes	1 Rarely	0 Not Certain
1. Define meanings of general words in context.				
2. Give definitions for specialized, technical terms.				
3. Recall explicitly stated information.				
4. State the main idea of a paragraph.				
5. State the central idea of a group of paragraphs.				
6. Succinctly summarize a chapter.				
7. State important details that support the main idea of a paragraph.				
8. State important details supporting the central idea of a group of paragraphs.				
9. Answer inference questions concerning the content, going beyond what was actually stated.				
10. Hypothesize as to the purpose of the material.				
11. Draw analogies from the reading (comparing the new to the known).				

Assessment Procedures

	3 Usually	2 Sometimes	1 Rarely	0 Not Certain
12. Apply what has been read in solving problems in daily life.				
13 Critically examine what writers have presented.				
14. Come up with alternative solutions that go beyond what was stated.				
15. Publicly state the value of choosing reading over other activities.				
16. Volunteer to answer classroom questions.				
17. Contribute to classroom discussions on the reading.				
18. Use mental imagery to picture the events, characters, and setting while reading.				
19. Self-evaluate reading behaviors when meeting a comprehension problem.				
20. Take appropriate action for alleviating a comprehension problem.				

Preorganizer 2
Study Reading Interview

Choose a partner and take turns interviewing each other. Ask the following questions orally, and write in the responses here. This may be handed in anonymously if desired, or used as a basis for small-group discussions.

1. How would you describe yourself as a reader? _____

_____

2. How often do you read purely for fun? _____
   What would you usually rather do than read? _____

_____

3. When you read for fun, what type of reading do you prefer (e.g.,
   magazines, newspaper sections, short stories)? _____

_____

4. What topics or subjects do you most like to read about? _____

_____

5. How do you usually prepare for a test? _____

_____

6. What special difficulty do you have with reading assignments?

_____

7. What do you think is the cause of that difficulty? _____

_____

8. Do you generally have trouble concentrating on your study reading
   assignments? If so, why? _____

_____

9. Which subjects/texts are the most difficult for you to read? _____

_____

   Why? _____

10. What might help you better understand that reading? _____

_____

11. What is your approach to reading an assignment? (What steps do you

    take?) _____

_____

12. What references (not your text or workbook) do you use regularly with

    ease? _____

_____

13. How do you go about finding needed materials in the library? ___

_____

14. Describe a typical day of personal and also study-reading. What

    is the balance? _____

_____

15. How do you feel, physically? Do your eyes bother you? Headaches?

_____

16. Describe your personal strengths and talents. _____

_____

17. Which of the following are your strongest and weakest reading areas?

    vocabulary _____ comprehension _____ rate _____

    concentration _____ recalling material read _____

18. When you leave school, will you be a voluntary lifelong reader of a

    variety of materials (yes/no/not certain)? _____

    Explain. _____

Preorganizer 3
Build Your Own Diagnostic Kit

As you read this chapter, make a list of tools you might find helpful for diagnosing your own students in the classroom. State your purpose for using each and place in the order in which you might administer these tools. For example, some possible categories include the following:

1. Examination of student records for information on standardized test scores, informal teacher comments, and so on.
2. Observation checklists
3. Pre- and posttests—types, length, and so on.
4. Interviews, conferences
5. Formal procedures
6. Informal procedures
7. Summary statements, conclusions
8. Portfolios of work

As an alternative, you may wish to take case studies and decide which procedures and instruments you would use with each case.

10
Assessment
Procedures

*As accountability systems accelerate educators must prevent
evaluation systems from eviscerating the curriculum.*
JOHN T. GUTHRIE, 1984[1]

INTRODUCTION

Effective teachers are those who systematically assess their students' needs,
levels, and interests and adjust their instruction accordingly. Assessment
can be formal or informal, objective or subjective. Formal assessment is
usually carried out at the end of a term and generally uses standardized
and objective tests. Feedback from a standardized reading test, for example, is given in a printout form with scores for strong and weak areas (e.g.,
vocabulary, comprehension, rate). Informal assessment, by contrast, may
be continuous throughout the term and may use subjective teacher-made
pre- and posttests, inventories, observations, and interviews. Feedback from
informal testing is more personal and detailed; it comes from student scores,
teacher notes and recommendations, and class charts—all in specific areas
teachers feel are important.

FORMAL TESTING: STANDARDIZED TESTS

Standardized test scores became popular around 1900 as a way to evaluate
programs, schools, districts, and systems by comparing them to a normal
population. Criticism of these tests became prevalent in the 1920s and 1930s
because the scores did not convey the complexity of reading levels or specify

reading difficulties. Many reading educators then turned to using teacher-made informal reading inventories, commonly referred to as IRIs, which consisted of series of graded paragraphs that individuals would read orally while the tester marked their errors. The levels established by these informal inventories were later converted into scores, and commercial IRI instruments were constructed. This meant that teacher-made inventories no longer dominated the field, because it was easier to use existing instruments. Unfortunately, in some cases the commercial tests did not measure the kind of material being read in classrooms. Next, new standardized tests were developed; they were supposed to give diagnostic information with "scientific precision and administrative efficiency."[2] Today we have a mixture of both commercial informal inventories and standardized tests.

Norm-Referenced Tests

In these standardized tests, students' performance is compared to that of others of similar age and grade level. These formal tests are normed over a broad population sampling. Commercially published, they use statistical procedures to try to achieve consistency in results. They are silent and generally group-administered. Norm-referenced tests were given initially to a sample of the population in order to compare students to the sample. One problem is that students vary considerably in previous instruction, background experiences, socioeconomic levels, and culture, making true comparisons difficult.

Standardized scores purport to be reliable (consistent) and valid (to measure what they are supposed to measure). Johnston (1984) has suggested that the issue of validity is broader, more important, and more complex than conventional wisdom has dictated. He suggests that we look at validity of the interpretation rather than the validity of the test, arguing that it is the outcome of the decision that should be judged valid or not, rather than simply a test score. All this suggests that teachers and administrators need to gain more expertise in interpretation in order to make valid decisions.[3]

Standardized tests tend to use brief passages, a reading sample not typical of the normal reading tasks of students. Most tests are timed, which tends to place the slow but accurate reader at a disadvantage. Group-administered, they fail to take into account the individual student's mental attitude, the testing environment, or students' emotional and physical state at the time of testing. Many school districts misuse scores that were intended to measure only general performance when making judgments about specific curricula or a particular school's population. When reading scores are given as reading grade norms, they should never be used to identify actual reading levels because they generally measure the frustration level of performance and are not statistically reliable as standard percentile or stanine (one step in a nine-point scale) scores.

There are, however, some advantages to using standardized tests. First, they are relatively economical and efficient to administer and score. Also, they come with an accompanying manual, which aids in interpreting test results. They may provide equated, alternative forms for comparable retesting at successive levels and multiple grade norms, which means that consistent and sequential comparisons can be made over the school years.

Criterion-Referenced Tests

In 1963 Glaser described an alternative to norm-referenced testing which he referred to as criterion-referenced.[4] Criterion-referenced tests (CRTs) check performance against a predetermined standard—for example, identifying eight out of ten related facts or main ideas. Results can then be used to direct specific skill instruction for those who need it. Although this saves instructional time, there are drawbacks. Criterion levels are arbitrarily set, there is little agreement as to what mastery really means, the items measured tend to be relatively low level skills, and they may not have reliability or validity. Teachers who wish to learn in detail how to construct appropriate criterion test items might refer to a source such as Norman E. Gronland, *Preparing Criterion-Referenced Tests for Classroom Instruction* (New York: Macmillan, 1973).

Minimum Competency Testing

Some states now require students to pass a test of minimum competency in order to graduate from high school. Usually criterion-referenced, these tests purport to measure either basic or survival skills, such as reading labels and schedules. Much controversy has arisen as local or state educational agencies have tried to decide what is the cutoff point for passing the test, what are basic skills, which competencies need to be assessed, how to meassure, and what to do with those students who fail.[5]

In 1979 the International Reading Association presented its official position on the matter of minimum competencies, stating that no *single* assessment measure or method should ever be used as the only criterion for student graduation or promotion.[6]

Aptitude Tests

Tests to measure intelligence quotient (IQ) were not designed to assess overall intelligence but were developed to show potential for success in school academic areas. Existing group tests tend to measure only language, reasoning, and mathematical abilities. They do not, as a rule, take into account other relatively independent types of intelligence such as spatial, musical, creative, kinesthetic, interpersonal, and intrapersonal. Think about your own strongest areas. Most of us are intelligent in a variety of ways, not just one.

One problem with group-administered intelligence tests is that students must independently read the test items. Thus, students with normal intelligence who are remedial readers may be rated as mentally retarded. Group IQ test scores share another problem with other standardized test scores: A variety of outside factors, such as one's emotional and physical state, or the testing environment, may influence results.

On the other hand, intelligence test scores can be useful in identifying potential underachievers, whose scores may indicate they are more capable than their actual class performance has shown.

Selected Standardized Assessment Instruments

Standardized instruments (listed and described in Appendix 5) show a range of tests being used in secondary schools today. As Karlsen (1981) pointed out, scores from these tests can be used to determine the level of specificity at which instruction should take place.[7] They should also relate back to the curriculum and the overall instructional objectives, or to the general ability levels of students. Obviously, some of these tests will be administered by specialists, with results having been placed in students' cumulative record folders. Secondary teachers need to know, however, how to interpret such scores in order to make a general assessment of their students.

Today, many norm-referenced tests have incorporated criterion-referenced interpretations, and we have criterion-referenced tests with norms. The tests described in this text are categorized as follows: attitudes, norm-referenced achievement, criterion-referenced, diagnostic–group, diagnostic–individual, group ability and intelligence, individual intelligence, and informal reading inventories.

SPECIFIC DIAGNOSTIC INSTRUMENTS

Miscue Analysis: A Qualitative Assessment

Although secondary students generally should not be asked to read orally without prior preparation of purpose, teachers (especially reading teachers) might make an exception when they want to discover individual student reading strategies. Goodman and Burke (1972) developed the Reading Miscue Inventory based on Kenneth Goodman's thesis that readers misread (or misunderstand) words for many different reasons, which he calls "miscues." These miscues are classified in relation to specific questions about how readers handle ideas and language, and what strategies they use.[8]

Because the inventory is time-consuming, it will be used only with specific secondary students or in special reading classes. Daniel R. Hittleman has modified this inventory to save some time.[9] His steps, adapted from *Developmental Reading: A Psycholinguistic Perspective,* include the following:

1. Use an audiotape or cassette recorder while a student reads orally an unfamiliar story that is mildly challenging but not frustrating— one where the student makes at least 25 miscues. Miscues include substituting one word for another; inserting an additional word; omitting words, phrases, or punctuation; reversing two or more letters; repeating one or more words; or using incorrect pronunciation or intonation.

2. Keep the recorder.on when the student finishes reading, and ask the student to retell the story. Use general questions to guide the student when necessary, such as "Tell me more about . . . ," "What else happened?," or "What kind of problem?" Use an outline of the story to record the information the student freely recalls.

3. Directions to the student before reading can be similar to the following:

   I would like you to read this story aloud to me. While you are reading I won't help you in any way, so if you come to a word you don't know, just do the best you can. Try to guess the word. When you are finished, I'll ask you to retell the story in your own words.

4. All miscues should be written on copies of the story being read, with each line numbered for reference. Use some commonly accepted markings such as those below.

Markings

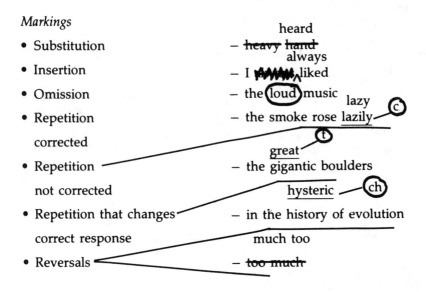

- Substitution
- Insertion
- Omission
- Repetition

  corrected
- Repetition

  not corrected
- Repetition that changes

  correct response
- Reversals

Quick-Score Achievement Test

The Quick-Score Achievement Test or Q-SAT (1987) is an individually ad-ministered, untimed test, constructed to measure achievement of students aged 7 to 18. It has two forms, which give scores in reading, writing, facts, and arithmetic, plus a general composite score. The reading subtest is ac-tually a test of word recognition only, not comprehension. Students read aloud from a graded word list. The writing subtest consists of having students write graded sentences from dictation. Each sentence has a punc-tuation or capitalization form and a spelling word taught at that grade level. The primary writing skill measured is mechanics. The facts subtest measures basic, school-taught facts. This Q-SAT was standardized in 1986 on approx-imately 1,500 students in 15 states. No information is given on socioeconomic status of the population sampled.[10]

Reading Style Inventory

The Reading Style Inventory (RSI, 1984) is an English or Spanish, individual or group, untimed inventory, purported to give information about how in-dividual students learn best. *Learning style* is defined as how well we learn under specific circumstances. The four major stimuli measured are (1) environment (music, talking, quiet); (2) emotional (peer or adult self-motivation, persistence, responsibility); (3) sociological (working alone, in groups, with peers, or with adults); and (4) physical (eating, drinking while reading, time of day for reading, amount of mobility allowed). This RSI is also supposed to describe students in terms of their auditory and visual strengths and their tactile and kinesthetic preferences. The questionnaire contains 52 multiple-choice items and is based on the premise that what students prefer gives an accurate indication of their learning style. In other words, it is believed that we tend to be most comfortable with what we can do well.[11]

INFORMAL TESTS: LEVELS OF READING PROFICIENCY

Informal measures, often teacher-made, can offer ongoing information about reading achievement, which can be content-specific, as well as information about attitudes, capabilities, interests, and behaviors that affect reading.

Before looking at some specific informal measures, let us think about what exactly we are trying to assess and how to assess it. In 1984 the National Assessment of Educational Progress (NAEP) described five levels of reading proficiency.[12] Table 10.1 shows these five skill and strategy levels, performance of each suggesting certain abilities, and specific tasks. This table can serve as a useful reference for making up information tests, as well as give insights into the vast range of reading proficiency.

THE CONTENT IRI OR CIRI

This is also referred to in the literature as a Group Reading Inventory or Secondary IRI. There is little doubt that of all the assessment procedures discussed previously, this can be the single most powerful tool for any secondary teacher. Unlike the individual tests that are used most often by reading specialists, this inventory is developed by teachers who use a text in their classroom. Its power lies in the fact that teachers know what skills and strategies they consider important, and they phrase their questions in the inventory as they would later on a class quiz or exam. The purpose of the Content IRI is to ascertain at the beginning of the term how well students can comprehend and use the class-assigned text, and what areas need further work by the teacher.

TABLE 10.1
NAEP's Levels of Reading Proficiency

Reading Skills and Strategies Level	Performance at this level suggests ability to:	Specific Tasks
1. Rudimentary	Carry out simple, discrete reading tasks.	Follow brief written directions; select words or sentences to describe a simple picture; interpret simple, written clues to identify a common object.
2. Basic comprehension	Understand specific or sequentially related information.	Locate and identify facts from simple informational paragraphs, stories, and news articles; combine ideas and make inferences based on short, uncomplicated passages.
3. Intermediate	Search for specific information, interrelate ideas, make generalizations.	Search for, locate, and organize information found in relatively lengthy passages; recognize paraphrases of what has been read; make inferences and reach generalizations about main ideas and author's purpose from passages in literature science, and social studies.
4. Adept comprehension	Find, understand, summarize, and explain relatively complicated information.	Understand complicated literary and informational passages, including material about topics studied in school; analyze and integrate less familiar material and provide reactions to and explanations of the text as a whole.
5. Advanced reading	Synthesize, learn, and recall from specialized reading materials.	Extend and restructure ideas presented in specialized complex tests such as scientific texts, literary essays, historical documents, and other materials like those found in professional and technical working environments; understand links between ideas even when they are not explicitly stated; make appropriate generalizations even when the text lacks clear introductions or explanations.

Source: Adapted from "Levels of Reading Proficiency as Described by the U.S. National Assessment of Education Progress, 1984," *Journal of Reading,* 30 (February 1987), p. 444.

Construction

To construct a CIRI, there are certain steps to be taken:

   1. Select a typical passage of approximately 400 to 600 words, taken from near the front of the text, unless the CIRI is administered later in the term,

when a passage not yet read by the class should be selected. The passage may be typed or students may read directly from their text.

2. The passage should be given a title, and a brief motivation/purpose paragraph should be composed and labeled. A background statement is made first about the topic, or a personal question is asked about it. Then, directly stated, is the sentence, "Read this in order to . . . ," giving readers a specific purpose for reading. The purpose for reading is *not* "for the test on Friday" or "to answer questions at the end of the chapter," but is connected to the overall comprehension of the passage. Questions concerning it will always be asked following the reading. An example of questions and statements concerning the purpose for reading follow:

> "Have you ever traveled to . . . , at least in your mind?"
> "This passage may surprise you with its description of . . ."
> "Read this in order to . . . describe the differences, or sequence events chronologically, or find out what happened to . . ."

Other frame-of-reference statements might begin, "Some people believe that truth is stranger than fiction," or "Arthropods play a very important part in the scheme of things."

This important paragraph introducing the passage should stir students' curiosity, or capture their attention, or help them tie into what they already know. Then the sentence should make very clear why the students are reading the passage—for what they will be held accountable.

3. Compose approximately 10 or 12 questions on the passage, divided equally among the categories of vocabulary meanings in context, literal comprehension (stated facts), and inferential comprehension (not directly stated in the passage but tied to what students already know). Vocabulary terms should always appear in at least the phrase in which they were used. Fact questions should be clearly stated. Inference questions should be worded so that readers realize there is not just one correct response—wording such as "Why do you suppose . . ." or "What do you think might happen if . . ." Critical/creative questions are important for discovering how well students can critique the content, discern between fact and opinion or fact and fantasy, give original conclusions, and so on.

4. Label each question with the letter V, F, I, or C outside the number. This will remind you later of the type of question. When students receive their inventories back, they can easily spot where they had difficulties.

Part I of the CIRI should take between 20 and 30 minutes, depending on your class, the length of the passage, and the number of questions asked.

Part II deals with specific strategy or skill areas in study-reading, -writing, and -learning that you believe are important for success in your classes. From the following list or from your own list, select three keys and develop 6 to 10 questions on each one. This section should also take approximately 20 to 30 minutes.

1. Reference skills (library, materials)
2. Parts of the text (text aids)
3. Rate of reading (adapted to purpose and difficulty level)
4. Listening/note-taking
5. Outlining
6. Content-specific terminology
7. Interpreting graphics
8. Following directions
9. Translating formulas, symbols
10. Finding main ideas, supporting details
11. Recognizing organizational patterns

12. Other _____

Administration and Scoring

When administering this inventory, tell students it is not a test to be graded, but a diagnostic tool. To score it, you will need to develop your own criterion levels of acceptability. For example, will three out of five mean successful completion?

A class profile is constructed from the results. The example in Table 10.2 is taken from Tonjes and Zintz (1987).[13]

A SECONDARY INVENTORY FOR READING/ENGLISH TEACHERS

When the goal is to discover how well students read a variety of materials, another type of inventory can be developed that is especially useful for reading and English teachers. This inventory can consist of several selections taken from different reading levels (e.g., from grades 5 to 12). Within each level are a variety of writing styles and types—fiction and nonfiction, and expository writing found in science, social studies, and math. An interest inventory can also be included here.[14]

TABLE 10.2
Content IRI Class Profile (Sample)

Name of Student	Part I			Part II			Overall Individual Needs
	Vocabulary (3 out of 3)	Fact (3 out of 4)	Inference (4 out of 5)	Parts of Text	Graphics	Study Strategies	
1. Margaret Jones	X					X	Some
2. Sue Jaramillo					X		Yes
3. John Johnson	X				X		Yes
4. Kevin Riley	X	X			X	X	Some
5. Arthur Chin	X		X	X	X	X	No
6. Janice King	X	X				X	Some
7. Loretta Lorrenzo					X		Yes
8. Jacob Kruger	X	X	X	X	X	X	No
Class skill needs	No	Yes	Yes	Yes	No	Some	

This profile may be used to determine classroom groupings. Skill centers may also be set up around the classroom for students to work individually on specific needs.

Source: From Teaching Reading, Thinking, Study Skills in Content Classrooms, 2nd edition, by Marian J. Tonjes and Miles V. Zintz. Copyright © 1987 Wm. C. Brown Publishers, Dubuque, Iowa. All Rights Reserved. Reprinted by permission.

Key: X means skill mastery.

THE CLOZE PROCEDURE

This deceptively simple diagnostic device can yield important general information about how well students read a particular text. Its beauty lies in its simplicity; it is simple to construct, to administer, and to score. There are no questions that readers might misinterpret, and they must be active readers, always thinking in English, in order to fill in the blanks appropriately.

Wilson Taylor originated the notion of cloze in 1953.[15] The term *cloze* comes from the Gestalt term *clozure* and means filling the gap, as there is a human tendency to complete an incomplete pattern or passage. As stated earlier in the text, specifically in the cloze procedure, every *n*th word is deleted (often every 5th word, or 7th for science), leaving the first and last sentences intact and using a twelve-space line for each deletion. No numbers are used in the passage as they have been found to be distracting, possibly even interfering with comprehension. Students are asked to fill in each blank with what they believe to be the exact word deleted. No synonyms are allowed when cloze is used for a readability match, but they are encouraged when it is used as a teaching device.

An abbreviated example of a fifty-blank cloze is shown here. It is taken from another selection in this text.

Enhancing Writing

English and Edwards describe computer programming as being similar to

writing a theme or term paper. It is necessary first _____ know the

audience, to _____ the subject, to limit _____ topic, to

control the _____, to organize the main _____, to out-

line, to write _____ then to revise. If _____ cannot

write it in _____, concise English they will _____

not be successful programmers. _____ of this requires precision,

_____ and orderliness on their _____. _____

have one additional step _____ writing, that of documenting

_____ in answering questions about _____ the program

functions, how _____ use it, the previous _____ required, any special features _____ pertinent information. In a sense it is like writing an advance organizer for what is to come.

For answers, see page 344.

Scoring of the cloze is based on the following criteria for determining levels of reading:

Accuracy	*Reading Level*
56 percent or greater	Independent
44 to 56 percent	Instructional
Below 44 percent	Frustration

A score falling in the range of the instructional level is said to be equivalent to getting around 75 percent on a multiple-choice test.

PreP: THE PREREADING PLAN

Langer (1981) describes a plan for an activity that may be used diagnostically to determine approximate levels of background knowledge students bring to their text assignments.[16] It is adapted here from "From Theory to Practice: A Prereading Plan" by Judith Langer, *Journal of Reading*, 25 (1981), pp. 152–156. PreP (Prereading Plan) gives teachers practical information on how well their students' concepts and language match the demands of the text. It encourages high-level thought by patterning.

Before beginning this activity, the text should be examined for key words or phrases representing major concepts to be developed.

> *Step I. Initial association with concepts:* "Say anything that comes to your mind when you hear the word _____ (e.g., *congress*). Jot responses on the board. This is students' first chance to tie concepts to prior knowledge.
>
> *Step II. Reflecting on initial associations:* "What made you think of _____" (response given)? This helps students become more aware of their own network of associations and others' views. They can then weigh, accept or reject, revise, and integrate ideas that occur.
>
> *Step III. Reformulating knowledge:* "Based on our discussion and before we start to read, what new ideas do you have about _____?" This allows verbalization of associations that have been changed or elaborated on through discussion.

By observing students' responses to this activity, teachers will be able to classify the level of students' background knowledge:

1. *Much prior knowledge:* Can define, draw analogies, make conceptual links, think categorically.
2. *Some prior knowledge:* Can give examples, cite characteristics of content; may not be able to make connections or see relationships between the new material and what they already know.
3. *Little or no background knowledge:* If they respond at all, they may make simple associations or may misinterpret the concept.

TEST QUESTIONS

Creating Test Questions

All teachers want to ask good questions. Here is a review of some notions about constructing good test questions for informal diagnosis. Sellitz et al. (1959) developed a checklist for improving these questions, which is still applicable today.[17]

1. Is this question necessary?
2. Is the point already sufficiently covered by other questions?
3. Should this question be subdivided for ease of understanding?
4. Does it cover the ground intended?
5. Does it contain difficult or unclear words and phraseology?
6. Could unintended emphasis on a word or phrase change the meaning?
7. Which type of question is most suitable to the learning purpose and nature of the task—multiple choice, true–false, matching, completion, short answer, essay?
8. Is the form of response easy, definite, uniform, adequate for the purpose?
9. Do earlier questions create a set that might influence this question?
10. Do earlier questions aid recall of ideas that bear on this question?

Types of Test Questions

Multiple Choice
The crucial thing to remember when developing multiple-choice items is to frame the alternatives carefully. This is one reason multiple-choice

questions are the most difficult to construct. Of the four to five choices, one must clearly be the best, whereas others should appear reasonable to the uninformed. Some authorities suggest including one choice that is almost correct and one that is clearly ridiculous. If you ask for "all of the above," or "A and C above"—this can also discriminate how well students know or have comprehended the material. The question itself should be longer than the choices, which should be short.

True–False
Use this form only for statements that are clearly, without argument, either true or false. Include only one idea in each question. Avoid negative statements when possible; if you do use them, be sure to underline the word *not*. Avoid involved statements with dependent clauses and complex ideas.

Matching
The column on the right is to be matched to the basic items numbered on the left. The right-hand column should always contain more choices than the left to hinder students from getting answers by the process of elimination.

Completion or Fill-in Questions
These questions may be the most difficult for some students because they generally require exact and correct answers: "Major types of literary genre include _____."

Essay Questions
These are subjective and require readers first to discriminate the exact task and then to outline the response before writing. Readers must recall the material and organize it before writing the answer. Examples of key terms used are:

- compare, contrast _____   Likenesses and differences

- define, describe, discuss _____   Clear definitions and key ideas

- enumerate _____   List, outline, show details and/or main ideas

- prove _____   Use facts and logic, justify, cite authorities

- evaluate _____   Make value judgments, pro and con

- summarize _____   Concisely restate main points

Levels of Questions

Bloom's taxonomy of the cognitive domain can serve as a useful tool for writing test questions at a variety of cognitive levels—knowledge, comprehension, translation and interpretation, application, analysis, synthesis, and evaluation.[18] The last three are often referred to as higher order comprehension levels and are not found as frequently in texts or tests as are lower level factual questions. The following can serve as a checklist for developing questions at many levels.

Taxonomy Level	Possible Verbs to Use
1. Knowledge	define, identify, label, list, locate, recognize, tell
2. Comprehension	convert, describe, expand, explain, illustrate, interpret, measure, summarize, translate
3. Application	apply, collect information, construct, demonstrate, find solutions, perform, solve, use
4. Analysis	analyze, debate, determine, differentiate, distinguish, figure out, organize, take apart, solve
5. Synthesis	compile, create, design, develop a plan, produce, synthesize
6. Evaluation	appraise (giving reasons), compare, conclude, evaluate, judge, rate

Asking the higher order questions gives students practice in being active thinkers, an important attribute for today's world.

INCONSIDERATE TEXTS AND FUTURE INVENTORIES

There is an alarming number of what are now called "inconsiderate" texts—those that are poorly organized, lack cohesion and transitions from one idea to another, and are inappropriate for their intended readers in terms of style, concepts, and developmental level.

Inventories of the future may select as writing samples both inconsiderate and considerate texts, in order to reflect more accurately what students must deal with in real life. This might reveal coping mechanisms not otherwise found in the usual inventory. Future inventories should also consider student interest in passages to be read and should ask students to read for a variety of purposes, such as getting the gist, locating specific details, critically analyzing, and generalizing.[19]

Instead of having students respond to comprehension questions from memory, future inventories might consider that because in the real world rereading is readily available, readers could also be asked to locate information while referring to the passage read.

Inconsiderate Text Sample

An example of an inconsiderate text follows. You might ask what exactly is wrong with it. Try to see how many examples you can find.

> If one were to teach the art of composition as a way conducive to enhancing students' inherent thinking processes it would conceivably be possible that those same self-selected students might ask why or why not; and thus we are beginning to discover the essential ties between writing and reading, as well as the other language arts. No piece of writing necessarily has the basic requirement. There should not be one and only one mode of thought, even though shifted within a single paragraph and carefully monitored. Parenthetical expressions and appositives, as we already know, make communication of meaning clear to all of us. [See the beginning of this section on inconsiderate texts for possibilities.]

ASSESSMENT TODAY AND TOMORROW

Warnings

As Farr and Carey (1986) point out, we continue to misunderstand the limited value of standardized test scores; we forget that they are only estimates of student achievement, and measure only some educational goals.[20] Recently there has been a resurgence of reverence for these tests as the ultimate accountability instruments. The motivation may be to placate the four Ps, press, politicians, parents, and public, who believe schools are failing to do the best job possible. The result is that tests may actually *direct* our curriculum ("teaching to the test") rather than just reflecting it. There is a pattern of pressure to all this, which we should note carefully.

Pressure Pattern

- The public becomes disenchanted with education because of reports of declining test scores.
- Politicians use test scores as a campaign issue, and promise reforms.
- Reform efforts focus on discrete, measurable education outcomes, using a task force of educators and lay people.

- The task force is asked to produce a framework for education in the state, to include broad goals and aims followed by specific behavioral objectives.
- Tests are developed to assess these specific objectives and thereby satisfy demands of the legislature and state department of education that they document the status of education with outcome measures to see if reforms have been effective.
- Schools are mandated to emphasize these frameworks (objectives); often, schools and teachers discover the test content in order to ascertain that their students receive practice on objectives, content, and format.
- As a result of this focused instruction, test scores rise.
- Policymakers and leaders then proclaim that their reforms have improved education.

As Farr and Carey further warn us, at the state level and in some large city school districts our education leaders are turning to tests to do more than just assess the curriculum.[21] They are actually using test scores to control what is taught in our schools. Will the schools of the future be nothing more than test preparation schools, where the curriculum is limited to what can be tested?

A recent movement of another nature, which could also have great impact on the way we test reading in the future, is the whole language movement led by such psycholinguists as Kenneth Goodman, Frank Smith, and others. They, like many other researchers today, are extremely critical of the ability of traditional reading tests to assess total language behavior. Researchers are now saying that we must go beyond the conventional paper-and-pencil, multiple-choice test mechanics and separate skills, and must test the process itself. This should lead to some creative new kinds of tests.

Glossary

A glossary is provided here to serve as a helpful reference in keeping the terms straight that have either been mentioned in this chapter or will be found in articles concerning assessment.

GLOSSARY FOR ASSESSMENT

Criterion: Relative standard or score implying sufficient achievement without reference to others' performance.

Criterion-referenced test: A test designed to measure the extent to which a student can perform a desired behavior. It is used to decide whether a student has reached a desired performance standard, which is based on the importance of the area.

Diagnostic test: Test used to determine specific skill strengths and weaknesses, thought to be independent.

Formal tests: Standardized, norm-referenced tests used to monitor students' progress.

Independent reading level: Level at which material is easily read with no assistance by the teacher needed.

Informal tests: Teacher-made or -published tests that use a criterion to monitor progress.

Instructional reading level: Level at which material is read effectively with teacher guidance.

Norm-referenced test: A test tried out with a sample called a norm group so that any one performance can be compared to that of the group.

Norms: Set of scores against which others' test performance may be compared.

Standard error of measurement: Variation or built-in error in standardized test scores.

Standardized test: Formal test using norms as a basis for comparing student achievement.

Stanine: One step in a nine-point scale of normalized standard scores, with a mean cf 5 and a standard deviation of 2.

Survey test: A test, usually standardized, which measures global areas of achievement such as comprehension and vocabulary.

SUMMARY

Assessment for study-reading is often a combination of formal and informal tests and inventories. Purposes of assessment are, first, to ascertain how well groups of students are doing in general, as compared to a similar normed population group, or as compared to students in previous years, using standardized tests. Second, informal measures such as inventories can be used to determine how well students read individually and what troublesome areas still need to be addressed. In order for teachers to construct their own informal measures, it is helpful to be aware of the levels of reading proficiency and of how to refine their questioning skills. Also, we need to be aware of a pattern of pressure that exists, which may cause standardized tests to direct our curriculum rather than just reflect it. Much careful thought should be given to assessment in secondary schools by all involved.

NOTES

1. John T. Guthrie, "Testing Higher Level Skills," *Journal of Reading*, 28 (2, November 1984), 188–190.

2. D. Resnick and L. Resnick, "Standards, Curriculum and Performance: An Historical and Comparative Perspective," *Educational Researcher*, 14 (1985), 5–20.

3. P. H. Johnston, "Assessment in Reading," in P. D. Pearson, ed., *Handbook of Reading Research* (New York: Longman, 1984).

4. R. Glaser, "Instructional Technology and the Measurement of Learning Outcomes: Some Questions," *American Psychologist*, 18 (1963), 519–521.

5. Betty D. Roe, Barbara D. Stoodt, and Paul C. Burns, *Secondary School Reading Instruction: The Content Areas*, 3rd ed. (Boston: Houghton Mifflin, 1987), p. 375.

6. *The Reading Teacher*, 33 (October 1979), 54–55.

7. Bjorn Karlsen, "Foreword," in Leo M. Schell, ed., *Diagnostic and Criterion-Referenced Reading Tests: Review and Evaluation* (Newark, DE: International Reading Association, 1981), pp. v–vii.

8. Yetta Goodman and Carolyn Burke, *Reading Miscue Inventory Manual* (New York: Macmillan, 1972), and Kenneth S. Goodman, "Analysis of Oral Reading Miscues: Applied Psycholinguistics," *Reading Research Quarterly*, 5 (Fall 1969), 9–30.

9. Daniel R. Hittleman, *Developmental Reading, K–8: Teaching from a Whole-Language Perspective* (Columbus, OH: Merrill, 1988), pp. 319–324.

10. Donald Hammill et al., *Quick-Score Achievement Test: (Q-SAT)* (Austin, TX: Pro-Ed, 1987).

11. Marie Carbo, *Reading Style Inventory: (RSI)*, revised. (Roslyn Heights, NY: Learning Research Associates, 1984).

12. "Levels of Reading Proficiency as Described by the U.S. National Assessment of Education Progress, 1984," *Journal of Reading*, 30 (February 1987), 444.

13. Marian J. Tonjes and Miles V. Zintz, *Teaching Reading, Thinking, Study Skills in Content Classrooms*, 2nd ed. (Dubuque, IA: William C. Brown, 1987), p.89.

14. Joseph L. Vaughn, Jr., and Paula J. Gaus, "Secondary Reading Inventory: A Modest Proposal," *Journal of Reading*, 21 (May 1978), 716–720.

15. Wilson S. Taylor, "Cloze Procedure: A New Tool for Measuring Readability," *Journalism Quarterly*, 30 (Fall 1953), 415–433, and John Bormuth, "Readability: A New Approach," *Reading Research Quarterly*, 1 (1966), 79–132.

16. Judith Langer, "From Theory to Practice: A Prereading Plan," *Journal of Reading*, 25 (1981), 152–156.

17. C. Sellitz et al., *Research Methods in Social Relations* (New York: Henry Holt, 1959).

18. Benjamin Bloom et al., *Taxonomy of Educational Objectives: Handbook 1, Cognitive Domain* (New York: Longman, Green, 1956).

19. William A. Henk, "Reading Inventories in the Future," *Evaluation in Reading, Learning, Teaching, Administering*, Sixth Yearbook of American Reading Forum (1985), 186–191.

20. Roger Farr and Robert F. Carey, *Reading: What Can Be Measured?*, 2nd ed. (Newark, DE: International Reading Association, 1986), p. 203.

21. Ibid., pp. 208–213.

RECOMMENDED READINGS

Bader, Lois A. *Reading Diagnosis and Remediation in Classroom and Clinic.* New York: Macmillan, 1980.

Cunningham, J. W., and Cunningham, P. M. "Validating a Limited-Cloze Procedure." *Journal of Reading Behavior,* 10 (1978), 211–213.

Drahozal, E. D., and Manna, G. S. "Reading Comprehension Subscores: Pretty Bottles for Ordinary Wine." *Journal of Reading,* 21 (1978), 416–420.

Dupuis, Mary M. "Diagnostic Teaching for Every Teacher." *The High School Journal,* 59 (November 1975).

Farr, Roger. "New Trends in Reading Assessment: Better Tests, Better Uses," *Curriculum Review,* 27 (September–October 1987), 21–23.

Farr, Roger, and Carey, Robert F. *Reading: What Can be Measured?* 2d. ed. Newark, DE: International Reading Association, 1986.

Fuchs, L. S., Fuchs, D., and Deno, S. "Reliability and Validity of Curriculum-Based Informal Reading Inventories." *Reading Research Quarterly,* 18 (1982), 6–25.

Gambrell, Linda B. "Minimum Competency Testing and Programs in Reading: A Survey of the United States." *Journal of Reading,* 28 (May 1985), 735–738.

Glazer, S. M., and Searfoss, L. W. *Reading Diagnosis and Instruction: A C-A-L-M Approach.* Englewood Cliffs, NJ: Prentice-Hall, 1988.

Glazer, S. M., Searfoss, L. W., and Gentile, Lance M., eds. *Reexamining Reading Diagnosis: New Trends and Procedures,* Newark, DE: International Reading Association, 1988.

Haney, W. "Validity, Vaudeville and Values: A Short History of Social Concerns over Standardized Testing." *American Psychologist,* 36 (1981), 1021–1034.

Haney, W., and Madays, G. F. "Making Sense of the Competency-Testing Movement." *Harvard Educational Review,* 48 (1978), 462–484.

Johns, Jerry L. *Basic Reading Inventory,* 3rd ed. Dubuque, IA: Kendall/Hunt, 1985.

Johns, Jerry L. *Advanced Reading Inventory.* Dubuque, IA: William C. Brown, 1981.

Johnston, Peter H. "Assessment in Reading." In P. David Pearson, ed., *Handbook of Reading Reseach.* New York: Longman, 1984, pp. 147–182.

Jongsma, Eugene A. *Cloze Instruction Research: A Second Look.* Newark, DE: International Reading Association, 1980.

Karlsen, B., Madden, R., and Gardner, E. F. *Standford Diagnostic Reading Test.* New York: Harcourt Brace Javanovich, 1976.

Kavale, K., and Schreiner, R. "The Reading Processes of Above Average and Average Readers: A Comparison of the Use of Reasoning Strategies in Responding to Standardized Comprehension Measures." *Reading Research Quarterly,* 15 (1979), 102–128.

Lerner, B. "The Minimum Competence Testing Movement: Social Scientific and Legal Implications." *American Psychologist,* 36 (1981), 1057–1066.

Lyons, Kevin. "Criterion Referenced Reading Comprehension Tests: New Forms with Old Ghosts." *Journal of Reading,* 27 (January 1984), 293–298.

Marino, Jacqueline L. "Cloze Passages: Guidelines for Selection." *Journal of Reading,* 24 (March 1981), 479–483.

McKenna, Michael C., and Robinson, Richard D. *An Introduction to the Cloze Pro-*

cedure: An Annotated Bibliography. Newark, DE: International Reading Association, 1980.

Messick, S., "Evidence and Ethics in the Evaluation of Tests." *Educational Researcher,* 10 (1981), 9–20.

Nelson Reading Test. Boston: Houghton Mifflin, 1977.

Peters, Charles. "New Directions in Statewide Reading Assessment." *The Reading Teacher* (April 1987).

Peters, Charles. "Comprehension Assessment: Implementing an Interactive View of Reading." *Educational Psychologist,* 22 (1987).

Pikulski, John J., and Shanahan, Timothy, eds. *Approaches to the Informal Evaluation of Reading.* Newark, DE: International Reading Association, 1982.

Readence, R. F., and Moore, D. W. "Why Questions? A Historical Perspective on Standardized Reading Comprehension Tests." *Journal of Reading,* 26 (1983), 306–313.

Schell, Leo M. "Criterion-Referenced Test: Selected Cautionary Notes." *Reading World,* 19 (October 1979), 57–62.

Schell, Leo M., ed. *Diagnostic and Criterion-Referenced Reading Tests: Review and Evaluating.* Newark, DE: International Reading Association, 1981.

Schreiner, Robert, ed. *Reading Tests and Teachers: A Practical Guide.* Newark, DE: International Reading Association, 1979.

Shannon, Albert J. "Effects of Methods of Standardized Reading Achievement Test Administration on Attitude toward Reading." *Journal of Reading,* 23 (May 1980), 137–155.

Shannon, Albert J. "Using the Microcomputer Environment for Reading Diagnosis." In S. M. Glazer, L. W. Searfoss, and L. M. Gentile, eds., *Reexamining Reading Diagnosis: New Trends and Procedures.* Newark, DE: International Reading Association, 1988, pp. 150–168.

Silvaroli, Nicholas J. *Classroom Reading Inventory,* 5th ed. Dubuque, IA: William C. Brown, 1986.

Stanford Achievement Test. New York: Psychological Corporation, 1973.

Summers, Edward G. "Instruments for Assessing Reading Attitudes: A Review of Research and Bibliography." *Journal of Reading Behavior,* 9 (1977), 137–155.

Tullock, Rhody R., and Alexander, J. E. "A Scale for Assessing Attitudes toward Reading in Secondary Schools." *Journal of Reading,* 26 (1980), 609–610.

Walmsley, S. A. "On the Purpose and Content of Secondary Reading Programs: An Educational Ideological Perspective." *Curriculum Inquiry,* 11 (1981), 73–93.

Weinshank, A. B. "The Reliability of Diagnostic and Remedial Decisions of Reading Specialists." *Journal of Reading Behavior,* 14 (1982), 33–50.

Ysseldyke, J. E., and Marston, D. "A Critical Analysis of Standardized Reading Tests." *School Psychology Review,* 11 (1982), 259–266.

Postorganizer 1
Sampling Standardized Tests

In small groups, examine several commonly used secondary standardized tests. Critique them in terms of appropriateness of the excerpts to your subject area, levels of questions, and the like.

Postorganizer 2
Developing Questions

With a partner, select a chapter or short story and develop a set of questions, making sure to use Sellitz's checklist found on page 334 and the suggestions for different types and levels of questions following it. Questions should be open, requiring more than a one-word response, and should reflect a variety of cognitive levels.

Postorganizer 3
Practice in Developing Informal Instruments

Individually develop a sample Content IRI and a cloze on a selected chapter or story in a secondary text or anthology. Discuss with your group or in class which is the more time-consuming and which is more useful to you as a teacher. What new ideas can you bring to these two informal assessment tools? This may serve as practice for developing these instruments for your classroom.

Postorganizer 4
Answers to Cloze

1. to
2. understand
3. the
4. purpose
5. ideas
6. and
7. students
8. clear
9. simply

10. all
11. logic
12. part
13. programmers
14. in
15. assisting
16. how
17. knowledge
18. and

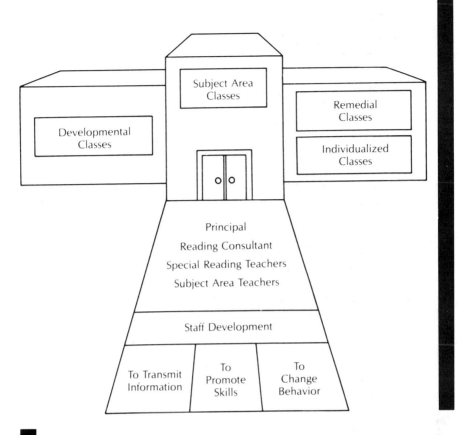

Subject Area
Classes

Remedial
Classes

Developmental
Classes

Individualized
Classes

Principal

Reading Consultant

Special Reading Teachers

Subject Area Teachers

Staff Development

To Transmit
Information

To
Promote
Skills

To
Change
Behavior

11

School Programs, Practices, and Staff Development

CHAPTER OUTLINE

Preorganizers
Introduction
Total School Study-Reading Programs
 Types of Programs
 An Individualized/Personalized Reading Program
 Secondary Study-Reading Goals
 Goals for Research and Practice
 Personnel Responsibilities/Requirements of Secondary Reading
  Programs
Staff Development for Secondary Reading
 Requirements
 A Staff Development Model
 Staff Development Programs
 Effective Leaders
 Unfreezing Staff Development Activities
A New Look at Secondary Reading
Grouping
 Grouping Types
 Cooperative Learning: Jigsaw I and II
 Competitive Grouping
Summary
Notes
Recommended Readings
Postorganizers

COGNITIVE COMPETENCIES

1. *Delineate* the types of programs possible for secondary study-reading, and select or combine the types you feel are most applicable or appropriate for the ideal school.

2. *Rank-order* Herber's study-reading goals, giving reasons for the order of importance.

3. *Reward* Siedow's staff development model so that you could present it to your principal.

4. *Develop* a mini-lesson using one of the types of grouping method explained here.

KEY TERMS

cooperative learning
developmental programs
effective leaders
group retellings
individualized programs

Jigsaw I and II
reading consultant
remedial labs
staff development programs
unfreezing

Preorganizer 1
Recollecting and Judging How You Were Taught

As a rule, we teach as we have been taught. After completing this questionnaire, you will be able to recall many aspects of how you were taught and decide which behaviors you do and do not wish to emulate. Ask yourself which behaviors especially lend themselves to meeting students' individual needs. Are behaviors very different in secondary schools than in college? Do professors in education teach differently than professors in other disciplines? Summarize your findings and compare them with your partner's.

Key: S = secondary school; C = college; E = education professor.

Generally, my teachers:	Usually	Sometimes	Rarely	Don't Recall
1. Lectured to the whole class				
2. Monitored activities while students did seat work				
3. Worked with small groups				
4. Worked with individual students				
5. Conducted whole-class discussions				
6. Previewed concepts to be developed later in the lesson				
7. Presented purposes for reading				
8. Presented key concepts within each lesson				
9. Spent time explaining or clarifying concepts presented within each lesson				
10. Evaluated students' understanding of concepts before moving on or formally testing them				
11. Provided feedback about learning of concepts				

	Usually	Sometimes	Rarely	Don't Recall
12. Used just one textbook in each class				
13. Used other collateral materials in addition to or instead of a textbook				
14. Reviewed and summarized major points and discussions				
15. Required us to develop concepts through outside reading assignments				
16. Allowed assigned reading to be done partly during class time				
17. Used study guides to help develop comprehension skills				
18. Used both small-group and large-group activities in the classroom				
19. Emphasized developing higher level as well as lower level comprehension				
20. Used reading and discussion as preparation for lectures or films as well as afterward				
21. Used advance or adjunct aids such as cognitive maps or other graphic organizers				
22. Encouraged capable students to help the less capable (peer tutoring)				

School Programs, Practices, and Staff Development   349

Preorganizer 2
Planning a Study-Reading, -Writing, and -Learning Program

You have just been hired (or transferred) to teach your major subject area and two periods of study-reading. Because of your knowledge and background in reading, writing, and learning, you are also expected to head a staff development committee to plan programs for the entire faculty throughout the school year. As you read this chapter, first briefly outline general overall plans, in rough draft form, of topics, materials, grouping, skills, and strategies you may wish to use for your two study-reading classes. How will you try to meet individual needs?

Next, decide how you will approach the task of heading the staff development planning committee. What initial steps will you take? The principal has already told you that the plan is to have a schoolwide program in whatever time it takes.

Finally, skim back over previous chapters to refresh your memory as to the key concepts, and use this chapter, too, as a resource for editing your rough draft. Role-play in small groups the total planning process and one example of a staff development session. (This pre- and postorganizer should take more than one class period and can be expanded to serve as an alternative final "exam," along with the posttest found at the beginning of this text.)

11
School Programs, Practices, and Staff Development

INTRODUCTION

Secondary teachers need to be concerned with the school programs, processes, and staff development models that help them be better teachers and their students better learners. The first section of this final chapter is concerned with the totality of secondary reading programs across the curriculum. This section is intended as a handy reference to consult when your school decides to augment its study-reading program. In order to have such a program, it is necessary to give careful thought to planning and conducting staff development programs. The second section describes some of today's requirements, possible programs to be adapted to your particular school situation, and ways of grouping for effective results.

TOTAL SCHOOL STUDY-READING PROGRAMS

Types of Programs

In those secondary schools that have a study-reading program across the curriculum, the program may be divided into subject area, developmental, remedial, or individualized phases. The subject-area phase includes the total school. Here, students are assisted by all teachers in using reading strategies with texts of varied content. Also, in subject-area classrooms attention may be given to recreational reading with some form of Sustained Silent Reading (SSR). In many schools specific short blocks of time are set aside each week in which all students in the school read a book of their individual choice without interruption.

Developmental programs are often designed as electives for average and above-average readers and writers, and are usually taught by English or special reading teachers. However, some schools will assign history, science, math, or art teachers to teach a developmental course if these teachers have some background in related courses. In these classes, reading and writing are processes taught together.

Remedial labs are designed for disabled readers, those who read two or more years below the level at which they are capable of reading—their capacity level. Special-education students who are not mainstreamed are handled by a special-education teacher. Remedial labs are primarily taught by special reading teachers. Skill deficiencies and motivation are the two areas of emphasis in reading labs.

An Individualized/Personalized Reading Program

In one successful high school reading program, described by Blow (1976), the overall purpose was to get all students reading for pleasure. The description here is adapted with permission of the *Arizona English Bulletin* from "Individualized Reading" by Barbara Blow.[1]

1. Students read books of their own choice, but with some suggestions and guidance from parents and teachers.
2. When students register, a note is sent home to parents explaining book choices and inviting parent participation in recommending books and also in reading with their children.
3. Teachers skim each book read by a student prior to a ten-minute individual conference discussion. (The same teachers handle several sections of this class over an extended time to allow them to build up a sufficiently broad familiarity with the books in order to talk knowledgeably with students.)
4. Teacher paraprofessionals handle clerical tasks—take the roll, schedule conferences, record grades, check out books.
5. Conferences are held in an adjacent office or screened-off area so as not to disturb students' reading.
6. Three to four days each semester, the librarian gives book talks. Otherwise, all class time is reserved for silent reading.

7. Classroom paperback collections are readily available, with multiple copies of popular books.
8. Lists of recommended books or those most frequently read by other class members are distributed at regular intervals as a source of ideas for future reading. (A paper can be passed around with students listing their favorite book title and author, plus a phrase as to why they recommend the book—for example, "a really humorous story" or "ties in nicely with what we're studying in history" or "exciting, suspenseful adventure.")
9. Students sign up one week in advance for conferences to enable teachers to prepare and to give students time to plan their approach to the conference, which will be graded.
10. Grades may include credit for such things as good attendance, number of pages read, quality of conference discussion, selection of challenging books, and the like.

Secondary Study-Reading Goals

Instruction
Herber (1988) has outlined the following goals.[2]

1. The instruction in study-reading should be integrated with instruction in course content in all subject-area classes and at all grade levels in secondary schools.
2. The reading strategies themselves should be integrated so they can be applied in all subject areas in logical combinations rather than in isolation.
3. Subject-area teachers should be the principal personnel for providing study-reading instruction in secondary schools.
4. The instruction in reading should be well articulated so students learn increasingly sophisticated reading and reasoning strategies as they progress through the grades within the various disciplines.

Curriculum

1. The reading curriculum should be embedded in the curricula of the various secondary subjects.
2. The resulting reading/subject-area curriculum should be conceptually based rather than informationally based.
3. Every student, through this curriculum, should be allowed access to the study of important ideas.

4. Resource materials that are considerate of readers should be available for use in the curriculum, but not so that they become substitutes for instruction.
5. The curriculum should be well articulated so students encounter increasingly sophisticated materials and ideas as they progress through the grades within the various disciplines.

Personnel

1. A long-term staff development program should be provided for all teachers so they can learn how to integrate instruction in reading with instruction in course content.
2. A staff development program should be provided for reading personnel to help them work in a facilitating role with other teachers in their efforts to integrate instruction in reading with instruction in course content.
3. The primary role of reading personnel, from teacher to consultant, should change so that they may better facilitate the work of other teachers in the reading program.

Organization

1. The integration of reading instruction with instruction in subject-area classes should constitute the basic and universal reading program for secondary schools.
2. Special reading programs for students should be *push in* rather than *pull out* programs relative to the regular curriculum.

Goals for Research and Practice

1. Standing should be given to practice in the practice-into-research-into-practice cycle.
2. Evaluations and assessments should be used as stimulants for growth and development rather than as deterrents.
3. What constitutes appropriate evidence for determining the impact and value of instructional programs should be established.
4. Informed intuition as a legitimate and valuable means of contributing to the evolution and refinement of instructional strategies and programs should be acknowledged and accepted.

Personnel Responsibilities/Requirements of Secondary Reading Programs

These are adapted with permission from *Secondary School Reading Instruction: The Content Areas*, 3rd edition, by Betty Roe, Barbara Stoodt, and Paul Burns, pp. 9–10, copyright © 1987, Houghton Mifflin Company, Boston.[3]

Subject-Area Teachers

1. Knowledge of reading skills needed by secondary students in order to read in their discipline
2. Knowledge of assessment measures to identify those who cannot read regular assignments, can read with assistance, or can read with ease
3. Ability to identify specific learning problems needing referral to specialists
4. Knowledge of ways to assist students in learning needed content-specific skills
5. Knowledge of study-learning strategies for increasing students' success rate
6. Knowledge of ways to differentiate assignments for different levels of reading proficiency
7. Willingness to cooperate with other school personnel such as the reading teacher in helping students reach their full study-reading potential

Special Reading Teacher

1. Works directly with students.
2. Has a graduate degree in reading (or its equivalent), along with several years of teaching experience, and is certified as a reading specialist.
3. Knowledgeable of reading skills, formal and informal assessment tools, and a variety of methods and materials for reading instruction.
4. Plans and teaches reading classes for disabled, average, and accelerated readers.
5. Supervises parents and paraprofessionals who assist in the reading program.
6. Works with content teachers whose students are in reading classes; assists content teachers in selecting appropriate instructional materials; when asked, helps content teachers develop and use study-reading strategies in their class.

7. Assists the reading consultant as a resource person and demonstration teacher.[4]

Reading Consultant

1. Works with administrators and other school personnel to develop and coordinate the total school reading program.
2. Is free from teaching special reading classes or regular classroom teaching.
3. Has a high degree of professional skill, knowledge, and years of formal study in reading and related fields. Has had several years of successful teaching experience and meets certification requirements of a special reading teacher.
4. Studies the population—both students and teachers.
5. Assists the principal in planning a comprehensive reading program, which includes basic skills, corrective and remedial, content-area, and leisure reading.
6. Orients beginning teachers to philosophy, procedures, and materials for a total school reading program and keeps everyone informed of new developments in the field.
7. Evaluates the program through supervisory activities and research, making recommendations for change as needed.
8. Provides in-service instruction—conducts workshops, seminars, and conferences on specific reading topics such as content, informal reading inventories, metacognitive strategies, and study-reading guides.
9. Evaluates and recommends reading materials.
10. Serves as a resource person with special cases where a high degree of professional competence is required.
11. Keeps the community apprised of the purposes and progress of the reading program.

Principal

1. Gives administrative direction and support.
2. Encourages staff.
3. Ensures that the reading philosophy is implemented in innovative, logical ways.
4. Provides the impetus for defining the philosophy of the reading program and facilitates it by extending it to the whole school.
5. Hires capable personnel.

STAFF DEVELOPMENT FOR SECONDARY READING

Requirements

According to Nelson-Herber (1988), a staff development program must meet the following criteria:

1. It must be addressed to the perceived and expressed needs of the target population.
2. It must be grounded in a theoretical framework and presented through a consistent information source.
3. It must be planned collaboratively with administrators, teachers, staff, and community.
4. It must be based on long-range goals and objectives.
5. It must be designed to take advantage of a multiplier effect.
6. It must be supported with sufficient resources.
7. It must be evaluated on the basis of defined goals and levels of use.[5]

More than anything else, it is the staff development model that can make the difference in determining the success or failure of a total-school study-reading program. Teachers need to learn how to incorporate needed reading materials, skills, and strategies as a normal part of their teaching; and they need demonstrations, opportunities for practice, and administrative support for change to occur.

A Staff Development Model

Siedow and co-workers (1985) describe a straightforward staff development or in-service model in six steps.[6]

1. *Assess needs.* A successful staff development program begins with a needs assessment, administered by coordinators or committee. Secondary teachers are interested in those areas that will help their students learn their subject. Giving them a say in what topics will be covered can serve as a motivator that leads toward their commitment to the process. Needs assessment instruments such as checklists or questionnaires will help teachers focus on specific need areas. Group discussion is a possible alternative and may be used in order to reach a consensus on critical needs.

2. *Formulate objectives.* From data received in the needs assessment, the coordinators or committee formulate program objectives that are reasonable

in terms of teacher beliefs, abilities, and practices as well as student learnings and behavior.

3. *Plan content.* Instructional strategies should first be selected that are (a) relevant and have the potential to be effective in the secondary classrooms, (b) easily learned, (c) easily blended with regular teaching practices, and (d) likely to show quick results in the classroom. Later, more demanding strategies can be used to help solve pressing problems and assist student learning.

4. *Select presentation methods and staff.* It is a good idea to demonstrate strategies first, and then provide opportunities for practice. Depending on the situation, staff may be experienced teachers, consultants, or university personnel.

5. *Evaluate effectiveness.* Ongoing evaluation can clarify the needs of teachers and students throughout the process. It also motivates participants by documenting growth in knowledge and skill.

6. *Provide follow-up assistance.* Coordinators or committees need to offer follow-up assistance in order to give assurance that the objectives are indeed met and continue to have impact. Change is a long-term process, so it should not be expected that teaching and learning objectives will be met during the staff development sessions.

Staff Development Programs

Three types of staff development or in-service programs are shown by Korinek, Schmid, and McAdams (1985), who reviewed the literature of more than 100 reports. The three types have different purposes—transmitting information, acquiring skills, or changing behaviors, respectively. Table 11.1 shows a comparison of these three types.[7]

The best staff development program includes some type of demonstration, participant practice, feedback, and coaching to find ways to apply or transfer new methods to the classroom. Such a program can be successful with both knowledge and skills. Behavior changes take time, patience, and a willingness to persevere. Teachers can become uncomfortable when trying new methods and may want to fall back on familiar ways of teaching. They need to know they have support, and they need to receive encouragement during the trying-out process. As with giving up smoking or drinking, or going on a diet, you have to feel worse before you can feel better. We all need the reassurance that mistakes are all right when learning something new and different.

TABLE 11.1
Features of Three Staff Development Programs

	Type		
Feature	Information Transmission	Skill Acquisition	Behavior Change
Time frame	1–3 hours per session	Multiple sessions of 2–3 hours	Multiple sessions of varying lengths
Location	Available meeting or conference sites	Usually school-based; occasionally conference sites	School-based home, school, or district
Content	Generally unrelated, self-contained, independent topics	Most presentations part of sequence, some independent topics	Interdependent presentations linked by common purpose
Audience size	No upper limit	Determined by ratio of session leaders to participants	No upper limit
Presentation style	Lecture, demonstration, or panel with passive audience participation	Demonstration, practice, feedback, active participation	All styles, both active and passive participation
Evaluation	Rating of usefulness or enjoyability	Demonstration of the skill	Measurement of change in teaching behavior and degree to which project objectives met

Source: Reprinted with permission from "Inservice Types and Best Practices" by L. Korinek, R. Schmid, and M. McAdams, *Journal of Research and Development in Education,* 18 (1985), 33–38.

Effective Leaders

Those who are most successful in leading staff development activities are those who do the following:

1. Arrange to assess participant needs in advance.
2. Provide a variety of activities.
3. Involve participants actively.
4. Tie topics directly to classroom examples.
5. Have a positive, supportive, enthusiastic attitude.
6. Are well informed and organized.
7. Keep within the time schedule and share the schedule.
8. Try to schedule programs during teacher release time, not after school or on Saturdays.

9. Explain clearly, answer questions directly, and give full directions.
10. Provide materials and allow participants to produce their own classroom materials.

Unfreezing Staff Development Activities

Unfreezing is a term used for activities that loosen people up at the beginning of a session or term, building interest and motivation for the activities to come. The idea is to unfreeze rather than unglue a group.[8]

Ice Breakers
These activities vary from 5 to 20 minutes in length, with the intent of involving participants in thinking about problems to be addressed during the session.

1. *Brainstorming:* Having identified a broad concept reflecting the main topic (e.g., vocabulary), participants work in small groups to generate lists of related words in a limited amount of time.
2. *Conceptual conflict:* To arouse curiosity about the topic, give teachers a description of a situation that will cause them to be puzzled, doubtful, surprised, or perplexed (e.g., a 16-year-old student who reads aloud with perfect pronunciation but little or no understanding of what was read).
3. *Magic circle:* Opening up communication, the leader starts off with light questions that lead to more probing ones (e.g., "What do you like best about teaching?" "If you were given $2,000 to spend on your classroom, what would you purchase?" "What are the most serious problems your students face in your subject area today?"). Each member has the opportunity to comment.

Vicarious Experiences
These are aimed at getting teachers involved with actual materials or strategies used with students. They serve as a demonstration of a generalization and take from 15 minutes to one hour. Instead of just being told about a strategy, teachers experience it themselves.

1. *Set up a hypothetical situation.* Describe the situation to everyone concisely, and then ask how this might have changed life as we know it or affected the results. After dividing the group into triads, allow five minutes for discussion and then pool answers on the board, forming categories. With this as practice, distribute to each triad a study-reading-related problem and proceed as before.

2. *Distribute a ten-statement prediction guide to reading instruction.* After they complete it independently, have teachers pair up and discuss their responses. A general discussion can follow—for example, decide whether or not they agree with the following: (a) students need to be told purposes prior to reading, (b) graphics in texts are usually self-explanatory, (c) most tenth-grade students should be able to handle a text written at the tenth-grade level.

A NEW LOOK AT SECONDARY READING

Monahan (1988) reported at a preconvention institute in Toronto, Ontario, on the new look in secondary reading in Orange County, Florida.[9] The new look came about because of the use of the Degrees of Reading Power program (DRP) by Reading Resource Specialists (RRS) in secondary schools. The College Board gave a full day's orientation to the DRP and its use. The results matched students' comprehension level with text materials. A reading resource specialist was assigned to each secondary school to work solely with secondary teachers. The RRS promotes a comprehensive reading program, supports existing remedial programs, assists in diagnosing and prescribing learning strategies in all subjects, provides staff development for the school staff, teams teachers with regular classroom teachers, and interprets the reading program to parents and community. During the first year of implementation, staff development sessions were held twice a month for full days. Topics included role interpretation, available resources, assessment computers, recreational reading, and leadership concerns.

Publicity ideas to sell their reading effort and to inform included newsletters, flyer posters, summary reports, test data reports, graphs, and charts. Recreational reading ideas included SSR (sustained silent reading), book fairs, trade-a-book day, promotional posters, bumper stickers, door decoration contests, guest readers, and recognition awards sessions.

A reading–learning–thinking strategy series was developed for a ready-to-use bank of ideas. These included many items discussed in this text, such as SQ3R, cloze, brainstorming, summarizing, graphic organizers, list–group–label, prediction, think-alouds, and vocabulary overview guides.

A strong focus is on interpreting and applying current research. Guest speakers in research areas are featured attractions. Touches that promote goodwill include serving refreshments at staff development sessions, taking photographs of teachers and principals in action, and sending flowers and letters of appreciation.

GROUPING

Small-group instruction has not been as popular in secondary classrooms and workshops as it is in elementary ones, even though it has been found to have positive effects on concept development and achievement. Grouping in staff development sessions should promote more attempts to use it in the regular classroom.[10]

Grouping Types

Wood (1987) has delineated several grouping types that have proved to be successful with secondary students.[11]

1. *Group retellings:* Have students work in pairs or triads, each silently reading a different piece of material on the same topic, with the purpose of being prepared to retell to their partner or small group what was read, in their own words. The others may add a similar fact at any point from their own reading. A final step could be a synthesis of findings.

2. *Associational dialogue:* This alternative to traditional testing assesses ability with expository material through free recall and associational thinking. First, give students a list of key concepts from the readings and have them take notes from the text, class lectures, and discussions using another sheet of paper. Organize details around each concept to form clusters. The original list is used for study. In class, students use their clusters to work on concepts in their own words. They then contribute information from their own experience to expand the others' view. Finally, discuss the results with the whole class.

3. *Paired learning:* Working in pairs, students begin by reading two pages of their text. One partner is the "recaller," who must orally summarize from memory what was read. The other is the "listener/facilitator" who corrects errors, clarifies concepts, and elaborates on the material. Drawings, pictures, or other media can be used to facilitate comprehension and retention. Partners then switch roles for the next two pages.

4. *Buddies:* Place together students of varied ability levels and tell them they are now responsible for each other's learning. This means giving help on specific assignments as well as reading and editing each other's work before it is handed in. In dividing the class, keep differences between ability levels to a minimum yet with sufficient differences so students can profit from each other. To do this, rearrange the class roll from the most to the least well prepared. Then divide this list into three groups, as for ability

grouping. Now place together the top students in each group, the second in each group, and so on, until the list is completely divided.

5. *Analysis/synthesis/problem solving:* Write specific thought-provoking questions on poster-size paper, one question to a sheet, and tape to walls. With twenty-five students, divide into five groups and use five questions, arranging five chairs near each question. This becomes the home base for each group member. Direct students to write their responses to the first question, and have one student record the answers on the poster paper. Direct groups to move around the room to each base, alternating recorders and moving every five minutes. Then all students return to home base to clarify and consolidate their lists. In the final presentation phase, a group member reports to the class the synthesized responses for each group's questions.

6. *Home groups:* Assign students to a home group throughout a grading period and call them together at specified time. One way would be to start the class by having groups meet for 5 or 10 minutes, greet each other, discuss progress toward a project, tell of an experience related to their assignment, share materials or books, or review for a quiz.

Most successful classes and workshops communicate a caring climate that encourages both individual thought and cooperative learning. When you group, at least at first, be sure to assign specific tasks to individual students. This keeps them on track and makes them accountable for their own actions. Tasks might include chair, recorder, reporter, time keeper, task minder, graphic designer, special researcher, and so on.

Cooperative Learning: Jigsaw I and II

There is a definite power in having peers help teach each other. Their interactions enhance learning as well as motivating those involved. This is true at the staff development level, too. Slavin (1989) describes two methods that have proved successful today with all levels of students.[12] The discussion here is adapted with permission from "A Cooperative Learning Approach to Content Areas: Jigsaw Teaching" by Robert Slavin, in *Content Area Reading and Learning: Instructional Strategies*, edited by Diane Lapp, James Flood, and Nancy Farnham, copyright © 1989 by Prentice-Hall, Englewood Cliffs, New Jersey.

1. *Jigsaw:* When readers must extract information from their text, you can use a method named Jigsaw. The basic idea is that each mixed-ability group member becomes an expert in one aspect of the topic being studied. Experts read information on their topic and then meet with other experts

from other teams asssigned to the same topic. The experts then return to their own team to take turns teaching their teammates about their topic. Students read individual sections that are different from their teammates'.

2. *Jigsaw II:* An adaptation, Jigsaw II, can be used whenever the study material is narrative in form. Thus, it can be used most appropriately with social studies literature and sometimes in science. Here, the assigned teams of four or five students represent a cross-section of the class. Students are assigned units or chapters to read and are given "Expert Sheets" with different topics for each team member to focus on while reading. After reading, students meet with like experts from the other teams to discuss for 30 minutes, then return to their own teams to teach the others about their topic. Finally, everyone individually takes quizzes covering all the topics. The scores then become team scores. High-scoring teams receive some type of recognition, such as certificates or mention in a newsletter or on a bulletin board. The key here is interdependence.

To construct materials for Jigsaw II, first select several chapters, units, or stories, each covering enough material for a two- to three-day unit. Selections to be read in class should not require more than 30 minutes to complete. Next, make an "Expert Sheet" for each unit, which points out what to concentrate on when reading. It also assigns expert groups and identifies four topics central to the unit. For example, in social studies, take a section on Indian tribes and assign pages to be read. Ask four questions to delineate topics that appear throughout the story or unit, such as "What were this tribe's customs and traditions?," not "What happened in 1878?" Finally, construct a quiz for each unit consisting of two questions for each topic, each quiz having at least eight questions that require considerable understanding and challenge and that focus on main ideas—for example, "What are norms of behavior?" Give four or five choices of answer. An alternative to quizzes might be a report or a craft project.

If some groups may need guidance in their discussion, discussion outlines can be provided listing main points to consider. For example, in the topic relating to establishing English colonies in America, the outline might be as follows:

Topic: How did religious ideals affect the establishment of settlements in America?
  • Puritan beliefs and practices
  • Treatment of dissenters
  • Quakers in Pennsylvania

To determine how to assign students to teams, you must take into consideration balancing students of low, average, and high performance levels, while making sure the average performance level of all teams is about equal.

Rank-order students from high to low performance and assign a team letter to each student. In a seven-team class, you would use letters A through G. Start from the top of the list with letter A. After you write G, continue lettering in the opposite order. For 28 students, the list would look like this: A B C D E F G / G F E D C B A / A B C D E F G / G F E D C B A. Next, look at the balance of each team according to gender and ethnicity, trading students of the same approximate performance level.

Team assignments can remain the same for six weeks, but experts within each team should be randomly or selectively changed for every unit. With classes of more than 24 students, there should be two expert groups on each topic so that there will be no more than 6 students in each expert group.

Finally, then, there is a regular cycle of instructional activities: reading to locate information; expert discussion groups dealing with the same topic; team reports by experts returning to their own team; test, paper, or project; and team scores and recognition. All teams can achieve awards; they are not in competition with each other. If your criterion is 80 percent for a great team and 90 percent for a super team, all groups will usually meet one criterion. If not, lower the level.

Competitive Grouping

To balance cooperative grouping, competitive groups can sometimes assist in students' intellectual, social, and emotional development. Such groups may involve tests or contests in which students compete against each other rather than cooperating toward a common goal. Following are some general suggestions for handling either cooperative or competitive groups.

At first, it may be helpful to move around to all groups, monitoring what is occurring and assisting when the need arises. This could mean answering or asking questions, giving guidance or suggestions, modeling how to make group decisions, or reminding groups of individual assigned roles. Students need to know that they are accountable for the assignment, that it isn't just a time-filler, and that they must understand clearly what the task is. Using 5 × 8 cards with names and roles on one side, along with basic instructions, provides a good reference for them. At the end of class the recorder can use the back of the card for reactions, a progress report, or questions for the teacher.

As students become more accustomed to small-group work with its roles and responsibilities, it is important that teachers back off and not interfere unless absolutely necessary. Small groups seem to function best with around five or six people per group. Larger numbers may mean that some will not get as actively involved as others.

There are also purposes for grouping other than ability level or skill needs. Interest groups can be very successful where students have a chance to select a story, research topic, or problem to solve that is of interest to them. Sometimes grouping for social or interpersonal needs can be helpful. Take, for example, a class that has a number of reserved students who rarely do any talking. Putting all the talkative leaders together can force them to learn to listen and respect others, while the shy ones are forced to talk and take leadership roles. For active class involvement, grouping is an important addition to the whole-class lecture–discussion organizational pattern.

SUMMARY

Areas of practical concern for secondary study-reading programs include factors in developing such programs across the total school curriculum and staff development guidelines for ensuring successful progress. Goals, instruction, personnel, and organization must be considered. Personnel requirements and responsibilities are of utmost importance, as is the way staff development programs are carried out. Grouping in its many forms is an effective device for accomplishing secondary study-reading goals.

NOTES

1. Barbara Blow, "Individualized Reading," *Arizona English Bulletin*, 18 (April 1976), 151–153.

2. Harold Herber, handout given at the Preconvention Institute, International Reading Association, Toronto Convention, May 1, 1988.

3. Betty Roe, Barbara Stoodt, and Paul Burns, *Secondary School Reading Instruction: The Content Areas*, 3rd ed. (Boston: Houghton Mifflin, 1987), p. 9.

4. Ibid.

5. Joan Nelson-Herber, handout given at the Preconvention Institute, International Reading Association, Toronto Convention, May 1, 1988.

6. Mary Dunn Siedow, David M. Memory, and Page S. Bristow, *Inservice Education for Content Area Teachers* (Newark, DE: International Reading Association, 1985).

7. L. Korinek, R. Schmid, and M. McAdams, "Inservice Types and Best Practices," *Journal of Research and Development in Education*, 18 (1985), 33–38.

8. JoAnne L. Vacca and Richard T. Vacca, "Unfreezing Strategies for Staff Development in Reading," *The Reading Teacher*, 35 (1980), 394–396.

9. Joy N. Monahan, handout given at the Preconvention Institute, International Reading Association, Toronto Convention, May 1, 1988.

10. Mark W. Conley, "Grouping," in Donna E. Alvermann, David W. Moore,

and Mark W. Conley, eds., *Research within Reach: Secondary School Reading* (Newark, DE: International Reading Association, 1987), pp. 130–140.

11. Karen D. Wood, "Fostering Cooperative Learning in Middle and Secondary Level Classrooms," *Journal of Reading*, 31 (1987), 10–18.

12. Robert Slavin, "A Cooperative Learning Approach to Content Areas: Jigsaw Teaching," in Diane Lapp, James Flood, and Nancy Farnam, eds., *Content Area Reading and Learning: Instructional Strategies*, (Englewood Cliffs, NJ: Prentice-Hall, 1989), pp. 330–346.

RECOMMENDED READINGS

Alvermann, D. E., Moore, D. W., and Conley, M. W., eds. *Research within Reach: Secondary School Reading*. Newark, DE: International Reading Association, 1987.

Anders, Patricia L. "Dream of a Secondary School Reading Program? People Are the Key." *Journal of Reading*, 24 (January 1981), 316–320.

Anderson, Richard C., et al. *Becoming a Nation of Readers: The Report of the Commission on Reading*. Washington, DC: National Institute of Education, National Academy of Education, 1985.

Bates, G. W. "Developing Reading Strategies for the Gifted: A Research-Based Approach." *Journal of Reading*, 27 (7, April 1984), 590–593.

Bean, Rita M., and Wilson, Robert M. *Effecting Change in School Reading Programs: The Resource Role*. Newark, DE: International Reading Association, 1981.

Bennis, W., and Nanus, B. *Leaders: The Strategies for Taking Charge*. New York: Harper & Row, 1985.

Brinkerhoff, R. "Evaluation of In-Service Programs." *Teacher Education and Special Education*, 3 (1980), 27–38.

Cook, D., ed. *A Guide to Curriculum Planning in Reading*. Madison: Wisconsin Department of Public Instruction, 1986.

Diller, Christine, and Glessner, Barbara. "A Cross Curriculum Substance Abuse Unit." *Journal of Reading*, 31 (March 1988), 553–558.

Downing, John, and Morris, Bert. "An Australian Program for Improving High School Reading in Content Areas." *Journal of Reading*, 28 (December 1984), 237–244.

Farrell, Richard T., and Cirrincione, Joseph M. "State Certification Requirements in Reading for Content Area Teachers." *Journal of Reading*, 28 (November 1984), 152–158.

Gardner, Howard. *Frames of Mind: The Theory of Multiple Intelligences*. New York: Basic Books, 1983.

Gee, Thomas C., and Forester, Nora. "Moving Reading Instruction beyond the Reading Classroom." *Journal of Reading*, 31 (March 1988), 505–511.

Gove, Mary K. "Getting High School Teachers to Use Content Reading Strategies." *Journal of Reading*, 25 (November 1981), 113–116.

Herber, Harold L., and Nelson-Herber, Joan. "Planning the Reading Program." In Alan C. Purves and Olive Niles, eds., *Becoming Readers in a Complex Society*, Eighty-third Yearbook of the National Society for the Study of Education. Chicago: University of Chicago Press, 1984, pp. 174–208.

Joyce, B., Showers, B., and Rolheiser-Bennett, C. "Staff Development and Student Learning: A Synthesis of Research on Models of Teaching." *Educational Leadership* (October 1987).

Larson, Janet J., and Guttinger, Helen Ireland. "A Secondary Reading Program to Prevent College Reading Problems." *Journal of Reading*, 22 (February 1979), 399–403.

Lehr, Fran. "New Approaches to Remedial Reading Programs at the Secondary Level." *Journal of Reading*, 24 (January 1981); 350–351.

Michigan Curriculum Review Committee and Michigan Reading Association. *New Dimension in Reading Instruction*, 1985.

Moller, B. "An Instructional Model for Gifted Advanced Readers." *Journal of Reading*, 27 (4, 1984), 324–327.

National Assessment of Educational Progress. *The Reading Report Card*. Report No. 15-R-01. Princeton, NJ: Educational Testing Center, 1985.

Nelson-Herber, J., and Herber, H. "A Positive Approach to Assessment and Correction of Reading Difficulties in Middle and Secondary Schools." In J. Flood, ed., *Promoting Reading Comprehension*. Newark, DE: International Reading Association, 1984, pp. 232–244.

Patberg, Judythe P., et al. "The Impact of Content Area Reading Instruction on Secondary Teachers." *Journal of Reading*, 27 (March 1984), 500–507.

Professional Standards and Ethics Committee. *Guidelines for the Professional Preparation of Reading Teachers*. Newark, DE: International Reading Association, May 1978.

Readance, John E., Baldwin, R. Scott, and Dishner, Ernest K. "Establishing Content Reading Programs in Secondary Schools." *Journal of Reading*, 23 (March 1980), 522–526.

Samuels, S. Jay, and Pearson, P. David, eds. *Changing School Reading Programs: Principles and Case Studies*. Newark, DE: International Reading Association, 1988.

Siedow, Mary Dunn. "Inservice Education for Content Area Teachers: Some Final Thoughts." In *Inservice Education for Content Area Teachers*. Newark, DE: International Reading Association, 1985, pp. 163–166.

Smith, Richard, Otto, Wayne, and Hanson, Lee. *The School Reading Program: A Handbook for Teachers, Supervisors, and Specialists*. Boston: Houghton-Mifflin, 1978.

Stallings, Jane A. "Effective Use of Time in Secondary Reading Programs." In James V. Hoffman, ed., *Effective Teaching of Reading: Research and Practice*. Newark, DE: International Reading Association, 1986, pp. 85–106.

Stallings, Jane A., Needles, M., and Stayrook, N. *The Teaching of Basic Reading Skills in Secondary Schools Phase II and Phase III*. Menlo Park, CA: SRI International, 1979.

Usova, George M. "Comparing Attitudes toward Reading Instruction among Secondary Principles, Reading Specialists, and Content Teachers." *Reading Improvement*, 16 (Summer 1979), 169–174.

Vacca, Joanne L. "Program Implementation." In *Staff Development Leadership: A Resource Book*. Columbus, OH: Department of Education, 1983, pp. 51–58.

Ward, Stephen D., and Bradford, Eugene J. "Supervisors' Expertise in Reading Affects Achievement in Junior High." *Journal of Reading*, 26 (January 1983).

Webb, N., and Kenderski, C. "Student Interaction and Learning in Small Group and Whole Class Settings." In P. Peterson, L. Wilkinson, and M. Hallinan, eds., *The Social Contexts of Instruction*. Orlando, FL: Academic Press, 1984, pp. 153–170.

Webber, Elizabeth A. "Organizing and Scheduling the Secondary Reading Program." *Journal of Reading*, 27 (April 1984), 594–596.

Wepner, Shelley B., Feeley, Joan, and Strickland, Dorothy, eds., *The Administration and Supervision of Reading Programs*. New York: Teachers College, Columbia University, 1989.

Whilhite, Robert K. "Principals' Views of Their Role in the High School Reading Program." *Journal of Reading*, 27 (January 1984), 356–358.

Postorganizer 1
Planning a Study-Reading, -Writing, and -Learning Program

By now you are able to summarize and make generalizations concerning all major facets of study-reading, -writing, and -learning. Refer back now to Preorganizer 2. After working cooperatively with a partner or small group, you must now decide how to present your information to the rest of the class. If role playing is not an option, you may wish to draw a cognitive map with a written explanation, or make a formal outline, or provide information in the form of a study-reading, -writing, -learning lesson plan, or develop a dialogue or skit. Try to be creative in the way you present your information, and enjoy this different way of synthesizing a body of knowledge.

Postorganizer 2
Posttest

Return to the beginning of this text and retake the pretest. Compare the results with how you responded on the pretest to measure quality and quantity of learning. The crucial thing is that you will now apply learnings to your classroom.

Appendixes

Appendix 1
The Barrett Taxonomy:
Cognitive and Affective Dimensions
of Reading Comprehension

1.0 *Literal Comprehension.* Literal comprehension focuses on ideas and information which are *explicitly* stated in the selection. Purposes for reading and teacher's questions designed to elicit responses at this level may range from simple to complex. A simple task in literal comprehension may be the recognition or recall of a single fact or incident. A more complex task might be the recognition or recall of a series of facts or the sequencing of incidents in a reading selection. Purposes and questions at this level may have the following characteristics.

    1.1 *Recognition* requires the student to locate or identify ideas or information *explicitly* stated in the reading selection itself or in exercises which use the explicit ideas and information presented in the reading selection. Recognition tasks are:

        1.11 *Recognition of Details.* The student is required to locate or identify facts such as the names of characters, the time of the story, or the place of the story.

        1.12 *Recognition of Main Ideas.* The student is asked to locate or iden-

Source: Reprinted with permission from a discussion of Thomas C. Barrett's "Taxonomy of Cognitive and Affective Dimensions of Reading Comprehension," in "What Is Reading? Some Current Concepts," by Theodore Clymer, in *Innovation and Change in Reading Instruction,* edited by Helen M. Robinson, Sixty-seventh Yearbook of the National Society for the Study of Education, Part II, 1968, pp. 1–30, copyright © 1968 by the University of Chicago Press.

tify an explicit statement in or from a selection which is a main idea of a paragraph or a larger portion of the selection.

1.13 *Recognition of a Sequence.* The student is required to locate or identify the order of incidents or actions explicitly stated in the selection.

1.14 *Recognition of Comparison.* The student is requested to locate or identify likenesses and differences in characters, times, and places that are explicitly stated in the selection.

1.15 *Recognition of Cause and Effect Relationships.* The student in this instance may be required to locate or identify the explicitly stated reasons for certain happenings or actions in the selection.

1.16 *Recognition of Character Traits.* The student is required to identify or locate explicit statements about a character which helps to point up the type of person he is.

1.2 *Recall* requires the student to produce from memory ideas and information *explicitly* stated in the reading selection. Recall tasks are:

1.21 *Recall of Details.* The student is asked to produce from memory facts such as the names of characters, the time of the story, or the place of the story.

1.22 *Recall of Main Ideas.* The student is required to state a main idea of a paragraph or a larger portion of the selection from memory, when the main idea is explicitly stated in the selection.

1.23 *Recall of a Sequence.* The student is asked to provide from memory the order of incidents or actions explicitly stated in the selection.

1.24 *Recall of Comparisons.* The student is required to call up from memory the likenesses and differences in characters, times, and places that are explicitly stated in the selection.

1.25 *Recall of Cause and Effect Relationships.* The student is requested to produce from memory explicitly stated reasons for certain happenings or actions in the selection.

1.26 *Recall of Character Traits.* The student is asked to call up from memory explicit statements about characters which illustrate the type of persons they are.

2.0 *Reorganization.* Reorganization requires the student to analyze, synthesize, and/or organize ideas or information explicitly stated in the selection. To produce the desired thought product, the reader may utilize the statements of the author verbatim or he may paraphrase or translate the author's statements. Reorganization tasks are:

2.1 *Classifying.* In this instance the student is required to place people, things, places, and/or events into categories.

2.2 *Outlining.* The student is requested to organize the selection into outline form using direct statements or paraphrased statements from the selection.

2.3 *Summarizing.* The student is asked to condense the selection using direct or paraphrased statements from the selection.

2.4 *Synthesizing.* In this instance, the student is requested to consolidate explicit ideas or information from more than one source.

3.0 *Inferential Comprehension.* Inferential comprehension is demonstrated by the student when he uses the ideas and information explicitly stated in the selection, his intuition, and his personal experience as a basis for conjectures and hypotheses. Inferences drawn by the student may be either convergent or divergent in nature and the student may or may not be asked to verbalize the rationale underlying his inferences. In general, then, inferential comprehension is stimulated by purposes for reading and teachers' questions which demand thinking and imagination that go beyond the printed page.

3.1 *Inferring Supporting Details.* In this instance, the student is asked to conjecture about additional facts the author might have included in the selection which would have made it more informative, interesting, or appealing.

3.2 *Inferring Main Ideas.* The student is required to provide the main idea, general significance, theme, or moral which is not explicitly stated in the selection.

3.3 *Inferring Sequence.* The student, in this case, may be requested to conjecture as to what action or incident might have taken place between two explicitly stated actions or incidents, or he may be asked to hypothesize about what would happen next if the selection had not ended as it did but had been extended.

3.4 *Inferring Comparisons.* The student is required to infer likenesses and differences in characters, times, or places. Such inferential comparisons revolve around ideas such as: "here and there," "then and now," "he and he," "he and she," and "she and she."

3.5 *Inferring Cause and Effect Relationships.* The student is required to hypothesize about the motivations of characters and their interactions with time and place. He may also be required to conjecture as to what caused the author to include certain ideas, words, characterizations, and actions in his writing.

3.6 *Inferring Character Traits.* In this case, the student is asked to hypothesize about the nature of characters on the basis of explicit clues presented in the selection.

3.7 *Predicting Outcomes.* The student is requested to read an initial portion of the selections and on the basis of this reading he is required to conjecture about the outcome of the selection.

3.8 *Interpreting Figurative Language.* The student, in this instance, is asked to infer literal meanings from the author's figurative use of language.

4.0 *Evaluation.* Purposes for reading and teacher's questions, in this instance, require responses by the student which indicate that he has made an evaluative judgment by comparing ideas presented in the selection with external criteria provided by the teacher, other authorities, or other written sources, or with internal criteria provided by the reader's experiences, knowledge, or values. In essence evaluation deals with judgment and focuses on qualities of accuracy, acceptability, desirability, worth, or probability of occurrence. Evaluative thinking may be demonstrated by asking the student to make the following judgments.

4.1 *Judgments of Reality or Fantasy.* Could this really happen? Such a question calls for a judgment by the reader based on his experience.

4.2 *Judgments of Fact or Opinion.* Does the author provide adequate support for his conclusions. Is the author attempting to sway your thinking? Questions of this type require the student to analyze and evaluate the writing on the basis of the knowledge he has on the subject as well as to analyze and evaluate the intent of the author.

4.3 *Judgments of Adequacy and Validity.* Is the information presented here in keeping with what you have read on the subject in other sources? Questions of this nature call for the reader to compare written sources of information, with an eye toward agreement and disagreement or completeness and incompleteness.

4.4 *Judgments of Appropriateness.* What part of the story best describes the main character? Such a question requires the reader to make a judgment about the relative adequacy of different parts of the selection to answer the question.

4.5 *Judgments of Worth, Desirability and Acceptability.* Was the character right or wrong in what he did? Was his behavior good or bad? Questions of this nature call for judgments based on the reader's moral code or his value system.

5.0 *Appreciation.* Appreciation involves all the previously cited cognitive dimensions of reading, for it deals with the psychological and aesthetic impact of the selection on the reader. Appreciation calls for the student to be emotionally and aesthetically sensitive to the work and to have a reaction to the worth of its psychological and artistic elements. Appreciation includes both the knowledge of and the emotional response to literary techniques, forms, styles, and structures.

5.1 *Emotional Response to the Content.* The student is required to verbalize his feelings about the selection in terms of interest, excitement, boredom, fear, hate, amusement, etc. It is concerned with the emotional impact of the total work on the reader.

5.2 *Identification with Characters or Incidents.* Teachers' questions of this nature will elicit responses from the reader which demonstrates his sensitivity to, sympathy for, and empathy with characters and happenings portrayed by the author.

5.3 *Reactions to the Author's Use of Language.* In this instance the student is required to respond to the author's craftsmanship in terms of the semantic dimensions of the selection, namely, connotations and denotations of words.

5.4 *Imagery.* In this instance, the reader is required to verbalize his feelings with regard to the author's artistic ability to paint word pictures which cause the reader to visualize, smell, taste, hear, or feel.

Appendix 2
The Basic Academic Competencies

A statement of what academic preparation for college ought to be, this is the collective judgment of over 400 school and university teachers and administrators.

Basic Academic Competencies are:

1. Developed abilities; outcomes of learning and intellectual discourse, acquired when there are incentives and stimulation to learning when there is an encouraging learning environment. Different levels of competency can be defined in measurable academic, basic terms.
2. Interrelated to and interdependent with the basic subject matter areas. Without such competencies, the knowledge of literature, history, science, languages, mathematics, and all other disciplines is unattainable.
3. Not substitutes for drive, motivation, interest, intelligence, experience, or adaptability. Nor are basic academic competencies social coping skills even though we recognize that coping skills are crucial to success in school, life, and work. Coping skills are simply another important matter which we have decided not to subsume under the area of Basic Academic Competencies.

Source: Reprinted from *Preparation for College in the 1980s: The Basic Academic Competencies and the Basic Academic Curriculum,* copyright © 1981 by College Entrance Examination Board, New York.

4. A link across the disciplines of knowledge, although they are not specific to the disciplines. Teaching that is done in ignorance of, or in disregard for such competencies and their interrelationships to each of the subject matter areas is inadequate if not incompetent.
5. A way to tell students what is expected of them. The knowledge of what is expected is crucial to effective learning; its absence deems much of learning useless.

How expressed?

Descriptions of each of six secondary competencies:

1. *Reading competencies*—ability to:
   - Identify and comprehend main and subordinate ideas in written work and summarize ideas in one's own words.
   - Recognize different purposes and methods of writing; identify writer's point of view and tone; and interpret writer's meaning inferentially and literally.
   - Separate one's personal opinions and assumptions from a writer's.
   - Vary one's reading rate and method (survey, skim, review, question, and master) according to the type of material and purpose for reading.
   - Use features of books and other reference materials (table of contents, preface, introduction, titles and subtitles, index, glossary, appendix, bibliography).
   - Define unfamiliar words by decoding, using contextual clues, or by using a dictionary.
2. *Writing competencies*—ability to:
   - Conceive ideas about a topic for the purpose of writing.
   - Organize, select, and relate ideas and outline and develop them in coherent paragraphs.
   - Write Standard English sentences with correct:
     - sentence structure
     - verb forms
     - punctuation, capitalization, possessives, plural forms, and other matters of mechanics
     - word choice and spelling
   - Vary one's writing style, including vocabulary and sentence structure, for different readers and purposes.
   - Improve one's own writing by restructuring, correcting errors, and rewriting.
   - Gather information from primary and secondary sources; write a report using this research; quote, paraphrase, and summarize accurately; and cite sources properly.

3. *Speaking and Listening Competencies* — ability to:
   - Engage critically and constructively in the exchange of ideas, particularly during class discussions and conferences with instructors.
   - Answer and ask questions coherently and concisely, and follow spoken instructions.
   - Identify and comprehend the main and subordinate ideas in lectures and discussions, and report accurately what others have said.
   - Conceive and develop ideas about a topic for the purpose of speaking to a group; choose and organize related ideas; present them clearly in Standard English; and evaluate similar presentations by others.
   - Vary one's use of spoken language to suit different situations.

4. *Mathematical Competencies* — ability to:
   - Perform, with reasonable accuracy, computations of addition, subtraction, multiplication, and division using natural numbers, fractions, decimals, and integers.
   - Make and use measurements in both traditional and metric units.
   - Use effectively the mathematics of:
     - integers, fractions, and decimals
     - ratios, proportions, and percentages
     - roots and powers
     - algebra
     - geometry
   - Make estimates and approximations, and judge the reasonableness of a result.
   - Formulate and solve a problem in mathematical terms.
   - Select and use appropriate approaches and tools in solving problems (mental computation, trial and error, paper-and-pencil techniques, calculator, and computer).
   - Use elementary concepts of probability and statistics.

5. *Reasoning Competencies* — ability to:
   - Identify and formulate problems, as well as propose and evaluate ways to solve them.
   - Recognize and use inductive and deductive reasoning, and recognize fallacies in reasoning.
   - Draw reasonable conclusions from information found in various sources (written, spoken, tabular, or graphic) and defend one's conclusions rationally.
   - Comprehend, develop, and use concepts and generalizations.
   - Distinguish between fact and opinion.

6. *Studying Competencies* — ability to:
   This set of abilities is different in kind from those that precede it. They are set forth here because they constitute the key abilities in learning how to learn. Successful study skills are necessary for

acquiring the other five competencies as well as for achieving the desired outcomes. Students are unlikely to be efficient in any part of their work without them.

One further difference must be expressed: Activities related to acquiring the basic studying competencies will fail unless students bear in mind the role of their attitude in the learning process. That attitude should encompass a sense of personal responsibility for their own progress, a desire to make full use of the teacher as a resource, and a willingness to conduct themselves in ways that make learning possible for classmates as well as themselves.

- Set study goals and priorities consistent with stated course objectives and own progress, establish surroundings and habits conducive to learning independently or with others, and follow a schedule that accounts for both short- and long-term projects.
- Locate and use resource external to the classroom (e.g., libraries, computers, interviews, and direct observations) and incorporate knowledge from such sources into the learning process.
- Develop and use general and specialized vocabularies, and use them for reading, writing, speaking, listening, computing, and studying.
- Understand and follow customary instructions for academic work in order to recall, comprehend, analyze, summarize, and report the main ideas from reading, lectures, and other academic experiences; and synthesize knowledge and apply it to new situations.
- Prepare for various types of examinations and devise strategies for pacing, attempting or omitting questions, thinking, writing, and editing according to the type of examination; satisfy other assessments of learning in meeting course objectives such as laboratory performance, class participation, simulation, and students' evaluations.
- Accept constructive criticism and learn from it.

Appendix 3
Reading Selections for Rate Adaptability Practice

Covered Bridges

Green Sergeant's Bridge was the first covered bridge I had ever seen, but the aura of history and nostalgia of American past grew upon me as the years went by and resulted in my collecting covered bridges in about a thousand paintings, even writing a book about them. Not far from Green Sergeant's Bridge was built the first covered bridge in America (in 1805). Originally uncovered, the builders were embarrassed about its cost (more than the national debt at that time), and decided to enhance its value in the public eye and call it, The American Permanent Bridge. Making the bridge appear "permanent" involved giving it a thick coat of cement paint and then covering it over with America's first bridge roof. Other bridge owners copied the idea and soon most all American wooden bridges became covered. Because animals often shy at crossing rivers, and a covered bridge resembles a barn, drovers enjoyed the fact that their herds willingly entered a roofed structure. The covered bridge became standard Americana.

Although most people consider the New England covered bridge just a way to keep snow out, most traffic was in winter by sleds, and the owner of each covered bridge was obliged, (sometimes by law), to shovel snow *into* their bridge! Some consider the covered bridge unique to Vermont, but that state is number five, with Oregon fourth; Pennsylvania was first, Ohio second and Indiana third.

Covered bridge portals were ideal places for advertising posters and local announcements. One bridge over the Delaware at Portland, Pennsylvania,

Source: Reprinted with permission from *Return to Taos: A Twice-Told Tale* by Eric Sloane, copyright © 1982 by Hastings House, New York, pp. 26–28.

sported the largest advertisement of its time. With the promise of the free coat of paint to preserve the wood, the Chamber of Commerce had consented to a four-hundred-foot Coca Cola sign. I guess the insurance company would not insure buses passing through so long a bridge for I remember passengers disembarking at one end and walking across the bridge while the bus went across empty. The Coca Cola bridge was not alone in advertising lore. Others still had remnants of old advertising signs and I recall several singing the praises of "Dr. Scott's Electric Flesh Brush." This proved to be no more than a metal-backed hairbrush. "It's power can be tested," the ad said, "by the compass which accompanies each brush. Massage the flesh with it to cure paralysis, toothache, constipation, malaria and indigestion."

The one sign that intrigued me most was an ad for "Mentholated Underwear Guaranteed to Cure Rheumatism." I'd almost rather have the disease! [415 words]

Stress

Every person on earth is under some degree of stress, as a result of physical, mental, and emotional factors, twenty-four hours a day, every day. First, physical stress. The degree of complex interaction among nerves, muscles and bones required to bring about even apparently simple body movements is truly incredible, even for such an apparently simple action as writing your name. This was brought home to me with great force near the end of my drinking days, when I found that, stone-cold sober and not suffering from the shakes, I could not write my signature in a form that could be identified as definitely mine. Too much alcohol had thrown my whole delicate muscle control system just a little out of whack—temporarily—and the result was shocking to me. Yet, under normal circumstances, we write our signature automatically, without thought or awareness of effort.

Our mental and emotional equipment runs in a similar manner, the operational units of each interacting together with amazing precision to achieve organized conscious thought and emotional balance. And here also we have become so accustomed to controlling these equally delicate systems that we operate them almost entirely *unconsciously* and *automatically*. . . .

Every person's level of stress is constantly rising and falling. In well-adjusted people, this process is easily kept within comfortable limits, because they have learned—without conscious thought—a whole array of attitudes and simple methods of reducing stress whenever it rises above a comfortable level. Occasionally, when really provoked, the usual attitudes and methods are inadequate and the well-adjusted person's stress level rises to "blowing point." When that happens, these people scream, swear, throw things, smash something, or hit out at someone or something. Others use more sophisticated techniques (take a walk, visit a friend, construct a model, paint a picture, bake a cake, write in a diary). But of whatever kind, these actions function to reduce the pressure to a manageable level. These are healthy safety valves. The heavy stress is over, gone, done with. [336 words]

Source: Reprinted by permission from *Addictive Drinking: The Road to Recovery for Problem Drinkers and Those Who Love Them,* pp. 20, 21–22, by Clark Vaughan, copyright © 1982 by Clark Vaughan. Used by permission of Viking Penguin, a division of Penguin USA.

Escapism to Wonderlands

When Alice fell down the rabbit hole, Lewis Carroll had "not the least idea what was to happen afterwards." At the time, 4 July 1862, he was probably too busy rowing Alice Liddell and her two sisters up the Thames from Oxford to Godstow to worry about it. But the fantasy that he began so casually has fascinated, delighted and disturbed children—and adults—ever since.

There is a deep divide between the character of the Reverend Charles Lutwidge Dodson, an Oxford mathematics dean for forty-seven years, and his alter ego Lewis Carroll, author of *Alice's Adventures in Wonderland* and its sequel *Through the Looking Glass*. Dodson was shy, stammering, reserved, pedantic. His life was tightly organized around timetables, registers and indexes, with every detail minutely ordered in advance. But in the company of little girls like Alice Liddell and her sisters he became completely transformed, entirely at ease, and a fascinating talker and storyteller. With them he lost his stutter, and his shyness and reserve, creating endless Wonderlands for their benefit.

Some commentators have claimed that Carroll's fantasy was not an escape from the dull routine of Victorian academic life, but rather, that the pedantically ordered world of the Revd. Charles Dodson, with his compulsion to relegate and interpret in mathematical terms, was a desperate attempt to escape the chaos revealed in the Alice books, and to exorcise the demons present in their metaphysical confusion. There may well be an element of truth in that. In both books, Alice is characterized as a straightforward, sensible and courageous girl, nicely brought up, who is plunged into a crazy world, and confronted with bewildering, often nightmarish situations. Her attempts to apply logic are constantly met with arguments that are pure nonsense. Perhaps the outside world looked just like that to the shy Reverend. But his main purpose was to entertain his impressionable companions—it clearly gave him great pleasure to do so—and he was well aware of the appeal which absurdity has for small children.

The young have always used fantasy to escape from a dull world ruled by adults. Dragons and witches are so much more exciting than teachers and postmen, and if the going gets too rough, one can always return to the comforting, if monotonous, reality of the parental home. The Grimm brothers and other collectors of folklore recognized this long before Dodson did, and countless other storytellers have added their own contributions since. [410 words]

Source: Reprinted by permission from *Fantasy: A Practical Guide to Escapism: The Lure of the Impossible,* by William Davis, copyright © 1984 by Sidgewick & Jackson, London.

Appendix 4
History of the
English Dictionary

History can help us appreciate what we too often take for granted. How much do you know about how our English dictionary evolved? Read this summary to fill in your knowledge gaps. What was each century's major contribution? Perhaps making a timeline would help to put things into perspective.

COMBINED DEVELOPMENT OF THE ENGLISH DICTIONARY: ENGLISH AND HISTORY

The history of the dictionary is a fascinating chapter in the history of ideas. Its beginnings are concerned with the international language of medieval European civilization: Latin. Our first word books were lists of Latin terms, difficult and usually taken from Scripture. These were accompanied by glosses in easier, more familiar Latin, and then in native English (i.e., Anglo-Saxon).

Around 1,400 isolated glosses were collected into a kind of Latin–English dictionary. In 1565 the first great classical dictionary, Cooper's *Thesaurus*,

Source: Adapted from the book, *Webster's New World Dictionary*, copyright © 1966, pp. xxvii–xxxiv. Used by permission of the publisher, New World Dictionaries/A Division of Simon & Schuster, Inc., New York, NY.

appeared. Its publication had been delayed five years because Cooper's wife, fearing that too much lexicography would kill her husband, had burned his first manuscript. None of the word books in the sixteenth century used the title *dictionary* but instead resorted to fanciful names such as *hortus* (garden) and *thesaurus* (hoard).

During the late sixteenth century, with the Renaissance in full swing, literary scholars preferred Latin or Greek to English. Because scholarly writing included many polysyllabic Latin and Greek terms, there was a need for explanations. Thus, the *Dictionary of Hard Words*, the real predecessor of the modern dictionary, was developed to provide those explanations. If the sixteenth century was the century of the foreign-language dictionary, the seventeenth century was one of hard words.

In the early eighteenth century there arose word books giving more attention to literary usage. Latin and Greek had either been absorbed into the language or been sloughed away. The French influence brought notions of simple elegance in syntax and a quiet effectiveness in words. Convinced that English had finally reached a high standard of purity, literary scholars were convinced that the brash expansionism and the new Industrial Revolution might destroy this hard-won high standard of literary refinement. What was needed was a dictionary to enshrine this standard for posterity. Nathaniel Bailey's *Universal Etymological Dictionary of the English Language* (1721), with illustrations by Flaxman (1731), was one of the most revolutionary dictionaries ever compiled. It paid attention to current usage and was the first to feature etymology, syllabication, illustrative quotations, illustrations, and pronunciation. Samuel Johnson greatly extended and refined Bailey's techniques and fixed the spelling of many disputed words in his *Dictionary* (1755). Johnson's book influenced English letters for a hundred years and, after revisions, continued in common use to 1900. As late as 1890 most Englishmen used the word *dictionary* as a mere synonym for Johnson's *Dictionary*. In 1880 a bill was actually thrown out of Parliament because one word in it was not found in "the Dictionary."

Johnson became a linguistic legislator in trying to remove "improprieties and absurdities" from the language. From these activities of his we still may get the notion that the dictionary is a "supreme authority" for arbitrating questions of what is correct.

In the second half of the eighteenth century the increasingly wealthy middle classes pushed to have a key to pronunciations acceptable in polite society. Pronunciation experts, usually of Scottish or Irish extraction, edited a series of pronunciation dictionaries such as John Walker's *Critical Pronouncing Dictionary and Expositor of the English Language* (1791). Walker's pronunciations and Johnson's definitions were combined into a dictionary that dominated the field in England and the United States until well after 1850.

The nineteenth century brought us the recording of word history through dated quotations and the development of encyclopedic word books. In 1836 Charles Richardson produced a dictionary completely lacking in definitions, *The New Dictionary of the English Language*, thus combining Johnson's perception with the findings of the new science of historical linguistics. Dated defining quotations were used to indicate the "senses and the historical evolutions of the senses." From this evolved the *New English Dictionary*, 1933 (N.E.D.) or *Oxford English Dictionary* (O.E.D.), which covered the words of English with a "completeness of historical evidence and discrimination of senses unparalleled in linguistic history."

The modern American dictionary is typically compact and relatively inexpensive, and contains spellings, pronunciations, limited etymologies, illustrations, selective synonyms and antonyms, and encyclopedic data (scientific, technological, geographical, and biological). It is indeed a storehouse of information, and is worthy of more than a casual perusal.

Appendix 5
Assessment Instrument
Listing

Attitudes

Estes Attitude Scales, 1981, Pro-Ed. Secondary Form, grades 7–12. Measures attitudes toward reading, science, math, English, and social studies.

Norm-Referenced Achievement

Assessment of Reading Growth, Jamestown Publisher. Level (age) 13–grades 6, 7, 8. Level (age) 17–grades 10, 11, 12, adult. Using items released by the National Assessment of Educational Progress, it determines silent reading comprehension and assesses literal and inferential comprehension.

California Achievement Tests: Reading, 1985, CTB/McGraw-Hill. Levels 10–20, forms E, F–grades K.0–12.9. Measures vocabulary and comprehension, and word analysis at levels 11–16.

Comprehensive Tests of Basic Skills: Reading, 1985, CTB/McGraw-Hill. Forms U and V, grades K.0–12.9. (Time for administering, 45–70 minutes.) Measures word attack, vocabulary, and comprehension.

Iowa Tests of Basic Skills, 1982, Riverside Publishers. Multilevel Edition, forms 9–14, grades K–9. (Administration time: 4 hours.) Measures listening, word analysis, language, spelling, capitalization, punctuation, usage, reference materials, and mathematics.

Metropolitan Achievement Tests, 1986 (MAT6): Reading Instruction Tests, The Psychological Corporation. Grades K.5–12.9. Levels 5.0–12.9 measure vocabulary and comprehension.

Stanford Achievement Test Series, 1984, The Psychological Corporation. Two alternative, equivalent forms, 10 battery levels, grades K–13. Reading test booklets include word recognition skills, vocabulary, and comprehension.

STEPTEST (Sequential Test of Educational Progress)—Reading, 1963. Levels 1–4, Cooperative Test Division, Educational Testing Service.

Test of Reading Comprehension, 1978, Pro-Ed. Ages 6½–17 years. It measures silent reading comprehension, the ability to identify words related to a common concept, understanding of sentences similar in meaning but different syntactically, and the ability to answer questions related to paragraphs. There is a special subtest for remedial students.

Wide Range Achievement Test, 1984, Justak. Level 2, for age 12 and above. Focus is on decoding skills, pronunciation of printed words only. This is an individual test, which takes approximately 10 minutes and can serve as a quick screening device.

Criterion-Referenced

El Paso Phonics Test, 1979, Allyn and Bacon. This is a part of the Edwall Reading Inventory—it measures initial and ending consonant sounds, initial consonant clusters, vowels and vowel teams, and special letter combinations.

Fountain Valley Reading Skills Test, R. L. Zweig Associates, Grades 1–12. Grades 7–12 measures vocabulary, comprehension, and study skills.

Multiscore, Riverside Publishing Company.

Objectives—Referenced Bank of Items and Tests (ORBIT), CTB/McGraw-Hill.

Reading Yardsticks, Riverside Publishing Company.

Diagnostic—Group

Stanford Diagnostic Reading Test. 1984, The Psychological Corporation. Grades 1.5–12. (Administration time: 15–40 minutes per subtest.) Brown Level (grades 5–8 and very low high school) assesses phonics; structural analysis; auditory vocabulary; literal and inferential comprehension of textual, functional, and recreational material; and reading rate. Blue Level (grade 8–community college) assesses phonics; structural analysis; word meanings and word parts; rate, including skimming and scanning; literal and inferential comprehension of textual, functional, and recreational materials.

Diagnostic—Individual

Gray Oral Reading Tests, revised 1986, Pro-Ed. Forms A and B have 13 graded oral reading passages in each. (Administration time: 15–30 minutes.) Measures oral reading; designed to identify readers who read less well than their peers; identifies individual strengths and weaknesses.

Reading Miscue Inventory, 1987, 2nd ed., Richard C. Owen Publishers. (Administration time: 1 hour.) This gives an in-depth, qualitative analysis of oral reading performance and comprehension.

Woodcock Reading Mastery Tests, 1973, American Guidance Service. Forms A and B, grades K–12. (Administration time: 30–45 minutes.) Detects reading problems; facilitates grouping for instruction; evaluates school reading programs, testing for letter and word identification, word attack and word comprehension, passage comprehension.

Group Ability and Intelligence

Cognitive Abilities Test, 1982, Riverside Publishing. K–12, levels A–H for grades 3–12. (Administration time: 98 minutes.) Measures verbal, quantitative, and nonverbal abilities.

Kuhlman-Anderson Tests, 8th ed., 1982, Scholastic Testing Service. Grades K–12, 9 levels. (Administration time: 50–75 minutes.) It measures cognitive tasks that assess verbal and nonverbal capacity.

Test of Cognitive Skills, 1981, CTB/McGraw-Hill. Five levels for grades 9–12. Each level has four tests for sequence, memory, analogies, and verbal reasoning. Grades 2–12. (Approximate administration time per subject: 6–10 minutes.)

Individual Intelligence

Slosson Intelligence Test, revised 1984. Infant–adult. (Administration time: 10–20 minutes.) Assesses mental ability; used to predict reading achievement and to screen students with reading problems.

Stanford-Binet Intelligence, 4th ed., 1985, Riverside Publishing Company. Forms L and M, ages 2–adult. Untimed. Measures verbal, quantitative, and visual reasoning; abstract and short-term memory.

Woodcock-Johnson Psycho-Educational Battery, DLM Teaching Resources, ages 3–80. (Administration time: 2 hours.) Measures cognitive ability, scholastic aptitude, academic achievement and interest level; tests visual matching, auditory blending, concept formation, reasoning with analogies, reading achievement, written language, knowledge, level of preference for participation in scholastic and nonscholastic activities, adaptive behavior, and mathematics.

Informal Reading Inventories

Bader Reading and Language Inventory, 1983, Macmillan Publishing. Preprimary–adult.

Classroom Reading Inventory, 5th ed., 1986, William C. Brown. Form C—Junior High, Form D—high school and adult, grades 1–adult.

Ekwall Reading Inventory, 2nd ed., 1986, Allyn and Bacon. Preprimer–grade 9.

Informal Reading Inventory, 2nd ed., 1985, Houghton Mifflin. Grades primer–grade 12.

Name Index

Subject Index